Isabelle Frohne-Hagemann (Ed.)
Receptive Music Therapy
Theory and Practice

Isabelle Frohne-Hagemann (Ed.)

Receptive Music Therapy

Theory and Practice

zeitpunkt musik
Reichert Verlag Wiesbaden 2007

Bibliografische Information Der Deutschen Bibliothek
Die Deutsche Bibliothek verzeichnet diese Publikation in der Deutschen Nationalbibliografie;
detaillierte bibliografische Daten sind im Internet über http://dnb.ddb.de abrufbar.

Gedruckt auf säurefreiem Papier
(alterungsbeständig – pH 7, neutral)

Dr. Ludwig Reichert Verlag Wiesbaden 2007
www.reichert-verlag.de
ISBN-13: 978-3-89500-564-0

Printed in Germany

CONTENT

PREFACE

In 2004, a collection of 21 contributions dealing with many different forms of Receptive Music Therapy was published in Germany. This collection was the first of its kind in Germany, and was meant to help Receptive Music Therapy to take up an equal and well-earned position alongside Active Music Therapy. In German speaking countries Receptive Music Therapy, like Sleeping Beauty, had more or less fallen asleep since the 1970's, a time when Active Music Therapy became a kind of must. The German edition was meant to introduce and take inventory of most of the best-known methods in Germany, Scandinavia, France and Luxemburg.

In order to support scientific communication among German and English speaking authors and therapists, we decided to translate the book and open the door to an international exchange about receptive forms of music therapy. This book contains 16 of the original articles from the 21 articles of the original German edition. Two have been added. Edith Geiger, for example, replaced her original article on the basics of Guided Imagery and Music with another touching on further leading themes in GIM.

What is the reader going to find? In **Chapter 1**, Isabelle Frohne-Hagemann *introduces Receptive Music Therapies* and provides a short overview of their history. She elaborates on some important concepts from the Ancient World and their development throughout the centuries, and looks for reasons why receptive forms of music therapy in German speaking countries, in contrast to Anglo-American Music Therapy, were often regarded to be less effective than active music therapy between the 1970s and the beginning of this century. She points to the influence of contexts and ecological thinking on the development of modern forms of receptive music therapy that made a revival possible. Furthermore, the author refers to some of the different functions of music within the different methods presented in this book.

In **Chapter 2**, Rosemarie Tüpker discusses "Listening as a Gestalt". A short introduction to listening as a field of research within music psychology is followed by an investigation of the psychological sphere of listening activities, based on descriptions of experiences. Different states, types and ways of listening are evaluated. Well-known forms of receptive music therapy are based mainly on a state of listening to music that uses a balance between listening as a figure and listening as a background in order to attain therapeutic goals.

In **Chapter 3**, Susanne Metzner presents "Some Thoughts on Receptive Music Therapy from a Psychoanalytic Viewpoint". In this article, she outlines the special chance of creating a 'potential space' and encountering the alien with the help of composed music in music therapy.

Chapter 4 by Lars Ole Bonde from Denmark deals with "Music as 'Co-Therapist'". He investigates the relationship between music and imagery in BMGIM, focusing on the role of music. The investigation is based on material from a study of BMGIM with cancer survivors.

Edith M. Geiger presents her research on “The Guide-Traveller Relationship as a developmental relationship for the Self” in **Chapter 5**. The intention is to understand the special quality of the relationship between therapist and client during the music listening period. She explores the quality of the ‘guiding-relationship’ using Daniel Stern’s theory of the infant’s development of the Self and the various stages of development.

In **Chapter 6** Dag Körlin presents *The Spektrum Group GIM Therapy*. This is one of several psychotherapeutic adaptations of Group GIM. The “Spektrum GIM Group” is an integrated part of the Spektrum program, which treats patients with trauma-related disorders in five-week closed groups consisting of 5 patients. However, the method can also be used by itself, and with other diagnostic groups, with the exception of schizophrenic patients. The main theme of the chapter is concerned with different methods of limiting and containing experiences in adapting to the general vulnerability of psychiatric patients.

Birgit Süselbeck-Schulz, a graduate of Integrative Music Therapy, presents a case study in **Chapter 7** “The Bonny Method of Guided Imagery and Music (BMGIM) and Grief Work” describes a GIM process with a young woman who lost two babies (one miscarriage and one stillborn child with heavy deformities as a result of a hereditary disease). The case study shows how the patient processed her grief and regained self confidence during a further pregnancy.

Carola Maack reflects on “Cultural Aspects of the Bonny Method of Guided Imagery and Music (BMGIM)” in **Chapter 8**. She discusses how the Bonny Method of Guided Imagery and Music (BMGIM) as therapy culture fits into different (sub) cultures. The following areas of BMGIM provide the focus for this concept: the therapeutic relationship, imagery and symbols, music, and altered states of consciousness (ASC).

In the lengthy **Chapter 9**, Isabelle Frohne-Hagemann presents “Receptive Music therapy as seen from the Perspective of Integrative Music Therapy (IMT)”. Biopsychosociocultural embodiment and conditions of illness demand different forms of receptive approaches for different patients in their therapeutic processes. Petzold’s spectrum of complex consciousness implies the areas of somato-, psycho- and nootherapy that should be considered under the aspects of “four paths of healing”. She then illustrates these theoretical concepts by introducing several case vignettes, which show how GIM and other receptive interventions can be integrated into a therapeutic process. Finally, some basic concepts of GIM and Integrative Music Therapy are compared.

Chapter 10 provides an introduction to “Sound-Guided Trance developed by Wolfgang Strobel”. Receptive music therapy with sound archetypes, an in-depth psychological method, presented by Andrea Schmucker. Monochrome sound structures not only induce altered states of consciousness but also open doors to varying areas of experience (specific to the particular sound). She describes how, due to the explicit characteristics of the individual tonal structures, which are produced on archetypal instruments, it is possible to target a defined theme (reaccessing repressed contents) and to influence it accordingly (leading to new corrective experiences). Five characteristic sound archetypes are presented and explained from the point of view of both in-depth psychological and transpersonal therapy, as well as from a shamanistic standpoint.

"Sound and Trance in a ritualistic Setting visualized with EEG Brainmapping" is presented by Jörg Fachner and Sabine Rittner in **Chapter 11**. They ask: What happens in the brain when perceiving monochromatic sounds on an imagery journey? How does one stay close to music therapy practice without disturbing the setting? The authors describe how, for the first time, laboratory brain research was brought into a realistic music therapy setting to show the effects of trance-inducing sounds on the brain. The explorative brain imaging study combined qualitative and quantitative research strategies. The authors analyze and compare the results of two receptive trance-inducing methods in regard to rest and trance.

In **Chapter 12**, Christoph Schwabe, the founder of "Regulative Music Therapy (RMT)" in the former GDR, describes the *milestones of a concept development.* He illustrates the conditions which have influenced the concept's development, and presents basic concepts about procedures and the role of the music.

In **Chapter 13**, Helmut Röhrborn presents "Regulative Music Therapy (RMT) in the dyad", and the essential characteristics of RMT and its criteria for indications and the symptom oriented concepts practiced within a concept for group psychotherapy in Erlabrunn (a hospital in East Germany). He describes the 6 steps of the perception oriented training program and gives examples for their realization within the treatment of somatoform disturbances, somatically ill persons with coping problems, patients with pain and relaxation problems, and patients with personality disorders.

In **Chapter 14**, Thomas Wosch presents his investigation of "Psychology of Emotion and its Meaning in Regulative Music Therapy (RMT) and Guided Imagery and Music (BMGIM)". He discusses the classification of emotions and a process of different emotions by comparing RMT and BMGIM, also in regard to altered states of consciousness. His results conclude differences between indications in both methods and in their application. In a typical emotional process, the focus of RMT seems to be the state of anxiety, which is treated specially. Wosch argues that GIM skips the treatment of anxiety when working in altered states of consciousness.

Chapter 15, written by Hans-Helmut Decker-Voigt informs the reader about "DRMT – The Methodology of Music Therapy and Depth Relaxation". This method is a modular system including 7 basic steps that relate to the respective physical and psychic-emotional states of mind of a patient. The author gives very concrete instructions regarding how to work within the seven steps, what to say and to suggest. He also concentrates on the role of the music used, not, however, describing the choice of the pieces themselves.

Receptive music therapy has a high significance in anthroposophic music therapy, and is presented by Monica Bissegger in **Chapter 16** "Receptive Music Therapy in Anthroposophic Music Therapy". The individual therapeutic pieces of music as well as direct, freely improvised play for the individual patient are based on the knowledge of the musical qualities and the phenomenological observation of the individual situation of the patient and his illness. The directly played music helps the therapist to get involved with the actual situation with the patient and to react to his/her play.

Receptive Music Therapy as direct play to the patient also has its value in **Chapter 17**, "The Therapeutic Use of Sounds in Earliest Childhood" (premature and newborn babies) by Monika Nöcker-Ribaupierre. The term music therapy is used in a complex meaning differentiating between medical music therapy and music psychotherapy. Both of these receptive approaches have different meanings of the situation and treatment of prematurity, but start from a physiological significance of music on the human organism. Based on biomedical organic prerequisites and the physiologic effectiveness of music, different receptive music therapeutic approaches will be described and critically examined.

Chapter 18 contains Lony Schiltz's presentation of "Psycho diagnostics, Psychotherapy and Research by means of Stories written under musical Induction". Her psychoanalytical approach is to restore the process of symbolization which is blocked or underdeveloped in many areas of psychopathological dysfunction. She describes her work with adolescents suffering from conduct disorders. By means of integrated qualitative and quantitative research methodology, she was able to prove that stories produced under musical induction function as a projective test complementary to the Rorschach and the TAT.

We hope that these 18 chapters will enable our English speaking colleagues to become more familiar with interesting European contributions to the theory and ways of using receptive forms of music therapy. Furthermore, we wish to motivate further exchange on the subject in the scientific community and among music therapy and psychotherapy practitioners.

We would like to thank all who helped translating the German originals. Special thanks also to Elizabeth Franzen for the final stylistic revisions of all English translations. It was a tremendous amount of work.

Dr. Isabelle Frohne-Hagemann
Berlin, November 2006

CH. 1: RECEPTIVE MUSIC THERAPY

An Introduction

ISABELLE FROHNE-HAGEMANN

If one were to ask a layman what Music Therapy is, the answer would have more to do with *listening* to music than with active improvisation. The idea of listening to music for therapeutic purposes is a reasonable one, considering that, although people listen to music daily, they experience the effects of making music themselves much less often (Bruhn; Frank-Bleckwedel 1994, 412). The idea that music can bring order to the human soul is thousands of years old, and one, which is deeply rooted within us. From antiquity up until modern times, composed music was regarded as a work of art, with the ability to affect us by means of its own internal structure. It is thus justifiable to ask how, and by what means music takes effect. It is also understandable that a patient might expect music in therapy to be prescribed like a medication, especially as this concept is still cultivated today. In his "musical apothecary for the home," Rueger, a music theorist, recommends for example that one listen to Chopin's Piano Concertos when suffering from melancholy (Rueger 1991, 158).

Such recommendations are rejected by most music therapists in Germany. Effects of music cannot be denied. However, music does not heal the individual per se, as though soul and body need only be "tuned", like a musical instrument. Although one *does* "feel music in one's fingers, music *does* elicit emotional response, acts as balsam for the soul, or is coupled with memories of a specific situation, calling forth corresponding moods and feelings: The *meaning* of these effects can never be separated from the context and the listener's listening habits.

In ancient times, music was an expression of cosmic harmony and symmetry. It was assumed that music was not an individual creation of humanity, but a representation of cosmic laws (Möller 1976b). The universe, or macro-cosmos, was thought to have been constructed according to a musical code. The individual, acting as a microcosmic instrument, was assigned to bring this macrocosmic order of the universe to sound. In order to do this, however, he had to be healthy. Health was equated with musical order, while illness indicated an improperly "tuned" instrument (see also Kümmel 1976a, 31 ff, 1976b, 29 ff). Music had a purely ethical and moral meaning and was to be utilised for educational purposes. According to the philosophic tradition of the Pythagoreans, of Plato and of Aristotle, music was assigned to guide the soul (psychagogia) towards concordance with a higher state of reality. This included soul-cleansing, or catharsis, whereby catharsis was not understood as ridding one of strong emotions, but more as purification.

Subjective reactions to music had no relevance to this metaphysically oriented view of the world, although the Sophists and the Epicureans, for example, did recognise the importance of the *experience* of listening to music, and thus of resulting sensual, subjective and hedonistic listening experiences and feelings. Permission to perceive and experience the world was not to be granted in the following centuries either, as according to the view of the world at that time, it was unthinkable to question the concepts of absolute truth, goodness and beauty (see also Frohne-Hagemann 2001). Before the background of an ancient pedagogic understanding of music, repeated attempts were made to develop theories regarding the question of the effects of music and their respective therapeutic relevance. As late as the sixteenth century, Zarlino warned against listening to music solely for pleasure, as the effects of sensual listening would corrupt the individual (see also Tatarkiewicz 1979, 267).

In the seventeenth century, Athanasius Kircher developed an interesting theory. With recourse to the ancient Hippocratic teachings of bodily fluids, he explained *how* music affected the so-called life-spirits, or *spiritus*, and how it could thus be used therapeutically (see Möller 1976a, 35 for more detail). Life spirits were the "vehicle of the soul". Their behaviour was influenced by the kind of bodily fluids, as well as their combination (which resulted in differences in temperament and degree of illness). The *spiritus* interceded between body and soul. Music was able to affect the life-spirits due to the phenomenon of *resonance*. Different types of musical vibration, caused by varying pitch and dynamic, led life-spirits within the nerves and the arteries to move in different ways. This resulted in varying states of emotion. Music affected the life-spirits in such a way, that a 'disorderly' combination of bodily fluids was brought back to normal. Calming, or trophotropic, music would bring a pathologically excited individual to reason, by causing his *spiritus* to move in a calmer fashion. Fast and stimulating (ergotropic) music would bring an apathetic, melancholic patient to quicker movements … and let him sweat out the fluids causing him to be ill" (Möller 1976a, 36).

According to the world view at *that* time, Kircher's ideas were a fairly plausible explanation of the way music worked, especially as the patient's individuality and his subjective experience were not taken into account. These ideas were, of course, rather unspecific. Kircher did not yet view the effect of music as dependant on factors such as context, culture, listening habits or biography, etc., as we do today. The notion that the way in which music took effect was dependant on, among other things, context, the patient's relationship to the doctor or therapist, as well as biographical factors and patient compliance, was inconceivable. Trophotropic (calming) and ergotropic (exciting) music only have an effect, where the patient is ready to get involved and accept change.

In France, the traditional model of music was still being used as late as the nineteenth century in psychiatric experiments with listening to music which were carried out there for the first time (Lecourt 1988). Music was regarded as the "method of choice for reaching emotional areas" (Möller 1976b, 40). The Frenchman Jean Etienne Dominique Esquirol, head doctor at the Salpetrière, had groups of patients perform programs of music, in order to influence their emotions. This was seen as ethical and moral upbringing, socialisation or "trâitement moral" (Lecourt 1988, 16). Esquirol's expectations were, of course, disappointed, as his patients' world of emotions could neither be normalised nor unified. He wrote: "As a result of this failure, I don't, however, conclude that it is useless to play music to the mentally deranged... Where music fails to heal, it distracts, and lessens bodily and mental pain; apparently it is useful in re-convalescence; its use should not be shunned" (as quoted [in German] in Möller, ibid).

It became clear that merely listening to music was not able to heal. It was no wonder that communal listening in a psychiatric context increasingly served as "entertainment" or the "interruption of pathological thinking" (R. Schumacher 1982 as quoted [in German] in Schumacher / Muthesius / Frohne-Hagemann 2004).

In 1954, the Frenchman Jacques Jost became interested in the effects of music on the individual, and began, with the help of modern technique, to take physiological measurements of various patients (Lecourt 1988), 16). These experiments were not particularly useful in psychotherapy, as Jost's understanding of music remained bound by the old concept of Sender-Recipient. Nevertheless, starting in 1963 he conducted experiments within individual and group therapy sessions, using 45 minute programs containing excerpts from larger works. The first piece was supposed to mirror the patient's current condition, the second to neutralise or alleviate (to cleanse in a cathartic sense). The third piece was meant to stimulate, mobilise or calm the patient therapeutically (Lecourt, ibid, 36).

While in Teirich's book (1958) ten out of eighteen articles still dealt with Receptive Music Therapy, it was increasingly rejected in German-speaking countries in the Sixties. Interestingly enough, this was not the case in the former GDR. Here Receptive Music Therapy flourished in the form of Regulative Music Therapy (RMT), as developed and practiced by Christoph Schwabe. Schwabe's work made reference to concepts concerning music and relaxation, developed, for example, by Teirich, Schultz, Jaedicke, Grote, Fengler und Blanke. It appears as though a bridge was built between the old concept of the "trâitement moral", or the wish to *regulate* the world of emotions, and the regard for subjective perception. Receptive Music Therapy was also able to retain its position in England and the USA (see Gembris 1993, 198 ff). Gembris emphasizes that intensive research was done, especially regarding the use of "background music", in pain relief, relaxation and the reinforcement of specific ways of behaviour. Music is viewed pragmatically, not acting 'per se', but as an "acoustic backdrop for therapeutic purposes, trusted and thus desired by many people" (Gembris 1993, 198 f). What had changed was the realisation that a piece of music neither had the same effects on everyone, nor did it always affect each person in the same way. Gembris indicated as early as 1981, that a model for the "constancy of receptive relationships" did not exist (German: "Konstanz der Rezeptionsbeziehungen") (Gembris 1981, 96). The pieces of music used in Receptive Music Therapy could for this reason, be merely "transitory, not final" (ibid., 97).

This statement, nonetheless, brings the problem to a point. One consequence could be, that as the effect of a piece of music could be merely temporary, as "music now indicated for a specific music-therapeutic purpose, could lose its therapeutic properties at a later point" (ibid, 97), music may only be used as background. This concept was taken over by practically-minded Americans, not in psychotherapy in the narrowest sense, but in functional therapy accompanied by psychotherapy. In the USA, intensive clinical research was done with musical parameters. A second consequence could be further research regarding how music is experienced. In the USA in the Seventies, for example, Helen Bonny examined the influence of music on individuals in altered states of consciousness (Bonny 1976). How was music perceived and experienced? What kinds of imagination were supported by the music heard, and how did this occur?

Receptive research is an interdisciplinary field of research, and deals with "perception, experience, and the effects of music" (Gembris 1996, 321). Since the Seventies, knowledge of neurobiological, developmental-psychological and emotional-psychological processes, which occur while listening to music, has increased immensely. At the same time, social psychology has enabled greater knowledge of the role of socio-cultural factors, which come into play while experiencing music, of listening habits, of the influence of medial realisation, and of a specific interpretation of a work of music, as well as, among others, the semantic function of music while listening (Bruhn et al. 1993). From a psychoanalytical point of view, the relationship between music, recipient and therapist has become an intensive object of research.

Apparently Anglo-American research is taken into little account in German-speaking countries. Gembris' accusation of 1993 is still valid today (Gembris 1993, 199): the importance of a professional exchange in the worldwide scientific community is recognised by only a very few music therapists.

The reasons for this are varied, and will not be discussed here. One should ask, however, why in German speaking courses of study in music therapy Receptive Music Therapy very often took a back seat (Oerter 1993, 340 ff). In addition to the rejection of the musical sender-recipient-model, the following culture-dependant factors play a role:

In the Seventies, many German music therapists rejected "prescribing" music: a result of the fear of manipulating experience and emotion, as this would increase the power of the therapist without stimulating the self-healing powers of the patient himself. Perhaps the Germans had become particularly allergic to all forms of manipulation because of their history. Perhaps they overreacted, and threw out 'the baby with the bath water'. Perhaps active music therapy gained the lead because freedom of speech and responsibility for one's own actions became a matter of course in a successful democracy, which promoted subjective experience and personal expression more strongly. The beginning of free improvisation's train of victory in West German music therapy could be an expression of the idea, that old metaphysical or authoritarian world views had been overcome. Personal feelings should and could now be expressed freely.

The need to experience music subjectively for *therapeutic* purposes, to actively create and be allowed to come to terms with music, did not start just by chance in the late Sixties[1]. Free improvisation in music therapy was 'invented' at the same time as old structures in jazz music were being destroyed and overcome. It promised freedom from fixed norms and systems. This was a phenomenon not only to be found in German-speaking countries. Active music therapy was discovered everywhere. It bloomed, and has been held to be the "real" music therapy by most music therapists up until today.

Nevertheless, the differing methods of Receptive Music Therapy discussed here have developed further in the shadow of active music therapy. Their current position shows how much, or how little, modern research in receptivity has been taken into account, although allowances must be made for the fact that these methods have only been cautiously introduced in professional discussion within the international scientific community. This is especially the case as next to no German music therapy findings have been published in English.

A broad spectrum of modern methods of Receptive Music Therapy has been portrayed in this volume. It is hoped that a better acquaintance with them will interest and enrich the reader. A better knowledge of the methods and their goals is meant to help in deciding which methods should be used when, and with whom, and how the needs of the patient or client can best be met.

Receptive Music Therapy encompasses a wide variety of clinical and anthropological objectives and fields of work. Recently, methods have been developed to meet specific clinical goals. On the other hand, existential crises of the senses in our society require modes of treatment which are oriented to mental and spiritual growth. Older shamanistic and spiritual traditions of Receptive Music Therapy, which have differentiated themselves from more modern methods, could be useful in these areas.

The function of music varies according to the method used, and methods are often combined with each other. Methods with clinical objectives use music as background, as a medium for training powers of perception (as in Regulative Music Therapy), as a means for learning strategies for deep relaxation (as in Music Therapeutic Deep Relaxation), or in order to assist narrative skills through listening to music (as in musical memory work with older individuals or in story-telling with adolescents).

In other methods, music itself is given more space and importance (in Guided Imagery and Music or Sound-Guided Trance, for example). Music is not only a medium, or the means to an end. It becomes an area of *musical experience*, or *container*, in which mental processes are able to occur. Transpersonal dimensions of the soul can also be affected, and other states of consciousness simultaneously

---

1 Translators comment: "68er Generation" is also an expression referring in German to those students active in rebellion against the older generation's attempts to hide and repress the later impact of the Third Reich in the late Sixties and early Seventies.

examined. Western society is defined by a one-sided and very particular mode of existence. Nevertheless, it should be considered that it might be necessary to develop very different kinds of mental abilities, in order to meet the demands of complex bio-psycho-social realities.

Receptive Music Therapy demands a *culture of listening*. This includes qualities such as listening, becoming responsive, giving oneself up to personal experience with the help of music, helping, and learning to find oneself. Listening is the process of becoming active, consciously perceiving and consciously experiencing. When so viewed, Receptive Music Therapy is an active therapy. And basically, each active music therapy contains receptive music therapy, as music can only come into existence when one listens, and allows oneself to get involved in the experience.

How then, does music take effect? The following quote is meaningful, and could be used as a maxim accompanying the reader through the chapters of this book: "The influence of music first begins with man's interaction with music. Music takes effect not by its mere presence, but in that a client seeks it out, listens to it or improvises actively" (Bruhn, Frank-Bleckwedel 1994, 416). The many-sidedness, with which this occurs in Receptive Music Therapy, as well as theoretical and, in individual cases, practical approaches, will be portrayed by the authors in the following chapters.

Acknowledgement

The author would like to thank Elisabeth Franzen for the translation.

CH. 2: LISTENING TO MUSIC AS 'GESTALT'

ROSEMARIE TÜPKER

1. Listening to Music as a Field of Research in Music Psychology

With the writings of Carl Stumpf[1] (1883, 1890, 1911) and Hermann von Helmholtz (1863) at the end of the 19th century, inquiries into the phenomenon of listening to music opened up the new field of music psychology, and have remained one of its central topics until today.

In music psychology the term 'reception of music' is understood as "the kenning and mental grasping of a piece of music" (Gembris 1999, 25). At first, emphasis was put on attempts to classify a typology of listeners (Besseler 1926, Wellek 1930/31, Adorno 1962). This increasingly led to the question of musical preference and the effect of music (which was dealt with less judgementally) [2]. In addition, there were inquiries into the ability to differentiate and the capacity of musical hearing.

Systematic musicology as a super ordinate field deals with questions of the perception of musical phenomenon according to psycho – acoustic and physiological aspects. It also deals with sociological, cultural and historical factors.

A clear separation between the different fields of systematic musicology does not seem to be possible or worthwhile. From the beginning we find a wide variety of approaches, those scientific and those based on the humanities, experimental test set-ups alongside gestalt psychological, psychoanalytical and cultural scientific discourses. Quantitative and qualitative methods of research of all kinds are applied.

In addition to musicologists, researchers of other disciplines have been and still are interested in this subject. A separate discourse among psycho – analytical authors can be pointed out, only rudimentarily taken in by musicology (see Oberhoff 2002a, b and 2003).

Recently, a scientific discipline has evolved under the keyword *sound design*. Based on the research and ideas of the Canadian composer and researcher Schafers (1977/in German 1988), one finds, in a kind of scientific "*crossover*", an interdisciplinary group which covers everything from composing to commercial applications, from technical gadgets to serious research, which could be of interest for music therapy.

---

1 For 'Gestalt' psychology Stumpf is of interest as he was the teacher of Berlin Gestalt psychologists Wolfgang Köhler, Kurt Koffka, Max Wertheimer, Kurt Lewin .

2 A review on perception and reception of music from a music-psychological point of view is offered by the annual "*Musikpsychologie*" Volume 14.

Within musicological research into the reception of music, it is not only the applied methods that are multi – layered, but also the leading research questions, as well as the applicability of results in pedagogical, therapeutic and commercial contexts. In a historical overview one may clearly observe a growing, if not always consistent, differentiation of views and approaches.

Initially, the effects of music were seen as biological reactions[3] and as an anthropological constant. Musical preferences were dealt with as characteristics. Newer research, for example, stresses the historical and cultural conditionality of experiencing music (Kötter 1996, Rejzlik 2001), its situational ligation (Lehmann 1994, Behne 1984, Gembris 1990, Müller 1990, 2000) or the aspect of the development of listening to music (Schwarzer 2000, Troué/Bruhn 2000). A similar differentiation is shown in some music psychological explorations relevant to music therapy. For example, Karow/Rötter (2000) examine the increase of tolerating pain through music not as in the effect of a remedy independent from a subject but dependent on certain factors like hearing strategies and how one approaches and turns attention to music. However, Gembris rightly criticizes the "one-sided prevalence of research approaches which are merely experimental and based only on cognitive theories", as well as the fact that the findings often lack relevance. Thus, he advocates a diversity of methods and a "parting from the general principle of experimental natural science" (Gembris 1999, 24). Some new approaches seem to be continuative, exceeding the classical musicological scope of *composition – interpretation – reception* (de la Motte-Haber/ Kopiez 1995). They extend to the vision of partial fields of musicology merging into an inter-disciplinary "systemic musicology" (Fricke 1989, Fricke 2003).

2. Listening to Music as a psycho-logical Entity

If we want to understand 'listening to music' as a gestalt in a psychological sense, we speak of an entity "*listening to music*" within our experience and behaviour. This entity is confined as a whole and can be characterised as something particular. This approach can be separated from that which assumes a work entity called a "*piece of music*" and asks *from there* how a human being receives, sees, accepts and conceives it. The latter perception looks at two enclosed entities (music on one side, listener on the other side) and inquires into the impact of the former on the latter. Here, we will examine, which facts come into view when we consider "*listening* to music" as a gestalt-forming entity that can be researched psychologically as an efficacious psychic occurrence.

Beginning with the basic principles of 'gestalt psychology' and 'morphological psychology' (Salber 1991), we shall inquire into the psycho – logic of the gestalt

3 Of course, this kind of research still exists. The fact that in taking blood – pressure (Dogiel 1980), performing an EEG (Petsche 1987) or doing magnetic resonance imaging (Janata et al. 2002) the newest arsenal of investigation is applied, sometimes indicates a rather extrinsic interest in research.

of "listening to music". This means that other questions, like those relating to sound propagation and musical acoustics, the physiological prerequisites of listening, sonic-processing in the brain or the effect on heartbeat or immunological status, will not be considered. Of course, this does not mean a negation of these phenomena, but can be understood as a limitation of the object of research (German: "Gegenstandsbildung"). "Listening to music" is, as the term implies, characterised as an object of investigation that cannot be considered without the listening human being.

With reference to Straus we could add: It is the human being who listens to music, not the ear or the brain (see Straus 1956, 112 ff). This is based on a notion of music that does not try to describe music by itself, but as an immanent cultural phenomenon, a shape that only comes into being between and for human beings. "It (music) is a configuration and is being configured (...). It is happening within the space of humans relating to each other, between player and listener, composer and interpreter, among two or more players (....). It allows the creation of a 'space of relating' and helps to internalise relationships as structures and to connect different 'inner spaces' with each other" (Tüpker, 2002, 100). In addition, this means that 'listening to music' cannot be described as an ahistorical phenomenon. Many of the phenomena to be described are dependent, for example, on the existence of machines for playing pre-recorded music and thus on the completely new availability of music. Moreover it means that we have to be aware that different kinds of listening to music are connected with certain cultural, social and economic prerequisites. This is why the following remarks only apply for a certain cultural environment.

Within our perception and experience, a gestalt is something that can be seen holistically (as an entity)as something specific silhouetted against something else. We can differentiate the gestalt of "listening to music" from the related gestalt of "making music" or, in reference to daily routine, differentiate the gestalt of "learning" before and the entity of "going to bed" afterwards. The gestalt of 'listening to music' belongs to those entities which can be understood and explained out of an actual event. On another level we can distinguish such "entities of action" (German: "Handlungseinheiten") from long-existing psychological entities like "character", "personality" or "neurosis" or from more all-encompassing "entities of interaction and co-action", such as "family", "institution" or "society", which extend beyond the personal. In classifying these different psychological entities we can state that listening to music belongs to the current genetically and self-configuring gestalts.

This indicates, referring to a term by Sander (1927), a gestalt formation in which the here and now of an activity defines its character, its 'form development' and its effect.; Other factors like character, personality, and musical preparatory training of the listener do have an influence, but only secondary, as a personal "refraction" or a certain way of listening. The morphologist Salber calls those 'entities of action' 'worlds of an hour' (German: "Stundenwelten") (1989). Something limited to a smaller time frame like an hour defines our experience and action, and thus forms a complete gestalt ("world") which can be described psychologically in its 'form development' and effect, its conditions and limitations, in its variations and its transitions to something other.

Listening to music creates a certain and ascertainable context of experiencing and acting which differs from other *'worlds of an hour'* like learning, cleaning up, cooking, playing the piano or painting, gardening or driving a car.

3. Listening to Music at the Centre of Experience

When considering different situations in which we listen to music, we can first think about two different combinations. We listen to music "live": musicians and listeners are in the same place at the same time. And we listen to recorded music: the musicians are not in the same place, usually their playing belongs to the past, often it did not even happen within the same time continuum. Thirdly, all those situations occur to us during which we do something and listen to music *as well, in addition to something else*: music is played in the background. First we will examine those situations where listening to music is in the foreground, at the centre of experience[4].

Music reaches our ear. We turn our attention to it and leave behind what we were occupied with before. We sit *expectantly, excitedly* in a concert hall or we *have made ourselves comfortable*. Everything is *adjusted*, we have *chosen the right moment*, the *remote control is arranged* in order *to experience the beginning consciously*.

Music *puts us under its spell*, *takes* us *in*, *carries* us *away*, and thus away from everyday life, away from what was just important and restricting, away from other obsessions and entanglements. Music releases us from these other realities. It *relaxes* us while taking us into its tensions, into its *skilful* and *ideal* change of tension and solution. We allow the music *to enchant* us. We *immerse* ourselves in the forms and movements it offers us. Somehow, this is always active and passive at the same time. Music *carries us away* and we *let* ourselves *be carried away*. This cannot be separated. Of course, we can, if we choose, work against this happening, and resist surrendering to the music.

When we do engage with music, we often avert our eyes from the world, unnoticeably. We look in front of us, or close our eyes. The gestalt of 'listening to music' is intensified when visual aspects are closed out. *Music is not outside* of us *anymore*, at the same time it *resonates in us* – or *are we in it?* Those determinations seem to be obsolete and futile. We avert our eyes, away from the world, and yet we feel innermost connected with it, with the musicians, the sounds and what

4 The following describing texts are unified summaries based on descriptions of experiences of listening to music. Characteristic phrasing of the texts is set in italics. The reader might wish to review how these descriptions correspond to his own experiences, whereby the descriptions may only partially apply.

they stand for. We give ourselves up to the arches and lines of the music, allow our experience to be put into rhythm and form by what we hear; we entrust ourselves with its enhancements and escalations, its solutions and twists which seem to be our own at the same time. When listening is successful, we ourselves *are all music; we are what we hear.* This can be *inebriant, overwhelming, thrilling, shaking, stirring,* or *still, comforting, resolving, inspiring* or *uplifting.* It depends on the music and on the listener. Often, the experience is conflicting for the listener: *painful and yet comforting, sad and consolatory, vehement and relieving, suspenseful and relaxing.* In addition, it does something to us physically: we get goose bumps, there is a shudder, a throbbing of the heart, afterwards the pain is gone or we feel hungry.

But yet, at the same time there is more: images arise, memories, things long forgotten, or something which has never been there, things unreal or utterly trivial. Music *shifts* and moves us into a different time or space, into a kind of dreamy state, into a landscape, into scenes and moods, exciting or uplifting, contemplative or sensuous. Feelings and sentiments emerge, may be those we believed to have forgotten or those we did not assume to have. Finally, we *can weep,* or *we have to move*, we want to dance, or tap with our foot, we *automatically* start *fidgeting* or rap out the rhythm. Preferably, we would now like to sing along or to conduct, and we do, if the situation allows us to. Or we realize that we have been thinking of something different for a while, something completely unimportant and ordinary. Through a surprising turn, the music retrieves us. Where have we been? Within ourselves, within the music, or somewhere completely different? Or we are annoyed that the movement has already come to an end. Why did we not listen "more thoroughly"? But this is only "bad" for the idealising images of a "good listener" we might have in our head. The gestalt of 'listening to music' endures those "distractions" without breaking apart. At the next moment the music has retrieved us. The next movement takes us in again. Music is not resentful, but the opposite. Music seems to have taken those "distractions" into good hands. Music has transformed it. Not only do we follow the music, but the music itself seems to contain our own experience, our current condition or our present situation in life. We *feel understood by it,* as if it *was written for us,* as if we *had invented it just now.* The music *carries* us *away*, we *let go,* but *we find ourselves in it again.* When we leave the gestalt of listening to music, we "*somehow*" feel *understood or consoled, animated or pacified, appeased or appalled, stimulated or composed:* transformed and having arrived at ourselves.

Variation: Not everyone listens to music alike

Of course there are different "types" of listeners. While one swears that he listens *to a complete opera with his eyes closed*, the other prefers a place where he has a good view or where he can look at the pianist's fingers. In a live situation – while opening and closing our eyes at will – we can move back and forth between two conditions.

With open eyes we experience the total work of art (German: "Gesamtkunstwerk") more strongly. We hear and see how the musicians play, how they express something through gesture and facial expression. When what we see and hear coincides, our experience is intensified and our pleasure increased. Then it feels *ideal, wonderful, and just perfect, how he plays.* When it *the person pushes himself into the foreground, fools around absurdly*, uses *continuously exaggerated gestures*, or *stands rigidly*, this will be more likely to disturb the impression of listening.

Not only are there different types of listeners, but also different types of listening where one attunes to the characteristics of a particular situation of listening and adapts them to the individual preferences. Sometimes we close our eyes unnoticeable when the music is growing more dramatically, more heartfelt, more complex or mellower and nothing new seems to happen on stage. Or we open our eyes because a new voice comes along and we want to know who is entering the stage. Or we want to see, in the case of New Music, for example, how a special sound, brought to our ear for the first time, is created.

One wants to hear the music *with his own ears*, the other one loves *his feet and belly to vibrate with the music.* One hears music more intensely when it is live, or is then more *tolerant concerning styles of music, mistakes or imperfections*, because he considers vitality of live music to be more crucial. Others feel disturbed by the many distractions of a concert situation: many people, the experience of being amongst others. Thus, they enjoy listening to a CD at home much more. This enables them to feel at ease with themselves and to experience with greater intensity. One *hears in images,* the other does not have images that surface with the music. One might suffer when listening to rhythmic music when the situation does not allow him to *rock with it*. Someone else might prefer sitting quietly, or *even better lying down* with the possibility of falling asleep. General idiosyncrasies of temperament, for example being extrovert or introvert, rational or emotional etc. can be found in the way people listen to music; there they find their expression or their balance.

Variation: Sometimes I listen like this, other times like that

As we have seen before, variations in ways of listening to music are only partly individual idiosyncrasies. Individuals do not listen to music in the same way every time, and most people listen to different styles of music differently. At times, music has an animating effect. At other times, we prefer listening while motionless, *going inward.* We might prefer to listen to classical music live, while with rock music we would rather remain *master of the volume control.* Although we actually prefer live music because there we feel a stronger vitality and liveliness, we can appreciate that with a CD we *become the prince* who can decide: "Now I want this piece of music!" – "The beginning once again please!" "The same piece again, but with a different singer." "I would rather have the last movement at another time." "With headphones, even in the middle of the night at full volume."

There is a significant difference depending on whether or not we have heard the music before. To listen to something for the first time might *open up a whole new world.* Gradually, of course, this depends on how new this music compares to previous aural experiences. And it depends on the life situation in which this is happening to us. The experiences with *music that we have never listened to before*, with a new style or with music from a different culture are often considered to be important turning points in life. In order for this to occur, the point in time has to be just right. Even if it is less significant a new piece of music, a new song, an unknown phrase ora sound never heard before can become a very special experience. Listening to music for the first time brings us to a point where it becomes possible for us to be moved internally, free from aim and purpose. Open for each (musical) turn we tune into a frame of mind of *astute calm and floating attentiveness,* where we are *taken by the music.* If we listen to a piece of music more often, this refers to *finding and remembering something again*. Sometimes we listen to a piece of music for so long that we *internalise it entirely*, until we *are full,* or we *suddenly tire of it.* At the same time this is psychologically, not only the piece of music we have taken in, but a whole complex of emotions, tensions, afflictions, joys and conflicts which gains form through repeated listening, and is thus able to find closure (gestalt closure). Now we own it. We cannot lose it anymore. It is solved, collected or, as Bion would put it, "contained" (Tüpker 2003,109 ff). Now it can remain as it is. We are free for something else.

When we have not listened to a certain piece of music for a long time or we deliberately choose to listen to it, we thus *prove* our *memory*, our *emotions*, and the *consistency of our inner world*. We examine how much we have retained. Why do we *now, of all things, want to listen to this music, this interpreter?* With the music we choose to listen to, we search to retrieve and restore something in us, and to bring it back into our experience. This does not always happen consciously. We want to put ourselves into a certain mood. Sometimes this does not work: the former *happy time, from which the music comes*, does not want to arise again, and this rather creates sadness. This is why any repeated listening is at the same time new listening. It is *rewriting* of former experience. Nevertheless it contributes to stabilisation (Tüpker 2002).

Variation: Biographies of listening to Music

Listening to music takes place as a current event, but each of us has his own listening biography. There are first listening experiences which opened our ears, and which we tend and save as *innermost* experiences, or those which have to be revitalised first so that we can recall them. If we encounter them surprisingly, this can evoke a *flash-like reviving* of an over-all atmosphere. Odours can evoke something similar.

Most people can describe different phases of listening to music during their lifetime. Often, the time of growing up is an important phase in which we search and find our identity, and in which listening to music supports us in that process. During that time, listening to music is a *hunger for something new, exciting, moving*, a *search for identification*, a *desire for home, which can be found and chosen by oneself*, a *stabilisation..* Music is considered to be something that *my friends and I sav*our and my parents do not, something the parents do not want to listen to, or at least not as often, and not as loud. Concerning today's youth in particular, Kühn describes the role of music as "furthering identity", being a mainspring of listening to, producing and exchanging music: "In the mirror of being affected by music I recognise the other and feel recognised by him" (Kühn 2001, 85 f).

Later transitional periods are also often characterised by a change in the manner of listening to music. One listens *excessively,* and the listening itself is especially intense and remembered lastingly. A new phase of life often means a different kind of music and a different kind of listening. This might be connected with an adjustment of identity in and through a new group one feels related to, and which listens to a different kind of music. Different phases of life *can be identified by one's record collection.* This is why we can use aural biographies in music therapy as a means to establish contact to someone and to reinforce memories.

Musicians sometimes describe the interrelation between different phases of listening to and making music and other parts of life as converse- Music does not follow life, but *music has always 'shown one the ropes'. First* there was *a leap*, *a radical turn, a widening of the horizon brought about during* the experience of music. After this turning point came different and more tangible changes brought about by life circumstances. It is hard to define what came first or was, in fact, more important, the new friend or the music he played. Sometimes, it is actually the new experience of music *that remains from a certain period.*

4. Listening to Music in the Background

Psychologically, we can differentiate between gestalt forms where listening to music is the entity-forming centre of the psychic context and those where other activities like driving a car, ironing, cleaning up, learning, cooking or eating are in the foreground, and music is heard *as well.* Sometimes this kind of background music is omnipresent, and only in a private space is it self-adjustable. For those who do not wish to listen to background music, this is a serious problem because music pushes itself into the foreground of one's experience. Then a disturbance, it cannot consciously be pushed back into the background (this is similar to the experience of pain that cannot be pushed into the background). Indeed, music was used in designing backgrounds in former times as musical entertainment: at deployments and processions, in so-called "promenade" and "garden concerts", in church and at court, and later as parlour music in middle class society. In these situations, equal emphasis was given to both the main event and the atmosphere of a specific occasion, thus achieving an expression of festiveness, luxury and abundance. Today, it is, of course, possible to listen to music *without the musicians being present.* We have the option of receiving the experience of music without the trappings of an occasion. Without the distraction of extra-sensory input, music can come to us in an uncluttered way. The stillness and simplicity of this experience has become a kind of luxury in itself.

From 'Musique d 'Ameublement' to 'Muzak' and 'Sound-design'

An example of a case of background music being used to an extreme is where it becomes omnipresent. The unnoticed "effect" of such music – especially commercial 'Muzak' – was probably highly overestimated by those who applied it with hope and those who felt exposed to it with some misgivings and a certain reluctance. Results of investigations increasingly show that the desired effect, like the increase of productivity or the disposition to buy, is difficult to determine (see Behne 1999, 7 ff).

However, these inquiries do not support the reverse, that this kind of musical background does not take effect at all. In fact, we create our own background music for everyday life through our personal CD collection or through tuning into a radio station that "supplies" us with an uncertain sequence of pieces of music (often with a well-dosed mixture of music and reports). The well-known problem of 'Muzak', a decrease in effect through habituation, is countered by radio stations with an appropriate proportion of new and well-known pieces of music. This is how *our* radio station *entertains* us the whole blessed day. The double meaning of the German word "to entertain" (to pay alimony, to nourish / to enjoy oneself, to amuse) mirrors the aspect of a successful psychological "accommodation". This is inexpensive and effortless, like nothing else in life. Music which continuously *moves along* in the background, which is *always* there without us having to deal with it, demands little, if anything, from us. We can understand preferring this kind of music psychologically because it offers us an animate and inhabited atmosphere, an atmosphere of not-being-alone-in-the-world. In this way, it is an experience of the *primary substance* (Balint 1973, 79 f) which we only become aware of in its absence. This is why the reverse becomes understandable: If that which continuously pours into us differs too much from that which we need and like, it soon becomes *unbearable* and turns into a *poisonous substance* from which we cannot withdraw.

Even in pubs and shops, the CD collection or chosen radio station has its source in the preferences of the innkeeper or shopkeeper, rather than a choice made according to the kind of Muzak or more modern variations from the 'Sound Designer's' workshop. However, the subjective assortment is probably the best choice because – in all its indefiniteness and haziness – it still creates a certain atmosphere, thus meeting *entertainment* in a double sense of the word. Aurally it contributes to people who feel connected to each other through a certain lifestyle, attitude, common tastes (and available goods or services). At the same time it marks a cut-off point from other groups. Here, one could compare the function of background music with that of interior decoration and furnishings. For this reason, it is similar to one of Satie's ideas. Satie, whose first and singular "performance" failed brilliantly describes, in my opinion, our contemporary exposure to background music accurately:

In 1920 Erik Satie realised the idea of a '*Musique d'Ameublement*' at a theatre soirée. The music was not supposed "to have more meaning than a piece of furniture in a parlour". It should "be part of the sound of the environment", "soften the noise of fork and knife", "furnish the burdensome silence between the guests", and "spare" the visitors "the usual banalities". Satie thought it to be completely aimless, pure "comfort", having the "same task as light and warmth", "like an armchair in which one sits or not", like "the pattern of a wallpaper" (quoted from Wehmeyer 1974, 227f). On the night of the soirée, the music composed for the occasion by Satie and Milhaud, was played in the hall during short breaks in between the scenes. The audience was prepared for the music by an (unintentionally?) paradoxical instruction: "We urgently ask you to not attribute any meaning to the music. During the breaks, do behave as if there was no music"(ibid.). This could only fail! Especially the emphasis on "urgently" foreshadows what Milhaud describes from memory of this "Performance of a Background Music": "Completely against our intention, however, as soon as the music started the audience flowed back to their seats in a hurry. Without success Satie exclaimed: 'Talk! Walk around! Do not listen!' Silently, they listened to the music. Because Satie had not anticipated the charm of his music, the whole effect was spoiled. This remained our only public experiment with this kind of music." (Milhaud 1962 in Wehmeyer 1974, 227)

In the category of 'listening to music in front of the background of experience', there are other psychological versions which can be worked out. Two other examples, which do not claim to be exhaustive, follow.

Listening to Music during Schoolwork, or "Music helps me to concentrate"

Many students experience that doing schoolwork is easier to music (Drewes/Schemion 1991, 46–66). With a Gestalt psychology approach we can understand that – in front of the background of music, and with its help – a certain psychological condition of concentration is reached. Paradoxically, music helps to maintain psychological attachment to the accomplishing of a task. This is managed in that music creates a condition that is full of relish, yet shields against other enticements, internal as well as external, like beautiful weather or particular inner impulses. Without music, pressure alone (external or internal) to finish the assignment, would not be sufficient. To put it differently, music helps to keep distracting impulses at bay, attaches them to itself and keeps them in the background. However, this condition is not stable. If a favourite song is played, the student will most likely be enticed away from his or her homework. We say: "The music is distracting." Psychologically, this means that the music enters the foreground, concentration and experience find another focus point, the psychological condition "tilts" to the side which is more pleasurable, more attractive. If the work can be completed, this is not necessarily a "problem". The music allows the student a break, probably not more than three minutes, considering the standard length of this kind of song. The student might then lean back relaxed, take a deep breath, dream a little, or move to the music. Then he is able to return to his task with renewed drive. If this *does not* work, it rarely has to do with the music alone. Most often, there are more serious reasons which might be biographical – a difficulty from daily life, or a challenging learning situation. When a student chooses to listen to music whilst doing homework, we can say that he is practising, in a sense, a kind of self regulation of his condition through music. It would therefore probably not be advantageous for him to disallow the option of listening to music in the hope that he would do his homework better, without distraction. A functioning "self treatment" with music comprises the knowledge that there is music which is less suited as a protective background, and that there are tasks during which the radio must be turned off.

All in all, the example of schoolwork stands for a certain "type" of listening to music which many adults use as well, and which could be summarised as follows: "Music helps concentration". The term "type" is meant differently here than when referring to "types" of listeners. Recapitulating, it characterises a kind of listening to music which can be understood in an actual context. It differs from other alternatives to listening, thus throwing light on certain psychological idiosyncrasies from different angles. Everyone is aware of these forms. What differs is personal preference.

Listening to Music while ironing, or, "With music everything is easier"

Related to the previous type are others like listening to music while ironing, cleaning, cooking or washing dishes. These have in common that they ask us to continue an activity, whereby music contributes to the process. They do not require much concentration. Far from it! Those activities are regarded as *boring, monotonous, and annoying.* They require repetition, and *are never ending,* because everything gets dirty again. Psychologically, these actions are about "worlds of an hour" ("Stundenwelten") which do not absorb our inner life or psyche completely. They *do not fill* us, and due to their redundancy leave *space for other things*: for daydreams, "rehashing" the day, unsystematic contemplation, or just listening. While daydreaming or pondering, we rely on ourselves. We have to create out of our inner self, and music can be of support here. This "type" of listening to music could address and effectively cater to too much "boredom" (which might feel threatening for different reasons) and what is experienced as too much "inner emptiness". The not yet formed psychological space, in which other things could rush uncontrollably, is kept, as it were, an appropriate size by the music. It still leaves enough space for "reverie" which is socialised by activities like listening to music. Thus, three things happen simultaneously. We have time to listen to music with relish, in daydreams we rehash our day, or we prepare a paper, in the course of which the flat is clean and the dishes or the ironing is done. Only the 'brownies of Cologne' could do better! (Translator's note: This refers to a folk tale in which small elves in the city of Cologne do all the work while the inhabitants are sleeping). Viewed closely, these three things are artfully interwoven: The cleaning can take up and transform different aspects of the music, for example its drive, tempo and rhythm. At one moment music might accelerate cleaning, at another it might allow us to daydream, to work thoroughly and slowly. This is why "everything works better with music". But is music really the reason we feel so much better afterwards? Or did the disregard of every day activities help us? During tidying up, thoughts and every day worries seem to sort themselves out. The accumulated trouble of the day has been cleaned up with the dishes. During ironing, our mood has been smoothed as well. Simply sitting down and listening to music could not, replace such complete pieces of artwork of everyday life (German: Gesamtkunstwerke). A dissecting scientific perspective would indeed like to know who is actually helping whom? Does music help cleaning? Does cleaning help listening to music? Is ironing helpful being in tune with affects? Does music help against boredom? The hybrid forms we create in our everyday life are artful and skilful. For many people, listening to music has become integral to accomplishing many areas of everyday life, and is part of 'self treatment'. "Every day, life laughs" about the questions of a form of science which wants it to be neat and unmixed, explicitly related and cleanly sorted. On a gestalt psychological level we can understand that the operating gestalt is intertwined here. The wholeness of "listening-to-music-while-cleaning-and-being-in thoughts" *is greater and different* (Ehrenfels) than cleaning plus listening to music plus being in thoughts. The question of whether it would *only* work in this way and not *differently as well* is posed only secondarily. Only when it does not work, when we realise that it used to work differently somehow, and that there are people who dislike background music, do we become aware that there is a possibility of it working differently – without necessarily having alternative ideas.

5. Miscellaneous in One

Listening to music in the fore- or background is only a first, rough approach to a diversity of forms in which we listen to music. Listening can be included in other activities or forms of experience; or states of abeyance of listening and something different come into being, as it is used in music therapy. Sometimes we hear music without there being an actual external sound. We hear something coming from inside as a catchy tune, a musical idea or memory both while awake and dreaming.

Listening to Music inclusive

Neither historically nor interculturally is it always appropriate to separate music from other things. Sometimes, music ethnologists find themselves in a paradoxical position when researching musical manifestations with musicological methods. They find that too self-evident conceptual classifications are debatable. This is because object and concept formation – not immanent in the researched culture – deforms the researched object a priori. Something similar becomes obvious when one researches music in myths. Historically, one discovers that "music" has not always been clearly separated, that it has not been abstracted out of the diverse manifestations in which it is found, has not been representationally generalised (see Tüpker 1999). This may lead one to consider that the act of listening to music could be "included" in a more comprehensive gestalt of experience. For example, all kinds of music-making or composing certainly comprise listening to music. Music belongs to dance as well. Both music and movement may be in the foreground. And in some circumstances it may be sufficient to listen merely inwardly. In free dance, there is an immediate transformation of 'listening to music' into movement. In ballroom dancing it is more a case of dancing *to* music. Then, whether we pay more attention to the music or to dancing might depend on our ability or physical condition. Or, both might recede into the background because we are talking inspiringly, because we are excited by or infatuated in our partner, or because we are concerned with the impression we make on other observers at the edge of the dance floor. Dancing is possibly that 'form development' where we most likely understand that, psychologically, music is not necessarily its *own* gestalt. We can understand dancing as an active form of listening to music. Our movements show how we hear the music. On the other hand, we can understand music as an internalised form of dancing, the gesture as an incarnated melodic phrase and the musical phrase as an incorporated gesture. There are hints of different, merging 'modes of senses', also identified in more recent infant research, and described as 'amodal perception'. Daniel Stern assumes the idea of a shared matrix of "gestalt forms" which differentiate further into modes of senses (1992, 74 ff). This concept sheds new light on the question of synaesthesia: experience is not explained by an additional link or particular characteristic of an individual, but is through recourse to a former mode of experience.

It is common practise for music to be added to the 'Gesamtkunstwerk' of opera and to most films. Even documentaries and news broadcasts are often accompanied by music. We only become aware of this when we reflect critically, for instance when the towers of the World Trade Center collapsed, or pictures of the war against Iraq were accompanied by background music. Research on film music scores shows how unconscious perception of music contributes to the effect and connotation of a scene. The music comments on and interprets scenes, substantiating meaning or making it more concrete. Music, for example, determines whether a gaze is an indication of threat or infatuation. There are yet other ways in which music can give meaning to scenes, in this case those which involve everyday life. Listening to a walkman might put us in a condition where we suppress the *"background noise of reality"*. At the same time, we let life float past us like in a film, its scenes accompanied and emotionally commented on by music.

Listening to Music in a State of Suspension

At the pivot point between foreground and background, we can constitute a condition of experience where we move as if in a (deciphered) "hidden puzzle picture" (German: "Vexierbild") between two focus points: now listening to the music, now focusing on something else. In a hidden puzzle picture. a figure "capsizes", like the well-known duck/rabbit figure, where the duck image turns into that of the rabbit (and vice versa). We probably recognise what has been described here from our own experiences during a concert, whilst listening to music at home, driving a car, dancing, or at the opera. When we observe and describe accurately what happens at these moments, we discover a particular abeyance: music enters the foreground of experience. At other times something else comes to the fore. In other words, this particular state of suspension could be called a "tilting" or "inverse figure", which relates to the "hidden puzzle picture". This abeyance can be experienced as a relaxed change in which the focus shifts gently between being-in-the-music and inner images, body awareness, thoughts and memories. At times we listen attentively, then we are concerned with something other than the music. Sometimes it more resembles a fast oscillation which creates the feeling that music, and the other point of focus work to keep each other in balance. At the same time they transfer us into it.

In everyday forms of self-treatment through music we do not consciously search for this condition, nevertheless it occurs on some level, without our knowing. This is different in 'Receptive Music Therapy'. In my opinion, this is exactly the condition being searched for to set the psyche in motion, to animate concealed feelings, to allow that what has been repressed to emerge to a compatible degree. In "*Regulative music therapy*" [5] (Schwabe) and other comparable music therapeutic relaxation methods, the patient is invited to similarly accept the change between perceiving music and relinquishing to body awareness, thoughts and emotions.
In '*Guided Imagery and Music*' (Bonny), there is an endeavour to bring inner images and music into an oscillating process of change. Additionally, patient and therapist talk with each other during the music, so that the two experiences, of listening to music and talking, – as fore- or background – move against each other.

Additionally, in '*Writing stories to music*' (Schiltz), '*Psychodynamic movement*' (Priestley) or '*Painting to music*' we hope for a condition that – in the space *between* the music and another media – searches for vestiges in the past, for things repressed

5 The music therapy methods referred to in the following text are described in this book more thoroughly. This is why references are being forgone here.

and lost – this is like a search for a new turn, for other potentials, so that the psyche can move into new directions.

Survey

Listening to music is a psychological gestalt which we connect with multifaceted experiences, everyday as well as extraordinary, irrelevant and trivial. and some of outstanding and delightful quality. This gestalt is agile and alterable, so that, once found, it survives, participates in and accompanies the vicissitudes of life. We use this gestalt in self-treatment, in everyday "*entertainment*" and background music, in the resolution of conflicts in times of crises, and in the finding and shaping identity and ensuring continuity. This self-treatment through listening to music probably forms the basic experience of 'Receptive Music Therapy'; even though only some forms qualify for integration in clinical treatment.

Acknowledgement

This chapter was translated by Jutta Groene. The author and the translator would like to thank Tana Lyons, Wellington N. Z.

CH. 3: ESSAY

Some Thoughts on Receptive Music Therapy from a Psychoanalytic Viewpoint[1]

SUSANNE METZNER

A personal experience

I have a very precise recollection of my first experiences with receptive music therapy, although over sixteen years have passed in the meantime. I made these experiences in a practical introductory course of training as a music therapist. The students split up into groups of two, each pair decided who would take on the role of the therapist and the patient, and then each pair settled down somewhere in the room. My role was that of the patient. Following a relaxation exercise, the trainer turned on the music, an orchestral song, which was unfamiliar to me. I imagined a sunny mountain landscape. Standing on a hilltop, I looked down into a valley and saw a wooden cabin lying somewhat beneath me, the entrance to which was not visible from where I was standing. My partner tried to help me discover which strivings, wishes, or feelings were lying in this imagined scene. I, however, was completely content with just looking at the scenery without any further inner involvement. After a while I noticed that tears were flowing down my face. I was not at all sad, but relieved. I was not conscious of the other persons in the room, and happily, my "therapist" remained silent. As the music ended, my tears ended too.

In the following conversation we reflected upon what had happened, but were not able to gain insight into the meaning behind it. It was not possible to discover any kind of connection whatsoever to my life at that time or to my past. However, I must admit that in the scope of this training group exercise, specific therapeutic techniques to access deeper, unconscious levels could not be used.

The piece of music we heard was one of the "Four Last Songs" of Richard Strauss, "Im Abendrot" (At Sunset), which is based on the poem with the same title by Joseph von Eichendorff. While listening to the music I did not understand the text, but I cannot exclude the possibility that it – or at least some of the words – possessed a subliminal meaning for me: wandering, time to sleep, losing one's way, solitude, peace, and death.

Approximately one year later I happened to visit a house in the south of Germany, in which Richard Strauss had lived for a while. A sign posted next to the door listed the works which he had composed during his stay there, one of which

1 The English version was first published in Nordic Journal of Musictherapy 13 (2) 2004, 143–150.

was the “Four Last Songs”. I was overwhelmed by a sudden realization: all I had to do was to look around in order to recognize the mountain scene which I had seen in my imagination. Soon afterwards I came to see another parallel between my feeling of relief and the personal meaning of this work for the composer: Eichendorff’s poem was the stimulus for a song cycle in his later years. Looking back upon a life marked by triumphs as well as illness and worries in later years, he composed these songs, which are far away from the pompous heaviness of earlier works. Instead, they are expressions of simplicity, tranquillity, inner peace, and relief.

Some Basic Prerequisites

The thoughts I present here are to be understood as a psychoanalytic look at existing concepts of receptive music therapy, not as a new development or description of a psychoanalytic concept of receptive music therapy. The following is based on the assumption that something very typical to receptive music therapy is reflected in the experience I made, namely – to put it in very simple terms – a shift of the relationship axis from patient-therapist to patient-music (respectively composer and interpreter). This leads to the question of the influence of composed music on intrapsychic and interpersonal dynamics within therapy, as well as its therapeutic usefulness for the process.

Basically, I do not use the term usefulness here as demanded and promoted in a large part by the scientific research community, which follows a tradition of natural-science predominantly concerned with the collection of quantitative data, but rather in the sense of a humanistic approach. This connection to a humanities tradition, which Pohlen (1999) generally demands of scientific psychotherapy, is fundamental to music therapy, because it uses art – per se an expression of the search for meaning and for human life conceptualisations. Music as an integral element in therapy should support individuals in their search for meaning and new perspectives for their lives.

Psychoanalytic reflection is surely not the only approach, but the one I favour. It primarily focuses on intra-psychic and interpersonal processes within a therapeutic framework. Although this is where psychoanalysis was originally developed, it is not limited to this area. In principle, psychoanalysis can be seen as a means to gain knowledge of all questions concerning the individual and his subjectivity within a continuing life story, and in the surrounding world and culture. Consequently, psychoanalysis can also be used as culture analysis.

Both art and psychoanalysis are critical interventions towards culture and convention. Art is an attempt to express a mystery, and psychoanalysis is an attempt to solve a mystery. This is of great importance for psychoanalytically informed receptive music therapy. It means that the psychoanalytic approach aims towards music in reference to the dialectics of manifest phenomena and their latent meanings. This implies that psychoanalytic reflection regards the object of analysis and all of its individual, situative, historic, and socio-cultural determinants as unique, and avoids generalizations.

This leads to the question of what is interesting about receptive music therapy from a psychoanalytic viewpoint. I will confine myself below to those music-therapeutic techniques which centre on listening to composed music while the listener is fully conscious. I will ignore the, in part, immense differences between schools of therapy, indications, and settings. Maybe this will help in identifying positions common to different therapy schools.

Consensus on Music in Therapy

In the course of the history of philosophy and musicology, diverse views, both different and controversial, have been expressed in answer to the question the essence of music. The circle of philosophers, musicians, music critics, and musicologists of past centuries has recently been broadened to include music therapists, whose thinking is based in many respects on the interface between the mentioned fields of knowledge and practical work. In 1998, the "Kasseler Konferenz", the association of music therapeutic organizations in Germany, was able to come to a general consensus, independent of school, on the definition of music in music therapy, as stated in the following thesis:

"*Thesis 4:* Music is sound created by man. As an acoustical, time-structuring event, music is the articulation of human experience with expressive and communicative functions. Music exists in the dialectic field of opposing forces of individual, namely physical, mental, spiritual, social, and socio-cultural determinants and is effective and significant there.

Music becomes a carrier of subjective meaning about the process of recognizing internalised experiences, which are connected with the history of mankind, the enculturation process, and the current situation." (Thesen der Kasseler Konferenz 1998, 233)[2]

---

2 The whole Thesis No. 4 in German: Musik ist vom Menschen gestalteter Schall. Als akustisches, zeitstrukturierendes Geschehen ist sie Artikulation menschlichen Erlebens mit Ausdrucks- und Kommunikationsfunktion. Sie befindet sich im dialektischen Spannungsfeld individueller – körperlicher, psychischer, spiritueller, sozialer – und gesellschaftlich-kultureller Bedingungen und ist dort wirksam und bedeutsam. Musik wird zum subjektiven Bedeutungsträger über den Prozeß des Wiedererkennens interiorisierter Erfahrungen, die im Zusammenhang der Menschheitsgeschichte, dem Enkulturationsprozeß und der aktuellen Situation stehen.
Zu "gestaltet": Bei der musikalischen Gestaltung werden Töne, Klänge und Geräusche in übergreifende rhythmische, melodische und harmonische Strukturzusammenhänge gebracht. Dieser Vorgang ist Grundlage aller künstlerischen Schaffensprozesse in der Musik. Gestaltung schließt auch unbeabsichtigte Schallereignisse ein, sofern diese vom Rezipienten als bedeutsam wahrgenommen werden.

The attentive reader will have noticed that nothing is stated in the thesis about the emotional effectiveness of music, although this often serves as a reason for using music therapy. The fact that composed music in particular (but improvised music as well) is complex, in other words, artistically polymorphic and full of conflicting movements, and that the emotional stirrings of the player or listener are not long-lasting, obviously makes it very difficult to find evidence of long-term emotional effects of music on the human being. In music therapy practice, the complexity and transitory quality of music are compensated, at least in part, by the conversation generally following music listening that focuses on the subjective meaning in the current situation. Thus, it would not have presented a problem for the authors of the Theses to assert such a relationship. This was not the real reason for not mentioning the subject. Rather, they were not able to achieve a consensus about the concept of effectiveness on emotions, due to the diversity of views on this topic.

Music and Semantic Meaning

For psychoanalysis, the meaning, rather than the effect of music, is in the foreground. Surely, this hermeneutic approach has consequences in reference to how music is dealt with and how therapeutic processes are understood. This approach is primarily based on theories of presentational and discursive symbolism (Langer 1954, 1984) and on theories of transitional phenomena (Winnicott 1985). In order to explain the psychoanalytic interpretation of the "Kasseler Thesis" cited before, it is necessary to take a closer look at the Langer's statement, often cited in the literature on music therapy: "If music has any significance, it is semantic and not symptomatic" (1954, 176). On logical grounds, Langer differentiates between the symbolized (a feeling or a thought) and the symbol (music or language). Especially in presentational symbol forms, the structures of the symbol and the symbolized are very similar. In the case of music and feelings it is, for example, the dynamics. Because of this, the symbolized is concealed in the symbol, which often leads to confusion. As a symbol, music is not the cause of feelings, but a logical expression

---

Zu "Schall": Schall ist die Bezeichnung für alle hörbaren Schwingungsvorgänge und schließt die Begriffe Ton und Klang als Phänomene universaler harmonikaler Gesetzmäßigkeiten und den Begriff Geräusch mit ein.
Zu "zeitstrukturierend": Musik beinhaltet Erfahrungen von und mit Zeit.
Zu "Artikulation": Diese Artikulation ist nonverbal und präverbal. Auch das Verständnis der Musik als präsentatives Symbolsystem ist darin enthalten (Maria Becker in: Lexikon der Musiktherapie 1996, 230); andere Zugänge sind aber ebenfalls abgedeckt, wie semiotische (Christoph Schwabe(1978): Methodik der Musiktherapie. Leipzig) oder ästhetische (z. B. Jan Mukarowsky (1971): Kapitel aus der Ästhetik. Frankfurt am Main; Georg Lucács (1972): Ästhetik, 4 Bände. Frankfurt am Main).

of them. In this connection, it is necessary to define the term feeling in a very broad way because it includes more than basic affects such as anger, joy, or sorrow. The entire spectrum of emotional states is meant. In other words, mental strain, moods, and mature sentiments are included, as well as strivings and stirrings with a primal, instinctive, vital and pre-rational character. Langer describes the latter as "something of the life rhythms we share with all growing, hungering, moving and fearing creatures: the ultimate realities themselves, the central facts of our brief sentient existence" (Langer 1954, 211).

In music, emotional experience is expressed, or, more precisely: In music, that is expressed what a person knows about emotive life and this is nobody other than the composer. However, composing cannot be seen as completely free self-expression. The composer or improviser works within a framework defined by the idiomatic forms of the prevailing (musical) culture at a particular time. Thus, the emotional content is placed within a context of social, socio-cultural, economic, and historic determinants. Therefore, composition is a search for an abstraction from the pure personal-ness and situative-ness of an emotional catharsis. I believe that improvising is not totally different to this, but that is not my subject at the moment.

Composed music understood as an abstraction, is not an expression of emotions, which have been pressed into a more or less rigid form. Rather, it communicates subjective experience within a socio-cultural context. Music is an expression and a product of the struggle for an insoluble alloy between content and form- It shows the hand of the composer and the mark of the times. A good or successful piece of music is a triumph – by all means an intellectual triumph – over all barriers to the expression "unspeakable" realities. At the same time, it is nothing more than playing with sounds.

Music (like art in general) is "measured" or in other words evaluated by its coherent consistency, not by its beauty, because a successful expression of incoherence or of failure can satisfy aesthetic needs as well, although not, of course, a need for harmony.

Furthermore, a developmental principle is inherent in music. Because in contrast to language it does not have a vocabulary, its contents do not have assigned or specific connotations. An individual piece of music acquires its individual-subjective meaning anew every time it is played even when we have known a piece of music for a long time. Other than that, it has no meaning. "Music is revealing where words are obscuring, because it can have not only content, but a transient play of contents. It can articulate feelings without becoming wedded to them." (Langer 1954, 198).

Finally, music also has an interactive power (see Niedecken 1988, 85), because through music an imaginary dialogue is begun between listener and composer. For the composer, this concerns the motivation to express something, as well as the decision to make available an interpretation other than the product of his or her creative process, which itself is open to a certain extent. This can be seen as a kind of transference. The dialogue partner, namely the interpreter or listener, produces empathic responses –not automatically congruent or enduring ones – to the content with which a composer has occupied himself, and to the form of expression he has chosen.

In therapy, the responses of the patient hearing the music can be seen as counter-transferences in accordance with the double meaning of this concept as we understand it today. On one side are assignments of meaning in the sense of transferences, which must be interpreted in order to acquire knowledge of one's own unconscious. On the other side, counter-transference is based on perceptions of the meanings hidden in the musical object, which must be understood and distinguished from individual and personal assignments of meaning in order to avoid confusions and misunderstandings.

Thus, in psychoanalytical informed receptive music therapy, attention would not focus solely on the emotional responses of the patient, but on the interactive process between patient and composer, which I refer to as fantasized dialogue. What is required of the therapist is not only to have profound knowledge of the pieces of music and their origin. He or she must also be able to become aware of personal counter-transferences in connection with the music and to distinguish these from those of the patient.

The use of music in therapy would inevitably lead to psychoanalytic critique in those cases where the music is fitted to the needs of the patient in a one-sided way. In other words, when the therapist does not adequately consider the specific musical structures and contents that are opposite to the deformations arising from subjective experience and projection. Likewise, critique would also be voiced in cases where the patient is matched with the music in a one-sided manner through the therapist's expectations of specific emotional reactions to a piece of music. This would be seen as insufficient consideration of the dynamic, ambiguous and multiple meanings of music.

Space within the Psychic Triad

The central idea behind the following thoughts is the concept of "potential space" (Winnicott 1985), which can be seen as an emotional state that plays an important role when music is heard. A number of dialectic relations underlie this notion, for example those between reality and fantasy, between self and non-self, or between the symbol and the object (see Odgen 1997, 1).

"Potential space" is first of all a term from developmental psychology, but Winnicott also uses it to describe the play space in general, the analytic space, the sphere of cultural experiencing, and creativity. The terms "transitional object" and "transitional phenomenon" are related concepts. These terms designate objects with a peculiar dual nature: On one side, they are objects or phenomena of the sensory world; on the other, they must first be created by the perceiving individual and are part of his or her innermost possessions. For this reason, the individual does not see transitional objects as something really external, separated from the self. At the same time, the function which they have for the individual is perceptible by the external world and – in favourable cases – is respected by it. Their entire meaning, however, remains in the dark.

To make a psychoanalytic view of music reception as suggested in the last section possible, music too can be seen as a transitional object, that is, a subjective assignment of meaning shaped by the objectivity of musical structures. In this act of acquiring and making music available as a transitional object, we are dealing with a dialectic process, which can be considered as a precondition to a lasting meaning or effect of the music therapeutic experience.

Generally, dialectic processes play a central role in the psychological construction of subjectivity. Subjectivity is seen in contrast to a state of reflexive reactivity. It can become evident in the barely noticeable feeling of self-being, which gives experience the quality of thinking one's own thoughts and feeling one's own feelings. Further, it becomes evident in the mature ability of intentional self-reflection. Inextricably linked with the construction of subjectivity is the development of a distinction between the symbol and what is symbolized. In concrete terms, this means the ability to separate one's own thoughts from what one is thinking, and to distinguish one's feelings from one's reactions.

This capability has its roots in early childhood in the first creation and use of transitional objects. From this point on it has lifelong relevance for the individual regarding how he actively organizes the external and internal world.

Between the symbol and what is symbolized there is an open space, which the individual, with his own interpretation, both builds and fills. By doing this, he constructs his own subjectivity. Herein lie the dialectics of potential space, which becomes very explicit if one uses negation: If there is no distinguishable space between the symbol and what is symbolized for the individual, than there is neither space between fantasy and external reality nor one between self and non-self, and vice versa!

Potential space, which, following Odgen (1997) I have described as an emotive state, constitutes spaces which emerge within the psychic triad consisting of symbol, symbolized, and the interpreting subject. I would like to explain this psychic triangulation with the example of listening to music. I have already mentioned that a successful piece of music is measured by its coherent consistence. However, this is only possible if the listener (the interpreting subject) is able to perceive the space between the symbol and what is symbolized, and to relate to the relationship between both. This, in turn, requires that the subject is able to differentiate his own thoughts and feelings from those contained in the music.

The creation of potential space, which has thus proven to be a process of triangulation, is by no means a rare occurrence. It is a fully normal and commonplace psychological process, which, however, can be disturbed (see Odgen 1997). By means of this process, we are able to enjoy a sad piece of music, or to listen to a number of pieces played in a concert that arouse a variety of emotions in us without having to remain in their grasp for a longer period of time. If the necessary distance is missing in order to make this differentiation, the listener would neither find access to the music nor to himself or herself, even if this may sound paradox.

However, it seems to be a particularly enjoyable experience for us humans to keep this triad of symbol, symbolized, and personal experiencing in a kind of floating state for a while and let the differences fade out. This is a psychic act, which I believe should not only be interpreted as regression, but as an activity of the primary process. In order to perceive the symbolized, the listener becomes one with the symbol by nestling himself or herself into its movements. The symbolized is then compared with personal interiorised experiences until, as a result of this integration process, a new dialectic relationship is finally established, namely the acknowledgement of the other through the creation of one's own subjectivity.

This would correspond to the general objective of psychoanalytic-informed receptive music therapy. In order to reach this goal, the therapist tries to help the patient build a "potential space" there, where he or she is not able to. In this process, the methods, techniques, or specific music pieces are not of central importance. Crucial is the empathetic offer of a relationship. In paraphrasing Winnicott (1985, 49) one could say that psychotherapy occurs where the potential space of the therapist and of the patient overlap.

Admittedly, the patient must be not too far away from being able to construct a potential space if he or she is to profit from the therapeutic use of composed music. With patients with ego-structure disturbances or so-called disturbances in early childhood development, psychotic and/or personality-disturbed patients, or severely traumatised ones, this is often not the case. Such persons have an acute pathology of potential space, because of their weak or temporarily impaired ego functions. These become evident, for example, in the missing distinction between self and non-self, or in the confusion of reality and fantasy. From a psychoanalytic viewpoint, composed music in therapy must always be regarded as a contra-indication if music is used one-sidedly as a projection surface for transferences or for projective identification instead of being used to develop the patient's ability to find a transitional object.

Encountering the Alien

What is special about the therapeutic relationship in music therapy from a psychoanalytic viewpoint? In the preceding thoughts, which dealt with the patient's dialogue with composed music, I mentioned some functions of the music therapist in connection with the statement that on the one hand, music is a symbol and has a meaning, and on the other hand that dialectic processes within potential space play a role when listening to music. Just the fact that the music therapist is also drawn into a dialogue with the music, underlines the complexity and ambiguity of the involved processes, without having mentioned the transference-counter transference relationship between patient and therapist, regressive processes, dealing with defence structures, or the role of resistance. There is no question that the significance and organization of all these process variants are influenced by including composed music, in the same way as in active music therapy with improvisation. Since each therapy takes a very individual course depending on the interplay of patient, therapist, and music, psychoanalytic interpretation would have to focus on each specific case. For this reason, I cannot discuss this in any more detail here. However, despite the complexity of the issue, there is something which is becoming clearer regarding therapeutic function in receptive music therapy, and which is unique to this form of psychotherapy. In order to explain this point further, I will focus on an important element of receptive music therapy, namely the selection of music.

In most cases, at least when there is no standard music program, the therapist chooses the piece of music or makes a pre-selection. Here, empathy plays an important role. Characteristic for the selection of music is that the therapist takes on an empathetic perceptive attitude and tries to understand the patient by relating to his or her inner world. This emotional and cognitive process of understanding includes being able to hear music through the ears of the patient and anticipating how the patient will hear the music, even if the patient is neither able to express this himself nor as yet has any thoughts about it.

However, Treurniet (1981), referring to Winnicott, states that the experiencing self of the patient is so unique that it places limitations on the therapist's empathic capacity. The fact that the pieces of music are also something quite unique makes it logical that there can never be a perfect fit between the selected pieces and the experiences and needs of the patient. From a psychoanalytic viewpoint, it is important that these limitations be recognized and respected. Otherwise, the therapist's self will intrude into the potential space of the patient. The attempt to deliberately apply empathy as a "method" can be seen as an expression of the therapist's desire to control the unconscious dynamics of the therapeutic relationship.

Wellendorf (1999) assumes that empathy, besides the personal and private ability of an individual to adopt an empathic perceptive attitude, is both the product and the specific quality of an intersubjective process. For this reason, he suggests a change of perspective: "We are dealing with a relationship that allows the analyst to use his self and his own experience (empathy) in order to understand the alien in oneself and oneself in the alien." (Wellendorf 1999, 16ff., translation by the author). Thus, empathy is a relational concept. "When we use it, we are moving in an area of mutuality and intersubjectivity." (Wellendorf 1999, 16ff, translation by the author).

For music therapists, this means that the selection of music must be seen as a product of an intersubjective process. Truly, this does not change the fact that the music therapist still does the selecting, but this occurs with a different attitude toward the patient. The music – regardless of whether the selection proves afterwards to be good or not as good– becomes the third party, the mutual reference point, simultaneously referring back to the therapeutic relationship. This opens up completely new dimensions regarding the choice of music. It is no longer limited to the conventional area of classical or romantic symphonic music, nor is it absolutely necessary that it corresponds to the music listening preferences of the patients. The deciding factor is, if it is possible to place the music in the position of the third party within the intersubjective relationship, or to work on making this happen.

What enters into the centre of attention is the differentness, which evades all attachment and integration, in other words, all empathy. The therapist's willingness to be empathic necessitates a counterpoint, namely the willingness to acknowledge the alien in one's own self and one's own self in the alien other. In every attempt at enlightenment something remains in the dark, a valuable remnant that should be preserved and not unravelled.

Composed music in particular provokes the (painful) experience that discontinuity is an integral part of processes, and that the dimension of alteration and dissent is an integral component of every relationship. Self-theorizations and illusions, which have been built up in relationships to an other are challenged, and with every step that we come closer to a deeper understanding, the mystery who we are, who the other is, and what the music is increases. In the encounter with a new, unfamiliar object, which cannot be completely occupied by conscious or unconscious fantasies, or with repetitions of past experiences, lies the changing power of composed music in therapy.

Acknowledgement

The author would like to thank Elenore Hertweck, Annweiler, for the translation.

CH 4: MUSIC AS CO-THERAPIST

Investigations and reflections on the relationship between music and imagery in The Bonny Method of Guided Imagery and Music (BMGIM)[1]

LARS OLE BONDE

Introduction. Is music experience only personal?

> "The metaphor (image) comes and undresses as it sheds meaning, meaning within meaning. Music as co-therapist reveals, closes, entices, expands, proposes, lulls, demands, challenges, confuses, opens, salutes, etc. The metaphor in response to music opens into the emotion. Sometimes the metaphor is not present. The emotion may be the metaphor, or emotion comes before metaphor (or vice-versa)." (Helen Bonny n. d.)[2]

In this quote Helen Bonny uses metaphor and image as synonyms, and she describes some of the ways in which music may function as a co-therapist in The Bonny Method of Guided Imagery of Music (BMGIM). The idea of 'music as co-therapist' is often present in the BMGIM literature (Skaggs 1992; Metzner 1996; Isenberg-Grzeda 1998), and it reflects the special role of carefully selected and sequenced classical music in BMGIM. More than 75 music "programs" are listed in the overview (Appendix B) by Bruscia and Grocke (2002), and new programs are developed continuously by BMGIM therapists and trainees (Bonde 2004). The literature includes analyses of some programs, and theoretical reflections on the relationship between music and imagery (Bonny 1978, Goldberg 1995, 2002). And yet, it is not easy to explain what actually happens in the music-listening period of the BMGIM session, when the client and the therapist explore the client's inner world as expressed in images, metaphors and emotions. Bonny described some of the things that the music 'does', however, it is certainly not a matter of stimulus (music) and response (imagery, emotion). Every "music travel" is different, and the client who listens to the same music several times in subsequent sessions does not repeat herself. What the therapist needs to know 'by heart' is the "image potential" of the music selection or program. The personal dimension of the music experience is well documented in Music and Emotion Research, with "person-centered" as an important keyword (Gembris: "Every person has her own music experience";

1 This chapter is based on material from a PhD dissertation (Bonde 2005)

2 Handwritten note dated N. Y. 12-1-89, in The Bonny Archives folder "Misc. Notes – GIM"

Ulich: "Every person has a personal response to music" – see Wosch's chapter in this book).

Nevertheless, I think that the relationship between music, imagery/metaphor and emotion is not purely idiosyncratic and personal. This is what the BMGIM therapist learns by experiencing (and later analyzing) the "image potential" of the music programs alone, and her clients' bodyminds. Music as 'co-therapist' does best when the 'primary' therapist has chosen a program or sequence suited to meet the needs and the ego strength of the client (often based on the Iso-principle, see Metzner's chapter in this book). However, even if the work of music as co-therapist is not a mystery, it is not easy to document and explain the common denominator of imagery among clients and even across cultures (Hanks 1992).

In this chapter, I will document and discuss how a BMGIM therapist or researcher may document and understand the image potential of music in BMGIM programs. First, methods and perspectives in BMGIM music and imagery research are presented. Then I will focus on one specific piece of music, and demonstrate its image potential in a multi-dimensional analysis. The next step is an analysis of the imagery of four cancer survivors to the same music. This material comes from a study of the influence of individual BMGIM sessions on mood and quality of life in cancer survivors (Bonde 2005). The imagery is presented in the format of a so-called Event Structure Analysis (Tesch 1990), followed by an analysis and interpretation of images as metaphors and the narrative configurations.

Analyzing music and imagery in BMGIM

Between 1973 and 1989 Helen Bonny developed, or "composed", 18 GIM music programs (Bruscia and Grocke 2002, app. B,; Grocke 2002a, 2002b). In the so-called "'Monograph' #2", Bonny (1978) described the therapeutic meaning of specific musical elements and designed a music-centered system of analyzing the music programs. Bonny identified the following characteristic features of the music used in GIM sessions:

"1) music is a catalyst for tension and release
2) the music is a container for the GIM experience
3) the music stimulates the flow and movement of the imagery
4) the music offers variability in the stimulus
5) the music conveys mood
6) the music belongs to the Western tradition of classical music"
(see Grocke 1999, 149)

The features of tension and release, variability, and mood are examined together with the primary musical elements of pitch, rhythm/tempo, timbre and melodic line for each music selection and for the program as a whole. These elements are primary, because they carry specific metaphoric implications for the listener, e. g. changing timbres may represent particular characters in the imagery experience. In her monograph, Bonny also presents the idea of the "Inner morphology" of a music program in graphic, "affective-intensity profiles" of selected programs. An example is given below: The music program *Positive Affect.*

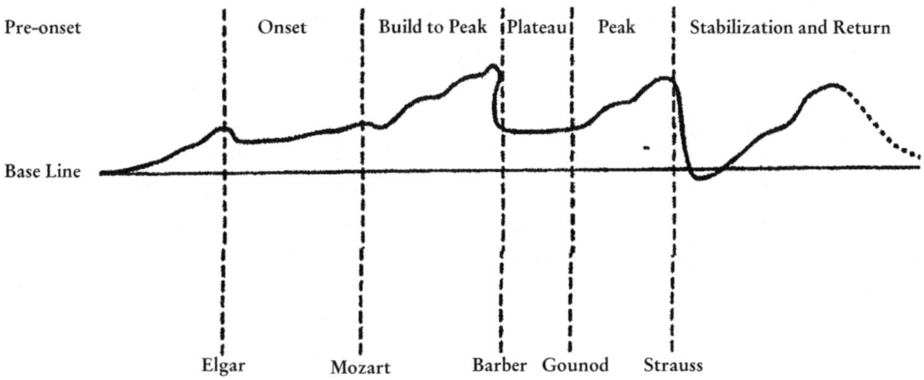

Fig. 1: The dynamic profile of the GIM music program ***Positive Affect.***

The X-axis is a timeline, including all 6 selections in the program. The Y-axis does not measure or indicate anything exact. It attempts a graphical representation of experienced affect intensity – the rising, stable or falling mood and energy levels.

Bonny's graphic charts ('contour model') give the reader an overview of how the music within a complete program is sequenced to facilitate a specific dynamic affective experience. Bonde and Pedersen (1996/2000) elaborated the method into a graphic description of single music selections, called *Dynamics of experience*. Their graph includes three levels of experience, and indicates on a timeline (with descriptive musical cues and references to the score) how the music unfolds affectively and dynamically, thus indicating an important aspect of the specific music selection's image potential.

Summer (1995) developed another music-centered method of analysis. However, this method focuses on the question of how well the music selections in a program meet the needs of a client. The two core concepts are *holding* and *stimulation*, providing the understanding of the music as a "space" where all sorts of experiences may develop. Holding music is characterized by relatively stable episodes, and gives the client a sense of safety, nurturance and "home", while stimulating music is less stable and invites the client to go beyond the present limits of her state and being in order to explore new possibilities within the imagery. The researcher identifies salient formal divisions in the music. She examines the musical elements within each division paying special attention to their metaphorical character of holding or stimulation.

Many researchers use the *phenomenological description of music* as part of their music research method. The description may or may not use specific music-analytic terminology. The purpose is to describe the unfolding music as heard in the lived experience of the listener/analyzer. Good examples are provided by Bonny and Grocke (see appendix 6 and 7 in Grocke 1999). Description of the imagery is the other core element in phenomenological methods. The "image potential" may be identified by the researcher through experiencing the music in a non-ordinary state of consciousness (from the client's perspective). Or, client experiences may be included in the analysis and correlated to the music. This will be demonstrated later.

Kasayka (1991) developed *a phenomenological method of analyzing GIM programs*. During the phase of exploring the music she follows the four steps of Ferrara's (1984) five-step procedure. In the phase of reviewing client experiences to a program she follows five steps inspired by Forinash and Gonzalez' (1989) procedure. Based on summaries from both phases, she investigates the interrelationships of music and imagery, and makes assertions on how the music may promote and support particular kinds of experience.

Grocke (1999) developed *A Structural Model for Music Analysis* (SMMA) as part of her study of "Pivotal moments" in BMGIM, and as fourth phase of an analytic procedure related to Kasayka's method. The SMMA leads the researcher to systematic comments and descriptions of the music selections in a program, addressing 15 parameters or categories: Style and form, texture, time, rhythmic features, tempo, tonal features, melody, embellishments, harmony, timbre/ quality of instrumentation, volume, intensity, mood, symbolism/association, and performance. The 15 categories were based on Bonny's unpublished sheet of nine "Musical Elements" (texture, tension/release, movement, mood/mode, structure, tonal, pitch, symbolic/associational, embellishments, composer's intent). The SMMA analysis of four musical selections underpinning the pivotal moments of four clients allowed Grocke to identify the following common features: "there was a formal structure in which repetition was evident; they were predominantly slow in speed and tempos were consistent; there was predictability in melodic, harmonic and rhythmic elements, and there was dialogue between solo instruments and orchestra, or between groups of instruments, or in vocal parts." She found that strong, structured music in a musical form and from the romantic period provided the necessary musical support for pivotal experiences. (Complementarily Lewis (1999) found that transformative BMGIM experiences of a spiritual nature were more likely supported by impressionist music.)

Grocke also introduced *Event Structure Analysis* (Tesch 1990) as a format facilitating the study of the relationship between music and imagery (coded as temporal or emotional events) as both unfold in time. SMMA and Event Structure Analysis were used by Marr (2000) in her analysis of the GIM music program "Grieving". She correlated the results of the SMMA analysis with the imagery of four clients, using the Event Structure Analysis format (as later in this chapter).

Affective-intuitive listening or "Body listening" is a heuristic method developed by Bonny (1993, 2002). It was designed to facilitate analysis from an experiential-embodied perspective. Bruscia labels the method "A music therapy version of embodied phenomenology" (Bruscia 2005). *Creative Music Analyses* inspired by Bonny's affective-intuitive perspective may use other modalities to gather information on the researcher's or the therapist's first-person experiences with the music, e. g. by making artwork, poetry, narratives or dramatic forms as interpretations of a music program.

Bruscia (2005; see also Abrams 2002b) developed the two most elaborate methods of music analysis, especially designed for research in music experiences in BMGIM: *Heuristic Music Analysis* and *Collaborative Heuristic Analysis of Music.* Both methods are aimed at understanding how the GIM music programs are experienced by client and therapist during a session, and therefore the analysis involves the researcher exploring the music in four experiential spaces: in an alert vs. in a deeply relaxed state X focusing on the music vs. on the imagery (see Figure 2). In the collaborative method the group of researchers experience the music program in all four spaces, both as guide and as imager.

A brief description of the research project BMGIM with Cancer Survivors. A Psychosocial Study of the influence of BMGIM on Mood and Quality of Life (Bonde 2005).

Six women, all cancer survivors, volunteered in the project. (The participants are introduced in Appendix A.) They received 10 individual standard BMGIM sessions over 4 months.

The research project used multiple methods. The influence of BMGIM on mood and quality of life was investigated in a quantitative study using standardized questionnaires (HADS, EORTC-C30, Antonovsky's SOC). Results included a significant reduction of anxiety from pretest to follow-up (as measured by HADS), and a significant increase in sense of coherence from pretest to follow-up (as measured by SOC).

The participants' experience of the therapy was investigated in an interview study based on Grounded Theory procedures. This study identified the following categories of self-perceived outcome: Enhanced coping, Improved mood, New perspectives on past/present/future, Enhanced hope, Improved self understanding, Coming to terms with life and death, Opening towards spirituality.

The relationship between music and imagery was investigated in a phenomenological-hermeneutic qualitative study, also based on Grounded Theory. Some of the results of the qualitative study are reported on here.

The complete dissertation is available as a pdf file at http://www.musik.aau.dk/research/musikterapi/gim-resource-center/index.htm
Other results are published in Bonde 2005b (A Case Study) and Bonde (forthcoming).

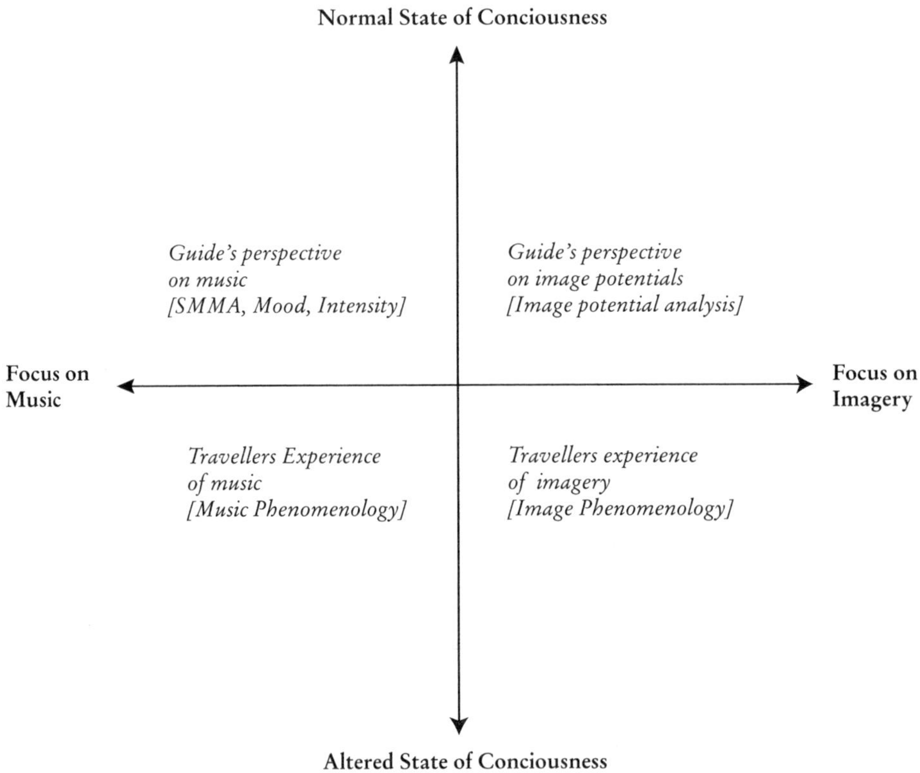

Fig. 2: Heuristic Music Analysis (HMA): Four analytic perspectives (Based on Bruscia (2005). [Methods in brackets added by the researcher].

Heuristic Music Analysis is (best) performed in dyads or in groups. Data from sessions are included and compared, and the results are brought together in a final synthesis. Bonde and Pedersen (1996/2001) present an example of an analysis of a full program (*Creativity 1*), performed in a dyad and inspired by an early version of the method. Further details on these and other methods especially designed for the analysis of music programs used in the Bonny Method is given by Abrams (Abrams 2002b).
In the following analysis, all four positions of the HMA are present:
1. (Lower left) In the phenomenological description of the music
2. (Lower right) In the imagery of four clients

3. (Upper left) In the SMMA analysis
4. (Upper right) In the description of the image potential

Heuristic Music Analysis: Music, Image Potential and Client Imagery in Brahms: Violin Concerto, 2nd movement

All music selections from GIM programs are included in the database "GIM Selections" (Bonde 2002), with data on the recording and the work, often including short characterizations by Helen Bonny or other programmers. The Brahms movement is described as "Pure, intense, romantic". However true this may be, it does not give the therapist sufficient information about the music and its therapeutic potential. A more comprehensive description can be found in Grocke (2002a, 117): "There is a classic structure to the music, with first and second themes, a development section, and a recapitulation". "It gives a soaring quality, a quality of peacefulness and rest, but also if an individual is ready for it, a peak experience" (Bonny and Mardis 1994). The second melody introduces a new aspect to the music, as if to offer a question and an answer. There is anguish, intensity, and strength in the violin part, as it soars throughout this section, building emotion and intensity in a dramatic and decorative way. The ending is particularly beautiful as the horns and woodwinds hold a long chord, and the violin has the final say."

Following the guidelines of HMA, the music will now be described from four perspectives. The first perspective is a phenomenological description of the music and some conclusions concerning the image potential of the piece.

Table 1. Phenomenological description of the Brahms movement (short version)

BRAHMS: *Violin Concerto D major, 2nd movement (in F major)*

A long oboe cantilena unfolds with stable woodwind accompaniment. The melody is simple, based on the three notes in the tonic major chord [a-f-c, often echoed by other instruments, before the melody continues], yet sophisticated: phrases may be prolonged or sequenced in an unpredictable, yet pleasant way. The slow adagio tempo makes it easy to follow both the core melody and the accompaniment. This is very safe – the only hint at tension and chromaticism is found in a) the transition bars between the melodic phrases, where bass and treble mark the dominant function in chromatic as/descending, b) the use of small crescendi-decrescendi. The entry of the solo violin and the strings (prepared by two string bars of tonic and dominant) is a beautiful restatement of the melody, with fresh echoes of the melodic core motif in woodwinds. However, this section (already shortly after the beginning of 2nd statement in F) takes the listener into new realms quite quickly: the key changes suddenly to the remote G flat/F sharp, not immediately identifiable as major or minor. The mood changes correspondingly (from mood wheel category 3/4 to 7), and the melodic line of the solo violin (even if the core motif is based on the 'innocent' motif cell of bar 10) becomes longing and plaintive, with many sighs (a falling semi-tone interval). This is intensified by an octave rise in the solo violin, by an unexpected fermata, by the many rather dramatic crescendos and the short melodic-harmonic sequences mowing upwards. The music is no longer stable and predictable, but ambiguous and filled with chromaticism and other musical surprises. The tempo also increases, until a calando brings the movement back to adagio and the tonic F major.

When the oboe sings the well-known pastorale theme the violin joins in with soft, eloquent embellishments of the melodic line. Diatonic and chromatic melodic movements are integrated on the firm harmonic basis of F major. The violin restates the core motif, and through a series of small variations/sequences the movement is brought to a comforting and affirmative close (with a surprising *piano* F minor chord (bar 113) as a last shadow of the drama from the second main section of the movement.

Conclusions concerning image potentials of the movement – are:

- The movement is in ternary form – A B A' – yet the predictability of the outline is 'blurred' (in a typical Brahmsian way) by the many unpredictable variations, especially in the B section.
- Major shifts with the potential for image transformation or changes are at 2:15 The violin entry, section B; 3:52 The mood and key shift to a more dramatic and tragic episode; 6:11 The return to a secure base, harmonically and melodically, with the two solo instruments in harmony, integrating diatonic and chromatic elements.
- The movement is basically supportive and lyrical-pastoral in character, but the B section brings some challenges for the listener in the form of tonal/harmonic drama, dynamic tension and melodic longing.

The musical perspectives are summarized in an "Intensity Profile" inspired by Bonny's "Affective Contour/Profiles":

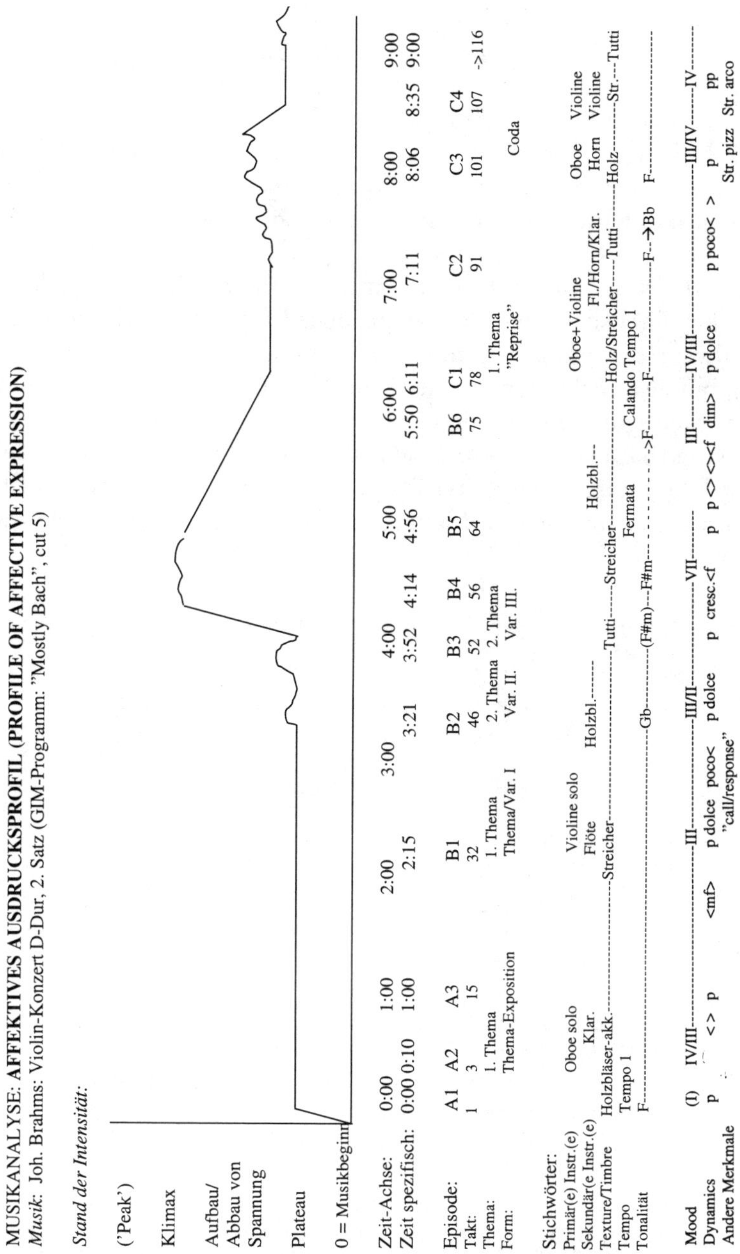

Fig. 3: Intensity Profile of Brahms ***Violin Concerto, 2nd. movement]***

This profile or map of the "inner morphology" of the Brahms movement is based on the following analytic procedures:

- Phenomenological description of the movement (Table 1)
- Analysis of the musical form (auditory and visually, consulting the score)3
- Mood Analysis (using Hevner's "Mood Wheel")[4]
- Analysis of the image potential.5
- Furthermore, I have integrated material from an analysis that was undertaken during a workshop with 12 music therapy researchers6.

The Intensity Profile is not an exact measurement of any single musical element. Tension and higher intensity level may be produced by volume (loud music is often, but not always experienced as more intense than quiet music; crescendos as intensifying), but also melodic movement and phrasing contributes (ascending movement often producing tension, descending relaxation), as do mood, texture etc. It is possible to make an exact graphic representation of the energy and tension level of the recording (measured in Volts) The *digitised wave-form* (DW) profile of the Brahms recording is presented in Figure 4, enabling a visual comparison with the Intensity Profile:

3 This analysis is integrated in the Intensity Profile. The recording used was a digital remastering of an analogue recording from the 1960s. Solist: David Oistrakh, conductor: Franz Konwitschny. DG 447 427-2. Score used: Heugel H 31406.

4 Also integrated in the Intensity Profile, Hevner's Mood Wheel is included in Bonny 2002 p. 309.

5 Based on the Phenomenological description and material from the workshop describe in note 4.

6 I would like to thank all participants in my workshop at the Ph. D.-course in Aalborg University, October 25th, 2003. The participants in this workshop listened to the Brahms movement without any introductory information about the music. Individually, they chose and worked through one of the following tasks: 1) Auditory Analysis of the music (identifying salient musical features) 2) Visual Analysis using the score (same purpose as a), 3) Mood Analysis (using the Mood wheel), 4) Analysis of the image potential (Questionnaire on the character of the listener's personal imagery or free indication/suggestion of image potentials), 5) Drawing a Mandala (+ comments).

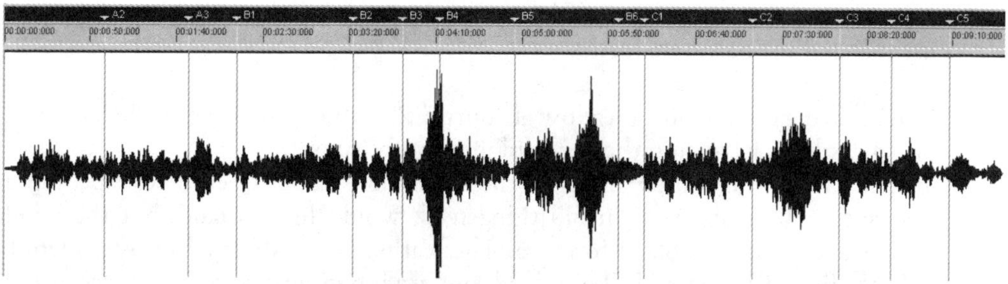

Fig. 4: The digitised waveform profile of Brahms ***Violin Concerto, 2**nd*

The DW-profile is close to the Intensity Profile in many ways: the climax is the same, and the three major shifts in intensity level are located the same places. However, there are important differences: The "peak point" indicated at the Calando is not reflected in the DW, as it is pp, and the intensity level of the B-section (higher than A and C) is not reflected in the 'mechanical' profile.

The Intensity Profile with cues makes it clear that the music is composed of three interconnected, yet rather different sections. The tonally stable, lyric-yearning first section leads directly – and rather unexpectedly (B2, bar 46) – into the second section, characterized by an initial building of dynamic tension and rather turbulent episodes (changing levels of dynamics and tension, alternation between major and minor, dramatic and passionate expression of the solo violin). Tonal and dynamic stability returns, and the movement finds perfect balance and rest in the third section, which has the character of a synthesis: the two solo instruments play together in dialogue (each leading or accompanying the other, obligato). In the orchestral accompaniment we hear both the wind chorus of the first section and the string chorus of the second.

Even if Brahms included a certain ambiguity of form in this movement – it can be heard as a movement in ternary form (ABA') or as a set of variations – this analysis points to a division in three sections, with the most prominent transitions in bars 46 (B2) and 78 (C1). The first transition is sudden and surprising, while the second is very well prepared (through the gradual slowing down of the Calando).

A very basic narrative pattern is found in this movement: A safe base → A journey/exploration or challenge → Return to base after new experiences. The image potential may be described in the following way: The stable plateau of the first section promotes a sense of security and confidence (e. g. positive memories) and the lyric-pastoral character may evoke nature scenes and landscape imagery. In the second section, new images are bound to appear: the idyllic atmosphere is destroyed or threatened, and corresponding moods and emotions may be evoked. In the final section, a return is likely, or maybe the resolution of or new perspectives on a problem.

Two examples from the material of the expert group may illustrate the image potential and the narrative form:

(A) 1. A loving couple on a meadow at sunrise; 2. A dramatic scene in the hall of an old castle; 3. Return to the peaceful meadow at sunset.
(B) 1. A tiny white feather floats in the sunshine over an open landscape and a forest. 2. It floats over an old thingstead, would like to land, but the wind blows it on, over a black forest. 3. The feather is transformed into two white butterflies. They would like to land, but are blown upwards. They freeze and fall to the ground in the forest as tiny ice crystals.

The indicated image potential makes the music suitable for several therapeutic purposes. In the GIM program *Mostly Bach* the Brahms movement is cut 5 (of 6), following 4 emotionally demanding compositions by J. S. Bach (in Leopold Stokowski's romantic orchestrations). It is quite common for clients to experience the Brahms movement as a great relief or even reward after a lengthy period of 'hard work', and this is confirmed or extended by the last cut of the program: the slow movement from Bach's *Double Concerto*. which This is almost exclusively in mood 4, and in many ways a perfectly balanced composition and program ending (An analysis of this movement can be found in Bonde (2005) chapter 8.3.1). The combination of safety/confidence and a certain challenge also makes the Brahms movement suitable for assessment. In this project, the therapist used the music to assess some of the participants, i. e. as the first piece of music in their GIM process. We shall now take a closer look at the imagery of the six participants as they experienced the Brahms movement for the first time, and how it relates to the flow of the music.

Event Structure Analysis (Brahms): The relationship between music and imagery

Tesch (1990) defines Event Structure Analysis (ESA) as a method to "examine and represent series of events as logical structures, i. e. as elements and their connections (including the assumptions that govern these connections) that can serve as explanatory models for interpreting actual or folkloristic sequences or events" (Heise and Lewis 1988 quoted in Tesch 1990, 29). ESA, or 'Qualitative Sequential Analysis', belongs – like Grounded Theory – to a specific type of Qualitative research: Research in which connections are sought between Identified and Categorized Elements (Tesch, ibd., 85). It uses events as the units of analysis. They are the elements among which the connections are sought. Events in real life or stories occur in chronological order. However, there is an underlying 'logical structure' according to which they happen. It would not make sense for some events to occur at certain points in time, because certain conditions have not been met. Furthermore, a story or actual event takes one turn every time a prior event is completed. At the same time, there are actually several possibilities of events that could occur instead. This is the kind of logical structure the event analyst is interested in. David Heise calls these logical structures "production grammars" (Heise 1988 in Tesch 1990, 88) They could also be called 'sets of rules'.[7]

Within qualitative sociological research, ESA is used by researchers who focus on chronological sequences and their relationship, based on choice making by people involved in the sequences. Abstract logical structures of events "can be generated and compared with actual events (...) Event analysis can be applied not only to actual incidents but to folk tales and other cultural narratives (Heise, 1988)" (Tesch 1990, 27)."…. preferred method of data display is 'directed graphs' in which 'nodes symbolize elements, and lines between nodes show relations'").

ESA can be considered a qualitative enrichment of the quantitative 'sequential analysis'. The focus of interest is "the dynamic aspects of phenomena, such as interactions between or among people, or *the unfolding of folk tales and other stories*. The objective is to discover the structure of these processes, i. e., the 'rules' that govern the sequence of interactions or events. Quantitative researchers use statistics like transitional probability or time-series analysis to discover regularities in the sequence of events. *Qualitative researchers are more interested in the conceptual logic of event structures, i. e., in models that show relationships between events….* A production grammar is expressed either as a list of relations between events, or depicted in a diagram" (Tesch 1990, 64, italics added by me). Tesch distinguishes between structural analysis and interpretational analysis, and ESA belongs to the first group.

Even if ESA is not defined by Tesch as a 'narrative method', it is obvious that ESA is well suited for the analysis of clinical events like BMGIM sessions. ESA has been used by Grocke (1999) in her study of "Pivotal Moments in GIM", and by Marr (2000) to analyse the music and imagery sequences of four participants 'travelling' to the music program *Grieving* (Keiser 1986). ESA was applied "to discover how the temporal music sequence, and specific musical elements, influenced imagery processes and development" (Marr 2000, p. iii). In this analysis, I use the same graphic table model as Marr, correlating musical episodes (based on the phenomenological description and the SMMA analysis) with the imagery sequences of the participants. The coding system is different from Marr's. She made a distinction between temporal events ("imagery as it occurred in time or as a chronological sequence") and Emotional events ("images reflect emotional or feeling content, or the participant described or expressed emotion"). I found these codes too broad for my purpose, so in this analysis I used the code column for a registration of image modalities, in order to study eventual patterns in the distribution. 'Comments' indicate important correlations between music and imagery, based on my own hermeneutic interpretations of the music.

7 Event Structure Analysis is not mentioned in the methodological handbooks of Banister (1994), Wolcott (1994), Creswell (1995) or Robson (2002)

A necessary precondition for the ESA is a complete and very precise transcription of the imagery as it unfolds in time. Only when this transcription is combined with the score is it possible to see exactly when, in a given episode, an image occurs – and how it occurs or develops.

The event structure analysis of the second movement of Brahms' Violin Concerto is portrayed in Table 2. The columns are defined in the following way:

Column 1: Episodes correspond with the phenomenological description and the Intensity profile (references to bars in the score)

Column 2: Coding of image modalities (V=visual, A=auditory, S=sensory-kinaesthetic, O=olfactory, G=gustatory, E=emotions, M=Memories, R=reflections and thoughts, T=transpersonal, Ot=Other, e. g. body tension).

Column 3: Cues referring to the phenomenological description and the Intensity profile Columns 4–8: Imagery of six participants (1,1=First session, first music selection). ANHO and SAAA say very little, and so they share a column (*ANHO in italics;* **SAAA in bold)**

Column 9: Hermeneutic interpretations of music and image potential.

Table 2. Event structure analysis. Brahms Violin Concerto in D, 2nd movement [Only a few guide's interventions are included]

Episode/Bars	**Code**	**Music**	**INLA 1,1**	**ESMA 1,1**	**PIJØ 1,1**	*ANHO 2,1* **SAAA 4,4**	**WIFU 3,3**	**Comments**
A1 (1-2)	V/E	F major chord			[Induction image: at the sea]		The little girl is always with me	The opening is really ”open”: ”What may come now?”
A2 (3-14)	V	Oboe cantilena unfolding, 1st section of melody		I can see them.				The ’safe base’ is established by this beautiful and predictable, yet flexible and dynamic melody in F.
A3 (15-31)	R/S G/S V E	2nd section of melody	Very nice. Not really happy music, but OK. It's very calming.	It is free. Good air. A little salt.	Sunset. A quiet day.	*[What are you aware of in the music?] (No answer)*	No matter where I go I just want to feel peace and calm inside. I feel calm...	The melodic line is expanded in a new way, and the melody comes to a perfect end in F
B1 (32-45)	R/M/S V/M V E/S	Violin takes over the cantilena and expands it. Many imitation of thematic core	Lovely music! Aahhh! The music is lifting me up now. Wings come to my mind – or I am drifting on a cloud. Wonderful lightness	I was thinking that I was walking at the beach, where a river runs out.	I see the light of the ocean. It twinkles down there. The last sunbeams make the surface twinkle. Fiery colours of the sun: bronze, red... Beautiful clouds above me.	I just sink down... in peace *[Is that what you need?]* I think so. *[Therapist checks in later, but there is no reaction apart from a smile and a relaxed body]*	.... in my whole body	Both a repetition and a new quality – of timbre and expression. Interaction of instruments

Episode/Bars	Code	Music	INLA 1,1	ESMA 1,1	PIJØ 1,1	*ANHO 2,1* SAAA 4,4	WIFU 3,3	Comments
B2 (46-51)	V/E Ot	Unexpected key shift to G flat major. A small motif (oboe bar 12) is transformed and elaborated.		In the middle of the river there are rocks, the water gushing over them. The river is deep; I won't risk jumping on the rocks to get over.		I feel tense, like if I have to produce something... and I cannot!		The first unexpected shift: without modulation the key changes to the dreamy world of G flat major. The violin responds by changes in the melody and the mood.
B3 (52-55)	E Ot V/E	Dynamic intensity and tonal shift. Crescendo < f			A sentimental mood.	You ask me: 'What do you see?' – And I see nothing, and then...	The girl helps me clear away...	Yearning and melancholy is intensified into a passionate expression
B4 (56-63)	R/V/S M/V E R/E	Violin presents theme variation in F3 minor. Passionate "Call-Response" dialogue between solo/woodwinds Surprisingly the episode ends with a fermata	I am aware of this violin being very comforting. It makes me think of.... dancing couples with swinging skirts – swinging to the music. But there is also melancholy in the music..	Reminds me more of a summer day with sailboats racing on the fjord. Old wooden ships. Great to watch them. There's a tongue of land where you can watch them from above	But also beautiful I think I am alone		I would like to have things cleared away...	The new mood is melodically explored, new image potentials. The surprising fermata enables reflection.

Episode/Bars	Code	Music	INLA 1,1	ESMA 1,1	PIJØ 1,1	*ANHO 2,1* SAAA 4,4	WIFU 3,3	Comments
B5 (64-74)	R M/R E Ot	Soft p start then dynamic changes < >, Melodic-harmonic sequences, crescendo culminating f (bar 73), transition to F under preparation	...pushing or stimulating other moods. I prefer the lightness. But I know the other mood very well. A lot of music evokes that melancholy. That's fascinating – but I prefer the other one, and I can stay with the lightness. There's aggression in this music also – spite!	The sails being filled by the wind. There can be more than 50 boats. There's something about this music: It gives an 'impetus' to the movement'. It is in the music.	It is OK to be alone.	[*Can you allow the music to surround you?]* Mmm. [*Let the music move you*] Mmm.		An episode with many events and dynamic changes – a lot of energy is mobilized (and may be mobilized in the listener) – and then the music slows down, preparing the way for...
B6 (75-77)	R V/S Ot	Long ritardando bringing music back to initial tempo, mood and key. Solo violin in its highest register. Misterioso	But now it's calm again		I am sailing in my kayak near (the coast at Moesgaard) Lyme grass. But no other people there.	[*Let the music give you what you need*] Mmm.		... new reflections. Without knowing for sure it feels like reapproaching the safe base.

Episode/Bars	Code	Music	INLA 1,1	ESMA 1,1	PIJØ 1,1	*ANHO 2,1* SAAA 4,4	WIFU 3,3	Comments
C1 (78-90)	V/R V/E V/E	Recapitulation and synthesis. First theme in oboe with violin embellishment, then roles change. Integration of diatonic and chromatic movements	Now, autumn leaves came. The last leaves are falling. The tree is tripped naked. A tree with big leaves – Maple! It's all orange. On the earth lie the orange leaves. It's beautiful, but also decline	I am walking on my beach. It can be rough down there sometimes. The wind is quite stiff. But you can go into the plantation and find shelter. Walk there and feel good. There are brackens and bushes and everything.	Now it's time for sunrise. It feels fine, not so sentimental anymore. It grows lighter.			In the recapitulation all elements of the movement is brought together in harmony. A beautiful partnership of the two solo instruments, joined by both groups of the accompanying orchestra. Serenity and harmony.
C2 (91-100)	R R V/S V/E	Violin restates first theme, whole orchestra accompanying. Pizzicato strings, great crescendo. Climax > p. Modulation to subdominant. Violin drops more than two octaves.	It is like a pleasant acceptation of the decline. I mean: autumn is the opposite of spring. In Spring everything grows, in Autumn everything is 'packed down' again.	You can always find shelter there, even if the wind is howling. I think this music was rather stiff; it reminds me of stiff winds – right in the face. But I can manage – I like it.	I am sitting in my kayak. The sea is dead calm; I can see the sea floor. I am paddling very quietly – making no noise.		I see the beautiful colours!	The last increase in intensity is created when both accompanying groups play together. The pizz. and the crescendo combined intensifies the energy. The imagery may correspondingly come to a final clarity.

Episode/Bars	Code	Music	INLA 1,1	ESMA 1,1	PIJØ 1,1	*ANHO 2,1* SAAA 4,4	WIFU 3,3	Comments
C3 (100-106)	R/E R	Oboe sings the core motif + the epilogue in tonic F, accompanied by arp. and emb. in the solo violin, first in low then high register. Sparse acc., only woodwinds	Actually I really like Autumn, like... accepting the melancholy. There is also death in this image: This tree stripped naked. But it doesn't die, does it? [No it comes back] It comes back; it just hibernates to come back next year.	I think this music changes a lot – between something stiff and something soft.				The music rests. The epilogue sounds confident first in the oboe...
C4 (107-116)	R R/E V/S	Solo violin sings the epilogue accompanied by strings (arco). A surprising f minor chord casts a shadow over the comforting and affirmative ending.	That cycle is absolutely fascinating! They are mutually dependent – of course I know!	Very good. This last bit was very comforting. Fine (laughs)	I start paddling down the coast ... near home, at Århus – Moesgaard beach.	I am relaxed now.		...then in the violin. The music comes to a harmonic closure, yet with a small reminder of the passion and the drama (the f minor chord).

The analysis of the unfolding imagery – or 'events' – may be done either vertical, i. e. following the imagery of one client, or horizontal, i. e. making comparisons between the clients within the episode.

Vertical observations of the imagery of six clients.

INLA initially focuses on the music and its features. A1→B1: She describes the mood of the music, which she likes, and allows herself to react spontaneously and bodily to the music. From the perceived beauty, she develops a feeling of lightness and freedom. When the music changes in B2→B3, she is silent, and then follows an image of a dancing couple (B4). However, INLA also recognizes other moods, which she identifies as melancholy (sadness) (B5, first part) and aggression (B5, second part). The Calando (B6) is recognized as a calm transition, and during the recapitulation (A') she experiences a sequence of Fall imagery with clear metaphoric significance. In C1, the image of a naked maple tree leads to reflections of decay. In C2, INLA identifies with the tree, and in C3 she confronts herself with thoughts of death/hibernation and rebirth/Spring renewal. C4 brings acceptance and recognition of this life cycle; a reconciliation with aspects of sadness, death and loss.

ESMA is taken to 'her beach' by the induction and the music. A sequence of associations and memories follows: The fresh air at the salty inlet (fjord) (A3), the difficulties and danger connected to any attempt to cross the river (B2→B3), a boat race with a whole 'armada' of old sailboats (B4), and reflections on the music that produces an 'impetus to the movement' (B5). In the recapitulation, ESMA finds shelter from the stiff winds in a nearby plantation (C1) where she reflects on the polarity of stiff ↔ soft in the music (and in the winds of the beach). In the pause before the next music selection, (Bach's *Double Concerto*, 2nd movement) she declares that she feels fine and calm.

PIJØ follows the induction image – being at the sea. In the first sequence of her journey (→B2) she experiences a sunset at a well-known beach, with much light and many colours. When the music changes (B2→B5), she reports on being in a sentimental mood and being alone, which she accepts even if it is obvious that she does not like this mood. As the music moves towards a climax (in B5) the experiential perspective changes, and active images of sailing in a kayak appear (PIJØ did sail in kayaks before she got cancer). Calmness and solitude returns (B6), and the recapitulation brings a sunrise (C1). The mood is no longer sentimental, and the experience of the last episodes is marked by a deep sense of calmness and clarity.

These three clients listened to the Brahms movement as the very first piece of music in their very first session. They were comfortable with the format and delved into their inner imaginative world without problems.

This was not the case for ANHO, who listened to Brahms as the first piece of music in her second session. In the first session it had already become obvious that even if ANHO was able to enjoy the music she had difficulties staying in ASC and holding on to the images. This was very frustrating for her. The theme of 'having to produce something' or 'not being good enough' is also evident in session #2, where bodily tension is reported in B2, when the music becomes more challenging. The therapist makes a choice and guides the client's attention towards the music, suggesting that the client take from the music what it can give her mind and body. In the end ANHO reports that she feels relaxed.

In contrast, WIFU, who listened to the Brahms movement as the third selection in her third session, went deeply into the process from the very beginning of the session. The ESA shows that she talked very sparsely, but from the therapist's log it is clear that this only reflects a need to be with the imagery without ,interruption' by the therapist. The emotional intensity is high, and the image of the little girl has great significance for the client. (In the interview she states that the girl represents her own intuition and total confidence). The feeling of confidence is embodied from the beginning (A→B1). As the music changes and becomes more challenging (B2→B4), WIFU reports that she is engaged in a process of clearing-out, assisted by the girl. A long silence follows. In C2, when the pizzicato accompaniment of the main theme begins, she talks about beautiful colours, whereupon a new silence follows.

SAAA listened to the movement as the fourth piece in her fourth session. At this point in the session she is already in a state of deep relaxation, beyond visual imagery, and she only reports verbally that she feels serene and calm in the beginning of the piece. The rest of the time she is silent and apparently very comfortable.

Vertical observation of similarities and differences.

Similarities: four of the clients (the exceptions are ANHO and SAAA) experienced predominantly visual imagery, developing in spirals with reflections and emotions. The music came to the foreground now and then, as described in Goldberg's holographic field model (Goldberg 2002). Three of the clients had nature experiences in which they were alone (it is not possible to identify the place of WIFUs imagery; however, it includes colours, maybe of flowers).

Differences: the focuses of the clients were of course individual, and so was the outcome of the imagery: Existential reflections (INLA, PIJØ), memories (ESMA), deep emotion (WIFU), psychodynamic awareness and frustration (ANHO) – as well as musical awareness (INLA, ESMA) and deep relaxation (SAAA).

Horizontal observation of similarities and differences.

Similarities: All imagery in episodes A→B1 is characterized by positive emotions and a slow tempo (of the imagery). The sudden changes in tonality, melody and dynamics from B2–B5 evoke new elements in the imagery: contrasts in mood, increased tempo, challenges, changing emotions. At the end of section B (B6) where the music is dominated by diminuendo, ritardando and calm, the imagery slows down and most of the clients are silent. In the synthesis or recapitulation (C – where elements of A and B are integrated) a (corresponding) synthesis of positive emotions, slow tempo and new qualities is seen: recognitions, acceptance, and awareness. Four of the six clients experience imagery closely connected with the musical sequences, and the development of the imagery reflects the inner morphology of the composition (Intensity Profile).

Differences: The information density and the image modalities are very different from episode to episode. WIFU and SAAA speak very little, ANHO does not experience any imagery, PIJØ's reporting is quite evenly distributed, and INLA and ESMA report very actively in some episodes (not the same). This makes the individual resonance to the music and the personal 'travel style' of each of the participants very clear.

This Event Structure Analysis shows that even if the imagery and 'travel style' of the clients is personal and individual, many similarities and correspondences can be observed. Of primary importance is the observation that the unfolding and development of the imagery is not a matter of coincidence. On the contrary it follows the morphology of the music closely. Another important conclusion is that four of the five clients are able to use the music in a therapeutically productive way, even in their first session (three clients), although they have no music therapy experience and no special musical background (ESMA even described herself as 'musically illiterate').

The next step in the investigation is an attempt to answer the questions of whether the imagery is related to the life world and problem focus of the individual client – directly or as metaphors, and whether or how images and metaphors are configured.

Metaphors and narratives in the music-listening periods

In this section some phenomenological-hermeneutic questions are addressed:

- Is it possible to identify different types or levels of metaphors in the material?
- What is the relationship between the images/metaphors and the problems/focus of the clients?

Images are – images! We cannot talk about metaphors before the images have been reported on verbally in the therapeutic dialogue, during or after the music-listening period (Bonde 2000). And we must distinguish between referential and metaphorical imagery. Parallel to image modalities we can operate with visual, sensory-kinaesthetic and other metaphors. Symbols form a special type of image/ metaphor: it cannot be reported or understood fully through being communicated verbally.

In Bonde (2000), three clinically relevant levels of metaphor commonly observed in the GIM literature were identified:

- The narrative episode configured round a core metaphor that characterized the client's problem in the real world.
- The narrative configuration of various parts of the client's self in relation to a life problem or a therapeutic issue.
- The complete narrative, based on the configuration of several metaphors into a coherent story.

Through the analysis of the imagery found during only one piece of music, it is not, in principle, possible to say anything definite about a client's life problems. All three types or levels of metaphors can only rarely be identified in an episode based on one piece of music or even in one single session (Bonde 2000, 2003). However, by including information from other sessions it becomes possible to say something about the significance of the metaphors presented in the ESA.

INLA: The naked maple tree is a core metaphor enabling the client to express her vulnerability. The recognition of the eternal cycle of Fall/Decline/Death and Spring/Rebirth/Life evoked by the tree metaphor is a good example of the second level of configuration: The client expresses her confidence in the music, the imagery and the metaphoric process.

ESMA: The experience of wind and sea at the "homely beach" is an episode configured around the core metaphor of the "beach wanderer": Within the surroundings of well-known and beloved nature, it is possible to reflect on the ups and downs of life; the wind blows cold or warm, and it is possible to find shelter.

PIJØ: The double position – and core metaphor of the "beach wanderer"/ kayak rower is characteristic of an episode where the client may learn something new about being alone or isolated (as a cancer patient in rehabilitation). Looking at oneself from the outside and inside out enables new perspectives to emerge.

WIFU: In this excerpt, only a flash of light is shed on the client's GIM process. In all ten sessions this woman is deeply involved and engaged in her imagery. Although she only speaks very little during the session, it is obvious that the interaction with the little girl has existential significance. The girl is a metaphor of a part of the client's self (intuition, self-confidence) and is configured in several sessions.

ANHO: No images are configured in this session, but the psychodynamic problem of "being good enough" (without producing images) is present and dealt with.

SAAA: No images or metaphors are configured; however the state of deep wordless relaxation is helpful for the client, who is often very demanding of herself.

Identifying processes of narrative configuration.

In the analysis, I have identified four narrative episodes configured round a core of self-metaphors. Two episodes were not of a narrative or metaphorical character. The ternary structure of the music mentioned in the music analysis has a parallel in a ternary dramatic structure in all four narrative episodes:

INLA: 1. Beauty (of the music)/Lightness/Dancing couples → 2. Melancholy/Mood of fall → 3. Naked maple tree: Death and rebirth/life cycle.
ESMA: 1. Relieving beach promenade/sailboats → 2. Stormy weather/full sails/needing protection → 3. Finding shelter in the plantation.
PIJØ: 1. Calm sea (seen from the beach) → 2. Sentimental moods and emotions → 3. Calm seas (seen from the kayak)
WIFU: 1. Intimacy with little girl → 2. Cleaning up (together with the girl) → 3. Seeing beautiful colours.
(ANHO: 1. No images, frustration → 2. Bodily tension → 3. Relaxation)
(SAAA: Apparently no development in stages or sections)

Bonde (2005, chapter 7) demonstrates in a more elaborate way how personal core or self-metaphors were configured during the therapeutic process, and how it was possible to identify emplotment. This analysis was based on Paul Ricoeur's theories. These processes are demonstrated in a case study (Bonde 2005a).

Discussion

There is no direct path leading from music to imagery - apart from the spontaneous, first order experience of what happens individually within the spontaneous BMGIM experience. It is not possible to infer the image (or therapeutic) potential of a piece of music from a phenomenological description or a structural analysis of the music. A combination of phenomenological, hermeneutic and heuristic procedures is needed when a therapist or researcher wants to establish a deeper understanding of the therapeutic potential of a music selection or program, or the role of music as "'co-therapist'". Music in BMGIM does not operate as a well-defined stimulus leading to a predictable response. The music stimulates supports and frames the multimodal imagery, and the images can serve as metaphors of psychological or existential problems and solutions. The music itself can also be experienced and understood as a metaphor of human being and interacting.

Hevner's Mood wheel is one of the oldest devices of experimental music psychology still in use. It was designed in the early 1930s, and is still used to identify one very important aspect of the affective expression of the music (for a discussion, see: Gabrielsson and Lindström 2001, Juslin and Sloboda 2001). However, a critical question is whether important affective qualities are missing in the mood wheel, and whether the 'wheel' construction is sufficiently validated (Bonde 1997; see also Wosch 2002 and his chapter in this book). It is especially relevant to make an inquiry about the qualities of anxious/anxiety and angry/anger in a mood analysis, as they seem to be missing in Hevner's system. A partial answer may be that Hevner designed the mood wheel to identify the mood expressed in the music (or better: the mood the music is expressive of), not the mood or affect of the listener, as influenced by the music. Music is not 'a sentient being' (Kivy 1990), and I agree with Hevner (and many others) that music cannot express anxiety or anger. However, music in mood category 7 or 8 may very well evoke or support feelings of anger or rage in a client (For example: The special GIM Program *Affect release* was designed to support anger work. It begins with the movement *Mars* from G. Holst's symphonic suite *The Planets*, followed by two movements from Orff's *Carmina Burana*). Anxiety may be evoked – or provoked – by music in different mood categories, often by music that is ambiguous, with more than one layer of expression and meaning, with alien timbres etc. (For example: 2nd movement of Menotti's *Piano Concerto*, and excerpts from Shostakovich's *5th symphony*, both included in the program *Emotional Expression II*).

Anxiety and anger are very important mood states or emotions in BMGIM therapy, and even if these states are not included in the mood wheel they can be evoked and supported by the music. Thus I find Hevner's mood wheel compatible with other systems of emotional categorization (see the discussion in Wosch 2002 and in this book). Anger or anxiety is not present in the music and imagery episodes analyzed here, however, these emotional qualities were present in other sessions, where they were framed and supported by matching music.

The multiple perspectives of Bruscia's Heuristic Music Analysis enable a rich understanding of music as an existential message and therapeutic agent. In many studies, Bruscia developed a theoretical, yet clinically based, understanding of analogies between musical elements and parameters ('components' in Hegi's terminology (Hegi 1998)) and existential-emotional qualities, primarily in his Assessment-System IAP (Improvisation Assessment Profiles) (Bruscia 1987, 1994). In his preface to the Norwegian edition Bruscia (1994) writes that"... each musical element provides a musical metaphor – or perhaps archetype – for expressing a particular aspect of 'being-in-the-world' (...) Thus, each musical element has its own range of possibilities for expressive meanings, which are different from other elements." Examples: Musical form may serve as a metaphor of 'being-in-the-world', texture (mono-, homo- or polyphony) as a metaphor of 'being-in-space', melody as 'expression-of-self' etc. Following Bruscia's hermeneutic interpretations of music as metaphor, the main theme of the Brahms *Violin Concerto*, 2nd movement might be characterized as an entity/being or gestalt with

- a clear identity
- an ability to collaborate
- a flexibility of structure
- an ability to re-establish balance after episodes of dynamic tension
- credibility and sincerity
- precision and shading
- organic yet complex features

All in all, these features are psychological qualities of the music's image potential.

Theoretical perspectives on music as metaphor and narrative

The early experimental music psychologists (including Hevner) reintroduced the study of music and emotion. And a few philosophers with an interest in music aesthetics and music experience continued the discussion of the relationship between music and emotion, including the ever controversial question of if and how music may 'express emotion'.[8] The first book in modern time addressing the relationship of music and metaphor was Ferguson's *Music and Metaphor* (1960). The book investigated how music can be considered expression, and how music may express emotion and meaning. Ferguson understands music as a means of communication. "It is the perception of a full reality of experience – an awareness in which our every faculty of sensuous, intellectual, and emotional perception is indeed focused to a point." (p. 16) Ferguson also investigated music as embodied emotions and the elements of expression in music. He identified two embodied elements of music: tension and motion. "Our hypothesis... may be summarized as follows: There are two fundamental elements of musical expression – tone stress and ideal motion. These elements may serve to portray, respectively, two of three elemental factors of emotional experience – nervous tension and motor impulse." (p. 87) Secondary factors enhancing the vividness of the elemental suggestions made by tension and motion are: timbre, register, dynamic or rhythmic inflection. The Epilogue uses the concepts of metaphor and analogy to show how

8 The study of 'Music and Emotion' throughout the 20th Century is summarized and discussed in the comprehensive textbook with the same title, edited by Juslin and Sloboda (2001). This volume includes perspectives from philosophy, musicology, cognitive psychology and music therapy (Bunt and Pavlicevic). From a music therapy perspective, Pavlicevic (1997) presented an overview of the music and meaning debate, including a presentation of her own concept of 'Dynamic form'.

> "Tension and motion... are characteristic of human as well as of musical bodies. In the musical body they function for structure. In the human body they function through its pre-existent structure as the translation into activity of impulses aroused in that body by what may be succinctly designated as experience." (...) "The 'thing' which motion and tension can portray will naturally be a thing of which motion and tension are themselves characteristic. Such a thing is the human nervous system under the stress of emotion." (p. 185)

The issues raised in Ferguson's book have been standard elements in the discussion of music and emotion, music and meaning, and the role of the metaphor in music understanding for more than 50 years.

> "The composer who strives to give musical expression to his mood or emotion manages to discover and mould, presumably in most cases quite unconsciously, a tonal design which resembles very closely the internal pattern of his own affective state. The music then sounds the way an emotion feels." (Pratt 1938, as quoted in Ferguson (1960) p. 27).

This characterization of what is often called "expressive form" is one of the earliest examples of a modern psychological understanding of the relationship between music and mood or emotion. Since Eduard Hanslick's *Vom Musikalisch-Schönen* (1854) it was a musicological axiom that music does not express or refer to anything external (including psychologically 'internal' emotions). This anti-representational, anti-expressionist and anti-metaphorical attitude is still quite common in modern musicology. However, things have changed with the entry of so-called ‚new musicology' (Ruud 2000, Ansdell 2001) and the opening of music science and aesthetics towards other disciplines, especially cognitive psychology[9]. Music therapists often (more or less consciously) adhere to the (opposite) notion that music – be it as sound symbols in clinical improvisations or as imagery evoked in receptive music therapy – is an expression of the inner world of the client, including resources as well as pathological aspects. However, the issue of referential meaning in music is still controversial in musicology.

In music therapy theory, the understanding of music as metaphor and narrative is still in an early developmental phase. I have argued (Bonde 2002c) that the study of music as metaphor or narrative should focus on the relationship between musical syntax and musical semantics, with a link to psychodynamic and humanistic-existential paradigms. In this chapter it is not possible to unfold

9 The European Society for the Cognitive Sciences of Music (ESCOM) was founded in the 1990'es as an interdisciplinary forum including music psychology, musicology and music therapy. The ESCOM journal *Musicae Scientiae* is one of the most important sources of knowledge on musical meaning, including metaphor studies.

this theoretical discussion, but I will make reference to a few relevant texts. With his theory of *analogy* Smeijsters (1999) formulated a general theory of music therapy, with the purpose of 'bridging the gap' between music in psychotherapy and music in special education. His theory is mainly based on active music therapy. However, his dual concept of "Pathological musical processes" and "therapeutic musical processes" is also relevant in receptive music therapy. Analogy means that pathological problems correspond with musical expression and – the other way round – that psychological problem solving is reflected and maybe anticipated in the music. Aldridge (1996; Aldridge and Aldridge 1999) sketches a musically based metaphorical and narrative understanding of the human being: "The perception of music requires a holistic strategy where the play of patterned frequencies is recognized within the matrix of time. People may be described in similar terms as beings in the world who are patterned frequencies in time." (Aldridge 1996, 31). – The theory of music as metaphor is a more narrow and specific clinical theory describing a) the psychological equivalence of musical elements – *music as metaphor*, b) how clients present their music experiences verbally using metaphors – *metaphors of music (experience)*, and how these metaphors have clinical value and significance as information on the client's sense of self. The metaphorical dimension of musical elements was presented above, related to Bruscia's IAPs. There are only few studies of metaphors of music in the music therapy literature, and only two of the authors relate to the cognitive theory of metaphors, dominating contemporary psychology (Bonde 2000; Jungaberle 1999, 2001). However, metaphoric projection is a very common feature in music therapy practice. In active music therapy metaphors are extensively used in verbal dialogue on the improvisations. *Examples:* "It was like being in a witches' cauldron", "I felt beyond time and space", "The melody hit me right in the heart". The "playing rules" of Analytically Oriented Music Therapy are often metaphorical (Pedersen and Bonde 2002). *Examples:* "Play how you feel right now", "Play the animal from your dream". An analysis of these metaphors not only shows very clearly how clients experience the music, but also how they experience themselves, and how they may (or may not) benefit from music therapy. From a more theoretical point of view, Aigen (2002) suggested the metaphors of "Groove" and "Vital drive", as proposed by Keil and Feld (1994) as well-suited to describe musical processes in clinical situations. Vital drive may be considered an aspect of groove, and Keil describes how the rhythm section of a jazz group may produce different types of vital drive to support a soloist in his more or less idiosyncratic melodic phrasing. Based on analogy, the client in music therapy is the soloist, while the therapist has the role of the rhythm section, providing stability (holding the 'groove') and balancing it with spontaneity. In the case study of Lloyd, Aigen demonstrated how the jazz style seemed to "hold" the client, and how he learned about staying in the groove and the flow of the music, thus enabling him to tolerate longer and longer periods of non-structured transitions, first in the music, then in his daily life.[10] – Jungaberle (1999, 2001) studied musical metaphors extensively, based on Lakoff and Johnson's cognitive theory. He first made an analysis of newspaper music reviews in order to identify conceptual metaphors in the descriptions of music and musical experience. Then he made an analysis of clients' verbalizations of their therapeutic experience of music. In the music review analysis a series of core metaphors were identified, based on the prototype "Music is xyz", e. g. "Music is space", "Music is a landscape", and "Music is water". These metaphors were also found in the clients' verbal reports on their music experiences, but they were even richer, containing four new conceptual metaphors (or "metaphor families" in Jungaberle's words). *Examples:* One family is "Music is energy and power" with subgroups like "Music gives access to the inner world" or "Music moves me". Other families were: "Music is interaction" with subgroups like "Improvising is combat"; "Music is space"; and "Music is a living being". A specific conceptual metaphor is "Music is language" with subgroups like "Music can hide truth" or "Music makes the ineffable understandable". Jungaberle attaches special importance to the metaphor "Music is a landscape", because it expresses the spaciousness of music – there is 'room for everyone', and most people can 'find their place' in the music. Jungaberle (2001) also related the metaphors to Johnson's image schemata. Most prominent were the vertical schema (up-down), the container schema (the body and the music is a container for feelings), and the compulsion schema (being moved by music as an external force).

Based on his study, Jungaberle formulated a theory of "the metaphorical circle":

1) Extramusical structures influence the music experience when we hear or project specific qualities from our life world into the music.
2) Intramusical structures (the music experience) have an impact on our life experience, when we extract or transfer qualities from the music that gives meaning to our life.

Structures are transferred both ways – through metaphor. And thus metaphors provide clients and therapists in improvisational group music therapy with "maps" of musical experiences. In receptive music therapy we find a similar "metaphorical circle": Listening to the music, e. g. in the music-listening period of the BMGIM session, extra-musical structures may influence factors such as image modalities and image configuration types, while intra-musical structures may influence the

10 In the Ph. D. course at Aalborg University May 26th 2004, Aigen presented a paper on metaphors and image schemata, based on Lakoff and Johnsons cognitive theory (Lakoff and Johnson 1980). He suggested that music therapy may give clients first-hand experiences with missing or undeveloped schemas. He paid special attention to the Container-schema and the potential of music therapy to enlargening the container and thus – metaphorically through the music – expanding the social situations a client may tolerate, as in the case of Lloyd.

emotional quality and the narrative process of the experience. Or, in Helen Bonny's words from the introduction: "The metaphor in response to music opens into the emotion".

Conclusion

In this chapter I have tried to demonstrate how a scientific study of the relationship between music and imagery in BMGIM can be conducted. It was shown that the imagery of six clients (cancer survivors) was not random or highly idiosyncratic, but closely related to the music and psychologically meaningful. Different methods of analysis must be integrated in order to reveal the image potential of specific music selections and programs, and these methods should reflect the experiential processes of client(s) and therapist. Such a heuristic methodology allows the researcher to explore the therapeutic meaning of the music experience, with metaphor and narrative as helpful theoretical and analytical concepts.

APPENDIX (Participants):

Table 2: Basic information on the six participants

Name	Age	Job status	Marital status	Children	Cancer type	Time since remissal	Surgery:
WIFU	59	Retired	Married	3	*	*	No*
INLA	44	Active (Teacher)	Divorced	2	Breast cancer	11 months	Yes
PIJØ	41	Active (Student)	Divorced	1	Abdominal cancer	6 months	Yes
ESMA	65	Pensioner	Married	3	Breast cancer	7 weeks	Yes
SAAA	46	Unemployed	Married	3	Breast cancer	21 months	Yes
ANHO	52	Unemployed	Divorced	3	Abdominal cancer	5 months	Yes

* *WIFU was diagnosed with an inoperable cancer (breast cancer cells) behind one eye. During the project she attended medical control.*

Acknowledgement

With many thanks to Prof. Tony Wigram as my language consultant.

CH. 5: THE GUIDE-TRAVELLER RELATIONSHIP IN BMGIM AS A DEVELOPMENTAL RELATIONSHIP FOR THE SELF (D. STERN):

Exploring the parallels between the early mother-infant-relationship and the relationship between traveller and guide

EDITH M. GEIGER

The intention of this article is to understand the unique quality of the relationship between therapist and client during the music listening period. BMGIM therapists maintain a different relationship to the traveller as a "guide" than they do in pretalk and post-session-integration. The author explores the quality of the 'guiding-relationship' using D. Sterns theory of the infant's development of the Self and the various stages of this development. The parallels between the triadic relationship between music, therapist and client and the early infant-parent -dyad will be demonstrated; the functioning interaction that furthers the infant's (and client's) self-development as well as problematic interaction patterns will be investigated.

BMGIM – The Method

BMGIM – the Bonny Method of Guided Imagery and Music – is a music psychotherapy method developed by Helen L. Bonny based on music-evoked imagery. It is an approach within a psychodynamic and humanistic psychology framework. After the pre-talk the therapist helps the client by means of an exercise and a mental focus into a relaxed state. The music-listening phase begins. While listening to the music the client should report all images, feelings and bodily sensations to the therapist, who supports this process by asking questions and giving comments for further exploration of the client's imagery and feelings. Client and therapist maintain an ongoing dialog. The therapists interventions are known as "Guiding". Therapist and client are called "guide" and "traveller" during the music-listening period. After the music has ended the therapist brings the client back to NSC and a post-session integration talk follows.[1]

---

1 For more detailed information about the method see Ventre (2002): The individual Form of the Bonny Mehtod of Guided Imagery and Music (BMGIM). In: K. E. Bruscia & D. E. Grocke (Eds.): Guided Imagery and Music: The Bonny Method and beyond (pp. 29–37). Gilsum, NH: Barcelona Publishers.

Introduction

There is no doubt that the heart of BMGIM is the music listening and imaging of the client accompanied by the therapist. The dialog between therapist and client during the music listening period makes up the difference to other methods using music and imagery. A brief look can tell us that the relationship between client and therapist during the pre-talk and post-session-integration is quite different from the one maintained during guiding. My hypothesis is that BMGIM therapists not only offer music and imagery to the client but also a *special kind of relationship as an essential part of the music listening period and as a main therapeutic agent.* Guiding interventions are dependent on different parameters, such as disorder, course of therapy, imagery and music. "Guiding" is not the correct word for what BMGIM therapists are actually doing. M. Ventre (2002) suggests "facilitating" instead of "guiding". The German word "begleiten" (= to accompany) seems to express more distinctly what we are trying to do on the level of relationship: accompany someone, be with someone in his imagery. The following case vignettes mark the two possible ends of a continuum: one in which the relationship is unbearable for the traveller and therefore has to be cut off. and the other where it is the most important experience of the travel.

- Mrs M. had been in therapy for some months when I suggested BMGIM. She liked the idea, however during her first BMGIM session Mrs M. was not able to speak and report her imagery – the music session had to be ended very soon. Afterwards she said that she liked her images and the music. During the post-session talk she found out that the relationship during the music listening period was too intimate for her and, unconsciously, she had to close up in order to protect herself.

- Mrs. B. answered the usual question after the music listening period about what was most important for her, "that I could listen to the music together with you". In this case, obviously my presence as therapist had been more important to her than her images – our relationship turned out to be the image.

The Guide-Traveller Relationship as a developmental relationship for the Self (D. Stern), based on "The first Relationship: Infant and Mother" 1977, and the Interpersonal World of the Infant, 1985.

Right from the beginning music therapists reacted with great interest when Stern presented his work about the parent – infant – relationship, talking in musical terms while describing this relationship in detail. His descriptions fitted well to the experience of music therapists while improvising with their clients. Early interaction patterns can come to life again in the musical improvisation between therapist and client. Schumacher explored the connections between Stern's infant research and musictherapy with autistic children (1991, 1999) whereas Frohne-Hagemann and Pleß-Adamczyk (2005) used Stern's and Petzold's concepts (Petzold 1993c,d) of self development as a theoretical basis for conceptualizing musictherapeutical diagnostics for psychological problems of children and adolescents. But how does Stern's theory relate to receptive music therapy and to listening and imaging to music?

My hypothesis is that Stern's concept also comes to life in the BMGIM process in yet another way. Stern's credit is to have proven the basic importance of parent-child-interaction for the infant's development. His view on this subject can help us to understand the interaction between therapist and client during the music – listening – period and its meaning for the therapeutic process. In some ways, we can consider the state of consciousness of the infant as a different state of consciousness than the adult NSC[2]. Stern called the early relationship "the dance" of interactions between parent and infant, and I wonder if this could serve as an image for the therapist – client – relationship as well: therapist and client dance together in the field of music through different ASCs. Doubtless, guiding is a piece of art. Many therapeutic schools consider the therapeutic relationship to be the main healing agent. In BMGIM however, we use different tools to establish our guiding relationship than during pre-talk and post-session-integration. I will look at this relationship and its tools and structure, not from a psychoanalytic viewpoint of transference and counter transference but from the point of view of self development.

Basic Similarities between the parent – infant relationship and the relationship between therapist and client during the music-listening period

Six main obvious similarities between these relationships can be seen. In the list below, part one is Stern's statement as described in his books "The first relationship: Infant and mother" (1977, 2002) and "The diary of a baby" (1990). Part two is the analogy to the BMGIM process.

1. **Stern:** Parents **act towards infants differently** than towards adults or older children. The space of interaction is more intimate. The parent has to move into the world and level of experience of the infant in order to communicate (Stern 2002, 23 ff).
   In BMGIM, therapists act differently towards the client during pre-talk and post-session-integration than they do during the music-listening period while guiding. There is more intimacy through direct reporting of the inner experiences of the client. The therapist has to move into the imagery world of the client in order to guide. There is a completely **different repertoire of behaviour**.

2 I will use the abbreviations NSC = Normal State of Conscious, ASC = Altered State of Conscious

2. **Stern:** Every stage of development of the child requires different patterns of interaction and leads towards a new stage of development.
   In BMGIM every pattern of guiding suits the ASC and imagery of the client within the therapeutic process and supports development in this area.

3. **Stern:** Both partners **continuously adapt their interaction patterns** (2002, 92 ff).
   In BMGIM both client and therapist continuously adapt their interactions patterns during one session and the course of therapy. The therapist adapts his interventions to the travelling style and current needs of the client, her ASC, the particular requirements resulting from the disorder, and so on. This means e. g. that he will avoid feeling questions if the client cannot answer them, or is in a different mode of experience. The client does notice if the interventions fit well, and reacts accordingly. She also tries to make herself understood, shows forms of imagery with her hands, or tries to describe in a way that the therapist understands.

4. **Stern:** Timing and Structure: Every interaction has a specific **well-timed vitality structure**. Periods of time, tempo, pauses and intensity are important parameters. (2002, 97ff).
   In BMGIM, the timing and vital structure of the dialogue is essential; the therapist has to adapt to the client's imagery flow and intensity. This is essential for a successful therapeutic process, for the evolving flow of the imagery and the deepening of the process.

5. **Stern:** An essential part of the parent-infant-dance is the **testing of borders**, the crossing of borders of tolerance. During development, this is necessary for the child in order to start an adaptation or counter-maneuver, which widens her area of tolerance (2002, 95).
   In BMGIM, the client's borders of emotional tolerance e. g. are tested, and defensive manoeuvres have to be created (Goldberg 2000, 364). The music and the therapist contribute to this process.[3]

6. **Stern:** The interaction takes place **via all senses;** the infant experiences sensorimotor and affective stimuli from the parent as a unity of experience (Stern 2002, 38, 122ff). The psyche of the infant builds preverbal RIGs[4].

---

3 The counter-maneuver of the baby has an organization-building and adaptive function. Goldberg states that the creation of defensive maneuvers in the BMGIM process are "... an adaptive means of coping with deeply emotional and potentially stressful or threatening experiences, essential to the avoidance of fragmentation or disintegration of the ego." The process described is very similar.

4 **R**epresentations of **I**nteractions that have been **G**eneralized

> **In BMGIM,** the client is asked to experience music and imagery with all senses, and the therapist supports a full sensory and kinaesthetic experience. Often it is a multisensory experience, which is hard to express in words. The therapist values and supports experiences which are hard to express, or cannot be expressed in words. We can assume that the psyche of the client also builds an inner representation of the interactions between client, his imagery, music and therapist during the music travel.

The construction of and performance within the two relationships are similar. Essential parts and concepts of the early parent-infant-relationship are also essential for a well functioning "guiding"-relationship. A closer look at Stern's concept of Self development is helpful for a further exploration of these similarities.

Sterns concept of early Self Development

A brief summary of Sterns concept of self development as described in "The interpersonal world of an infant" and "Diary of a baby" will be given first.

First of all, Stern conceptualised 4 senses of the self in infancy. The "sense of self is not a cognitive construct, it is an experiential integration" (Stern 1985, 71). Later he broadened his concept to include the narrative self, and called this "world of stories (Stern 1990, 129ff). While passing through the various levels of self development, all the previous are still present in the child (Stern, 31ff). The development of the self continues through the whole lifetime.

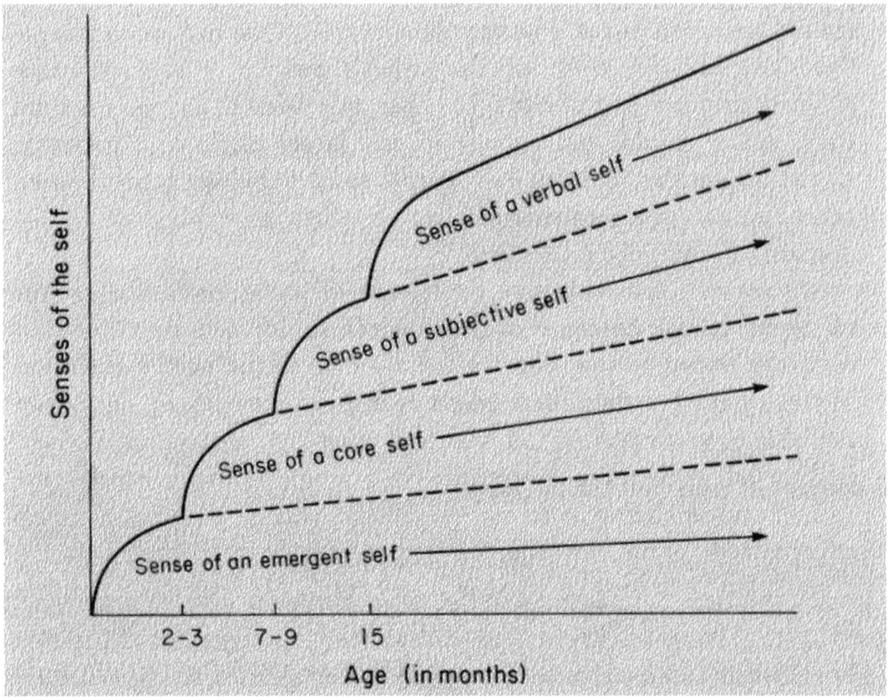

Fig.: Senses of the self (Stern 1985, 32), sense of narrative self has to be added

1: Sense of Self is emerging (0–2 months)

This means an emerging integration of networks, not yet based on one organizing principle. The infant is actively developing a sense of this organization, which is in the process of formation. Parents social behaviour (rocking, touching, soothing, talking, singing, making noises and faces) serves as physiological regulation to a great extent, but at times parents treat the infant as a child with a Sense of Self (e. g. "That's what you want to see" etc.)

From birth, the infant is able to sense with **Amodal Perception**; the infant has the capacity to transfer perceptual experience from one sensory modality to another, e. g.: what has been touched can be discriminated by seeing. Via **Vitality affects,** the infant senses his social world (how he is touched and treated by mother versus father, strong, tender etc.).

2. Sense of a Core- Self, Self vs Other, Self with Other (2–7 months)

"There is, for one, the physical self that is experienced as a coherent, wilful, physical entity with a unique affective life and history that belong to it. This self generally operates outside of awareness. It is taken for granted, and even verbalizing about it is difficult. It is an experiential sense of the self that I call the sense of a core self." It is important to notice that it is more cognitive function than "body ego" and sensorimotor schema, since it includes affective features (Stern 1985, 26). The infant begins to sense the difference between self and (the self regulating) other. The sense of a core self includes **self-agency** (authorship of one's own actions), **self-coherence** (being a physical whole), **self-affectivity** (experiencing patterned inner qualities of affects that belong to other experiences of self) and **self-history** (continuity with one's own past). From month 2–6 the infant's interest is very social, focused on people. From month 7 on, inanimate things become more important. The core-self is a necessary prerequisite to intersubjectivity.

3. Sense of a Subjective Self (7–15 months)

The infant discovers the subjectivity of the Other, her feelings, motives and intentions; it is the domain of intersubjective relatedness: Mental states between people can now be "read", matched, attuned to (or misread, mismatched and misattuned). Through affect attunement between parent and infant, intersubjectivity is experienced and developed.

4. Sense of a Verbal Self (ca.12–18 months)

Language helps to share experiences and create new meanings within a relationship, but it also brings alienation from the preverbal domains of experience like body sensations. The sense of a verbal self introduces a new way of two persons being together, where **meanings** are developed together.

5. Sense of Narrative Self (18. month–4 years)

The child learns to organize his own experiences and intentions in the form of stories. Motives and deliberate wishes of acting persons and rising and falling tension of the plot can be created within stories. Personal history is given meaning through the creation of stories.

Senses of Self and parallels to the BMGIM process

We create the Guiding relationship in BMGIM not only verbally or (sometimes by touching) but also by choosing the music. A triadic relationship between music, client and therapist is established. Through using the nonverbal medium music BMGIM therapists bring to life the world of experience of early infancy: Music can be sensed with the body both physiologically and kinesthetically. The sphere of vitality and categorical affects is embodied in music. Like the child moving through various domains of senses of self, the client wanders through various states of consciousness. Through verbal dialog between client and therapist, domains of verbal self and narrative self are addressed. During the imagery process, all senses of the self are continuously touched, developed further, expanded, and new experiences are integrated. Especially the conceptualisation of the vitality affects, the amodal perception and affect attunement show analogies to the BMGIM process and the guiding relationship. In BMGIM, we offer a multidimensional field of experience which in many ways goes back to our earliest forms of experience and perception.

Ad 1

Amodal Perception

The infant has the capacity to transfer perceptual experience from one sensory modality to another. What has been touched can be discriminated by seeing. **Cross-modal capacities** suggest that some properties of people and things, such as shape, intensity level, motion, number and rhythm are experienced directly as global, amodal perceptual qualities. This kind of perception is the prerequisite for understanding metaphors.

In the BMGIM process, our work with metaphors is directly connected to this early way of perception. Different modalities are explored using questions like "Is there a form for this feeling?" "Can you sense the texture?" The music might be perceived as bodily vibrations, and can then take on other forms of imagery like colours, feelings etc. The cross-modal capacities help to connect the direct music experience with personal history.

Vitality affects

are qualities of experience involved in all vital processes of life, such as breathing, getting hungry and waking up, which are best described by expressions like "surging", "fading away", "fleeting", "explosive", "crescendo", "decrescendo", "bursting", "drawn out" (Stern 1985, 54); categorical affects are more common like angry, sad or happy. Experiencing vitality affects is building structure and creating organisation for the infant. The description of the vitality affects an infant experiences (intensities, time gestalts like duration, rhythm, tempo, accelerando, ritardando, pitch, tone colour) reminds us of qualities of which music and the imagery process consist. Images and feelings evolve in time and have intensities, and are also important during the guiding dialog. Vitality affects, as well as music and imagery, consist of qualities which are hard to describe in words.

In the BMGIM process, we work in this area through using music and imagery where vitality affects are a main parameter. We also use this quality a lot in our guiding interventions. Often, the most important characteristic of our interventions is the quality of our mmh's, aha's, etc. and not the content. Using the vitality affective quality, we create different expressions of these reflecting words. Guiding questions are often directed towards the "how" of the experience and are aimed at the quality of the experience. The vitality affective quality plays an important role on different levels: music, imagery, therapist's voice and interventions.

Ad 2

Sense of a Core Self

This period is characterized by the regulation of excitement, activation, stimulation and tension of the infant. Through this regulatory process between infant and parent, the Core-Self of the infant is developed.

In BMGIM therapists work on this level by using the music to regulate excitement, activation, stimulation and tension, but also by using guiding interventions, which help the client in self – regulation of parameters in the imagery process.

Ad 3

Sense of Self with Other – Intersubjectivity

"Both infant and caregiver regulate infant's attention, curiosity and cognitive engagement with the world. The caregiver's mediation greatly influences the infant's sense of wonder and avidity for exploration." (Stern 1985, 103)

In BMGIM, client and therapist regulate the interest and engagement of the client in her imagery process. Stern notes that the caretaker in her role as mediator influences the explorative behaviour of the infant. The therapist has a similar role in engaging the curiosity and explorative behaviour of the client during the imagery process. The music turns into a "Self regulating person-thing" (Stern), because music can change the self dramatically. Music is suited very well for this function, because it has qualities like rhythms, movement, energy, expressive possibilities. BMGIM therapists reconnect to these early learned mechanisms with guiding interventions. They focus on the music, and give music the qualities of a person by asking questions like "Is the music saying anything to you?", "Can you tell the music …?"

Affect attunement

refers to parental empathic responsiveness and mirroring. It is a complex process where "first, the parent must be able to read the infant's feeling state from the infant's overt behaviour.

Second, the parent must perform some behaviour that is not a strict imitation, but nonetheless corresponds in some way to the infant's overt behaviour.

Third, the infant must be able to read this corresponding parental response as having to do with the infant's own original feeling experience..." (Stern 1985, 139)

This is the way in which being with somebody can be experienced, in which a common shared inner experience can be felt.

In BMGIM

- the guide must be able to read the traveller's state of feeling from his report of imagery and body expression,
- the guide must perform a guiding intervention, corresponding to the traveller's imagery and body expression (e. g. "mmh" with a matching vitality affect, verbal reflection with empathic sound, "you're big") and,
- the traveller must be able to read the corresponding response of his guide.

Affect attunement takes place between traveller and guide but also between traveller and music. The basic guiding intervention "mmh" can reflect the experience of the traveller and make her feel understood – or not if the "mmh" doesn't match; the affective colour (both vitality and categorical) of the "hm" is the important information which brings the feeling of being understood. The inner experience of the traveller has been *shared*, or not. The client also experiences affect attunement to a certain extent with the music; she can find her state of feeling mirrored by the music, and feel understood in her feeling. In this case, the guide might be witness of a shared experience or the experience is shared between traveller, guide and music.

The Triadic Relationship in BMGIM
Imagery as an Intersubjective Creation between Therapist, Music and Client

Seen from this perspective, the imagery of the client can be seen as an intersubjective creation between therapist, music and client. Imagery in BMGIM develops in quite a different way than during a day- or night dream. Perilli (2002, 433) states that metaphors are created within the relationship between therapist and client. Stern (2000, 109) himself says that sharing imagery in symbol drama creates a strongly intersubjective field. In BMGIM music *and* imagery is shared, the intersubjective field gets even stronger. The therapist induces the ASC and chooses the music. The client "reacts" with imagery. Then, the music is played continuously, and therefore influences the imagery of the client indirectly or directly when the client refers to the music itself. The therapist influences the imagery of the client by her comments and questions. The client's imagery develops within the relationship towards the therapist and the music.

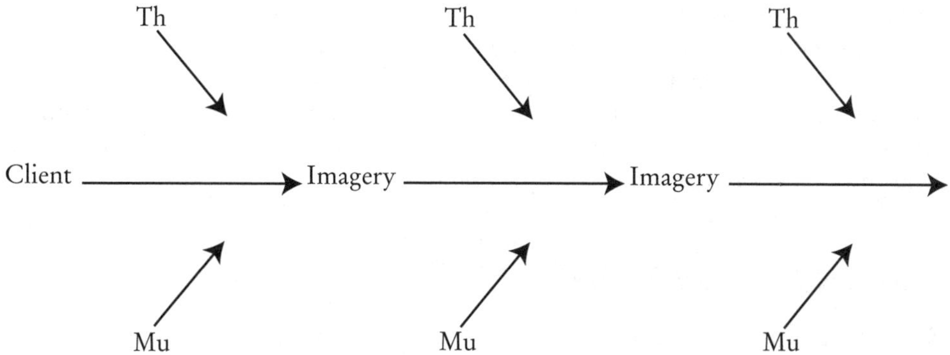

Ad 4

Verbal Self

Words always come into being in an affective way, only the affect gives them meaning; an island of intersubjectivity is created between child and parent. BMGIM therapists work on a similar level when they encourage their clients to find words for their imagery-affective experience. Often, words for an experience are found for the first time, or new meanings of words are discovered. The transition from the imagery experience to its verbalization is very interesting: sometimes it takes time until words arise; often it is necessary to stay in the experience instead of verbalising it immediately. The sharing of images in the verbal dialog is essential for the BMGIM process; the traveller constantly transforms an imagery experience, which most often is experienced in another modality than verbal, into words and often stories. The music may support this process from feeling and experiencing into language indirectly, e. g. words come up in the imagery process or the music itself "speaks" and conveys meaning.

The world of stories (4 years–)

The child learns to organize his experiences and intentions in the form of stories. He can create motives and desires of acting persons, falling and rising tension of a plot within stories. One's own story gets meaning through inventing stories. (Stern 1990, 129ff) Small entities, so called narratives, are co-constructed by children and parents. (2000, 109)

In therapy, creating a new story about oneself is essential. In BMGIM this takes place in a very immediate and direct way through the creation of imagery within the triadic relationship as mentioned above. The basic units of music are small – comparable to narratives; they are creatively transformed into imagery during the

BMGIM process and explored ideally through guiding. The music itself can serve as a story with rising and falling tension, with intentions etc. and thus promotes imagery stories. The imagery process itself as a whole is a process of creating a new story about oneself. It leads to reflexive self-knowledge and insight, either during the music listening or afterwards. Through verbalizing the imagery experience it turns into a shared experience with the therapist.

Problematic Interaction Patterns

We can see also similarities between the parent-infant-relationship and the "guiding"-relationship when looking at problematic interaction patterns. In the following, the problematic interaction patterns during the 5 levels of the Self development described by Stern will serve as a base for discussing problematic "guiding" interaction patterns between therapist and client in BMGIM.

Constitutional Differences and Emergent Relatedness

Constitutional differences like temperament influence the parent in relating to the child. There are differences in tolerance of stimulation and different thresholds of tolerance for different kinds of stimulation (e. g. acoustic, visual, tactile).

In a first BMGIM session the therapist might be surprised and puzzled by her client in different ways: his travelling style, his voice in ASC, body movements, tempo of imaging and reporting imagery. In general, his temperament during moving into ASC and the client's behaviour during ASC can differ from NSC. As therapists we need to get used to all characteristics the client shows in ASC. There is also a difference in tolerance of stimulation (music and imagery) due to temperament. Different degrees of tolerance for instruments and voice, as well as for several musical parameters like volume or dynamics are experienced. Depending on the temperament and state of mind of the therapist, it might be difficult for him to adjust. The ability to speed up or slow down, as well as great flexibility in pitch of voice of the guide can be helpful.

Core-Relatedness

According to Stern (2002, 95f) an essential part of the parent-infant-dance is the **testing of borders**, the crossing of borders of tolerance. This is necessary for the infant in order to start an adaptation or counter-manoeuvre. Expectable and tolerable overstimulation is part of a normal parent-child-interaction.

The following deviant interaction patterns can be observed:

- intolerable overstimulation
  *intrusive overstimulation is later followed by overavoidant behaviour of the infant
  *through a controlling parent the self-regulation is lost, the infant has learned that self-regulation is mainly done by the other, he is giving up; he experiences excitement not as something regulated by two people.

- intolerable understimulation
  A depressive parent might be unable to give enough stimulation due to lack of energy and empathy; depending on the infant's temperament he will make a lot of efforts in order to move his parent or react in a depressive way. The latter option means that the infant cannot develop the full spectrum of experience regarding the regulation of excitement.

In the BMGIM process we already find parallels to this regulatory process during the induction, as the relaxation directly focuses on the body. Also, the music has a component with a strongly physiological effect. The regulation of the imagery flow (intensity, tempo, number, quality etc.) takes place between client and therapist; the therapist contributes to the regulation by the music choice and her guiding interventions. Successful interaction takes place when the therapist is able to help the client in his self-regulation with imagery and music, when the induction and music choice is appropriate (niveau of stimulation, volume, orchestration-voice, etc.). Also, the client's borders of emotional tolerance are tested: some over-or understimulation helps in creating defensive manoeuvres and is a necessary part for the therapeutic process (see also Goldberg 1992). In BMGIM, over-or under-stimulation can take place through

- the choice of induction (relaxation and focus),
- the choice of music (through the various parameters like level of energy, tension, tempo etc.),
- guiding interventions

Intolerable overstimulation through music includes a music choice which is too challenging i. e. the container is too big, the music listening phase is too long, the music is too energetic, emotionally laden or not structured enough, and therefore overruns the clients borders of tolerance. The volume is too high, or the choice of instruments is part of an overstimulation due to the musical history of the client. Voice can often be an overwhelming musical stimulus. Overstimulation through guiding interventions includes what sometimes is called "overguiding": too many interventions within too short time intervals. Overstimulation can also be transferred by the voice of the therapist, if it is too loud, too high-pitched, or if there is too much energy in her voice as compared to the voice of the client and the sound of the music. The therapist can be controlling in her guiding interventions through "overguiding", or directive guiding when this is clinically not necessary;

this means that she does not allow the client to develop his flow of imagery and take part in regulating. It can also be controlling to perform a relaxation exercise, or to put on a calming piece of music, when anger is the main feeling of the client needing to be expressed. The client reacts towards intolerable overstimulation or controlling behaviour by not producing imagery or ending the imagery process, opening her eyes, refusing to answer questions, asking for different music, having emotionally overwhelming imagery, pulling back from the relationship to the therapist, orstopping reporting imagery.

Understimulation through music choice includes a music that has too little energy, emotional expressivity, movement, tension or complexity to meet the needs and emotional state of the client. This can also be true for the induction, when there is not enough energy or tension for the needs of the client. The therapist can cause understimulation by speaking too low, thus transferring lack of energy or pulling back from the imaginative and emotional scenery as it can be seen in counter transference reactions. Too few guiding interventions can contribute to understimulation, as can late timing. The client might go out of ASC, leave her imagery scene, and produce everyday thoughts and memories as a reaction. Understimulation through music choice often prevents clients from actually entering their imagery scene, or quickly leaving it after the music begins. If understimulation only occurs in one area, music or guiding, the other area might be able to compensate. Clients whose predominant experiences during the time of Core Relatedness in infancy have been over-or understimulated, might react towards the therapist in an over-avoidant way during the music-listening period, as the therapy set-up, especially the "guiding" relationship, triggers these experiences more quickly than the "normal" therapeutic relationship. The intimacy of the relationship, together with the early sensing patterns, increases the need to protect oneself as it has been in infancy. (See case vignette at beginning).

Intersubjective Relatedness:

The focus moves from **regulating** the infant's experience to **sharing** it. During the formative phase of the intersubjective domain, quite a few deviant interaction patterns can be found. Those highly relevant for BMGIM will be presented now.

Selective attunements

Through their expectations and repeated reactions towards a certain behaviour of the infant, the parents form a level of expectation within the infant: the building of a "False Self" begins (Stern 1985, 207ff).

During the music listening period, a kind of selective attunement can take place in the therapist: there are images she picks out as important and reacts to with a guiding intervention, others she leaves unnoticed. There are some feelings she reflects on more than others. A certain level of expectations can be formed in the traveller by the expectations or avoidances of the therapist.

Misattunement and Tuning

"Misattunements are covert attempts to change the infant's behaviour and experience."(Stern 1985, 213) One possible reaction of the child is that he doesn't see it as attunement; another possibility is that he might adapt to his parent's behaviour and allow her to "steal his feelings" because of his need of attunement.

In BMGIM this can take place if the therapist makes attempts to change the client's imagery experience. The client might not react to this intervention and just continue his travel; in this case he doesn't see it as attunement. The client adapts himself to the expectations of the therapist and the music choice, which does not resemble the client's state of feeling. In this case, a "False-Self" image is created, e. g. letting go of images he felt drawn to explore, or staying in an image without really wanting it.

Authenticity

During the domain of intersubjectivity, authenticity of the parents' behaviour is a very important factor. Non-authentic attunements can take place. This is also true for the therapeutic relationship between traveller and guide. During a BMGIM travel, the client is more sensitive towards the therapist's authenticity; non-authentic attunement attempts can happen.

Verbal Relatedness

Problematic interaction patterns happen if words are not used congruently: if they contain a double-bind message, or if misunderstandings are created between the actual experience and its naming. If, as Stern (1985, 226f) called it, a false self has been developed so far, it now gets semantic construction, and is therefore consolidated. The true self is cut off verbal expression, as the denied self experiences of the former periods cannot be encoded by language.

In BMGIM, during most of the travel the imagery experience of the client is reported to the therapist by words, sentences or coherent stories. Through reflecting phrases of the client with his own, different wording, the therapist prevents the client from sharing the meaning of words. Insecurity may arise in the client. The therapist needs to be open and sensitive to how the client experiences the meaning of words, not narrowing or changing it by means of his own meanings, associations etc.

World of Stories – Narrative Relatedness

Stern did not describe any deviant patterns during this domain. But we can think of parents who are not open for their child's stories, or who cannot give enough support for developing stories as a problematic interaction: nobody wants to listen to the story, or understands the meaning of the story within the world of the child.

Music consists of narrative units which create stories; it can help the client to find and create his own story. In BMGIM, therapists need to be open to the client's story and the symbolic language which creates his story, instead of having her own story of the music or symbolic interpretation in mind. As therapists, we need to let go of our own favourite musical pieces and stories connected to certain pieces of music during a client's travel. Sometimes it is necessary to hold the tension of not knowing the meaning of the story for a while before it reveals itself, instead of filling it with our own meaning.

Summary – Conclusions

Stern's description and conceptualisation of the parent – infant dyad can serve as a model for the "guiding"-relationship between therapist and client in BMGIM in many ways. The BMGIM setting brings – through ASC – a closer and more intimate relationship between therapist and client because of the client's immediate sharing of his inner experience. Higher attention and reagibility are established in the guide, like the heightened awareness of the mother towards her baby.

The musical-imagery field of experience opens up a broad spectrum of experience, which reminds us in many respects of the infant's perception capacities: the importance of body perceptions, vitality affects and affect attunement. The focus on this kind of perception and interaction during a music travel in BMGIM helps to activate these levels of experience and helps a post maturing of self development or further self development. Seen from a relational point of view, the client's imagery can be considered an intersubjective creation between music, therapist and client. The parent-child-relationship can be considered to be the prototype/archetype of a developmental relationship. The music-imaging process in BMGIM, guided by the therapist is a similar relationship. Apart from the complex triadic transference relationship, the BMGIM setting also continuously offers a healthy relationship model to the client suitable for her self development. In BMGIM, intersubjectivity is also necessary for the development of the transpersonal self: the therapist can allow and give space to it, or hinder it. So, he can help the client to get into contact with transpersonal and spiritual experiences and support their integration in the client's personality, or prevent him from doing so. The theory of D. Stern can help us to realize these parallels. As BMGIM therapists we gain a better and more conscious understanding of the kind of relationship we maintain during guiding, and of how it can be disturbed easily. The image of parent-infant-interaction can support us in maintaining the best possible guiding relationship. Being a non-manipulative guide is a permanent challenge.

CH. 6: THE SPEKTRUM GROUP GIM THERAPY

DAG KÖRLIN

The Spektrum Group GIM Therapy, to be described in this chapter, is one of several psychotherapeutic adaptations of Group GIM. Group GIM was originally created by Helen Bonny on the road to her individual form, now renamed the Bonny Method of Guided Imagery and Music (BMGIM) (Bonny 1978a, 1978b, 1980). Although Bonny continued to work with Group GIM, she did not consider it as therapeutically effective as the individual form, and presented it mainly for non-therapeutic purposes (Bonny 2002; Bruscia and Grocke 2002). Nevertheless, a number of successful psychotherapeutic adaptations have been developed by others for different clinical populations (Summer 1981, 1988, 2002; Short 1992; Goldberg 1988; 1994; 1995; Blake and Bishop1994; Justice 1994; Körlin, Goldberg and Nybäck 2000).

The Spektrum GIM Group is an integrated part of the Spektrum program, which treats patients with trauma-related disorders in five-week closed groups consisting of 5 patients. The Spektrum concept is to process the patient's issues through different functions and "languages" of the mind. Themes are worked through in a weekly schedule of GIM, Expressive Arts, Body awareness, Psychodynamic, Cognitive and Psycho-educational groups. The patient group is protected by a strong framework and held and cared for by a special "continuity person".

The Spektrum GIM Group, which comprises only five sessions, has been developed during the treatment of 300+ patients in more than 250 sessions. It has also been successful as a standalone outpatient group therapy, in which case more sessions are needed. Spektrum GIM is characterized by a pronounced individual-in-group focus which means that imagery focuses on the history and issues of the individual. Here, this is called "individual imagery", to be distinguished from "group imagery" which primarily concerns relationships within the group. Both take place within the mind of the imager. In the Spektrum GIM Group, individual imagery is protected by the framework, and promoted by the members learning to process each others imagery. These are the key factors that permit psychiatric patients to regularly have transformative and even transpersonal sessions (Körlin 1999).

The defining element of Helen Bonny's individual and group forms may be described as widening and exploration of consciousness through spontaneous individual imaging and experiencing evoked by music. Group and individual BMGIM share this essential feature, but differ in other respects. In both forms, listening to carefully selected music in a relaxed state induces a spontaneous and creative flow of emotions, thoughts, memories, sensory and symbolic images. The two forms also have the same general session structure of pre-session, relaxation/

induction, music listening, and post-session integration. Group GIM also requires competence in the guiding techniques of the individual form.

The main difference between Group GIM and BMGIM is in the guiding and the length of the music experience. In the individual form, the therapist or guide is in a non-directive and empathic dialogue with the traveler as the experience is unfolding. Supported by the dialogue, the client can encounter difficult relationships, self-images, affects and traumatic experiences as well as inner strengths and potentials. As the music session deepens, a wide range of altered states of consciousness may be evoked, making healing, transformative, archetypal and spiritual experiences possible.

In Group GIM, it is impossible to have a non-directive dialogue with several spontaneously, individually imaging group members at the same time. Instead, the experience is re-explored afterwards with each group member, using the same guiding techniques as in the dyadic session, e. g.: exploration (asking for sensory description), allowing (to acknowledge the experience), deepening (fully being with the experience) and bringing in the music (in the group, mainly to ask for connections between music and experience).

Another difference is that the music phase of a group session is relatively short, 6–8 minutes on the average, compared to the 30–55 minutes of the individual session. But in these few minutes of music in a group, imagery goes quicker and deeper per second compared to the individual session, and the full range of experiences described for the individual form happen. To go to the same depths and intensity of experience without the support of the guide requires safety, group cohesion, and trust in the leader to guide the experience after the music. The guide must be competent in recognizing affects and bodily and sensory images that are difficult to verbalize, as well as transpersonal experiences that go beyond words, and help patients acknowledge and explore them.

To apply Group GIM to a patient population, and a clinical context, the therapist can vary a number of adaptive principles and techniques almost indefinitely, and, as long as the essential elements are maintained, the result is defined as a Group GIM Therapy (after Brusica 2002 and Blake and Bishop 1994). The adaptive elements have two purposes: one is to contain the full range of BMGIM experiences to manageable proportions for clinical populations, the other to utilize the group process for therapeutic work. The adaptive elements may be summarized as:

- width of musical and session container
- amount of group reflection and interaction
- resource mobilization
- nature of the therapeutic framework.

Musical container

Psychiatric patients often have limitations in creating, maintaining and developing the music-evoked symbolic images that are the main integrative elements of GIM.

The length of imagery is an issue in itself since the initial symbolic nature of an image may quickly degrade into overwhelming affects and traumatic memories (Goldberg 1994). This may result from too much texture, harmonic change and structural development, as well as uncertain tonality and unpredictability of the music (Summer 2002). Symbolic images like snakes or arrows may quickly become intrusive or degrade into traumatic re-experiences, especially in the presence of strong dynamic changes, which function as "alarm bells" in the music. Also, transpersonal experiences are more prone to assume destructive qualities in the psychiatric than in the high-functioning traveler (Körlin 2002).

A piece of music with these characteristics is defined as a "wide container" (Summer 1989), to which the present author would add, "high in information content". An important therapeutic principle of GIM is to gradually help patients manage "wide container" music by beginning at the other end with "small container" music, which this author would define as music with "low information content".

In a "small container" (Summer 1989) – low information music is short, and with a narrow range in almost all musical elements. The shorter the piece, and the more consonant, repetitious and predictable it is, the smaller the container. Such music is more likely to preserve the initial symbolic quality of the music, and at the same time is less likely to stimulate development and transformation of imagery (Goldberg 1994). Since there is a limited supply of these qualities in the classical repertoire, minimalist new age and world music have been included in the small container repertoire.

Session container

The limiting strategy has been expanded to all the other components of the session, to form a total "Session container" (Goldberg 1994; 1995), again with the intent to limit the amount of information to be processed. Shortening or focussing the pre-session discussion, doing a brief relaxation, and sitting in chairs all limit the experience. Continuing the induction into the music, termed a "talk-over", lets the therapist's voice serve as a support. At the same time, verbal instructions may limit the development of imagery. The talk-over may leave a "window" of varying length for free imagery. Another way of limiting imagery is to make patient's paint, or even write, to on-going music. Also, the post-session artwork may be brief or substituted by writing.

Group reflection and interaction

The amount of group reflection and processing is essential to limiting or expanding the session. Generally, it takes more ego strength in the members to process group issues, especially if group members are free to take or not take time in the group.

This evokes issues of sharing and competition that are difficult to handle for vulnerable patients. Another difficult process is the victim-perpetrator shifts that occur in groups with traumatized patients (Söndergard 1987). This may threaten the cohesiveness of the group. On the other hand, group processing may offer great opportunities for change in clients with good ego strength (Goldberg 1994; 1995).

In the Spektrum Group, the strategy is to minimize problematic group process, without ignoring it. This is done through strict sharing of time and structured sharing of group member's reactions towards each other. This approach is chosen in order to leave as much space as possible for individual in-depth imagery and processing in the limited time available. Introspection is used, however, to focus separation issues in the later phases of the program.

Constructive group interaction, essential for the development of cohesion, may be fostered in different ways. Patients may for example participate in formulating the focus, or theme of the session, or they may create a group painting during the music, or afterwards together create a poem about the music experience (Summer 2002). Constructive interaction increases the individual's security to contact and afterwards share difficult imagery, but at the same time limits the space available for individual imagery.

In the Spektrum GIM Group, interaction is mainly fostered by teaching the members to guide and process certain aspects of each other's imagery. This is made possible by dedicated psychoeducational sessions, which help patients understand how the elements of imagery form a narrative, and how to be curious about this narrative and its possible meanings. This also helps patient's engage in sometimes complex individual imagery.

Resource mobilization

Mobilization of inner resources is important in helping patients preserve symbolic imagery, and in meeting and managing difficult affects and traumatic memories. Inner resources that are silent during ordinary consciousness may become conscious during the GIM experience of music in an altered state (Bonny 1988; Borling 1992; Tasney 1993; Picket and Sonnen 1993; Goldberg 1992; 1994; Bishop 1994). Bishop (1994), reporting from Individual GIM in a treatment program for abused women furthered understanding by describing a cyclical process of mobilization, followed by confrontation with traumatic material, ending in resolution and then new mobilization as a preparation for the next challenge. During this process, improvement of defenses can be observed. Examples from the Spektrum GIM Groups are bodily manifestations with qualities of warmth, energy, strength, nourishing (case 1), and movement (case 2). For example, gently swinging in the branches of a tree, feeling safe, and hearing mother's voice in the music, may reflect good moments of being with mother. Meeting a bear, feeling its strength in the body, may manifest the traveler's mental and physical resilience. As emphasized by Goldberg (1994), Bishop (1994) and Körlin (2002), the resource experiences go beyond the psychodynamic dimension into healing, archetypal (Jung 1959) and transpersonal realms (Körlin 1999).

Therapeutic framework

Finally, a strong therapeutic framework makes it possible to use "wider", more evocative music which promotes the meeting with, and transformation of, difficult imagery. The Spektrum GIM Group is protected by the framework of the Spektrum program.

The Framework of the Spektrum GIM Group

Spektrum is a time-limited 5 week program, for closed groups of 5 patients. At the beginning of the first week, they meet for the first time, and they separate as a group 5 weeks later. The "continuity person", who cares for and monitors the group between sessions embodies the integrative principle of the program. The idea is to process the same psychological content through different functions and "languages" of the mind. The program addresses implicit (non-verbal) memories and analogic (imagery) symbols (Langer 1956, Siegel 1999) through imagery in the GIM Group, Body awareness group and Expressive arts group (Körlin et al 2000; Rudstam 2002). These modalities also provide external manifestation of imagery through artwork and metaphor (poetry, enchantment). Language, concepts and affects are addressed through dysfunctional cognitions/affective schematas in the "Attitude group". In the psychodynamic group, social functioning is examined in a situation that promotes transference. Frequent issues here are taking/giving space and dominance/submission. The program thus adresses all aspects of the "symbolization triangle" (Körlin 2002).

The bridging and translation of themes between sessions and modalities is essential. The "continuity person", follows the group through most of the sessions, the staff meets twice weekly, and there is a movable screen, where art work and written material accumulates. This screen follows the patients into each session and is also present in team conferences and supervision.

A further continuity factor lies in the integration with the psychoeducational group, also performed by the author. Concepts of imagery, implicit memories, symbols, affects, resources, and cyclical process are explained and exemplified through GIM and other experiences documented on the screen. This material is then integrated with facts about anxiety, PTSD, affective states and other dignoses that may be represented in the group. The educational group thus relieves the GIM-group proper of the need of some educative ingredients, and promotes patient's participation in post-music guiding.

The program is evaluated with the SCL-90 (Symtom Check list-90), IIP (Inventory of interpersonal problems) as main effect measures and the RSQ

(Relationship Style Questionnaire, built on attachment theory) and the DES (Dissociative Experiences Scale) as independent variables, along with a checklist for separation and intrusive trauma.

Positive results have been published from the first year on, with a somewhat different program (Körlin et al 2000). We now have preliminary 6 month results for 50 recent patients, who also serve as their own "wait-list" controls. Most of these patients have been in "treatment as usual" both in the period before and after the 5-week group phase. The clients do not change before treatment, but go from pathological to normal SCL-90 values at the 6-month follow-up. One recent group was also evaluated with ORT (Object Relations Test) and Draw–a-tree test. which were scored using a narrative focus. The result was that all patients significantly increased their capacity to give a complex and holistic narrative of themselves, and that their self-confidence and self-image had improved (Åkerlind 2003). One of these patients will be presented as a clinical vignette (case 3).

Patients

The Spektrum program treats two kinds of patients: those with trauma-related disorders in a wider sense, and those who have strong potential for development, that for various reasons has not been realised. Schizophrenic psychosis, on-going substance abuse and sociopathic disorder are contraindicated.

Regarding trauma related disorders, it is now widely recognized that psychological trauma results not only in PTSD (Post Traumatic Stress Disorder), but also in a host of other conditions like anxiety, depressive and personality disorders (Foa, Keane, and Friedman 2000). Trauma-related disorder in the wider sense are often caused by a combination of separation trauma and intrusion trauma, where intrusion is a common denominator for the invasive nature of physical, sexual or psychological abuse as well as accidents, complications of somatic disease, traumatic childbirth etc. In the Spektrum program, separation trauma carries a more favourable treatment prognosis, while intrusive trauma has a greater association with disorganized attachment disorder, dissociative reactions and features of PTSD. In "full" and "complex PTSD", there is a stricter requirement of treatment continuity before and after the Spektrum program, and often a need for complementary EMDR, Cognitive or Cognitive Behavioural treatment (Körlin, manuscript).

The patient with an unrealised potential of psychological development may belong to any diagnostic category. Such persons may have grown up in emotionally or intellectually limited or rigid families, or some form of handicap has hindered them. Dyslexia is an interesting variant of the handicap theme – these persons often have a cognitive style characterized by thinking in images, which may explain their good treatment results in the Spektrum program.

The Spektrum GIM Group

The screen and the physical setting

The screen, which accompanies the group into the GIM sessions, contains pictures mainly from GIM and Expressive arts sessions. Previous individual experiences, as well as group themes manifested in the pictures, are regularly referred to in the pre- and post-session of the group GIM session. The group members are seated in a semicircle in front of the screen, thus interacting with each other, their individual imagery and group imagery on the screen columns (fig 1).

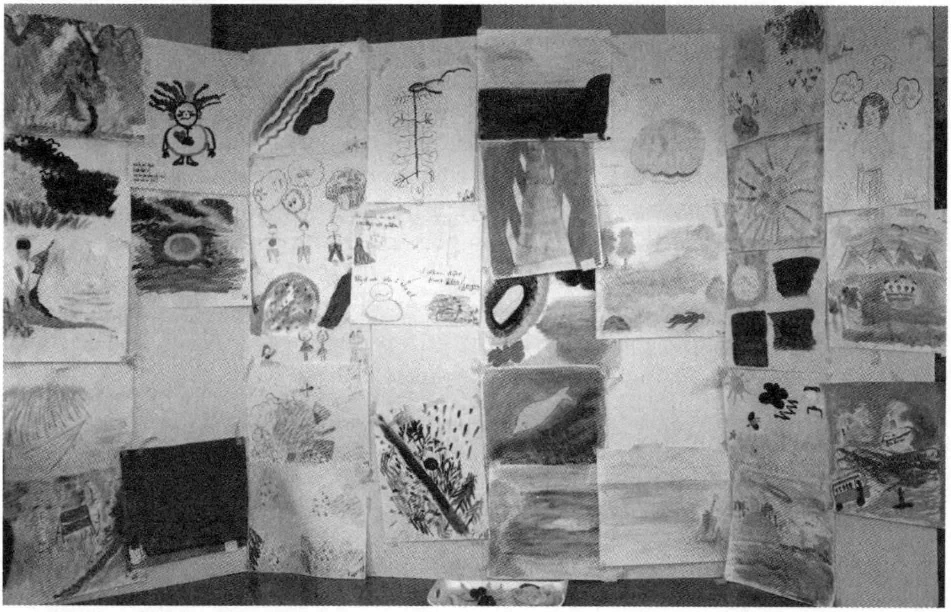

Fig. 1

To stress the perspectives of continuity and ownership and to expand the range of experience that can be reflected upon, everybody is required to sign and date their session pictures and put them up on the screen irrespective of content. A beautiful painting can be reflected upon just as well as a blank page (which is seldom), or one torn to pieces (which is also seldom, but tolerated as long as it gets up on the screen). Putting an image on the screen with the blank side facing outwards is also allowed. This happens now and then.

Treatment phases

The Spektrum GIM Group consists of only five weekly sessions. In these sessions, the group moves surprisingly fast through it's phases of cohesion building, work, and closure.

The first session, painting to ongoing music, is about building trust and cohesion and presenting oneself and ones issues. The second and third sessions are about widening and exploration of both resources and problematic aspects. Inductions tend to be open, and music is more evocative. By the third week, patients begin to feel separation anxiety, anger and insecurity about the future, which needs to be adressed in the remaining sessions. From the fourth week, the sessions become more structured and specific, although there is always space given, or taken, for spontaneous imagery. The themes in pre-session, inductions and talkovers are: summary, strategies for the future, and separation.

In the fourth session, this process is begun by invoking the metaphor of collecting important discoveries in some form of container (basket, rucksack, etc.) to bring into the future. It is suggested that some items that have been carried through history may now be left behind. This session sometimes has a talk-over at the beginning or end of the music, accompanied by regular, safely moving music with limited evocative potential.

In the fifth session, the focus is aimed at giving opportunity to work on separation, e. g. through the image of the group on a beach. Again, talk-over of varying length at the beginning and end of music is used.

Structuring of time, containment of group process, and fostering of interaction

The therapist takes the responsibility of keeping the time frame of the different session phases, and allots fairly equal time for each patient. Although the primary focus is on the "individual-in-group", the group members are invited to reflect on one another's experiences in the post-session and also, when indicated, in the pre-session. In the pre-session, group reflection is invited only when "hot" subjects come up, like strong experiences and symptoms, suicidal ideation and open group conflicts. The group processing is not "set free", however, as the leader still takes responsibility for fairly equal and short sharing of feed-back from the group members.

In the pre-session, every member makes a short summary of her/his current process and what is uppermost in his/her mind. This can last no longer than 30 minutes, which allows approximately 6 minutes for each member. In the music listening phase, the ingredients of relaxation, induction, music listening, closing of the experience and coming back from the altered state can take no more than 10–12 minutes, which gives room for 6–7 minutes of music. Creating a picture of the experience then can take no more than 20 minutes, including setting up tables, distributing paper and colours, painting, and finally returning to the semicircle for the post-session. The post-session sharing has to be completed in one hour, thus giving each member approximately 12,5 minutes of sharing time.

This tight schedule also has the effect that some interventions have developed into a standardized procedure, approaching protocol.

The container, (basket, or drawer), is also used as a metaphor in clarifying boundaries and limiting group process. For assessing feedback from group members, and therapists, the"Yes", "No" and "Maybe" baskets are offered as metaphoric tools. Without these, patients are prone to accept or reject feedback or interpretations for a variety of reasons other than their relevance. Feedback can be accepted, for example, out of submission, or out of feeling sorry for the other, or just because of a lack of a cognitive tool to slow the process. Reflections that are obvious projections of the other person may be put in the "No" basket, and those that are "spot on" may be put into the "Yes" basket. Reflections that belong to the "Maybe" basket are perhaps the most interesting. This is the place for feedback that evokes ambivalence. By placing something in the "Maybe" basket, it is stored for further consideration, strengthening the reflective ability of the patient. This also contributes to the safe space for personal imagery.

Group interaction is fostered above all in that patients learn to participate in the post-music guiding, and also in painting at a shared table.

The first session

The first session is different from the following four. Here, the first hour is spent with the group sitting at a table, painting to 20–40 minutes of ongoing music. First, a short presentation of imagery and implicit memories evoked by music in the altered state is given, along with the idea that these experiences can be used for understanding strengths and problematic areas in the person. The pre-session then focuses on expectations and reservations that the group members have about the method. The idea of imaging to music is unfamiliar to many, and anxieties of not being able to image or make drawings are frequent. Many have fears about what may emerge in the form of affects and memories. Therefore, the resource perspective of imagery is stressed, and also the basic GIM notion that anything and everything that is experienced is OK as a GIM experience, and can be worked with.

The music often consists of a full GIM program for example the "Peak Experience", thus music is more evocative than in the following four sessions. This is balanced by the mobilization of ego functions during simultaneous music listening and painting and by the support of the group sitting at the same table during the music. It is common even in this contained situation. with strong individual experiences, often in the form of emotionally laden memories that need post-music guiding. The post-session is done in the same way as session 2–5.

There are several reasons for this form. The first is to gradually aquaint the patients with the idea of imagery and creative expression and to start the individual process. The second is to build cohesion through group interaction. The third is diagnostic. The risk of overwhelming is less, thus more evocative music can be used. By focussing on reactions to musical container elements, strengths and vulnerabilities are assessed.

The second to fifth sessions

In the following four sessions the clients are seated in a semicircle in front of the screen during the pre-session, music listening phase, and post-session sharing.

To start the pre-session, the therapist says (wording may vary): "Let's begin with a status report – how are each of you right now? What have you been thinking, feeling, dreaming, doing since the last session? Has anything important happened in your life since the last group? Is there anything particularly evocative in the images on the screen right now? Who wants to begin?"

The group members then take turns in reporting their current experience, during which the leader inwardly ponders the themes, strengths and vulnerabilities of the individuals, the group, and the current phase of the group's life in the Spektrum program. Resource experiences or other important themes are commented on by the leader during this general inventory. In the fourth and fifth session, the themes of summary, strategies for the future, and separation are brought up

As a result of this evaluation, induction and music is chosen (see below). However, even when fairly detailed inductions or talk-overs are employed, the members are expressively allowed to follow emerging spontaneous imagery. After return from the music, and the altered state, folding tables are set up and paper and painting material is produced. After 15–20 minutes of painting, the group reassembles in the semicircle with their drawings behind the chairs.

The leader starts the sharing phase by saying (with variations): "Now, each of you has about 12 minutes to share your experience with the group. When you listen to each person's story from the music, imagine that he or she has been to a movie, only this movie is inside and consists not only of visions but also of other sensory experiences, emotions, memories, thoughts, and even sensations that may be hard to describe. Your job, and mine, is to be curious about this movie and ask more about what happened, and what it was like. You, who are in the centre, be aware of your freedom to leave out things that you don't want to share, and be mindful of the yes, no and maybe baskets when listening to the reflections of the others."

The group members then take turns in putting their picture in the centre and tell their story of what happened in the experience, which is, as a rule, incomplete. The leader usually asks an initial open question, and then invites the other group members by saying: "Curiosities, questions in the group about this experience?" The patients then start to ask for more detail, mostly doing explorative guiding interventions. The leader focusses on the allowing, or "owning" of experiences, interactions with the music, and has antennaes raised to detect implicit and ineffable experiences. Reflections about meaning are referred to the next phase of the post-session.

When the patient's story is satisfactorily guided, the leader says: "Let's put the picture on the screen", and then proceeds to help the person with this, one holding the paper in place, the other fastening it with tacks. When returning to the seats, the leader says: "What are your thoughts about the meaning of this experience?" After the patient's answer, which normally contains a new view or an interpretation of meaning, there is time for similar remarks from the other patients. Only at this stage does the leader attempt an open-ended "interpretation" that always includes a resource perspective. After every patient has shared, there is time for a concluding interpretation from the leader, who again emphasizes individual resources and issues as well as shared group experiences. For example, after the first session the leader will at least say: you have now presented yourself to each other. Or in the third session: "you all seem to have discovered a protected place in the music, but each one was different".

Inductions and music choice

As described, the pre- and post-music phases are fairly standardized, which leaves a variability for inductions chiefly in the second and third sessions, and for music choice in the second to fifth sessions. The planning of these elements is influenced by: 1) strengths, vulnerabilities and issues of individual group members. 2) group process and cohesion.

Strengths, vulnerabilities and issues are judged through observing imagery in relation to music, and imagery in itself. Reactions are observed to formal musical elements in the first, and these are tested in subsequent sessions. Critical musical elements, outside of those mentioned by Goldberg and Summer. are dissonance and dynamic change. The effect of such elements on imagery are constantly evaluated. Particularly, sudden or dynamic music sequences polarize imagery into mobilization of either power or alarm. Is the person managing or being overwhelmed by affective reactions? What is the balance between problematic and resource experiences in the imagery? How flexible are the defences?

This aspect of the session could easily be the subject of a full chapter, so I will limit this section to a few principles and to examples given in the case vignettes. When there is need for autonomy, or when group members have divergent issues, the focus may be open, or determined individually with each member already in the pre-session. If there are obvious similarities in the member's issues, they may be adressed in a shared induction. If possible, these are combined with a safe place induction during the second or third sessions. This can be done either when the safe place theme is suggested in previous imagery or life story, or when it is judged that the group is in a positive cycle phase. Movement is often employed in a negative cycle. Possible music choices for the themes of safe place and movement are given below. Other inductions that can be used, individually or combined, are also described below, along with some useful combinations with music. As a general rule, a wide induction tends to be combined with a smaller music container, and vice versa.

Inductions

A certain repertoire of well-known GIM inductions have crystallized as being useful: regulating, grounding, tree, movement safe place, and opening/widening. Movement, and to a lesser degree safe place, helping figure and nurturing are the resource qualities that can be evoked with some certainty (see discussion).

Regulating induction: To this induction, which is useful with PTSD patients, music with little development, a steady rhythm and movement compatible with breathing is used, and may be begun even before relaxation is started. Relaxation is then paced to attune to the music. After a brief grounding with the floor, seat and back of the chair, attention is brought to the steadiness of breathing. Then it is suggested that music and breathing move together. In sessions 4 and 5, this induction is often used as a lead-in to the talkovers of these sessions, which also need steady rythm.

Grounding induction: A grounding element is generally useful, particularly with insecure or vulnerable persons, and can be combined with all other inductions. Attention is brought to the contact between feet and floor, body and seat, and body and back of the chair. It is suggested that exhalation help the body feel a little heavier and increase the sense of contact.

Body-focussing induction: May be begun by suggesting a tensioning of the legs bringing pressure on the back of the chair followed by relaxation, feeling the body settle in the chair, a little heavier every time.

Tree induction: It is suggested that the patient begins the journey sitting with his back against a tree trunk. The tree image, as expected in theory, regularly manifests positive and negative self images.

Movement induction: Suggestion to follow the movement of the music, or particular instruments.

Safe place induction: Often combined with a grounding or regulating induction, after which it may be suggested that the patient find a safe place in nature, let the music create a safe place, or both.

Opening/widening induction: It is suggested to let the fantasy create a room where affects, memories and images can meet the music. May be combined with a breathing induction where it is suggested that the inhalation opens up the creative space.

Music

In the Spektrum GIM Group, the following musical pieces, mostly from the standard GIM repertoire (Grocke 2002), are used on a regular basis. In the small container range there is steady modern serious music with minimalistic features like A. Pärt's Spiegel im Spiegel. The Swedish movie music composer Stefan Nilsson has several small container pieces with some evocative ingredients. Still more evocation is possible in the Pachelbel Canon, Bach's Air, Corelli's Concerto Grosso or in similar baroque pieces. The orchestral Bach renditions by Stokovski then offer a gradual widening of musical containers. If a lighter texture and looser structure is needed, the music of Delius is useful, particularly pieces from the "Florida Suite". The "La Calinda" piece from Coanga, particularly the slower version arranged by Fenby, is a good piece for mobilizing movement in a non-forcing way. Some of Delius' music can be used in evoking safe places. Another good "movement" piece, with additional potential for inner dialogue, is Massenet's "Meditation" from Thais. The "Rhosymedre Prelude" by Vaughan Williams is one of many examples of small container string orchestra music. Music with female voices, like Puccini's "Humming Chorus" tends to have a nurturing, holding quality and the female voice in general is a strong vehicle for identification and connection. Other useful "middle container" music is Vaughan Williams "Greensleaves", Britten's Sarabande from the "Simple Symphony", Haydn's Cello concerto in C and the universally usable 2nd movement of Beethoven's fifth piano concerto. The most evocative piece of music used is Shostakovich's string quartet # 3, used only with inductions that intend to focus the experience on movement, and in groups with strong cohesion.

Clinical vignettes

Case 1: Safe Place-Nurturing

A 45-year old social worker and fugitive from a Middle East country, who had been imprisoned when her son was new-born. She was never personally traumatized in prison or otherwise, but witnessed several fellow prisoners taken away for torture or execution. Among those was a woman whom she thought could comfort her infant son better than she could herself. Highly intelligent and gifted as a child, she experienced herself as "not seen" by her mother and disfavored vis-à-vis her elder siblings, one of whom was imprisoned and killed before her own arrest. She married her son's father, who was also oppositional to the regime, for reasons that she described in terms of social compassion and politics. They separated in connection with their arrests, and were divorced several years later, having fled to different countries. During the last ten years, she had several periods of quite severe depression with fairly evident connections to her life situation and history. Antidepressants had little effect. She maintained that her depression had to do with her life being a failure, and that she couldn't understand why she was spared when more worthy persons were tortured or killed.

In the Spektrum program, she held herself back and generally took her turn among the last. Her work revolved around the issues outlined above, involving the aspects of separation. She could gradually allow herself to be emotionally touched. Her self-image, appearing in the second session, was that of a hawk: dominant, with overview, and control. She acknowledged the distance of the hawk, but denied that this was a problem. Due to her sense of failure, she did not paint the hawk, which was discovered by another group member in the post-session guiding. In the third session, induction was open, for several reasons. The individuals of the group were working on different issues, and this particular patient, with her autonomy, was resistant to being "directed" in her inner spaces. Music was Vaughan Williams "Rhosymedre Prelude", also for several reasons. One reason was to balance the open induction space with a small musical container. The second reason was that this piece provides possibilities for tender feelings.

In the music, she experienced soft stroking of her hair, and experienced a surge of longing and deep comfort combined with sadness, manifested by a tear on her cheek.

Fig. 2

In the fourth session, a "summing up" focus and smaller container music, Pärts "*Spiegel im Spiegel*" was used. She experienced moving between two positions: the lake, with sadness and tears, and the abyss, which at the same time has the shape of a Hawk.

Fig. 3

This symbolized contradictory aspects of the Hawk, (autonomy but also intellectualisation and isolation, in the boxed-in signs).

This sequence illustrates a processing cycle from the initial hawk image, that at the time gave an uncomplicated sense of control and courage, which enabled her to meet the avoided affect (=mixed emotions), evoked through an implicit memory (the stroking of the hair). The hawk, the loneliness and the accepted nurturing then were integrated in the next, summary, image.

Case 2: Mobilization of movement and energy.

A 40-year old woman, living alone with her son from a previous marriage. Her upbringing was dysfunctional with a physically abusive, alcoholic father. Since her divorce, she had had a stormy relationship with a man, who had an alcohol dependence and regularly disappeared on drinking sprees. Sensing one of these coming, she told him never to come back again if he intended to drink. He took the weekend ferry Stockholm-Helsinki, got drunk, and on the way back took his life by jumping off the ship. This sent her into a long-standing depression characterized by emotional and bodily numbness, receiving only partial help from SSRI's. In the Spektrum GIM Group, she manifested difficulty in perceiving resource aspects of her imagery. Mobilization of inner movement that is relatively easy to evoke through the motoric element of music was attempted. The Massenet "Meditation" was chosen, and in the induction, it was suggested to let each of the instruments evoke an experience of movement. In her imagery, both the fluite and the harp had legs, and took long lustful jumps at the same time as her body was filled with pleasurable sensations and she felt an urge to take part in life again.

Fig. 4

In the next session, the Pachelbel "Canon" evoked imagery of painful places in the body, pains that she had ignored in her depressive state, along with the pleasurable body experiences. This body awakening signalled an improvement of her depression, and gave her courage to start acknowledging her physical symptoms. The sequence also illustrates a positive-negative phase of a GIM cycle.

Case 3: Transpersonal-dissociative experience with psychodynamic work

A 37-year old woman, with a highly traumatic upbringing with a physically and mentally abusive mother, who actively encouraged sexual abuse by her uncle. She was married and had two children with an alcoholic man. After her first childbirth she no longer never enjoyed sex . After a TV-program about incest 8 years before her Spektrum treatment, she started to have stronger flashbacks with memory fragments of abuse by her uncle. This led to increased rumination about shame, guilt, and rage with a deep-seated sense of being worthless and deserving the treatment she had endured. In addition, she experienced an increase of phobic symptoms and, at the time of admission. deteriorating teeth due to untreated dental infections and severe agoraphobia, which required daily support by a social worker. She had never functioned in work-life, and was referred for psychiatric evaluation since her social security case manager thought she needed a disability pension. She was accepted into the Spektrum program due to strong indications of unrealised potential.

In the group, she was one of three women with varying degrees of PTSD as a result of sexual and physical abuse. Due to this, regulating inductions with breathing-music attunement and initial talkover were used for the several of the sessions. In the third session however, middle-container music in the form of the Haydn Cello Concerto in C, second movement, was used. In a talk-over, it was suggested that the traveller find the movement in the music to help the group members move into the experience, and the leaders voice returned towards the end of the music to guide them out. During the first notes of this piece, she was walking into a church with empty benches, the door slamming shut behind her. She was frightened, and split into three persons (this was her first acknowledgement of frequent dissociatve experiences), but the group leaders voice gave her strength to realize that they were all part of her. The music encouraged her to progress into the church towards a wonderful light that grew in intensity as she approached the altar, with a stronger experience of being one person as she progressed. At the altar, there was a coffin with two flowers, signifying mother and uncle To the side there was a book turned to an empty page. A voice told her that it was time for her to bury her ruminations about her childhood, and turn to a new page in her life. With the help of the leaders voice, she was able to move out of the church, the door closing behind her with the last note of the music.

She was shaken, but more and more relieved as the experience was guided in the post-session Understanding increased as the concepts of cyclicity, dissociation and transpersonal states were explained in the educative session. During the following three weeks of the program, she could intentionally turn on this experience and lay memories and issues vis-à-vis her mother and uncle to rest, as they were evoked in the Spektrum program. After termination of the five weeks, we had an individual session, with re-guiding of this material and additional artwork. She was able to leave her rumination behind and move on to other issues. She could meet the eyes of people in streets and subways, and learned, in the GIM sessions, to manage some of her anxiety through her breathing.

This woman was part of the evaluation with Tree-drawing and ORT mentioned before, which showed substantial improvement in both tests.

Findings and conclusions

Individual in-depth processing and expansion of consciousness

The priority of the Spektrum GIM Group is to foster the defining elements of Group GIM: individual inner exploration through spontaneous, creative music listening in an expanded state of consciousness. This is most pronounced in the middle two or three sessions of the series. All other aspects of the Spektrum Group are subordinate to this aim, and have the function of providing a safe space for it.

This allows sessions that are evocative with a fair amount of work with traumatic imagery, shadow aspects, transpersonal experiences and transformations. In groups with strong cohesion, up to 25% of sessions may have transpersonal features. In figure 1, most of the yellow colors represent such experiences (Körlin 1999). The tendency in previous literature has been to deem this not possible or constructive with psychiatric patients (Summer 2002; Goldberg 1994; Clark 2002).

A number of features contribute: the redefinition of consciousness, the treatment phases, the group interaction in post-music guiding, the containment of group process, the screen, the tight structure and other session containing elements, the total framework, and the management of resource experiences.

Redefinition of consciousness

The results show that it is possible for psychiatric patients to develop through expanded consciousness. This is possible because the experiences of altered states in the music are explained through pedagogical information, pointed out in the guiding, and manifested on the screen. The GIM Group experience is also defined to include not only the music experience but the whole setting: images and thoughts during the pre-talk; the relaxation and induction; and after the music phase proper. With this widened notion of experience, even non-participation, a blank experience or a white paper are manifested on the screen, and provide fruitful material for processing. This goes hand in hand with demonstrating the existence of the inner life, and of encouraging the "owning" and management of experiences.

In the pedagogical situation with Spektrum patients, expanded consciousness is termed "widening of experience". It is a revelation for most to realize that experience includes not only ordinary consciousness but also all sensory qualities of imagery, unclear affects, ineffable experiences and thoughts, clear or jumbled.

Group phases – the temporal space

The phases of the Spektrum group are first, trust and cohesion building, second in-depth work, and third, closure. In such a short and intensive setting, these phases can be speeded up, in fact almost compressed into each other. The initial cohesion building and the concluding summary and separation work form the temporal enclosure of the creative space.

In the first session, where the patients paint to on-going music for 30 minutes and afterwards share their experience, group interaction and sharing of individual imagery are combined in building group cohesion. The metaphors introduced during the last two sessions further summary and closure.

Group interaction, screen, containment of group process and use of group introspection.

Group interaction and reflection are not used to explore the group process but to support cohesion, the individual's safety space, and the group's involvement in individual imagery. This involvement is primarily due the fact that group members learn to participate in the post-music guiding, and then the search for meaning. The systematic approach to this is perhaps unique to the Spektrum Group, and would not be possible without educative elements and the "movie" metaphor. The involvement in imagery addresses the traditional drawback of individual-in-group therapy: unenthusiastic listening to long life histories (Yalom 1995) and complex imagery (Summer 2002). The meaningfulness of individual imagery is also manifested by the continuity of imagery on the screen.

Group process is contained by the tight session structure, which safeguards equal time for each, minimizing issues around giving or taking time. Another part of the safety lies in trusting the leader to address and share tensions in the here and now. By doing this in a structured way, he also saves time for individual exploration. Individual boundaries are supported through the "yes", "no", and "maybe" metaphors. Group reflection is evoked in a limited way by focusing on shared experiences in inductions (resources and the separation issue)

Session containing elements

In previous paragraphs on the method, and in the case vignettes, some principles of varying the group and session containing elements were outlined. In the individual-in-group context, it is important to point out that the desired outcome is not a limited experience by itself, but a manageable transforming experience. This may contain all the experiential elements of the individual BMGIM session, and may be achieved also in a talk-over session as in case 3.

Framework

The Spektrum program is a planned setting, with a closed group going through a predictable schedule of events in a safe physical environment. The coordination of sessions, the presence of the continuity person, the continuity of themes, and the growing patterns of artwork on the screen add to the sense of safety and planning. This makes it possible to use quite wide musical containers, open-ended inductions and long spaces of "free" creative imaging in the music.

Resources and cyclicity

The abundant examples of resource mobilization (documented in photographs from about 1500 sessions) may be ordered into the following categories: Movement, Protection, Helping figures, Nurturing, Energy and Transpersonal. Several of these were illustrated in the case examples. The cyclical interaction with problematic experiences is obvious in the group process. For example, it is common for a nurturing experience to prepare the way for an experience of separation, and for an experience of protection to be followed by a re-experience of abuse. The awareness of cyclicity helps in attuning to the group process.

In the GIM group, resources and cyclicity are constantly fostered and interpreted, to impart hope and encourage continued processing in the face of difficult experiences. In the educative session of the Spektrum program, cyclicity is an excellent metaphor to explain the importance of owning both "positive" and the "negative" experiences. It is important if you feel "good" or "bad", but it is equally important to live through both, reflecting and learning along the way

Resources may be intentionally addressed in the pre-session discussion, induction, and talk-over, and they are actively interpreted in the post-session. However, it is not so easy to intentionally mobilize resources in the music experience. Movement is the easiest to access, through the movement of music itself. Protection, in the form of finding a safe place in the music, Helping figures and also Nurturing require that timing is right. Energy and above all transpersonal experiences are impossible to evoke intentionally, they come according to the wisdom of the inner growth process, provided there is enough trust and group cohesion.

Also, the resource concept is not straightforward. Emotions, resources and defenses perceived to be positive may be problematic in themselves. Each of them has a problematic or even shadow, backside. These may be sketched as: protection – isolation; nurturing – overfeeding; movement and energy – different qualities of flight; and transpersonal – spiritual by-pass[1]. Nevertheless, the positive quality has priority because of the strong tendency among psychiatric patients to regard themselves as powerless, worthless, negative and destructive. Inner experiences are frequently perceived in negative terms as meaningless, useless, un-manly, toxic etc. It is also a common conception that shortcomings are topics desired by therapists.

1 Spiritual by-pass, originally a Buddhist concept ascribed to the master Chogyuan Trungpa, is a term within transpersonal psychology. It refers to people using spiritual experiences to try to step over negative intrapsychic content or painful biographical events.

Thus, it is the first priority in consciousness-expanding GIM work to investigate the patient's ability to perceive, acknowledge and use also the positive sides of GIM experiences. However, it is important to be aware that mobilization of resources is not only supportive, but an integral part of the widening of consciousness.

Group GIM Therapy – a complex system

There are several things to bear in mind that limit any strategy to intentionally contain or widen the experiences. One is that group members with an acute need to process something particular will do so regardless of the therapist's intentions, as exemplified by case 3. A second is that some patients, for example those with a strategy of controlling others to prevent intrusive behavior may react negatively to limiting interventions. A third that, in talkover sessions, the leader's instructions may not limit, but the voice may be used for support of a wider exploration. A fourth, that the reaction to music may vary with the same music from one session to another. This happens because the patient goes in cyclical process with the music, alternating between resource and problematic experiences of the same musical elements. One example is for a traumatized patient to experience the Pachelbel Canon first as protective, and the next session as persistently invasive.

As in individual and group GIM, it is essential to always give the Group GIM Therapy patient a choice. It may be to open his eyes to defend against too difficult music, or it may be to allow a necessary experience to happen regardless of the therapist's intention. In my opinion, it is thus impossible to totally safeguard against the individual in-depth experience in the music, and thus skills in BMGIM guiding and processing are always required.

Conclusion

As a Group GIM Therapy, the Spektrum Group is far towards the end of the continuum where spontaneous individual music experience in an altered state of consciousness is emphasized relative to group interaction and reflection. In the middle two or three of the five sessions, confrontation with traumatic memories, conflict material, transformative imagery and even short peak experiences are frequent. Those sessions are the nucleus of the Spektrum Group series, and every other element of this GIM application can be seen as successive protective layers around this creative seed. The total framework of the Spektrum program, and the psycho-educative elements, make these experiences manageable, comprehensible and meaningful for mid-functioning psychiatric patients.

CH. 7: THE BONNY METHOD OF GUIDED IMAGERY AND MUSIC (BMGIM) AND GRIEF WORK

A Case Study

BIRGIT SÜSELBECK-SCHULZ

During training in Integrative Music Therapy at the *Fritz Perls Institute for Integrative Therapy*, I had the opportunity to follow a long-term Integrative Music Therapy with the 35-year-old client Anna (name changed) and her therapist Dr. Isabelle Frohne-Hagemann, in which 12 BMGIM-sessions were included. At the request of the client, her BMGIM-sessions were tape-recorded. After terminating therapy, the client released the tapes for research purposes and allowed her therapist to use them, together with the therapy notes and transcripts. A case vignette by Frohne-Hagemann (2001) and the tapes and notes from the BMGIM-sessions within the Integrative Music Therapy allowed me to describe the therapy process as an outside witness and to explore if it was comprehensible and compatible with the concepts of Integrative Music Therapy. The latter, however, will not be the theme of this chapter. Written permission was given by the client and her therapist to describe the course of therapy in this chapter.

The Bonny Method of Guided Imagery and Music (BMGIM), developed by Helen Bonny in the USA, is an integrative method, which in many aspects fits with the concepts of Integrative Music Therapy (see also the chapter by I. Frohne-Hagemann in this book). I would like to emphasize common concepts of openness for different psychotherapeutic concepts, centering on the differentiation of somatic-emotional experiencing, holistic orientation, the openness to work in different states of consciousness (for example waking consciousness, intuition, synergy, and the noetic), focusing on the here and now while simultaneously working on the biographic backgrounds and the transference process, and the conviction that therapy is in accordance with a Heraclitian principle, which develops along spirals and not in a linear way (Petzold 1993).

On the Grieving Process in Women with Miscarriage and/or Early Death of a Child

In this case study, the grieving process after a miscarriage and a stillbirth is described.

Confrontation with the death of a person with whom we have a relationship is a liminal experience, and is always also an encounter with ones own death. The ability to grieve gives us the opportunity to encounter this extreme situation, the death of a person, and to work through it in the grieving process with its different grieving phases (Kast 1982, 13f). It becomes problematic if grief cannot be allowed, for example due to a taboo of death and dying in society, or due to fear of stigmatization (Jerneizig 1991, 12). Especially with the early death of a child, grief work becomes more difficult because of these factors, like for example the "lack of appropriate grieving rituals"[1] (Nijs 1999, 16). Kast writes about the problem of helplessness among family and friends, which is supposed to repress ones own grieving: "Grieving that it is possible that birth can be death, and in a broader sense grieving that life cannot be without death, that hope so easily gives way to fear and resignation."[2] (Kast 1997, 64) The taboo, devaluation of the loss by society, lack of shared memories of the child (often the parents did not see their dead child), and isolation, lead into a vicious circle in which women often do not have the courage to show their grief (Lothrop 1998, 223). The very close participation of the mother in the death of her child (as it died in the womb or during birth) often leads to feelings of guilt which can be an expression of a deep crisis of identity (Kast 1997, 69). The relationship of the dead child to both parents, especially the bodily relationship to the mother "is a very intense relationship closely linked to the life of the couple and the expectant family. The loss of an expected child is a very severe one, and needs intensive grieving if trust in life should be possible again."[3] (Kast 1997, 65)

In therapeutic work with grieving mothers and fathers, the first goal is to get beyond speechlessness. The grieving persons should be allowed to talk repeatedly about the loss of the child and to cry about it (Jeneizig 1991, 77). Trust in the therapist is the basis for a successful grieving process in which the trauma is dealt with and where the person concerned can "relate as a changed person"[4] (Jerneizig 1991, 29).

In current music therapy literature, there is little exchange of experiences dealing with this issue. I would like to mention the grieving seminars by Jorgos Canacakis. Canacakis (1987) includes the ritual Greek laments, the *Myroloja* in his grieving therapy. The *Myroloja* are poems, laments with a meter of eight syllables. Melody, text, rhythm, and volume emerge and change with the mood of the personalities who take part in the singing (Canacakis 2002, 89). "The grieving persons can freely express pain, anger, protest, feelings of guilt, and despair towards the dead person. But they can also express their love and sympathy. Often a dialogue evolves; a talk

1 Original: "Fehlen von angemessenen Trauerritualen"

2 Original: "Die Trauer darüber, dass es möglich ist, dass die Geburt ein Tod sein kann, und weiter gefasst die Trauer darüber, dass Leben überhaupt nicht ohne Tod ist, dass Hoffnung so leicht der Angst und Resignation weichen kann."

3 Original: "eine sehr intensive Beziehung, die auch mit dem Leben des Paares und der werden Familie in engem Zusammenhang steht. Der Verlust eines so erwarteten Kindes ist ein sehr schwerwiegender Verlust, der intensiv betrauert werden muss, soll Vertrauen ins Leben wieder möglich werden."

4 Original: "als veränderte Person neue Beziehungen eingehen"

with the dead person, but also with persons alive."[5] (Canacakis, 117) During the singing, daydreams often appear. Kast points to the fact "...that in the surrounding of experiences of death people dream a lot, that the unconscious gives instructions for grieving, and through this a new identity of the grieving person is built"[6] (Kast 1982, 25).

Also, working with BMGIM is a good way of working through grief. The work with music-evoked imagery accompanies Anna's grieving process, which I will describe below.

Assessment

When Anna (the oldest of three sisters) was 15 years old, her youngest sister died of a lengthy illness. Anna was in puberty then. Many conflicts and insecurities were in the foreground, so that she could not properly grieve over the death of her sister. She repressed her sorrow and did not communicate due to the fear of becoming an outsider. She was proud of being brave and of dealing well with the loss. She did not grieve over her sister's death well enough within her family. Strong emotions, tears, and pain were not shown. There was a deep fear of being swept away by emotions. So, everyone was brave, and they almost never spoke about the dead child during the next years.

When Anna was 35 she had a miscarriage. Shortly after that she began (active) music therapy, but could only open herself to it in a limited way. Apparently at that time it was necessary for her to protect herself through dialogue from closeness and repressed feelings. After nine months she became pregnant again and lost that baby, too. He was born in the 7th month of pregnancy with severe deformities and died during the delivery. It appeared that the cause was a genetic disease detected through genetic testing both in Anna and in her husband.

Two years later a healthy daughter was born, which was a great joy for her parents. During all this time Anna was in therapy, with the goal of finding resources and grieving. During the course of therapy, receptive music therapy played a more and more important role. About a year after the stillbirth the BMGIM-cycle of 12 sessions started. There was a session every 4–8 weeks. Around the birth (of the healthy daughter) there was a break of 8 months. The long periods between sessions were due to her moving to another city. During the course of therapy it became evident that Anna could open herself more to receptive music therapy than

5 Original: "Die trauernden können dabei frei ihren Schmerz, ihre Wut, ihren Protest, ihre Schuldgefühle, ihre Verzweiflung dem Toten gegenüber ausdrücken. Sie können aber auch ihre Liebe und ihre Sympathie zum Ausdruck bringen. Es kommt oft zu einem Dialog, zu einem Zwiegespräch mit dem Toten, aber auch mit den Lebenden."

6 Original: "... dass im Umfeld von Todeserleben sehr viel geträumt wird, dass das Unbewusste Anleitung zum Trauern gibt und sich dadurch eine neue Identität des trauernden Menschen aufbaut"

to active music therapy, in which contact to the therapist is much more direct. She had never learned to share her feelings of grief with others, and she held a deep fear that with too much closeness she would be swept away by these feelings. By experiencing music and imagery, she made contact with repressed feelings. By bypassing direct contact with the therapist, Anna could allow her grief to exist, and she learned to slowly express and share it.

In the following, I describe Anna's therapy process with the focus of grieving over the deaths of her sister and her two children. Not all BMGIM-sessions will be described. Some sessions are summarized. In those sessions, issues apart from grieving were important. They will not be described in detail here. To connect the therapy process and the music, and to describe this connection in words, I describe the music used without attempting to deal too deeply with musicology or become too subjective. Those descriptions were created afterwards, influenced by my empathy with the patient and by the therapist sharing her experience of the music. Of course, all descriptions are shortened.

1st Session

The stillbirth happened 15 months ago. Grieving appears to be the main issue. For the first session a music program was chosen that can offer space for issues like loss and grief.

Music: Loss[7] *(designed by S. Stokes-Stearns) (25.44 min.)*

All pieces have a slow tempo. Low tones and a supportive and heavy bass produce a pious mood. Here, the feelings that can be expressed and accompanied by the music can deepen.

1. Albinoni, Adagio (9.35 min.)
2. Bach, Come Sweet Death (5.06 min.)
3. Bach, Mein Jesu (BMV 478) (5.11 min.)
4. Bach, Orchestra Suite # 3 (BWV 1068), Aria (5.52 min.)

1. Albinoni, Adagio

The slow pulse of the organ-bass makes one quiet and invites one into its depths. While the bass-line descends, the organ-melody provides simple movement. Then strings are added very gently and consolingly. A short pause before the solo-voice softly asks the traveler: "Why?" The whole phrase is repeated. The question is now asked more energetically and accusingly by the violin. The organ supports that with a low sound, above which the violin expresses deep feelings. The movement is slow, but it arrives at a heart-rending intensification in

7 The names of the music-programs for BMGIM just serve as a general orientation. They do not suggest any expectations of what the client is supposed to experience.

the strings. The grief is simultaneously consoled by the organ-accompaniment. The end of the piece is heavy and full of tension.

Summary of imagery: Albinoni's music helps Anna to talk about her experiences. She feels pain and can communicate it to the therapist. Lovingly, she describes how the deformed child looked, and that she felt he had some similarity with her dead sister. The fact that Anna saw her dead child after it had been born helped her to acknowledge the reality of death which is an important step in the grieving process (Jerneizig 1991, 107).

2. Bach, Come Sweet Death
Low tones with strings descending above them. Very slow tempo, the movement is like a misty weaving. Sepulchral mood like under the earth, the depth is like death. In the background, other instruments give the impression of life on earth. The traveler is held in a place of sweetness and sadness (playing with major and minor). The melody (cellos) is suggesting the necessity for acceptance.

Summary of imagery: Anna imagines going to the grave of her baby together with the therapist. Behind the tombstone she sees her dead sister waving at her. She is happy that she came (that she remembers her?).

3. Bach, Mein Jesu (BWV 478)
The energy is now brought up from the depths, allowing issues to be worked through, and feelings of grief, despair, and melancholy to be released. There is more movement in the music than in the 2nd piece. There is a balance between major and minor. The music is like a great consolation. One may feel understood.

Summary of imagery: During this piece, Anna feels shock about the loss. With the support of the music and the therapist, she can express the pain through crying. She just wants to cry, and above all be allowed to cry.

4. Bach, Orchestra Suite # 3 (BWV 1068), Aria
This piece has healing and grounding qualities. The steady pulse in the bass carries through the piece like a heartbeat, and gives stability and safety. The warm melody-line in the strings is rocking, consoling, and strengthening. It is possible to rest, reflect, and look back.

Summary of imagery: During this music, the imagery is intensifying. Among other things, Anna sees a red heart clasped by something black, and she senses an inner urge to free herself from that clamp.

For the first time, Anna can show the depth of her grief, cry while another person (here the therapist) is present, and allow herself to be comforted. The feelings surrounding the death of her child and her sister are closely related. Is she crying vicariously for her family? She senses the pressure of unprocessed grief, of the long silence in her family, and finds a way of releasing some of it by talking about it in this session. Shortly after this session, Anna dreams that she is in an airplane's belly: "There I am now, and I am scared to death. I do not know if I can get out of here safely. Then I look around in the airplane's belly." When working with this dream, the therapist asked her to look closer at what is in the plane's belly. Due to time reasons, BMGIM was not used during this session. Anna describes: "It is musty here, a disgusting brown carpet. It needs renovation and cleaning-up." To the question of how Anna would want to decorate the room, she answers: "Paint everything in a light color and furnish it with light-colored furniture, line the room with ermine." The plane's belly symbolizes her own belly, her womb. Inside her, it looks uncared-for and gloomy after the painfully terminated pregnancy. When working with the dream, she cleans up her insides, and lovingly decorates this inner space in a cozy way.

2nd Session

About two months later the second session takes place. Grief, pain and unclear feelings are the issues. The therapist chooses a music program that does not have too much depth, but offers space for many different sensations and imagery.

***Music: Quiet Music** (designed by H. Bonny) (34 min.)*

1. Debussy, Danse sacre et profane (10 min.)
2. Debussy, L'après-midí d'un Faune (10 min.)
3. Holst, The Planets, Venus (9.5 min.)
4. Vaughan-Williams, Fantasia on Greensleeves (4.5 min.)

> 1. Debussy, Danse sacre et profane
> The strings start in unison and broadly, opening a wide inner space. Then, a darker quality appears with a kind of knocking in the bass. Everything stays at a vague, somewhat mysterious level.

Summary of imagery: At the very beginning, Anna bursts into tears. She sees her younger sister playing on a meadow with her children. She watches it sadly and feels that she does not belong to it. She senses a lot of seriousness. But she notices that it gives her quite a headache to always think about her past.

> 2. Debussy, L'après-midí d'un Faune
> The flute starts with a chromatic melody-line sliding up and down. The orchestra chimes in with a boiling up and down movement, which raps with a lazy, sultry, lusty and erotic mood. The air swims, a floating and sliding appears, and the faun rises from the sultry orchestra sound with his instrument which accompanies the traveler like a magic flute.

Summary of imagery: The flute melody reminds Anna of her own inner liveliness. She feels "okay" with what has happened. She says, "I did not turn into a dark creature. The lively voice is still there, it is familiar to me."

3. Holst, The Planets, Venus
A slow upward movement in the horn and the orchestra is descending from above. The below and the above meet here. The horn and the flute meet. The mood is very delicate, almost ethereal. It is as if heaven and earth are touching each other.

Summary of imagery: "The music is good, it is comforting." Therapist: "Allow yourself to be comforted by it." Anna cries. Then she can say: "A light, a gift, it is like a blessing."

4. Vaughan-Williams, Fantasia on Greensleeves
This piece gives time to gently finish the traveling, and space for reconciliation. It has a rather contemplative beginning, and then pushes forward to some extent. In the middle part there is again a resting place, where contemplating and remembering are possible.

Summary of imagery: Anna imagines: "Now I am on my way, and well equipped. Wherever the way is leading, I got a lot on the way: the blessing, the knowledge that somebody is there with me. And the knowledge that I can *receive* (emphasized by B. S.-S.) it, but just do not open myself for it."

Looking back at the therapeutic process, it becomes evident that this session is very important because a contact with the transcendent level becomes possible. Anna can open herself completely and senses a deep feeling of belonging. A few days later she reports that she is pregnant again!

The first months of this new pregnancy – besides all the joy – are also determined by deep fears for the life of the unborn child. Anna has to endure some important medical check-ups to make clear that the fetus is healthy. The first examinations show comforting results. However, the autopsy report of the dead child reveals that both parents have the same genetic illness, a very rare coincidence. It is a great relief for both partners that they both have the same illness because each stops making the other guilty. Another thorough examination of the fetus shows that the child is healthy.

During the 3rd month of pregnancy some music therapy sessions take place, but BMGIM is not used so as to not endanger the development of the fetus due to possibly stirring experiences.

3rd Session

The 3rd BMGIM-session takes place four months later. Anna is in the 4th month of pregnancy, and wishes for more calm during the next months. The focus of the session is: letting go of old worries.

***Music: Nurturing** (designed by Bonny/revised by Bruscia) (26 min.)*
The music-program provides a protective ground for things to be worked on. The slow and tender pieces are not stirring; there is no striving towards a climax. They are like a hug, like nurturing for the soul. They are uplifting and strengthening.

1. Britten, Simple Symphony, Sentimental Sarabande (6 min)
2. Walton, Touch Her Soft Lips and Part (1.5 min.)
3. Fauré, Cantique de Jean Racine (6 min.)
4. Fauré, Requiem, Pie Jesu (3 min.)
5. Puccini, Madame Butterfly, Humming Chorus (2 min.)
6. Massenet, Orchestra Suite # 7, Sous les Tilleuls (4 min.)
7. Schumann, 5 Stücke im Volkston op. 102, Langsam (4 min.)

> 1. Britten, Simple Symphony, Sentimental Sarabande
> The strings play a light and tender melody. It sounds like dancing. It is supported by the bass and radiates longing. The middle part becomes more vehement and serious. After pausing and questioning, the piece proceeds softly.

Summary of imagery: Anna sees herself and her husband as bride and groom in front of the altar. She says: "It is appropriate that the two of them go towards the altar and receive the blessing."

> 2. Walton, Touch Her Soft Lips and Part
> This short piece picks up the mood of the preceding piece. The music is very tender.

Summary of imagery: Anna experiences her own wedding, and once again senses the power of the ceremony, which also gives strength for the couple's shared experiences.

> 3. Fauré, Cantique de Jean Racine
> Deep organ-sounds make one quiet. Now the choir sets in, first the male voices, then the female voices unfold like a hug between mother and father. The music gives a feeling of safety and understanding.

Summary of imagery: Anna reports: "Before we got married we had already lost our first child. The voices touch me very much. I am also singing it for my husband."

4. Fauré, Requiem, Pie Jesu
This piece is a very moving piece for solo-voice. For Anna, it is as if the soprano-voice, as a mother, asks for a blessing for her children.

5. Puccini, Madame Butterfly, Humming Chorus
It is like an echo of the preceding solo-voice. One has time to be with what was heard.

6. Massenet, Suite # 7, Sous les Tilleuls
First there is an introduction of sustained strings and bells. Then the violin starts with a motif like an encouraging, inviting call. One is called back into life, it goes on.

Summary of imagery (4.–6.): Anna re-experiences the happy initial time of her marriage. She had not experienced this light-heartedness since the first miscarriage. Experiencing this happy time is like a resource.

7. Schumann, 5 Stücke im Volkston op. 102, Langsam
The piece starts with a melody in the cello that rises from the depth, and is accompanied and supported by ascending chords in the piano.

Summary of imagery: Through the vivid memory of the initial time of her marriage Anna now also senses closeness to her child: "Experiencing how a new life is growing is a miracle. She has her own soul, and it is bright. She has nothing to do with all the heaviness and only needs my body at the moment. She says I can develop well with you."

By identifying with the cello-part, Anna senses that the soul of the child is carefree. This is very important for Anna and gives her a lot of strength for the following months of the pregnancy.

4th, 5th, and 6th Session

In the following three sessions, which took place in shorter intervals, the theme was the changing of the different identity areas that take place during a pregnancy. In the 4th session for example, Anna deals with her role as mother. The focus of the 5th session is the physical change, and the focus of the 6th session is the change in outside circumstances (moving, job). Again and again, she deals with worries about the health of the child. The positive support through BMGIM throughout the months of pregnancy cannot be described here in more detail. But it should be mentioned that Anna had very vivid imagery of her newborn, healthy child that gave her a lot of strength and hope for the pregnancy. She can sense herself as a woman carrying healthy life within her. During the 6th session, she sees herself resting in the palace gardens of Sanssouci (English translation: "without worries"), enjoying the light-heartedness and joy of life, which she had lacked for a long time.

7th Session

About four weeks later Anna is in her 7th month of pregnancy, and she is fine. A new (old) issue appears: At the beginning of the session, she reports about meeting persons in her everyday life to whom she feels she does not measure up to mentally. She describes her insecurities and fears when in contact with them, and that this hinders her so much that she cannot stand up for her own interests and ideas anymore.

The focus of this session is the question: "How can I manage to not be intimidated by authorities?" During the BMGIM-session it appears that this problem has to do with unprocessed grief for her dead sister.

*Music: **Searching** (Designed by K. Bruscia)*

The chosen music-program with its richness of different atmospheres and soundscapes offers space for opening up. There is much time for development even though the direction is not yet known.

1. Liadov, Enchanted Lake (7.5 min.)
2. Vaughan-Williams, Symphony # 2, Lento (12 min.)
3. Holst, The Planets, Venus (8 min.)
4. Holst, The Planets, Neptune (7 min.)
5. Grieg, Cradle Song (4 min.)

1. Liadov, Enchanted Lake
It starts with a sustained bass-sound, which suggests depth. Out of this mysterious and yearning depth, a colorful richness of sound with different atmospheres arises. In between, it becomes more thrilling, as if creatures are coming out of the thicket, and the flute keeps suggesting light-heartedness.

Summary of imagery: Anna sees herself sitting at the shore of a big lake, happy and one with nature. Then clouds appear in the sky. Something is brewing. Anna senses tension in the body. What does it remind her of? Of school, where initially she was eager to learn and bright and could perform well. From grade 11 on, this was gone. The therapist asks her to say more about this time.

2. Vaughan-Williams, Symphony # 2, Lento
The orchestra carefully introduces this piece with the first three tones of a wide, sad theme. The second part starts with a fine melody in the violin. The tension

finally builds towards a touching peak. The violin bridges into the third part. The first motif appears, and the piece gently fades.

Summary of imagery: The music takes Anna back to school when she was about 15 years old. Exactly at this time, her sister died. She is very afraid to be asked anything, and stay silent. She can show her feelings neither at home nor at school. During the music, Anna experiences – and here it shows how she has to fight her feelings – how she closes down and refuses to perform even though she is eager to learn. During the BMGIM-session, this experience shows her what she really would have needed back then: compassion, understanding for her situation, and consoling.

3. Holst, The Planets, Venus
(Description see 2nd session)

4. Holst, The Planets, Neptune
This piece is mysterious. It sounds like music of the spheres, is staggering and irritating, like time and space dissolving in the cosmos. Then it slowly fades into silence.

Summary of imagery: Anna goes back to an exam. First she feels completely upset and dependant on the goodwill of the examiner. Out of this experience grow the impulse, and the insight into how important it is to act responsibly and take oneself seriously.

5. Grieg, Cradle Song
After the last piece of music, this one is restfully clear and one returns to earth. It is comforting and freeing, and it gives hope.

Summary of imagery: Anna now can imagine how she could make the examiner interested in her ideas.

7th and 8th Session

The issues of taking responsibility for oneself and releasing old patterns are worked with further.

9th and 10th Session

Since the last session 8 months have passed. Anna has given birth to a daughter, who is now 4 months old. In the meantime, Anna has moved further away to another city, and has kept in contact with her therapist by telephone. During this session, Anna talks about the first happy months with her baby. But she also has the need to rest and calm down. As she finally has the long wished for child, Anna now thinks that she has to be a perfect mother, not allowed to complain, and always thankful.

Summary of imagery: During the 9th session Anna's needs as a woman, mother, and wife become clear. Loving feelings towards herself and the baby free her from the feeling of having to be perfect. Also. the 10th session deals with finding her identity as a competent woman.

11th Session

Three months have passed since the last session. Anna talks about her everyday life as a housewife and mother, which is not fulfilling for her. She compares herself with other women who have jobs in addition to their families. She feels weak and insufficient; she "also" wants to be something very special. She seems dissatisfied and tense. The focus for this session becomes: Being independent from the ideas of other people, staying with herself, not needing to be something special.

*Music: **Reflections** (designed by S. Stokes-Stearns)*

The chosen music program goes into depth (2nd piece) after a contemplative beginning. The 3rd piece leads upwards again from depth, and one is held and strengthened by the following pieces.

1. Respighi, Pines of Rome, Gianicola (6.5 min.)
2. Debussy, Engulfed Cathedral (6.5 min.)
3. Holst, The Planets, Saturn (9.5 min.) (added to the program)
4. Holst, The Planets, Venus (8 min.)
5. Mozart, Serenade for Winds, Adagio (5 min.)

1. Respighi, Pines of Rome, Gianicola
This piece starts in the depths with a dazzling piano cadence. The clarinet, oboe, and violin spin fine threads of melody. The orchestra accompanies very tenderly. The mood is "as if everything is sleeping". The pines sway softly in the wind. Then it becomes livelier, something moves. At the end – one thinks the piece is over – the clarinet raises its voice again, the nightingales sing, the day rises and one becomes alert:

2. Debussy, Engulfed Cathedral
The orchestra rises. as if out of nothing. The bass smolders below, one senses something; the mood is mysterious. Then, tension rises, one comes closer to the

thrill, descends, bell-sounds make the mood more tense. It becomes more and more intense till something glorious appears like a revelation. One hears the bell of the engulfed cathedral with all its glory, the mood is solemn. Then the door slowly closes, the mood changes; melancholy is expressed by the orchestra, the music becomes darker, the melodies in the horns and the orchestra become more hollow. Drums in the bass communicate depth, bell-sounds talk about lost glory. In this way, the piece fades away.

3. Holst, The Planets, Saturn
The dark mood of the Engulfed Cathedral is continued. Something approaches, first hesitantly, then firmly as if coming from afar. It goes deeper, the footsteps become heavier and heavier, one cannot get away. Strings and bells make the mood more intense and stirring; a short while later it calms down again. Higher tones accompanied by a low bass lead upwards again. The mood now is tender, wide, and bright, but tension does not dissolve completely, and stays till the end.

4. Holst, The Planets, Venus
This piece has already been described in the 2nd session. There is an initial calling from the horns, and an answer from the strings. After the Engulfed Cathedral, one is torn upwards while the bass is still present. The mood is longing and tender.

5. Mozart, Serenade for Winds, Adagio
The character of this piece is set by a light, pulsating rhythm, which is constantly present. On this ground, two clarinets meet, complement each other, and play together. In the end a single clarinet unfolds on solid ground.

Summary of imagery: Anna floats in this imagery like a bird in clear air. She allows herself to float through the jungle into a cave. There, nice experiences from the past are revived. But then she feels drawn away from it. She finds herself in an art museum and looks around with her therapist. She sees pictures in golden frames in the style of Rembrandt with her family on them. First, she stays with the picture of her mother. She has a smile on her face, which appears stiff. Then the face becomes sorrowful and worrying. Anna knows this expression from the time of her sister's illness. She becomes aware that her mother also lost a child, and she feels a deep connection with and understanding for her.

Now she proceeds to her father's picture associated with the imagery of the picture by Spitzweg: The Bookworm. She looks into the face of this man and sees something unfathomable, something like a secret. To the therapist's question whether she wants to explore this secret, she says: "The music says that I do not need to know it. I wonder if I really have anything to do with it. He had a difficult childhood during the war. I guess I took up some of my father's feelings and suffered with him, and I do not need to do that anymore … he can deal with it himself."

Anna can get away from the sadness and heaviness, which had been passed on to her. Also, reconciliation with her mother takes place. It becomes clear to Anna that she is responsible for her own life in her own family, and that she does not have to carry feelings delegated to her in childhood.

12th Session

This session is the final BMGIM-session, and also the final therapy-session. Anna comes into the office for the last time, and the theme of parting from a long time of therapy is present. Due to the long distance and the long periods between sessions, this theme has already been prepared internally during the past year. Leaving and her perspectives for the time after termination of therapy are the focus of this last BMGIM-session.

***Music: Expanded Awareness** (designed by L. Keiser Mardis) (49 min.)*
1. Vaughan-Williams, Fantasia on a Theme by Thomas Tallis (16 min.)
2. Vaughan-Williams, Symphony # 5, Romanza (13 min.)
3. Vaughan-Williams, Lark Ascending (16 min.)
4. Vaughan-Williams, Fantasia on Greensleeves (4.5 min.)

1. Vaughan-Williams, Fantasia on a Theme by Thomas Tallis
The piece starts full of expectations and a bit mysteriously. Through the instrumentation an impressive stereophonic effect is achieved. The music gives no direction, stays unconcrete, and keeps all possibilities open. The traveler has time and space to approach gropingly, try out, and take everything in. The violin introduces the final chord in major which gives hope.

2. Vaughan-Williams, Symphony # 5, Romanza
The beginning is like drawing from the depths. Then slowly the theme develops, very intense and touching. It gives an idea of mental richness and beauty. The middle part is stronger and there is a quarrel. The ending is sad and consoling like a gentle caress.

Summary of imagery: Anna looks back at the last years, at the difficulties she had, and the help from therapy. The music is now with the therapist and the client, who part from each other in a very personal and good way. Sadness and letting go of each other are allowed. During this parting, Anna feels grown-up and independent, free, and still connected. She has the feeling that the shared sadness and also the experiences of comforting were given a good place here, which she is now leaving but can still remember.

3. Vaughan-Williams, Lark Ascending
First, the mood of the previous piece is continued. Then the violin grows and starts unfolding, first very hesitantly, gropingly, and playfully, then more certainly and full of joy.

4. Vaughan-Williams, Fantasia on Greensleeves
The piece already described in different sessions

Summary of imagery (3. and 4.): Anna takes the music in and feels like a bird that starts exploring the world. But she also senses a clear connection with the earth, senses inner strength and movement, sees herself joining people, looks for her place, and finds it. She has the feeling that she can co-create her surroundings.

Then she meets her husband. Both look at shared life-history and have the feeling that there will be a lot of good things for them in the future.

In this last therapy session Anna looks both backwards and forward. The feelings when parting are clear and real. There is nothing unspoken in the air. The therapist can let Anna go, and trusts that she will go her way. Anna senses this, and feels grown-up and responsible for her own life. Despite all the independence, she senses a deep connection with other people and with good forces.

Summary

Anna's mental development in the therapeutic process through BMGIM was described. During the presented BMGIM-sessions, Anna learned to express unprocessed grief, old and new. This was not only grief over her two lost babies; it also became clear to her that she alone was carrying part of her family's grief for her sister. The BMGIM-process within the context of the whole therapy helped her to free herself from delegated feelings. First, she was dealing with the grief over her own children.

The BMGIM-sessions, together with other elements of Integrative Music Therapy, opened a space for new experiences. In the 2nd BMGIM-session, Anna experienced a deep feeling of connection and being alive. She could open herself for new experiences. Immediately after that she became pregnant again (with a healthy child). During pregnancy, working on grief was still an issue in therapy. By saying good-bye to her two children and her sister, Anna got the feeling that the developing child in her uterus was not burdened with the past (3rd session).

Over time, Anna developed a new female identity. She experienced how she developed into a woman who carried healthy life and gave birth to it, took part in social life, and also looked for mental exchange and stimulation.

It should be emphasized that Anna's imagery, which could express itself and develop with the help of the therapist in and through the music, continued to mobilize an inner source of strength (Reddemann 2001) and pointed to solutions.

There was space for issues like death, grief, and parting as well as for confrontation with existential fears and for the blessing of hope, confidence, and new life.

Acknowledgement

The author would like to thank Carola Maack for the translation.

CH. 8: CULTURAL ASPECTS OF THE BONNY METHOD OF GUIDED IMAGERY AND MUSIC (BMGIM)

CAROLA MAACK

In this chapter I will show how the Bonny Method of Guided Imagery and Music (BMGIM) as therapy culture fits into different cultures. Culture is commonly defined as "the entirety of typical ways of living of larger groups, including mental activities, especially general values."[1] (Der Neue Brockhaus 1985a, 281) Stige (2002) defines culture in the context of culture-centered music therapy as "the accumulation of customs and technologies enabling and regulating human coexistence." (Stige 2002, 330) I will look at culture in four areas of BMGIM:

1. the therapeutic relationship
2. imagery and symbols
3. music
4. altered states of consciousness

For those readers who are not acquainted with BMGIM, I suggest reading Edith M. Geiger's chapter in this book first.

1. The Therapeutic Relationship

Independent of the setting in which BMGIM takes place, there is always a therapist-client-relationship with existing transference processes. The relationship is formed by the theoretical orientation of the therapist, for example Jungian Analysis, psychodynamic psychotherapy, Gestalt Therapy, transpersonal psychotherapy, etc. In BMGIM, transference and countertransference occur between therapist, client, music, and imagery (Bruscia 2002, 234f). In the context of the therapeutic relationship, I will focus on the cultural dimensions of transference and countertransference between therapist and client.

What does it mean if therapist and client come from different (sub-) cultures or from the same (sub-) culture? Hutterer-Krisch (2001, 137) holds that a therapist can help a client best if she comes from the same culture or subculture. Big damage would be done if the therapist, who came from a different (sub-) culture than the client, "does not see the inequality and considers it to be self-evident that he can empathize with the most foreign patients."[2] (Greenson in Hutterer-Krisch 2001,

1 Original German quote: "die Gesamtheit der typischen Lebensformen größerer Gruppen einschließlich ihrer geistigen Aktivitäten, besonders der Werteinstellungen."

2 Original German quote: "von der Ungleichheit nichts ahnt und es für selbstverständlich hält, dass er sich in die fremdartigsten Patienten einfühlen kann."

137) On the other hand, Suzan, a research subject in Yehuda's (2002) qualitative study of multicultural encounters in music therapy, says: "... there is an optimal amount of it [strangeness] that I deliberately choose, because it can serve as a stronger mirror of myself." Personally, I hold that in different phases of therapy more or less strangeness in the therapist might be helpful. For example, many female survivors of sexualized violence prefer working with a female therapist in the beginning stages of their therapy. In later stages they might prefer a male therapist. While I, as a client, worked on my family history during the Nazi-period, I preferred working with therapists from other countries in order to bring the perspective of another culture into the work. But I consider it very important that therapist and client are aware of their own cultural backgrounds and are open for the cultural background of the other. Occasionally, this should be talked about in therapy sessions. Lu, Lim & Mezzich (1995) describe possible problematic transferences and countertransferences if client and therapist come from a different or from the same (sub-) culture:

- Possible intercultural transference: overcompliance and friendliness; denial of ethnicity and culture; mistrust, suspicion, and hostility; ambivalence.
- Possible intracultural transference: omniscient-omnipotent therapist; the traitor (for example, if a Kurdish therapist also has Turkish clients, a Kurdish client might see her as a traitor); ambivalence.
- Possible intercultural countertransference: denial of cultural differences; clinical anthropologist syndrome; guilt; pity; aggression; ambivalence.
- Possible intracultural countertransference: overidentification; us and them; distancing; cultural myopia; anger; survivor guilt (if both therapist and client are survivors of violence); hope and despair.

Tienhoven, Waning & Veen (2001) describe other possible intercultural countertransferences:

- A feeling that the client was too different and therefore not accessible for the therapist.
- Through oppression, for example by colonial rulers, all people of that culture were permanently damaged (therapist's erroneous assumption). This assumption is pathologizing
- the client, and his individuality and dignity and his personal problems are no longer seen and valued.
- The arrogant and omniscient therapist.
- Making an island of the treatment situation: discussion about cultural differences is avoided which means the therapist identifies with the client's culture and denies her own culture.

In the setting of BMGIM training, the method is used among the trainees in dyads to try it out with each other with the help of the trainers. My very first BMGIM "client" in my first training workshop in the United States was a Jewish concentration-camp survivor (I am German). There was no time to talk about the cultural aspects of this pairing before going into the experience. While guiding him,

I noticed in myself collective guilt; pity; anger with the Germans who did that to him; fear of not being good enough or of being the wrong "therapist" because I am German (even though he had chosen me as a dyad-partner); and I tended to see his culture as the better one and to rather identify with his culture. During the music listening period, neither the fact that he was a survivor, nor my being German came up. Maybe he wanted to spare me. Or maybe he just noticed that it would go far beyond the setting of the training workshop. If I would work with him as a regular client, it would be very important to reflect on these issues during the pre- and post-session. It would also be very important for me as therapist to look at these issues on a regular basis in my supervision and maybe work on it in personal therapy. As BMGIM can lead into archetypal realms, I as therapist would have to be able to hold the energy and even be able to support my client if, for some time, he would see in me as German the embodiment of the collective shadow.

Another important aspect of culture is thinking and language. A colleague from Southeast Asia, who has lived and worked in Germany for many years, told me that during her personal therapy she tries to think and speak the way her German therapist thinks. That means: if therapist and client come from different cultures, they are always in the process of translating, even if they speak the same language. Western thinking and speaking is analytical; it therefore divides things into parts in order to understand them. Asian thinking and speaking is synthetic. Moods are described in an intuitive way without even trying to understand or explain them from an observing perspective. In Asia, the focus is to be in the mood and express it from there. A possible expression could also be silence (Suzuki 1988). For BMGIM, it means that the whole therapy process does not only have to be translated from one language to another, but from one culture to another. An intervention such as "What are you feeling?" is a useful intervention in our Western culture. It guides the client's awareness towards his feelings, which he can notice and communicate to the therapist with words. For an Asian client living in a traditional culture, this intervention might not be useful, as she would have to leave the mood and look at it from the outside to answer the question, which does not go with her way of thinking and culture. The client might even perceive the intervention as rude, intrusive, disturbing and/or damaging to the experience. It is important that both therapist and client are constantly aware of this translation process. It is almost impossible to get to know a different culture so well and to be able to live it, that therapist and client would no longer notice that they come from different cultures. Sometimes it is necessary to name cultural differences and give space for exploring them. And sometimes it is necessary to accept both cultures and let them be there, understanding them intuitively or not understanding them, without having to or being able to analyze or understand them.

Lu, Lim & Mezzich (1995, 477ff) suggest discussing cultural aspects in intercultural discussion groups. "Intercultural" here can also mean from different subcultures. The authors suggest the following items, which could also be useful for supervision or personal therapy:

- What is your cultural background? What has it meant to belong to these cultural groups? How has it felt to belong to your cultural group? What do you like about your cultural identity? What do you dislike?
- Where did you grow up. and which other cultural groups resided there?
- What are the values of your cultural group?
- How did your family see itself, as similar to or different from other ethnic groups?
- What was your first experience with feeling different?
- What are your earliest images of race and color? What information were you given about how to deal with racial issues?
- What does your nationality mean to you? What do you think it means for your client? What do you think your client's nationality means to him/her? What does it mean to you?
- Discuss your experience as a person having or lacking power in relation to the following: nationality, race, gender, profession, in the family, in society.

Spering (2001) describes the following tendencies in relation to cultural differences:

- Individualism vs. collectivism
- Confrontational vs. modest and tender
- Strong future orientation (planning, investing in the future) vs. weak future orientation (shorter thinking, instant gratification)
- Little gender differentiation (women have equal status to men) vs. high degree of gender differentiation (men or women have higher social status)
- Safety (order, structure) vs. uncertainty (strong tolerance of ambiguity)
- Equal power (egalitarianism) vs. distance to higher powers (obedience towards superiors is expected)
- In-group collectivism (pride in membership in small groups like family, organizations, etc.)
- Altruism, caring, and support vs. self-enhancement, assertiveness and importance of material possessions.

All these polarities and factors can influence the therapy process and the way clients see their therapists, or the way clients express things. The therapeutic relationship in BMGIM should always be reflected on the basis of nationality and cultural-historical development. BMGIM is a method that was developed in our Western individualistic culture. Often, goals in BMGIM therapy are individuation and self-actualization. For example, if I work with an Asian client who lives in her collectivistic culture or wants to return to it, it is important to explore together if she wants to walk a Western path of individuation and what that would mean for her life in her culture. If she chooses not to, maybe BMGIM is not the right method for her. According to Wilber (1979, 1995), stages of psychological development on a superficial level have different implications in different cultures, but underneath they have a common structure. Different kinds of therapy would be needed to treat

different layers of the personality. Leading BMGIM therapists, however, hold that BMGIM – sometimes using modifications of the method – can be used to treat all layers of the personality (Goldberg 2002).
When one works with a client who lives in a dominant culture that is not his own culture (for example a Kurd in Germany, a Native American in the USA, a homosexual in a mainly heterosexual society) or when one is a therapist from a non-dominant culture, developmental stages of cultural identity have to be taken into consideration in the therapeutic work:

1. Acceptance and conformity with the dominant culture.
2. Conflict between one's own culture and the dominant culture.
3. Resistance against and rejection of the dominant culture.
4. Introspection: both cultures can exist side by side but the dominant culture is irrelevant.
5. Integration: good and bad aspects of both cultures can be accepted. (Lu, Lim & Mezzich 1995, 477ff)

Those developmental stages can influence transference and countertransference and, if possible, should be brought into awareness. The therapist might temporarily be rejected as "something from the dominant culture". For the client, this can be an important step towards integration. (Of course, the reasons for rejecting the therapist might also not be based on cultural issues!) For the same reasons, a therapist might temporarily reject a client from the dominant culture. This should be dealt with in supervision or personal therapy.

Finally, I would like to mention some aspects of diagnostics. The more organic a disorder, the less it depends on culture and visa versa. Therefore. disorders like dementia or Creutzfeld-Jakob Disease are found around the world with exactly the same symptoms. Disorders like anorexia nervosa or Koro[3] only exist in certain cultures. In between one finds disorders like post-traumatic stress disorder (PTSD). Its symptoms of flashbacks, nightmares and fear are present in all cultures because they cannot be influenced or changed voluntarily due to neuropsychological processing. The approach to and the meaning of shame, guilt, fear, and somatization on the other hand is culture-dependent (Draguns 1996). For treating PTSD with BMGIM it means that the phases of reintegrating traumatic information as described by Körlin (2002, 406) (1. transformation of traumatic imagery into symbolic imagery, 2. establishment of cognitive memory and understanding, 3. integrating the resulting discursive symbols with analogical symbol and affect) can be processed in therapy around the world, but the meaning of imagery, symbols, and affect is culture-dependent.

3 Fear that the penis would withdraw into the lower abdomen and one would die from it. This disorder is found among men in Southeast Asia.

2. Imagery and Symbols

In this section, I will describe how we work with imagery and symbols in the BMGIM-culture, in contrast to other therapy cultures working with imagery. Then I will deal with the general cultural meaning of symbols and imagery.

Imagery plays a central role in the BMGIM-process. The meaning of imagery here is very broad. It can be inner pictures, memories, fantasies, emotions, body-sensations, intuitions, perceptions, inner dialogues, energy phenomena, etc. (Perilli 2002). These are seen as keys for self-knowledge and psychological growth (Toomey 1996/97). In BMGIM literature, we find different models that explain how imagery together with music can have healing qualities, for example neuropsychological models (Goldberg 2002, 361f; Körlin 2002), Jungian models (Ward 2002), psychodynamic models (Bruscia 2002), models of transpersonal psychology (Abrams 2002a), energy work (Carlsson 2001/02), etc. In these areas, further research is necessary. These models are expressions of different therapy cultures which can be integrated into BMGIM, and which again are determined by higher cultural-historical values and traditions.

Meadows (2002, 79f) compares BMGIM with other therapy methods that use imagery. He elaborates on five thematic areas:

1. Imagery experiences have layers of meaning. Some schools only use certain layers of meaning. In BMGIM one image can have very different meanings, often even several meanings at the same time. All layers of meaning are equally valued.
2. Imagery allows access to both conscious and unconscious material. Within the unconscious, there may be layers of levels of experience. Examples of this can be found in Bonny's *Cut Log Model of Consciousness*. By making unconscious material conscious, progress can be made in therapy. This process of bringing unconscious material into consciousness with the help of imagery plays an important role in BMGIM.
3. Each method uses techniques of moving in and out of the imagery experience. In BMGIM relaxation and concentration are used.
4. In each method. the therapist takes a role related to the client, and the client's imagery experience. The role of the therapist in BMGIM is to support but not lead the client. The imagery process is guided by the music, which was chosen by the therapist, and by the client herself.
5. Each method has its own attitude towards music. While many methods do not use music (for example Freudian Analysis), music has a central position in BMGIM.

As mentioned before, in BMGIM therapy, we find transference onto the therapist, the music and the imagery. Transference onto imagery can be a manifestation of transference onto the therapist, the music, or both. But it can also exist independently as pure imagery transference, especially if the client defends himself against transference onto the therapist or the music. (Bruscia 1995; 2002)

On the other hand, we can find countertransference onto the imagery of the client. A BMGIM-specific supervision method that works with this is Bruscia's (2002) re-imaging. Here, the therapist delves into the client's imagery in a short BMGIM-session. The same music is used as in the original session with the client. The therapist goes into the scene and makes contact with the imagery. Then the therapist analyses his imagery and compares it with that of the client to identify transference and countertransference. Of course, it is also possible to work with countertransference onto imagery in a traditional supervisory setting.

Working with imagery in BMGIM usually also means working with some kind of symbols. Therefore, I would like to proceed with the cultural meaning of symbols. Symbol is defined here "in the broader sense as a sensual carrier of meaning or opinion; in the narrower sense as a word, form, thing, or procedure which does not just stand for itself, but means, expresses, or represents something else on a hidden, deeper level."[4] (Der Neue Brockhaus 1985b, 207) Archetypes, on the other hand, are "original and ancient types, i. e. universal pictures from ancient times. ... The archetype essentially represents an unconscious content, which is changed according to the individual consciousness in which it appears when becoming conscious and when it is perceived."[5] (Jung 1988, 12f) Signs are "sensually perceived forms, which are vicariously used for content."[6] (Der Neue Brockhaus 1985b, 640) Kreitler & Kreitler (1972, 312) describe the difference between symbols and signs as follows: "Signs stand for relatively specified references on the basis of a rather arbitrary convention, while symbols evoke less specified and more personal or subjective meanings on the basis of relations other than strict convention between the significant and the signified."

Symbols have a central role in cultures: Through symbols, social order and structures are contained and passed on. By working with symbols or with their socio-cultural meanings in context, cultural structures can be solidified or changed. By using symbols from other cultures, parts of these foreign cultures can be integrated which might also change the foreign culture (Frohne-Hagemann 1991/2001, 120; Jung 1964; Kramer & Alstad 1993). The latter happened, for example, during the Christianization of the Teutonic tribes: The Teutonic culture radically changed through Christianity, but Christianity also changed through the use of pagan symbols (the Easter bunny, the Christmas tree, etc.). So, symbols

4 Original German citation: "Sinnbild, im weiteren Sinn der sinnliche Träger einer Bedeutung oder Meinung; im engeren Sinne Wort, Form, Gegenstand oder Vorgang, der nicht nur als solcher für sich allein besteht oder auftritt, sondern noch etwas bedeutet, ausdrückt oder darstellt, was in einem verborgenen, tieferen Bereich liegt."

5 Original German quote: "urtümliche Typen, d.h. seit alters vorhandene allgemeine Bilder. ... Der Archetypus stellt wesentlich einen unbewussten Inhalt dar, welcher durch seine Bewusstwerdung und Wahrnehmung verändert wird, und zwar im Sinne des jeweiligen individuellen Bewusstseins, in welchem er auftaucht."

6 Original German quote: "mit den Sinnen wahrgenommene Form, die stellvertretend für einen Inhalt eintritt oder verwendet wird."

influence culture and culture influences symbols. From a therapeutic point of view, it is important to see how symbols, processes of symbolization, and their manifestations in work with imagery in BMGIM are assessed differently in different cultures. In some cultures, dreams and visions are seen as more important than outer reality. In other cultures, like in our Western culture, dreams are often done away with as illusionary (Edgar 1994, 3). Jung (1964, 83) distinguishes between natural and cultural symbols. According to Jung (1964), natural symbols come from the unconscious, are variations of archetypes and are often of archaic origin. On the other hand, cultural symbols express "eternal truths" (Jung 1964, 83) within a cultural context. Often they became collective symbols within this culture and have a numinous quality. They can evoke strong emotional reactions in persons from that culture. If repressed or neglected, they disappear into the unconscious with unpredictable consequences. When spiritual/religious values of tribal cultures were repressed by colonial forces, the people lost their meaning of life, their social order and structure, and their morals decayed (Jung 1964, 84).

For the BMGIM therapist, it is important to know or be open for the cultural symbols and myths of the client's culture, and to discuss them with the client. For immigrants or refugees, working with symbols from their own culture and from the host country's culture can lead to better social integration on deeper levels. For the therapist, this work with the client's symbols and myths might mean that parts of him are mirrored in the "other" that might never have been mirrored by his own culture. This could provoke defenses, but could also be a huge enrichment for the therapist.

Porat & Meltzer (1998, 46ff) describe three social-political layers of the psyche which illustrate how unspoken cultural values can influence the imagery process. Their model of the psyche is Jungian (see Jung 1969). I will not describe the Jungian model of the psyche here, but proceed directly to social-political layers:

1. The person experienced a particular collective event (for example being a soldier in the Gulf War).
2. The person is affected by a social-political event as a member of the collective (for example hearing about the Gulf War and reacting to it).
3. The unconscious of the person is connected to the unconscious of the collective, where hidden collective themes, problems, feelings, and attitudes are expressed through personal images. Variations: A.) The image pertains to an intrapsychic issue but converges synchronistically with social-political issues. B.) Personal images tap into a transpersonal level of awareness and pick up anticipating events that have not yet fully formed from the unconscious of the collective, or attitudinal and emotional undercurrents being denied in the collective.

In therapy, these areas are often linked together. I use a fictitious example of a female client who seeks therapy with a male therapist after a rape. The therapist has been angry for a long time that society keeps seeing men as perpetrators and women as victims. The client experienced the rape herself (aspect 1) and reacts to it accordingly (aspect 2). For example, in therapy she reacts to strong music with flashbacks. Also, her direct environment, like her partner, friends, family, colleagues, etc., reacts to the rape (aspect 2), which in turn influences the client. Maybe other intrapsychic aspects are reflected in the working through of the rape (aspect 3A), for example the feeling of frequently being treated like an object, feeling inferior, etc. The client also perceives social attitudes and emotions connected with rape which are denied by society (aspect 3B), for example indirectly blaming the victim, or the attitude of "women are always victims and men always perpetrators anyway".

The therapist did not directly experience the rape. But through his client he is again confronted with a female victim and a male perpetrator. This might lead to his openly blaming the victim or playing down the effects of the rape (aspect 2). He might be reminded of his mother, who played the victim in order to dominate the male persons of the household (aspect 3A); or he might start confronting unconscious and denied attitudes of society too early, while for the client it would be important to work through her experience on a personal level, get rid of possible symptoms, and to reintegrate. All of this would have consequences for work with BMGIM, because during the music listening period, while working directly with imagery, transference and countertransference are perceived more strongly (also by the client), which in this case might bring therapist and client into a very delicate situation.

3. Music

Music always emerges in and from a culture. Music reflects the composer as an individual in his culture, the musicians as individuals and as a group in their culture(s), and the listener as an individual in his culture (Wilber 1997, 103ff).

In LSD-research, from which BMGIM later developed as a therapy method, music had the following therapeutic functions:

1. Music helped the patient relinquish usual controls and enter more fully into his inner world of experiences.
2. Music helped to focus awareness and to heighten concentration.
3. Music helped to facilitate the release of intense emotionality.
4. Music contributed toward a peak experience (Maslow 1968). Music and spiritual/religious experience have been closely linked at all times and in all cultures. Today and in our western culture, music is seen less and less as a religious experience, neither is it closely connected with healing, even though music therapy gives people a chance to reconnect with that.
5. Music provides continuity in an experience of timelessness.
6. Music gave direction and structure to the LSD-experience. (Bonny & Pahnke 1972, 65f)

As both in BMGIM and in LSD-therapy altered states of consciousness are used, those functions of music are also very important in BMGIM. In BMGIM, music evokes and guides imagery and the inner process. Unlike many other therapy methods that use music, BMGIM uses music not mainly for relaxation or as background music.

Besides transference onto the therapist and the imagery, in BMGIM we often see transference onto the music, our co-therapist. The music is usually chosen by the therapist. Possible transference onto the therapist may be projected onto the music. On the other hand, music offers possibilities for transference not offered by the therapist. A low and strong male voice like, for example, Susanin's Aria from "Life of the Tsar" by Glinka offers possibilities for transference onto a man. I, being a female therapist might never elicit this transference. Another important factor is the therapist's transference onto the music. Expressed or not, it is often perceived consciously or unconsciously by the client. In addition, there is the danger that the therapist cannot concentrate on the client well enough if she is dealing with her transference onto the music.

The following exert from a session with a client who spent her childhood in East Germany shows transference onto Russian songs:

Russian Folk Song: O the Steppes:

Cl.: That is Russian.
Th.: How is that for you?
Cl.: Not unfamiliar.
Th.: Where do you know it from?
Cl.: From soldiers with green and gray uniforms with red and golden shoulder straps. I see one with a uniform. He is just standing around.
Th.: Where are you?
Cl.: Outside. He cannot see me.

Russian Chant for Vespers: The Joy of Those Who Mourn:

Cl.: The voices are beautiful.
Th.: How are the voices for you?
Cl.: No feeling.
Th.: Do the voices feel something?
Cl.: No. The soldiers in uniforms are singing. They are singing this chant.
Th.: How is it to listen to the chant?
Cl.: Nice but somehow also strange.
Th.: Strange?
Cl.: It reminds me of something, but I do not know what. It is so familiar to me, also the language. But I do not know why.

To understand transference onto music in the cultural context, it is important to take a closer look at functions of music and their meaning within cultures. Merriam (1964, 209f) describes functions of music that are the same in all cultures:

1. Music serves emotional release. The way emotions are released or expressed. and how those emotions are judged and interpreted depends on the individual culture.
2. Music as aesthetic enjoyment. It is important to take into account that, for example. Asian aesthetic is determined by different patterns of experience than European aesthetic, and that in some cultures there is a complete lack of awareness for aesthetic.
3. Music as entertainment.
4. Music as communication.
5. Music as symbolic representation (for example rain dance or opera). Music as symbol (example see below).
6. Music stimulates physical response (listening to some pieces of music, it is difficult to sit still).
7. Music enforces conformity to social norms (for example music in social or religious rituals).
8. Music contributes to the continuity and stability of the culture (results from 1.–7.).
9. Music contributes to the integration of society (results from 1.–7.).

Some years ago, a Japanese woman asked me for a single BMGIM-session. For the session I chose the program "Creativity I" by Linda Keiser Mardis. The program consists of the following pieces:
1. Sibelius, Symphony No. 2, Allegretto
2. Vaughan Williams, In the Fen County
3. Delius, Koanga, La Calinda
4. Kalinnikov, Symphony No. 2, Andante
5. Yamada, Aka Tombo

The last piece of a music program usually serves for integration of the experience and for grounding. Music for that purpose has to offer safety in rhythm, tonality, dynamics, form, and melody. "Aka Tombo" by Yamada has a very clear rhythm, a simple, pentatonic melody line, mainly in major with a middle part in minor, an ABA-form, and no big dynamic changes. It therefore is an ideal final piece of a program. In Europe it is a rather unknown piece without any cultural symbolism. But in "Aka Tombo", Yamada used a Japanese folk song, which is very well known in Japan. The symbolism of the song corresponds with the text (which was unknown to me):

Dragonflies as red as sunset
Back when I was young
In twilight skies, there on her back I'd ride
When the day was done

Mountain fields in late November
Long ago it seems
Mulberry trees and treasures we would gather
Was it only just a dream?

Just fifteen she went away one day
Married then so young
Like a sister lost, I loved and missed her
Letters never seemed to come

Dragonflies as red as sunset
Back when I was young
Now in my eyes, when I see dragonflies
Tears are always sure to come

This is not only a very sad song that is almost experienced sadder and more touching due to the major mode, in the end Yamada also breaks it off in the middle of the stanza in his arrangement. I was confronted with a sad and confused client, who did not have a feeling of closure at all. This piece is not always contraindicated for Japanese clients; however, for the therapist it is important to know the cultural meaning of this piece and its lyrics. Vocal music in the client's native language or instrumental arrangements of pieces of which the client knows the lyrics have a leading effect on the imagery. For that reason we usually avoid those pieces altogether in BMGIM.

Altieri, a Mexican colleague, told me (personal account) that in Mexico mainly intellectuals and artists listen to western classical music. Classical music is usually seen in an intellectual way in Mexico. Clients from other subcultures, for example peasants, sometimes feel overtaxed when classical music is used in their BMGIM-therapy ("I am at loss with this music."). The music appears strange to them. Here, the transference onto the music can point to problems between socio-economic classes or between subcultures. It may also generate transference onto the therapist who has chosen the music. This transference might never have emerged without this music. It can lead to problems, but it could also be a chance to reflect upon things that otherwise might never have become an issue in therapy. For the client, it can also be relieving to hear that intellectual knowledge about the music, for example, the composer's name and the name of the piece, is not important in BMGIM. Important are images, feelings, etc. It might also be interesting to try out traditional Mexican music in BMGIM here.

Another thing to consider is the role of music in different cultures:

1. Music as aesthetic expression, concerts, l'art pour l'art. Cultures with this attitude towards music have more distance to music. Usually the focus is on intellectual analysis of the pieces and on knowledge of who wrote or played it when, etc. There is less focus on the emotional impact on the listener or on

how the listener perceives it. Music in connection with imagery or emotional experiences might appear strange in these cultures.
2. Music as a form of energy (Carlsson 2001/02). Here, music is seen as energy that has an influence on other energies, for example those of human beings. Within this concept music can heal as well as create illness.
3. Making music as a collective event (in the sense of Stige's "musicking" [Stige 2000]). People with this cultural understanding are very familiar with emotional experiencing of music, and with music as a means for communication and for physical expressions. The process of BMGIM can easily be accepted here.
4. Music as a living being (Gouk 2000, 19). Here music is seen as the numinous, as a good or evil spirit. Music has great power independent from the composer or the musicians. If BMGIM were to be used in cultures that have these magical, animistic ideas, one would have to be ready for extremely strong transference onto the music, and music would have to be used very carefully.

In BMGIM, music more familiar to the client offers more safety. The less familiar the music, the more ego-strength is necessary. If the client has enough ego-strength, unfamiliar music can be very helpful in discovering new parts of the psyche which could not have been discovered with familiar music (Summer 1995). If the music or musical style is familiar to the client, his associations to the music are important: Is the music perceived as pleasant, supportive, safe, or rather as conservative, negative, or threatening? Is it music from the client's culture, or is it familiar music from another culture? If it is from another culture it can be used for cultural integration or for confrontation with that culture (Yehuda 2002). Is the music maybe a symbol for the client's own but lost culture (for example a Taiwanese whose original culture is americanized listens to traditional Taiwanese music)? Here one might expect reactions of grieving in the BMGIM-process (Hanks 1992). Stige (2000) points to the problems that arise if a client listens to the music of the occupying power after a war. What does the music of the conqueror mean to the client?

4. Altered States of Consciousness

During the music and imagery phase of the BMGIM session, the client experiences a more or less altered state of consciousness (ASC) induced by relaxation and concentration. To describe different forms of ASC, Bonny (1978) developed the Cutlog Diagram.

Clients with little experience with ASC usually first go into areas close to the normal waking state. Gradually, they proceed into areas farther away from normal waking consciousness and experience more and more dimensions of their consciousness. Clients decide themselves where and how far they want to go. This decision, however, is made through a complex process which can be unconscious to the client. Exploring more and more parts of the psyche and bringing them into consciousness is seen as healing in BMGIM.

Many cultures integrate different states of consciousness into everyday living. Dreams and visions are seen as important sometimes more so than outer reality (Edgar 1994). In the western culture of the industrial countries, often only normal waking consciousness is generally accepted. Other states are often seen as not important (for example dreams) or even pathological (Eliade 1999). Eliade (1999, 33f) describes that ASC observed in Shamans were seen as psychological disorders by western anthropologists until the 20th century. The disease was explained for example by vitamin deficiency in Arctic shamans.

The embodiment of concepts of ASC through BMGIM in our western culture therefore is sometimes more difficult than in other cultures, where ASC are judged as more normal and important. In the western culture, ASC are accepted in certain subcultures like in certain schools of psychotherapy (hypnotherapy, etc.) and in some religious groups (for example meditation groups). In the area of religion, working with ASC is often seen as an indication for sects or cults. Here, the importance of ASC for our health is underestimated. (People, who are forbidden to sleep or to dream, thus going into ASC, experience spontaneous ASC during normal waking time.) I see indications of sects or cults rather in authoritarian, hierarchical power structures as described by Kramer & Alstad (1993).

ASC are experienced in a cultural context, need to be understood with their cultural-historical background, and again have to be integrated into a cultural context. People in an ASC experience everything present inside and outside more vividly. Therefore they are more receptive for everything that is carried from culture, be it through the therapist, the music, or the surroundings. There is a big difference in whether I conduct a BMGIM session in a room of a psychiatric ward in a hospital, in my private practice, or in a Hawaiian roundhouse. In addition, things that are present in the therapy room can become very meaningful for the client.

In BMGIM, the transition into ASC happens through the induction and the beginning of the music. The transition back to normal waking consciousness is marked by the end of the music and instructions by the therapist. The integration of the experiences in the ASC happens in the post-session processing.

Rules that apply to some states of consciousness do not necessarily apply to others (Kramer & Alstad 1993; Walsh & Vaughan 1993). Kramer & Alstad (1993, 301ff) are warning for example against a wrong assessment of unity consciousness in normal waking consciousness. Unity consciousness is sometimes experienced in BMGIM. In ASC, unity consciousness has the following signs (Kramer & Alstad 1993, 301f):

1. Experiencing being in the eternal, a place that always was and always will be.
2. Great energy that breaks through boundaries, while awareness expands till it seems to include everything.
3. Separation between me and not-me momentarily disappears or becomes ambiguous.
4. Deep feelings of identification with the cosmos.

5. The place feels foreign and yet familiar.
6. Awe and feeling of personal insignificance. Mundane concerns and emotions around self-enhancement and self-protection seem trivial.
7. No fear because death feels unreal or one feels as if one already died. This creates a feeling of deep relaxation.
8. One feels immune from being affected by the judgment of others, and free from vengeance and competitiveness. "Negative emotions" like anger, jealousy, etc. seem to be unnecessary and out of place.
9. Recognition that one is an aspect of God.
10. Everything (including oneself) is seen as perfect.

People who have experienced unity consciousness often desire to stay there. They want to transport the rules that apply to unity consciousness into normal waking consciousness. But we live in a world where we need to protect ourselves and therefore need boundaries, and where competition is common. Kramer and Alstad (1993, 314) describe three errors that result from this:
1. Experiences of unity consciousness are more real than ordinary reality, and so unity is superior to diversity.
2. It is possible to be in the mystical state all the time, and the more one is there the better.
3. The path to unity is through negating individuation.

Through these errors, new hierarchies (unity is better than diversity) and new competitions (one is a better person the more one is in the mystical state) are created. Kramer & Alstad (1993, 326) write about the integration of unity consciousness: "The One and the Many, unity and diversity, are opposites only when so framed by either/or thinking. A more inclusive dialectic framework sees them as interweaving poles within the process of existence. A view of spirituality and morality is needed that does not prioritize one pole over the other. … The mystical experience does not end with unity; it begins there, and then must be integrated into the equal reality of individual daily life."

The meaningful and responsible role of the therapist related to cultural issues also asks for a thorough discussion of professional ethics. I will therefore proceed to ethical questions in the work with clients in ASC. Because of the intensity of the work and the depth of transference and (unrecognized) countertransference, ethical problems can arise more easily than in regular psychotherapy. Taylor (1995, 38) describes four additional areas of ethics in the work with clients in ASC:
1. The therapist needs to have experience with and profound knowledge of ASC.
2. The therapy training of the therapist should have dealt with ASC.
3. There is a greater need for a safe therapeutic setting.
4. The potential for stronger and more complicated transference and countertransference should be kept in mind.

In BMGIM, areas 1 and 2 are covered well in the BMGIM-training. In the training, possible dangers in the therapeutic setting are also reflected. Transference and countertransference appear anew and in new depth every time. Therapists have to keep reflecting on it. Money, sexuality, and power are possible areas of ethical problems in every psychotherapy. Most professional codes of ethics deal with those areas. When working with clients in ASC, they could mix with spiritual longings and fears. Taylor (1995) adds the following areas of possible problems for the work with clients in ASC:

1. Love (fear of intimacy, fear of separation, jealousy, longing for spiritual connection, longing to be compassionate, desire for openheartedness, desire to be cherished)
2. Truth (fear of punishment, fear of criticism, fear of responsibility, fear of being unmasked, longing to be a conduit of spiritual truth, desire to speak and act with integrity, desire to be free of convention)
3. Insight (fear of seeing, fear of losing denial, fear of misusing spiritual powers, longing for mystical understanding, longing for psychic powers, desire to understand the client's therapeutic process)
4. Oneness (fear of losing self-identity, fear of losing God as Other, longing for union, longing for transcendence)

Here is a fictitious example: A BMGIM-trainee experiences painful memories. The trainee does not have much money. The BMGIM-trainer offers him a free BMGIM-session instead of suggesting an ongoing psychotherapy at the place where the trainee lives, which would have been paid by the health insurance but most probably, would not have been BMGIM-therapy. The trainer most probably has unconscious problems in some of the following areas: fear of insufficiency, desire for change (money); fear of losing control, fear of having no effect, longing to be a healer, desire to control the trainee's process, desire for the trainee's respect, desire for status (power); jealousy (of the possible other therapist), longing for spiritual connection, longing to be compassionate (love); fear of criticism (for example from another therapist), desire to act with integrity, desire to be free of conventions (avoiding dual relationships as convention) (truth); fear of seeing, longing for mystical understanding, longing for psychic powers (a single BMGIM-session could never be sufficient as therapy for the trainee), desire to understand the trainee's therapeutic process (insight). This mixed with idealization of the trainer or a negative transference from the trainee and unequal power relationships between the two can lead to severe damage for the trainee, both in the areas of health and career.

Finally, I would like to mention that a cultural understanding of the therapeutic process is very important. If this understanding is present, music, imagery, and symbols from one's own or from another culture can be used and interpreted consciously, and cultural differences and similarities between client and therapist can be consciously dealt with, thus enhancing the therapeutic process.

CH. 9: RECEPTIVE MUSIC THERAPY FROM THE VIEWPOINT OF INTEGRATIVE MUSIC THERAPY (IMT)

ISABELLE FROHNE-HAGEMANN

Some basic concepts of Integrative (Music) Therapy, which have already been described in more detail in other publications, are briefly referred to here, in order to better understand the application of receptive methods in IMT (Petzold 1993, 2001; Frohne-Hagemann 1990/1999, 2001).

Integrative Music Therapy (IMT) was developed at the beginning of the eighties, and modelled on Petzold's Integrative Therapy. The term, "Integrative Therapy" was used by Petzold as early as 1965 to designate a program of work, which would treat the whole individual with a combination of *somatic therapy*, *psychotherapy* and *nootherapy* (Petzold 1965 as quoted in 1993, Vol. 2, 976). A core concept of Petzold's theory of personality is the *bodily state*, or *body* of the individual (German: der Leib, das Leib-Subjekt). This is of central importance to Integrative Therapy. The term 'body' identifies the individual as a *"subject in possession of body, soul and spirit, interacting with its environment within a social and ecological context"* (ibid). Therapy must take the individual's embedment in culture and its traditions of thinking, feeling and doing into consideration. The individual is permeated with "collective reality". He is not only part of a culture, but creates culture. *"Personality embodies culture, is culture incarnate. However, during a life-span, culture is also created by individual personalities"*. (Petzold 1975, as quoted in Petzold 2002, 39). In this sense, therapy can be understood, not as *psycho*therapy, but as "*Human Therapy*"(German: "Human Therapie"). It refers to psycho- socio-therapeutic treatment of the individual in all cultural-historic and socio-culturally influenced areas of opinion, relationships, ways of experiencing and behaviour, and systems of values.

The many-layered model of Integrative Therapy portrays the individual and his surroundings in staggered relationship to each other; as figure and background in space and time, or context and continuum.

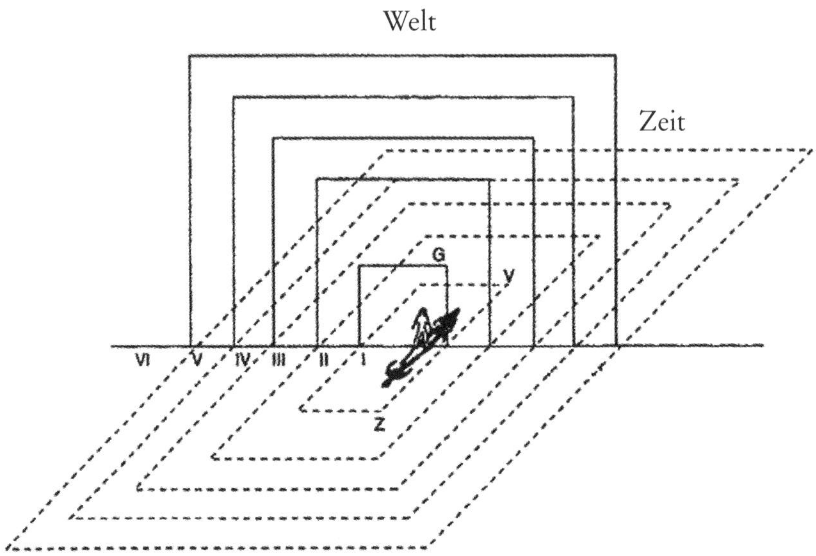

Legend: German: "Gegenwart" = Presence
German: "Vergangenheit" = Past
German: "Zukunft" = Future

German: "Welt" = World
German: "Zeit" = Time

I Individual in the front of the backdrop of the present, or the "here and now"
II Family Background
III General living conditions
IV Class Background and level of society
V Cultural Background
VI Mundane Background (German: mundaner Hintergrund)

Fig. 1: Many-Levelled Model (Petzold 1974, from Petzold 1993, 601)

The categories within Contexts I–VI (The present, the family, general living conditions, class and level, cultural background, everyday and global relationships) extend backward and forward as dimensions of time, as perspectives into the past and the future. Past experience and future possibilities are constantly to be found within the individual (Petzold 1993, Vol. 2, 601). Man is *embodied culture*, both within a personal context and a continuum.

Even when referred to as a "heavenly power", music is anchored in culture. The meaning of music is dependant on where, when, how and in what form it is created, how it sounds, and how it is heard and experienced. The 'many-levelled model' illustrates three-dimensionally, and by the use of various layers, how individually and culturally embodied experiences of music connect with each other.

In receptive music therapy, it follows that the use of music must refer not only to the six contextual categories and their respective time-frames, but also to personal, familiar, class-specific, cultural and biographical-historical dimensions. What are the listening experiences, together with their biographical context, which have had a socialising effect on the individual? What has impressed his way of experiencing and feeling? When, and in what contexts, familiar, public, etc. did an individual hear an emotionally moving piece of music? Where are incompatibilities to be found, (a child, for example, who can only listen to *his own* music secretly at the neighbours, because he is ridiculed for it at home) that result in dissonance between emotion and cognition? That is, certain feelings are permitted in one context, but not in another. These are important questions, when considering the form receptive music therapy should take, and the method to be applied.

The many-levelled model in music therapy shows that a large role is played not only by the present and past context in which a piece of music was heard, but also by the music itself. This can also be viewed in itself as a many-layered relationship. Human experience and expression speak out of music, emerging from past musical epochs together with their varying cultures and traditions. The many-sided, culturally and historically embodied perception of qualities of emotion "meets" an individually-coloured, collectively-embodied culture within the individual. This may or may not correspond to a particular epoch or musical style. It must be discerned, which past musical epoch (renaissance, baroque, romantic, impressionistic, etc.) or present style best relates emotionally to the individual and his habits of listening. To which music has resistance been built up, because emotional content has not been, or was not allowed to be embodied, or because of negative experiences? One must ask how or whether it is possible to develop an emotional acceptance for music, which at first hearing is foreign or strange, which could, however, be used to widen cultural horizons.

In referring to both context and continuum, the many-levelled model supports a broad understanding of therapy. Therapy must be oriented to psycho-dynamics and deep psychology, as well as to social psychology, in order to ensure that *identity* can be developed and differentiated in reference to its *biological, psychological, social and cultural background*. In the past few years a paradigm change has occurred in music therapy, prepared, for example, by Ruud (1980) and labelled "Ecological Music Therapy" in 1998 by Bruscia (1998). Stige also broadened the music therapeutic understanding of therapy with the grounding of "Culture Centred Music Therapy" (Stige 2002) and "Community Music Therapy" (Stige 2003). Receptive music therapy does not only take traditional clinical diagnosis into account. One must also consider anthropological goals, such as the abolishment of societal and cultural *alienation*[1], and the development of a sense of social and intellectual *belonging*, which could well include a spiritual, nootherapeutic dimension. The term "Human Therapy" can be seen as expressing a paradigm

1 Alienation: "man does not experience himself as an active agent in grasping the world. The world remains alien to him, in work, in religion and in one's fellow men (Koschnik 1992, Vol. 1).

change. Using perspectives based on ecology and the social-sciences, it redefines the pathologically fixated concept of illness theoretically and methodically in a new and health-oriented, or salutogenic way.

It is not easy to combine such perspectives and goals with each other in a meaningful way. In order to find theoretically and methodically corresponding concepts, various theories, methods and procedures of psychotherapy must be examined. Many pluralistic, combinatorial and eclectic forms of integration (see Petzold 1993a for more detail) merely *coincide* theoretically, *add* methods to each other without actually integrating them, or *intuitively* apply various techniques, without taking their theories of reference into account. The concept of "Integration" in Petzold's Integrative Therapy attempts to combine concepts from various procedures and methods where they actually coincide. This is, of course, often problematical. Sometimes, the only possibility is to agree to disagree.

Integrative Music Therapy (IMT) also attempts to integrate compatible ideas from other "schools" of active and receptive music therapy, based on the concept of integration in Integrative Therapy (Frohne-Hagemann 1996, 166 ff). In IMT, very little has been written about *receptive music therapy*. As it is the case that the effects of music and listening to music are not only therapeutic, but exist within a cultural context, each interpretation of an experience of music must be viewed in reference to its situational context *and* culturally embodied ways of feeling and thinking, i. e. not only according to psycho-dynamically oriented psychotherapy, but also contextual and cultural concepts (see also the article by C. Maack in this volume).

Integrative Therapy is used in therapies with both clinical and anthropological orientation. Petzold described *four* interlocking *Paths of Healing and Support* (Petzold 1988, 248 ff) with individual emphases, goals and methods, also used by Integrative Music Therapy (Frohne-Hagemann 1990/2001, 103 ff):

a) Psychotherapeutic work on consciousness and meaning, including nootherapeutic treatment, examination of unconscious perceptual content and ways of behaviour, and processing of traumatic experiences;
b) Somatic- and psychotherapeutic development of original trust, basal work on relationships and re-, or additional socialisation of individuals with early disturbances;
c) Psycho- and social-therapeutically oriented self-experience and of personality; activating experience and unfolding creativity in a group, according to the concepts of "co-creativity" and "conflux" (Petzold 2002, 67):
d) Socio-therapeutic, ecological and socio-cultural experience of solidarity, development of meta-perspectives of culture and society, cultural and political activism.

While a) and b) are more oriented to somatic-. psycho- and nootherapy, c) and d) are more socio-therapeutic in nature. As 'Human Therapy', however, they belong together.

The patient or client's therapeutic needs must be diagnosed, together with the context in which therapy occurs, for example, support, empowerment, broadening, mastering conflicts, etc. and the manner in which music is to be applied. The paths of healing and support, as well as the form of music therapy, whether active or receptive, can then be decided upon.

This article concerns itself solely with *receptive* music therapy. An overview of the respective emphases of receptive music therapeutic methods on each of the four paths is presented below with brief case vignettes.

The First Path of Healing and Support

Receptive methods of music therapy on the First Path of Healing and Support serve to locate the senses through

- Work with consciousness;
- Examination of the consciousness spectrum;
- Work with memory.

Receptive forms of music therapy are often based on differing models of *consciousness*, thus leading to a differing understanding of therapy. For this reason, the concept of consciousness of Integrative Therapy is briefly introduced here.

An individual is provided with a complex consciousness, which is anchored in the body. According to the theory of Integrative Therapy, there is no "spiritual primate" (Jung, M. 2001, 237), or transpersonal dimension. "Higher" knowledge and opinions can be obtained by an "informed" (socialised and enculturated) **body** (Petzold, 1993, 1155). The body's spectrum of consciousness reaches from the depths of the unconscious to the heights of no-consciousness (see Diagram Nr. 2). The body is "fundamentally ontogenetic and phylogenetic. From the beginning, the body has been capable of co- response, and is thus comprehending, communicating and expressing. It is memorable, valuable and creative. ... 'The body's knowledge' enables cause and effect, colour, bright and dark, rhythm, gravity, and qualities of gestalt to be experienced in a basal manner" (Jung, M. 2001, 237). With the body, one is able to see oneself from a higher perspective, through the eyes of another. This is shown in the following vignette. In this example, Julia also comes into contact with spiritual dimensions. By means of the archive of the body, doors can be open to a more complex consciousness.

The figure below shows the Spectrum of Consciousness, and the points at which it coincides with Somato- Therapy, Psychotherapy and Nootherapy.

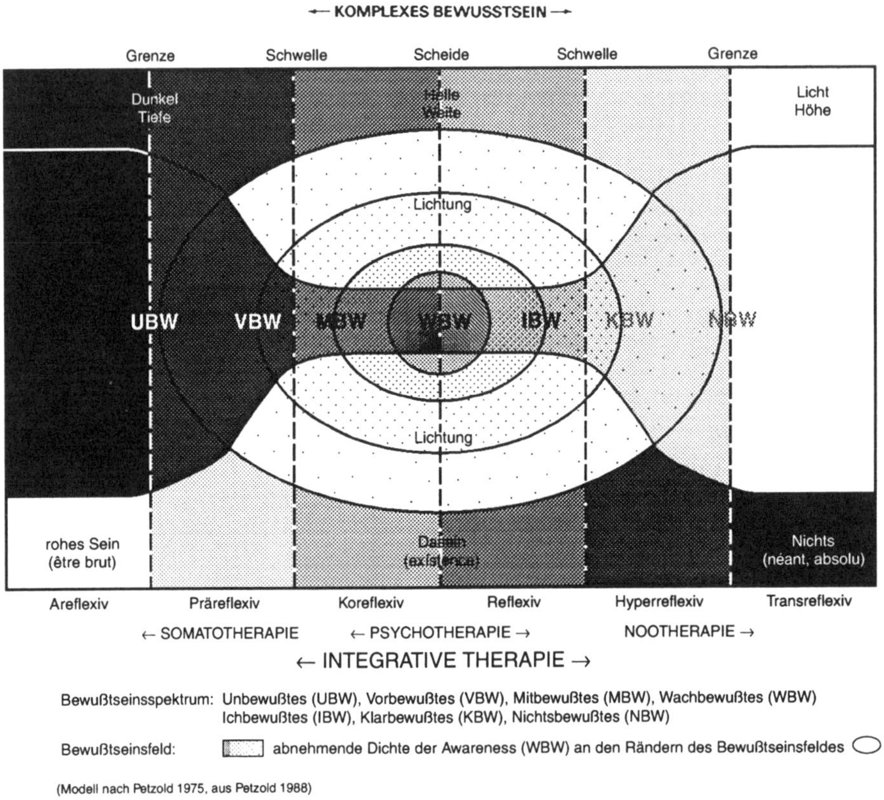

Fig. 2: The complex consciousness

Border Dark Depth	Threshold	Division Brightness Breadth	Threshold	Border Light Height

← SOMATIC THERAPY ← PSYCHOTHERAPY → NOOTHERAPY →

I ← INTEGRATIVE THERAPY →

Spectrum of Consciousness:
UBW: *Unconsciousness (a-reflexive)* – **VBW:** *Preconsciousness (pre-reflexive)* – **MBW:** *Co-consciousness (co-reflexive)* – **WBW:** *Awareness* – **IBW**: *Ego-Consciousness (reflexive)* – **KBW:** *Hyperconsciousness (hyper-reflexive)* – **NBW:** *No-Consciousness (trans-reflexive)*

German: "Rohes Sein" (French: être brut): Raw Existence; German: "Dasein" (French: existence): Existence; German: "Nichts" (French: néant, absolu): Nothingness; German: "Lichtung" = Clearing

Field of Consciousness:

Decreasing Density of Awareness (WBW) in the Margins of the Field of Consciousness

(Model according to Petzold 1975, from Petzold 1988, 278 ff)

The Spectrum of Consciousness is explained by Petzold as follows:

"The Spectrum of Consciousness stretches from *a-perceptive, a-reflexive* ... 'depths and darkness' of the Unconsciousness (German: **U**n**bew**usstes, **UBW**) and its individual (ontogenetically and collectively phylogenetically founded) strivings, to the *trans-perceptive* and *trans-reflexive* heights and 'dreams of life' (a metaphorical description) of No-Consciousness (German: **N**ichts**bew**usstes **NBW**). The Unconsciousness can be called "raw, unformed being" (*l'être brut et* sauvage, according to Merleau-Ponty) ... No-Consciousness, in contrast, is the *absolute nothing* (*néant absolu*), from which no statement comes. ... In the centre of the Spectrum of Consciousness is *Awareness*, grounded in bodily existence. We also call this perceptive consciousness (German: Wahrnehmungsbewusstes, **W**ach**bew**usstes **WBW**), encompassing the sensory, the perceptual, the affective, and the mnestic. The perceptive consciousness spreads in both directions with decreasing density, as a field of consciousness in both directions (UBW → NBW). Awareness is marked by a BOUNDARY LINE. Awareness can be pre-receptive and co-reflexive (MBW → UBW), or it can be both perceptive and reflexive (WBW → NBW).

Central Awareness extends in concentric circles, creating groups of awareness of varying density. Towards the Unconsciousness (German: **U**n**bew**usstes **UBW**), Awareness includes *co-receptive* and *co-reflexive* **Co-Consciousness** (German: **M**it**bew**usstes **MBW**, *Rohracher*), that is, all that is not focussed on, but momentarily included in Awareness. This can be accessed at any time. *Pre-perceptive* and *pre-reflexive* Pre-Consciousness (German: **V**or**bew**usstes **VBW**) is separated from Co-Consciousness by a threshold. For its part, Pre-Consciousness contains material from superficial layers of *a-perceptive* and *a-reflexive* **Unconsciousness** (**UBW**), which tries to filter through to consciousness, or even to Awareness (**WBW**) and Consciousness (German: **I**ch**bew**usstes **IBW**). The existence of this material might already be felt or suspected. On the other hand, Pre-Consciousness contains material which has sunken out of Consciousness (Awareness/ Co-Consciousness), but is not yet lost in the chasm of **Unconscious**. If the THRESHOLD of the *Pre-receptive* and *Pre-reflexive* is overcome by means of therapy or self-exploration, **Awareness** (**WBW, IBW**) forces its way up to **Pre-Consciousness** (**VBW**) and is refracted at the BORDER to the *A-reflexive* and *A-perceptive*. As its structure is too archaic and foreign, it cannot be accessed in depth by *perceptive*, *affective* and *cognitive* forms of **Awareness** (**WBW**) or by *full-perceptive* and *full-reflexive* **Consciousness/Ego-Consciousness** (**IBW**). Another set of senses and means of understanding are required. They must undergo qualitative transformation (through verbal or active interpretation, for example), in order to be able to be grasped and understood by **Awareness** and **Consciousness/Ego-Consciousness**. The

> Unconscious filters into Consciousness with decreasing density. That is, it is present in Consciousness up until the BORDER of the *Trans-Reflexive* (**NBW**).
>
> Awareness (**WBW**) extends towards *trans-perceptive* and *trans-reflexive* **No-Consciousness** (**NBW**), by leaving the *co-reflexive* and *co-perceptive* milieu of passive-receptive sensory perception (it comes to my notice, it sounds in my ear, it goes up my nose). *Active* perceptivity and reflexivity (*I* see or smell, *I* hear, *I* act) increases until a *full-reflexive* **Consciousness** (**IBW**) is attained (I am aware, *that* I see, smell, taste and act, and *how* this takes place). Within Consciousness, dulled Awareness is sharpened, decreasing, however, in volume, breadth and density (as shown by the decreasing punctuation in the diagram). Fully reflexive Ego-Consciousness is not only organic, but also *inter-subjective* (Mead 1934, see also Tugend hat 1979, 249 ff). It grows, due to the experience of 'you' (Buber) and of a 'generalised other' (Mead) ... *Pre-reflexive* Awareness (**WBW**) corresponds to a perceiving physical self, according to our theory of personality, to the 'total organ of the senses of the body'. Should this intensify to a ... fully perceptive and fully reflexive Consciousness (**IBW**), Ego-Consciousness is the result, encompassing both cognition and, in part, intuition, and becoming part of the ego. If **WBW** and **IBW** are integrated ... a THRESHOLD is crossed, making a *hyper-reflexive* condition which we call the **Hyperconsciousness** (German: **K**lar**bew**usstes **KBW**) possible. **WBW**, **IBW** and **KBW** are characterised by the metaphor of 'brightness' and the quality of 'breadth', just as **UBW** is characterised by darkness/depth and **NBW** by light/height.
>
> **Hyperconsciousness** encompasses intuitive and synoptic-synergetic abilities, attainable in creative and contemplative action. In Hyperconsciousness, crossings, complex synopses, broad-reaching, many-sided perspectives, synaesthesia and synergy are possible. The *clearing* within the field of consciousness broadens up to the BORDER of the *trans-reflexive* (**NBW**) ... Even **Hyperconsciousness** (**KBW**) breaks down at this point, as trans-reflexive universal structures of the absolute elude cerebral possibilities (the extension of the universe, for example, cannot be comprehended in depth). It might be possible through the idea of taking part (we are part of the cosmos) to have an idea of, and feel, this dimension of **No-Consciousness** (**NBW**) in a state of meditation. This paradoxical term is used purposely to name the apophatic quality of this incomprehensible and unlocated dimension. We then speak of *trans-reflexive participation* in being, in the absolute, in nothingness, as reported by great spiritual mystics. (The term mystical or trans-reflexive *experience* is insufficient, as we are dealing with areas on the far side of any experience *in sensu strictu.*).
>
> **UBW** and **VBW** are close to the body, and can be accessed by forms of somatic-therapy (for example, manual medicine, massage, relaxation techniques, breathing therapy, water therapy, meditation). Psychotherapy includes **UBW**, **VBW**, **MBW**, **WBW** and **IBW** [using cognitive, affective and symbolic methods]. **WBW**, **IBW** and, especially, **KBW** – **NBW** with some restrictions – are subjects of nootherapy (in creative and meditative practices ...). The entire **spectrum of consciousness,** or field of consciousness, is thus an area of work for "Integrative Therapy" and its methods, forms and media ..." (Petzold, Sieper 1988, 278 ff)

The division of the fields of consciousness using concentric circles makes it similar to the "cut-log" diagram (a ring-model of consciousness) used by Helen Bonny in Guided Imagery and Music (GIM). The ring-model, however, does not include a bodily dimension, and fails to depict how physical, intellectual, mental and neurobiological levels interlock with various forms of reflexivity. It gives the impression that the physical condition is unimportant. This is, however, not the case, as Bonny strongly emphasises bodily perception. It supports, however, transpersonal and spiritual leanings in the therapy culture of GIM, quite separate from the individual body embedded in culture. In my opinion, this could lead to a one-sided view of the subject, similar to viewing music taken out of its cultural context, as an "object as such".

Music is able to reach all dimensions of the spectrum of consciousness. Towards the left, it reaches somatic and vegetative areas, far away from awareness and Ego-consciousness. Towards the right it reaches the transcendental. We assume that work with consciousness and on locating the senses using receptive methods always include *somato-*, *psycho-* and *nootherapeutic* dimensions. These three areas, integrating the dimensions of ecolology and social culture, can never be separated completely, and are described here individually solely for didactic purposes.

The point of view of *somato- therapy* focuses on accessing knowledge of the body, and opening the bodily archive and memory. Breath, speech and emotion are closely interlocked. Through executing musical forms by means of respiration and the body, psychodynamic material can be activated, made conscious, and named. Work *on* the body affects respiratory and muscular tension, conflicts, etc. which are held fast *within* the body. In contrast, somato-therapeutic work on the body to music on the second path of healing is much more functional in character. The first path focuses on supporting breathing, with the goal of using music to free emotions. This can be accomplished by setting movement to music (expressive dance), or by stimulating bodily perception and imagination, while listening to music in a sitting or lying position. Information is thus provided regarding what has been experienced (see also the ideas of other authors regarding physical therapy in this volume, for example in the chapter by A. Schmucker).

From the *psychotherapeutic* point of view, a steady goal of receptive music therapy is the differentiation of emotions. Theoretically, our approach speaks of "emotional styles" as "non-linear schematic chains made up of multiple corresponding, resonant and evolutional processes. Information is connected by a network, and accumulates and transforms unforeseeably" (Petzold 1993, 829). The term 'emotion' was broadened by Moscovice (1984) and Halbwachs (1950) to include social and ecological dimensions (see Petzold 1993, 831). Emotions are dependant on the importance they are given within the "context of a 'social world' or system of values" (ibid). "Feelings as phenomena of resonance are ... characterised by culture and tradition. They flow not only out of the individual memory ('mémoire'), but also out of a 'collective memory' ('histoire')". Emotions are constantly anchored in the body. Their intensity and shade is determined in a neuro-physiological layer of the amygdale, before becoming conscious in the neocortex.[2]

2 Fundamental neurobiology requires complex explanations, which will not be further discussed here

The differentiation of emotion can be effected by work with memory, for example, by listening to emotionally meaningful music, as already seen in the treatment of older people (see Muthesius 1990). In IMT the *Musical Life Panorama* (MLP) can contribute to effective work with and on memories (Frohne-Hagemann 2000/2001, 175 ff). Meaningful pieces of music from one's personal biography are re-experienced. This frees important memories, together with their emotional meaning, out of the memory of the body, which allows traces left on personal biography to be explored.

Patients bring music that has been meaningful during their lives. Together with Doris, 67, we hear a popular song she had listened to repeatedly during puberty: A young man sings ardently of his love for a girl. He complains that their love has been forbidden by their parents because he and the girl are too young. Doris is very moved as she re-experiences feelings connected with this song and shares them with others. After all, she is dealing with feelings she had at that time: an undelivered princess, longing for love, but held a prisoner.

Jürgen, 28, brings sacral music to the group, but is very hesitant to share this, for him very intimate and precious music, with the others. He would interpret a negative reaction to the music as criticism of what he held to be valuable and beautiful. This leads to a discussion of the theme "esteem".

MLP can be prepared by the patient at home in that he records important pieces of music sequentially onto a cassette or CD. With this step, the process of tackling the past has already begun. The entire cassette/CD is then heard by the group. The patient relates, without stopping the cassette/CD, the atmospheres, feelings, emotions, pictures, scenes and thoughts that occur to him while listening. This technique is similar to GIM, especially if the therapist stays in verbal contact with the patient.

Imaginative psychotherapy with or through music is a valid method on the First Path of Healing, as it brings unconscious and preconscious material into "lighter" areas of complex consciousness. He who has learned the method, *Guided Imagery and Music*, can apply it here to great effect[3]. The GIM music programs consist for the most part of classical works. These represent 'containers', which allow an immersion into the deepest areas of embodied culture. Deeply embedded emotional processes are brought into movement. "Anna", the case study in the chapter by B. Süselbeck-Schulz in this book, describes a segment of therapy in which GIM greatly assisted the mourning process.

GIM can also enable contact with cultural elements of the psychodynamic process. The following vignette illustrates a problem concerning German history.

3 Let it be said here, that this method cannot be applied adequately without proper training. The impression should not be given that integrative music therapists can do everything. The purpose is to show how GIM is compatible with and enriches IMT in many ways

The problem is embodied in the patient, and influences her ways of feeling, thinking and behaving:

Julia [4], a 58-year-old doctor, wants to learn to understand her life better with the help of ambulatory music therapy. Since having an upsetting experience as an emergency doctor, she has had dreams, which have motivated her to think deeply about certain subjects. She decides to begin a therapy. Julia, a post-war child, grew up at a time, in which the Third Reich was not mentioned. She was raised in the complete silence of an apparently perfect world. She knew next to nothing about her father's activities during the Nazi era, whether he was a war criminal, a hanger-on, or a resistance fighter. But she developed an early interest in people who were suffering, as though attempting to peer behind the perfect world.

During music therapy sessions, Julia showed an immediate interest in the instruments, and was fascinated by music-therapeutic improvisation. She was able to bring past experience into the here and now without distorting it verbally. Through playing, she was able to open up unconscious archives of the body, and remember forgotten childhood experiences. She was not, however, able to come in contact with atmospheres felt within the silence of her parent's generation. At least, she had the feeling of not being able to translate these atmospheres into music, or to hear them within the improvisations. Julia's inexpressible themes concerned abysms, and things which had happened "behind the scenes", both collectively and in society. For this reason, the therapist felt that the use of imaginative processes, with and by means of music, could be indicated in helping Julia to process and integrate the unheard-of and unsaid. She suggested GIM.

Fantasies about the Third Reich appeared repeatedly during the GIM sessions. Julia was made to observe, that she was suffering, under the surface, both from feelings of a collective guilt, as well as from feelings of innocence, which she found embarrassing. She realised, why she had rebelled intensively against authoritative structures in the past. Her imaginations during the GIM sessions brought her into contact with existential themes. She lived through various facets of the experience of death, for example dying on a battlefield, being buried alive, or starving in a dungeon. She immediately brought these in connection with the Second World War. She identified herself, however, more with the young German soldiers than with the Jewish victims. Julia was born at the end of 1945, and thus felt close to the child soldiers who had been drawn into the war shortly before its end. In her opinion, which she was unfortunately unable to express, the soldiers belonged to a generation which had been made guilty through no fault of its own. Of course, Julia's themes were also related to her own biography. Julia knew that in 1944 her mother had had a miscarriage in the fifth month. It is possible, that the death experiences during the GIM journeys had to do with this sibling, who had not been allowed to live. It is also possible, that this sibling appears in the sessions described below. Mainly, however, Julia was suffering under the collective German biography.

The dimensions of suffering resulting from an inability to speak, both about the identification with German civilian victims, and about the tragic circumstances surrounding under-age soldiers, are probably much greater than is now recognised. In foreign countries, the question is beginning to be raised, "what proportion speaking of

4 Name changed

or emphasising suffering within the German civil population during the war should take within the process of coming to terms with German crimes during national socialism" (Neue Zürcher Zeitung, 7/24/03, 17). This presents the question, of whether one is allowed to beg for pardon, and if yes, who should do the pardoning.

A description of a GIM session dealing with the question of guilt follows. Julia's soul finds a solution in a higher instance, of an angel who bestows upon her a feeling of forgiveness. Sacral music (Nos. 4 and 5) helps to move suffering to a different emotional level[5].

The following dream provided a point of departure for the session:

"I had parked my VW in the police parking lot, because I wanted to report something. But I don't know what. The police didn't listen to me at all. Instead they locked me up, because I had parked in a no-parking zone. In the cell there was a glass container containing a foetus swimming in formaldehyde. It was as though I was daydreaming in the cell. Through a crack I could see a group of people outside, celebrating happily. I want very much to go outside to the group, and I do go out, briefly. I cry bitterly, because I want to belong to the group. But I have to go back into the cell."

The dream leaves behind strong feelings of despair and longing. For this reason, the therapist selects the GIM program, "Sorrow"[6]. The therapist's protocol of the session follows:

1. Marcello: Oboe Concerto in d minor (Adagio)
(subjective description, I. F.-H.)
This piece begins with a plaintive strings entry, a trembling standstill on one, then two notes (the interval of a second), begging to be released. After 0, 20 minutes the oboe begins a sad story of pain and longing. It is carried by the strings, which provide a foundation on one note. Musical movement remains gentle until the end of the piece, but supports the expression of pain and sorrow from the oboe. The orchestra supports the oboe's story with a steady beat. At the end, one is left standing and, in a way, waiting.

...[7] (what do you perceive?)[8] I see the baby. It's in a glass container, like in anatomy (how is that for you?) a bit eerie... ... Now I'm far away ... I see the scene from far away, as though behind glass ... (what do you see?) Now I see Julia sitting in the cell. It's as if she is anaesthetised. She's waiting and waiting ... (what is she waiting for?) She wants so much to belong to the group. (How does that feel?) I feel for the woman

5 It must be said in answer to the objection that the client has been manipulated through the music, that the therapist does not suggest a particular imagination at the beginning of a session. The client projects what is momentarily of importance to her and what she needs onto the music. She can reject the music, when the conflict of being allowed to feel forgiveness, is either unable to be overcome, or not yet possible

6 designed by Sierra Stearns (excluding No. 3)

7 ... indicates a pause in speech

8 Text in parentheses: Therapist's intervention

in the cell. She doesn't know why she isn't allowed to belong. Now I see the VW. An old model. I can see exactly where it is parked in front of the police station. She parks, absolutely legally, in the parking lot, so that she can ask the police for help. She wanted to report something, but instead she was punished and put into jail. She can't speak, or explain why she needs help. She also doesn't know why she parked the car wrong. [Thoughtfully] She drove that Volkswagen, an old model from – oh, yes – Nazi times! ... No one wants to know that, one shouldn't say that aloud ... For many people a Volkswagen is still something to be especially proud of. But the car's dark side, no one should see that.

2. Elgar: Cello Concerto Op. 58, First Movement
The cello continues the oboe solo from the first piece at a high dynamic level. Beginning in a very low register, it opens up an area for emotions on a much deeper level. The strings and winds begin after 0,35 minutes. The cello then tells a story in a solo, and the strings answer with a wavelike melody. This gives the cello a foundation upon which it can continue its story. The orchestral music intensifies dramatically at 2,30 and 7 minutes. The expression of pain is intensified by the cello. The cello narrates the story repeatedly by taking up impulses from the orchestra, and vice versa. It resembles the experience of resonance in group therapy. Short moments of hope are sensed repeatedly to the quick minor-key music. The end of the piece is indeterminate, and has an urgent feel.

... (What is happening now?) ... Julia is still in the cell (how does she feel?) Hmm, she also feels a bit proud ... a certain pride in being strong (where do you feel it?) in my head, a kind of defiance ...I don't know what to say, at the most I could talk about my sadness, but no one understands that ... The people outside encourage me to speak, but I hesitate ... I'm so sad. (Let the music accompany your sadness! ... [client cries] ... I can narrate the facts, but ... I just want to be understood ... Hidden behind the facts is so much I can't say at all ... I've heard, "Those are your people. You Germans started the war, it serves you right when bombs fall on you" so often ... I feel so sad about it. I want to be forgiven ... I feel helpless, and useless ... I have to go back to the cell. I have to allow myself to be punished in place of all Germans. I'm sitting there ...

3. Barber: Adagio for Strings
In this piece, dynamic and tension increases continuously in waves from minute 4,00 on. At 4,57 a general pause allows room for a catharsis. For 30 seconds, the sounds of strings support a feeling of rest. Up to the close of the work, dynamic movement develops again in an upward direction.

My parent's generation kept silent. I always tried to be a good German, especially abroad. To make a good impression. But some people humiliated me a lot (how does that feel now?) ... I have to bear it ... [at about 4,00 minutes] Something opens ... I see light in my eyes, a greenish-grey light ... I'm lying on the floor of the cell ... the ceiling is white ... it opens ... [at 4,57 minutes] there isn't a wall around me anymore ... the sky is there [the client opens her arms upwards, her eyes remain closed]. I can see my arms, I can really see them ... a shadow ... fog ... there are angels too (can the angels see you?) Yes ...

4. and 5. Swiridow: Excerpt from Three Choruses for "Czar Feodor Ivanovich" (Second and Third Chorus)
The deep men's voices indicate a possibility of moving from sadness to hope. The voices gradually broaden and intensify, allowing comfort and a certain sense of elevation to be experienced. At 2,00 minutes, an alto voice takes over. The men's voices and the solo woman's voice sing resolutely, and open up the possibility of dealing with religious aspects, if necessary. The fifth piece begins with a high woman's voice supported by men's voices. It is as though the woman's is able to express pain and sadness when carried by the men. The end remains open, floating. A feeling of longing remains.

... The angel understands me ... a feeling of forgiveness ... [cries] .... This brings me to the point where I can forgive X [an English friend]. (Can you tell him that?) ... [Apologetically] During the war he was just a little boy. He lived in London. The Germans were his enemies. We can speak with each other better now. I think he understands me a little better ... [cries] ... I'm only a human being, I can't always be 'above everything' ... (can you feel forgiveness?) yes, forgiveness: I hold it in my heart ...

6. Mozart: Ave verum Corpus, KV 618
Choir and orchestra convey deep emotion. The calm music, simple in its spirituality, comforts, and integrates all emotions. The major key provides absolution and a feeling of hope. The rocking rhythm provides support and stability. It is both the highest form of spiritual nourishment and balsam for the soul, and able to elicit a deep feeling of thankfulness.

... I am so moved by this wonderful music ... [cries] ...How is it possible for someone to simply sit down and compose something so profound! ... I see the baby again in the glass container. But now the baby has an old face, a senile face ... This glass container is outer space. Somehow it has the quality of the depths of the heavens ... Yes, that is the gift. (Can you take it with you and keep it when you return to reality?) Yes, I can.

With the help of GIM, Julia went deep into the experience of her feelings of guilt, and thus experienced something one might describe as grace: as she was able to recognise relationships as a whole as seen from a perspective of awareness (KBW) and to find a higher authority which understood her, she could work through her feelings of guilt.

The Volkswagen plays a key role. Interestingly, Julia was not consciously aware of the fact that the first VW was actually constructed by Porsche in 1934 (after Hitler's takeover of power). During the GIM journey it became a symbol for the successful German, silent about his own dark past.

Many themes were lived through during this session:
- Anaesthetising feelings guilt, through no fault of one's own;
- Having to be a good German, to make something good again (helping, like a doctor);
- Being misunderstood, being punished for telling the truth;

- Having to bear everything alone, not receiving any help;
- Loneliness, and longing to belong to a group;
- Inability to integrate the continuing existence of national socialism (symbolised by "Volkswagen");
- Ability to forgive a friend who judged all Germans on the basis of his own personal injury;
- Forgiveness from "above";
- The baby in the glass container as a symbol for child murder, or for life not allowed to be lived; the baby with the senile face as "archetype of the god-child" (C. G. Jung), understanding matters from a distance and guiding the client (see also Frohne-Hagemann 2002, 13).

This course of therapy also included nootherapeutic aspects. In addition to GIM, trance-stimulating music, as well as the monochord or gong played by the therapist, can lead into **nootherapeutic** work, in which journeys are made into hyper reflexive states (see also the chapter by A. Schmucker in this book). When deciding whether to use music from a CD or played by the therapist, the patient's problems, the therapeutic relationship, the situation and other factors which cannot be gone into in further detail must be carefully reflected. Usually psycho- and nootherapeutic aspects overlap.

As a further example, a (highly-shortened) case vignette by Integrative Music Therapist Matthias Witzel follows. With the assistance of a Bach Cantata, a space is made ready, in which the self can be deeply experienced, and spiritual growth can occur.

> "A 73-year-old woman ... (is) facing a difficult operation ... (wants) to explore meaningful questions regarding the meaning of life and death. Part of her difficulty is that although she is able to "grasp" and understand sensory matters, she has not been able to *feel* anything properly for a long time. (This is a problem of emotional anaesthesia, probably also brought about by the shock over the loss of her husband).
>
> As early as the second session she brings a dream, which she very much wants to relate:
>
> "I dreamt about a meeting with a group of people, at which we were introduced to a piece of religious music by J. S. Bach. We then spoke about what we had heard, a bit like music in school earlier. I know that in the dream the music was the first chorus of one of the church cantatas. A piece I had already heard many times. I am the only one of those present who is familiar with the music. But that is my secret. The cantata is about rejoicing over the coming of Christ to the world; a saviour in the midst of apocalyptic events. The title is something like, 'Rejoice and sing, play with trumpets and trombones'. In the morning I don't remember either the exact title or the music. It sounds like something from far away. What remains, is the knowledge that the music resembles the beginning of J. S. Bach's Easter Cantata. I feel as though something has be bestowed on me. I am a bit shaken, but happy. I look up the title the next day in a catalogue of Bach's works, but don't find anything similar".

The conversations with the client, of course, provide a series of possible interventions, which indicate themselves, according to what the client offers. The dream suggests using methods from the dream-work according to I. T. [Integrative Therapy] and IMT (see Frohne-Hagemann 1990). "Emotional Differentiation" (Petzold 1993) offers many possibilities of working with anaesthetised bodily perception, the theme "named" by the client. These might include work on the ability to perceive blocked breathing; perception of the body; esteem for physical sensation; investigation of biographical scenes evoked by bodily-oriented work; perception and esteem for what the client experiences emotionally in contact with the therapist, when investigating themes which might incorporate feelings of shame; physical reactions to the preceding). Also indicated ... is an examination of the client's religious beliefs, feelings, thoughts and actions, which may be used to block feelings of fear. In my opinion, this does not exclude letting the patient direct the focus of the session, if only briefly. It also does not exclude taking the patient's goals and intent seriously.

Since being confronted with illness, it has been important for the patient to "prepare herself well for death". By this she does not mean the physical process of dying, but the actual moment of "going over". ... The message of the dream is crystallised for the client, as a "message from the soul", comforting her and, in her words, providing a sense of calm and composure.

After focussing to regulate breath flow, the client is asked to centre her imagination on the J. S. Bach's church cantatas, which she knows in part and likes to listen to. The client ... chooses ... Cantata 173 (BWV 173: "Elevated Flesh and Blood"). Interestingly, the Cantata ends unusually, not with a "mere" peaceful, freeing Chorale. At the end of this Cantata, composed for the second day of Pentecost, Bach launches an exhilarating, dance-like choral movement. The structure of the movement, clad in simple homophony, as in many final chorales, strongly conveys happiness and reconciliation. At the same time, the chorale is integrated in an instrumental work with the strong dance character of a Polonaise. After a dance-like instrumental introduction, the choir urgently takes up the orchestra's melody. The simultaneous combination of chorale and dance, as well as the switch from instrumental dance to marked entrance of the choir entrance touches the client deeply as she listens.

She feels that her "intuitive choice" corresponds to the many-faceted synergy of text and music. It relates to her present theme, and leads her into a two-sided state of emotions. On the one hand, she feels a never-before-experienced deep feeling of consolation, together with warm feelings of sorrow relating to the loss of her husband. She is well-acquainted with sorrow. It is, however, usually cold and unpleasant. On the other hand, she feels a child-like cheerfulness, simultaneous with a vigorous and joyful composure. These feelings alternate, pulsating and quick, and resemble what she felt in the dream.

Questions regarding the sense of life and death remain unanswered, but, and this weighs more heavily, a fertile soil of comfort and trust in life is laid, in which these questions can continue to grow. The client takes the text of the music back into her daily life (Chorus from Cantata BWV 173).

Stir our spirits, Almighty God,
So that the gifts of the Holy Spirit
May work within us.
As your Son taught us to pray
They will come through the clouds
And bring us increase.

The client hardly wants to speak in the fifth and last therapy session before her stay in the hospital. She doesn't want to actively express her state of mind, whether instrumentally, in form or in movement. She merely says, that she was able to find consolation at home in Bach's music in moments when she felt afraid of the operation. She does not want to improvise with the therapist. She says, she is able to feel little, apart from physical heaviness and tension. She feels number again. I relate to her the impressions I have, of concordance between what she says and what she feels. It is perfectly okay to be "speechless" here. She relaxes a little, and we remain silent together for a few minutes. Together, we share the space, which is filled with an atmosphere of held-back melancholy, helplessness and tension, probably mainly due to the forthcoming operation. She nods in answer to my question, whether she is ready to listen to some instrumental music together. Her answer is confirmed by her posture and mimic. ... The listening period is preceded by a short introduction, which helps in becoming consciousness of the momentary mood. It also promotes "inner mindfulness" (Petzold 1983e). She expresses no personal preference, and so I select the Largo in d-minor from the Concerto for 2 Violins by J. S. Bach. This middle movement, fairly long for Baroque standards, is characterised by a powerful, carrying ground beat, a slowly rocking rhythm in 3, and a filigreed, but quite intensive, melodically flowing violin part. The client: "... as though it could carry me forever ..." The structure of the composition allows the listener – in spite of the minor key – to be affected by many qualities of emotion simultaneously. The calm and intimate musical flow touches the client deeply. She cries freely, and rocks herself increasingly "within". Afterwards, she relates seeing, in slow-motion and with great intensity, the garden of her childhood; how she played with her older siblings, and how they tenderly and lovingly danced with her. She felt the pain of frequently having been alone. At the same time, she was happy about being able to feel pleasant bodily sensations while listening to the music. She physically felt the animation of the playing child. She felt an impulse to move. She breathed deeply, and asked if she could listen to the music again. She would like to move a little bit to the music. A tender and cautious "Improvisation with movement" in one place follows to a repetition of the music. In the conversation afterward, she indicates that she has come into contact with her fear of the operation and felt liberation of the body. She is determined to take the music to the operation with her ... The session ends with a overview of the preceding sessions, including the aspects which have been important to her: being taken seriously on her search for spiritual orientation ...; esteem for her intuitive competence regarding her choice of spiritual path; the very moving experience of feeling consolation through Bach's music in an existential crisis; re-experiencing emotion through contact with music. Especially in this last, she begins to uncover, experience, express, share and, finally, process anaesthetised (Petzold 1993) emotions" (Witzel 1999, 276 ff).

Second Path of Healing and Support

Somato-, psycho- and nootherapeutic aspects also come to bear on the Second Path of Healing and Support.

Receptive music therapy focuses strongly on work on the body as *bodily re- and additional socialisation and enculturation*. Especially when treating individuals with damages in early relationships, fundamental work with the body in music therapy is necessary, in order to neuro-biologically anchor healthy experiences with relationships, in which security and original trust can be felt. The patients are repeatedly requested to "*get in touch with*" emerging feelings of the self, in order to develop a feeling and mindfulness for their own body. This is theoretically related to Sterns (1985) concepts of self-awareness and self-relation belonging to the "emerging self" within the "world of feelings". In therapy, this corresponds to "immersing oneself in one's feelings", and is necessary for developing self-coherence and -assurance. The musical selections transmit qualities of emotion, which can then be experienced and named, often for the first time.

Receptive music therapy helps in finding eutonia, or "good" bodily tension. This can be described as a desirable rhythmic balance between polarised elements (Frohne 1981). "Relaxation" is not necessarily the main objective, and can only be set therapeutically for overly tense individuals. Trophotropic music is used to bring about a more appropriate state of tension. Relaxation is counter-indicated for individuals with too little tension. They require just the opposite: exertion until a state of eutonia is reached. Ergotropic music used in the "vehicle function" can be used in this case (Frohne-Hagemann/PleßAdamczyk 2005).

When dealing with perception, music often functions "merely" as a shroud or background, filling a room with sound and providing a frame (as a background) for work on feeling (as a figure). In this case, music must be quite redundant, lacking strong emotional and dynamic movement, as in music by Klaus Schulze or Deuter, for example. As in GIM, classical music with a clear structure, for example Pachelbel's Canon, can also be used. In this case, the therapist supports the patient with music-related interventions as in "let the music carry you, comfort you, nourish you ..." which help to neuro-biologically anchor feelings of well-being and security, and store them emotionally. The function of music is not that of directing or "moving" the patient. When dealing with traumatised or fearful patients, it is important at the beginning to develop a sense of bodily security, and not to force an inter-affective relationship to the music (or the therapist).

On the second path of healing, receptive work also has the function of *sensitising and differentiating perception*. The perception of where a sound originates and how it disperses, the perception of the expectations and feelings it causes, the perception of where a sound or rhythm is felt and located within the body. All these "exercises" activate the senses, as well as bringing about a certain perceptive "level-headedness". At the same time they form a bridge to the third path of healing, which deals with learning how to listen in new ways.

On the second path of healing, trance-promoting music (for example, "Hanging Gardens" by the group, "The Necks") is not necessarily indicated, as it contributes to a loss of the certainty of being physically present. The Second Path is concerned with basal work on the body in its physical, mental, social and cultural dimensions (German: "Leibarbeit"). The functional goal is to provide the bodily self with contour. Individuals with less-well developed bodily identity are provided with firm ground under their feet. For this reason, trance-promoting music is seldom used within the context of functional relaxation in the here and now. On the First Path of Healing it can be used with patients with a sufficiently developed ego, who are setting out to investigate the spectrum of their personal consciousness.

Transfer and Counter-Transfer

As a general rule, transfer and counter-transfer must be considered on *all* paths of healing, whether from the patient onto music and/or therapist, or from therapist onto music and/or patient. Transfer and counter-transfer can be quite intensive during work on the second path of healing, and the decision to use active or receptive music therapy is often dependant on the intensity and quality of *transference*. The "Assessment of Relationship Qualities" (ARQ) according to Schumacher and Calvet-Kruppa (2001) can help greatly in accumulating theoretical background knowledge of the subject. These researchers differentiated between phenomenologically perceptible qualities of relationship between therapist and patient. Based on Sterns research with infants, qualities of relationship are divided into 8 contact-modes. Direct interaction, or interaction characterised by inter-subjectivity and inter-affectivity between therapist and patient, is possible from Mode 4 onwards.

The conclusion could be drawn that receptive music therapy is most indicated where it is too early for direct dyadic improvisation using inter-subjective and inter-affective means of contact, where this would be too threatening, or where active music-making in Modes 0 to 3 is not possible for other reasons. This is often the case with patients with early disturbances, and those suffering from fear (Frohne-Hagemann/Pleß-Adamczyk 2005). In such circumstances, receptive work is indicated, with the therapist functioning more as accompanist than opponent, and where the patient can use the therapist in order to better feel himself. Through receptive means, a therapeutic relationship is experienced, in which the patient is not confronted by the therapist, but held by means of her *presence*. This is the prerequisite for building a physical basis upon which feelings of original trust (certainty of existence) can develop, as well as for developing or mobilising resources, making it possible to confront existentially threatening fears. Only then can one allow oneself to be emotionally transported by the music, assured that it provides a secure time-frame and container, in which strong feelings can be experienced, relived, and processed. Interventions such as, "Can you allow the music to carry you?" or, "Can you breathe into the music?" intensify emotional experience. The music should not be experienced as an aggressor. One should bind oneself to the music's power and experience, and store it as personal bodily energy. In order to attain this goal, it is necessary to do good work with the body. In GIM, *physical interventions* support musical experience, and it is often a good idea to help the patient to experience his body as coherent and belonging to himself while listening. He should not use his imaginations in order to "drift away". In order to experience his own energy, the patient can, for example, kick or stamp on pillow held by the therapist, wring a towel, etc. in time to (or "against") the music.

Dorothee[9]9, 33, comes from an eastern European country. She is one of many women who were not permitted to live their own lives, as women in her country have many duties, but few rights. As a person with German origins she was accepted as a fellow citizen neither in her former country, nor in Germany. Out of shame, and fear of being flooded by uncontrollable feelings of pain, she rejected everything capable of expressing emotion. This included active music therapy. On the other hand, an inlet to music therapy was provided by the fact that she liked listening to music. What are Dorothee's needs? Applicable would be work on a sense of identity, which would convey the certainty of her bodily existence (i. e. by integrating her cultural roots from both the East and the West as well as experiencing existential assurance and the feeling of being able to influence matters personally. In order to reach a state of health, she should be allowed to experience respect and esteem for the way she is. Dorothee is physically quite tense, and would like to be more relaxed. However, she is ambivalent as regards letting go of tension: holding on protects her against feelings of coming apart. *Functional Relaxation to Music: Relaxation Training according to Music Therapeutic Aspects*, or *Music Therapeutic Deep Relaxation* (see the chapter by H.- H. Decker Voigt respectively in this volume) is not (yet) applicable, as the patient would follow all instructions automatically as a result of her belief in authorities. She would, however, suppress personal impulses, thus resulting in further tension. Receptive music therapy could be a fundamental consideration, as it protects against too precipitate vis-à-vis situations and interactions with the therapist. Receptive music therapy can provide a space in which Dorothee can experience personal feelings, for example with closed eyes and covered with a blanket.

The therapist decides to use GIM with the patient sitting, to provide her with a container in which she can seek *her own* way. In the assumption that on the Second Path of Healing the patient was able to mobilise her own inner resources through the music (and not through the therapist), so experiencing "re-nourishment", the therapist twice presents a program made up of small, more trophotropic, containers. This, however, has the result mentioned above: it confronts Dorothee directly with the embodied conflict. The music is experienced as a friendly *expectation*, which she is meant meet. [In therapy, she *thinks* she is expected to feel, in the family, she is expected to live life in a preordained way]. Her solution is to tense up physically. This allows her to avoid both expectation and personal emotions. She gradually becomes more and more conscious of her inability to defend herself. Insight and consciousness, however, do nothing to help her face up to her fear. Neither using a large, nor a small container is GIM indicated at the moment.

9 name changed

Work with the body is necessary, with music functioning as a *background*, shrouding and filling up emptiness. Work with the body means finding ground under one's feet, discovering the body (awareness of what is underneath one, of the form of the body while standing, sitting or lying, massaging the feet, listening to the heartbeat, etc.) while in the presence of the therapist. At first, the therapist is "simply there". Later, the therapist, for example, lays her hand on the patient's breast-bone or on the patient's hand, letting the patient experience touch and being touched. This allows the patient to open up space for her *own* personal experiences, *without* having to react to the therapist. Dorothee experiences tender feelings of closeness and distance without losing herself. She develops a greater natural sense of the certainty of her existence.
After a few months, GIM is able to be used again.

A short GIM session is held using music from Holst's, 'The Planets: "Mars"' and the Larghetto from Elgar's Serenade for Strings. This enables the patient not only to feel personal strength and feelings of identity won during therapy, but also to express these externally. This is necessary in order for her to overcome her fear of rejection. The first piece functions as a vehicle and catalyst. The patient uses the music's energy to defend herself against feelings she might be otherwise flooded by. In so doing, she kicks away a pillow held out by the therapist. Feeling the resistance necessary to kick the pillow away she comes in contact with her own body and strength. She is able to react in a more relaxed way to the following music, as she is more present in the body. A foundation is laid for dealing with early experiences of always having had to *function*. This is a script which continues to determine her experiences and actions today.

Physical bodily experiences, in which resources are mobilised, are fundamental for patients with problems with self-esteem or fear of destruction, especially when these are caused not only by familiar, but by societal and cultural conditions. Used as background, music can take over an important function in filling up abysms of space. It can also, as in GIM, act as a co-therapist, bringing the patient into contact with his own strength and emotions, and allowing him to experience self-effectiveness without personally interacting with the therapist. Experience of the self is only possible when the external world is unthreatening, when one is able to "get in touch with oneself". This is sometimes better served by receptive music therapy than by dyadic improvisation in active music therapy. In any case, active music therapy with Dorothee would not have been possible.

The Third Path of Healing and Support

On the Third Path of Healing, receptive methods are used whereby listening to music serves to open up personality, "co-creativity", and "conflux", and activate experience in group situations. Receptive and active methods are frequently combined and deepened by means of *indirectly connecting inter-medial paths* (Petzold 1993, Vol. 3, 1224), or by combining the arts (Frohne-Hagemann 1983/2001, 71 ff, [10]10).

10 this article was recently republished in English (translated by Elizabeth Franzen). In: Nordic Journal of Music Therapy, 14/2, 2005, p. 165–178

For example:
In a group situation, music can be heard in a state of relaxation. The group's fantasies are later drawn; the drawings are then put to music by the group. This "inter-medial" procedure allows the group to grasp certain themes more easily, as they are transferred from one sense to another, for example from hearing to sight to movement, from receptive to productive and vice versa, and from individual subjective experience to group resonance.

Techniques using dancing or painting to music, that is, where musical parameters are experienced in a sequential order in space, or their expressive content portrayed, are also receptive-active in nature. Associations can be gathered to different styles of music, out of different cultures. These associations can be made into a poem, and set to music. This allows the group members to start a conversation with each other. The experience of music serves less a deep-psychological uncovering of individual biographical elements, as an opening of individual creativity, which can then be broadened and shared. Themes can also be suggested by the therapist, for example, 'what kind of music is erotic?' Many aspects of the theme can be touched upon through exchange. These can reach from personal experience to culturally conveyed norms and gender-specific differences concerning what is, or should be considered erotic.

Many examples for creative ports of entry can be found in the work of colleagues, working with other methods (see, for example, L. Schiltz in this book). Their methods also provide material which can be used on the First and Second Paths of Healing and Support

The Fourth Path of Healing and Support

Listening to music as a group, usually during group music therapy, deals less with personal biography as with experiencing differences and similarities from a meta-perspective. It deals with learning about other tastes, other processes of socialisation, other cultures and habits of listening. Sharing emotionally-laden musical experience can help one to experience a humane way of coexisting, as well as tolerance and esteem. In listening to one another, one shows esteem for the other's musical taste without putting one's own culture first. The personal meaning which music can have for an individual must be understood from many perspectives (See Figure 1, The Many-Layered Model). One perspective is that of age. Older people are quick to complain when younger people only listen to techno music. They might find it worthless, as it is not differentiable. In fact, however, young people need this music because it allows them to feel vital physical-bodily elements of the self better, and helps to build bodily identity. Other individuals might need the music of Bach, especially when they reach an age at which they need to experience transcendental spiritual aspects. Sharing such needs is important for developing personality in the sense of differentiating culture. This refers to getting to know and enquiring about one's own traditions of thinking and feeling, in order to learn to understand what is foreign. On this path, patients can learn not to denigrate things, which do not correspond to their own way of living. Receptive music therapy is oriented towards promoting solidarity. Music is listened to consciously, to bring people closer to each other socially and behaviourally.

In practice, all four paths interlock with each other.

Similarities and Differences between Receptive Integrative Music Therapy and Guided Imagery and Music (GIM)

In conclusion, I would like to return to the idea of integration. By means of a few examples in sketch-form comparing some concepts of IMT and GIM, I would like to show how, and by what means, GIM can enrich integrative music therapy and vice versa. The same process should also be applied to receptive methods dealing with different themes (see also the chapter by T. Wosch in this volume, comparing RMT and GIM according to emotional-psychological aspects). However, space does not allow for such considerations here.

Frame of Reference

GIM (or the Bonny Method GIM), like IMT, attempts to integrate of different psychotherapeutic points of view theoretically, for example, Jungian (Ward 2002, 207 ff), psychodynamic (Bruscia 2002, 225 ff), Gestalt-therapeutic (Clarkson 2002, 245), and spiritual Orientation (Kasayka 2002, 257 ff). It is not clear, however, exactly how this happens in theory and in practice. For example, GIM borrows interventions from Gestalt Therapy without taking the theory of Gestalt Therapy into consideration.

Work with Consciousness

The GIM method is described by Ventre as a procedural occurrence and "integrative" process. That is, "a multidimensional, integrative process in that the imagery and symbols that arise may be experienced on many levels at once, from the concrete to the abstract and from the personal to the transpersonal" (Ventre 2002, 29). Openness exists for the idea that perception and experience can occur on many levels. The term, 'imagination' is broad, and includes kinaesthetic, visual-pictorial, auditory and scenic aspects, as well as those of thought during the experience of music. This corresponds to the inter-medial approach, which also attempts to enable patients to experience on many levels of the senses, in order that they are able to understand their experience according to different perspectives. In both methods, what has been experienced can be drawn, danced, or put into movement or a poem, before being reflected.

Work with Identity

Work with identity, in conjunction with the anthropological goal of work on the entire body, is the same in both methods, even though the complete concept of the "body" (as understood in IMT) does not seem to be known in GIM. Both Integrative Human-Therapy and GIM combine somato-, psycho- and nootherapy. Some representatives of GIM in America, however, lay the *main* emphasis on the transpersonal and spiritual. GIM serves "to claim our latent power to touch what is holy, to walk with the holy, to manifest the holy in our daily lives" (Kasayka 2002, 268). This type of therapeutic understanding is not compatible with the nootherapeutic method as taught by Integrative Music Therapy in Western Germany. Integrative Therapy, to be sure, includes existential questions about values, the meaning of life and life-goals, birth and death, transcendence, mysticism, contemplation, etc. in nootherapeutic treatment. This is especially shown in the vignette by Matthias Witzel. Angels are also welcome, as shown in the work with Julia. However, all forms of religious expectation from the part of the therapist and the resulting influence on the patient are avoided.

Work with the body in other, or altered, states of consciousness complies with IMT's concern. GIM, with its practical emotional work with differentiation, encompasses de facto the *entire* spectrum, from the darkness of "raw being" (French: "l'être brut") to the lightness of "nothing" (French: "néant absolu"). A GIM session usually affects the body's vegetative system, also when dealing with transpersonal experiences. It not only happens that the patient has to use the toilet because the kidneys have been brought into intensive action by the session. In my experience, GIM sessions also apparently heighten the readiness to receive (see the case study, "Anna" in the contribution by B. Süselbeck-Schulz in this volume). On the other hand, patients repeatedly, realise things during a GIM journey, which they are not conscious of in daily life (for example, that Volkswagen was constructed as Hitler was in power, or that Julia was able to understand, from an eccentric point of view, the nature of her problem).

Work with Emotion

The goal of GIM is, as in IMT, intensive work on the differentiation of emotions. In both methods, the goal is not to "get a grip on" or neutralise emotions before they have been lived through. The function of music is to allow emotions to be experienced bodily and lived through in their own time-frame. This endows them with form and contour. Pent-up emotions such as anger or sorrow, for example, can be lived through and processed with the help of music functioning as a vehicle or catalyst (ergotropic music). Julia's example also shows how music used as a container provides a time-frame, as well as an area in which differentiated feelings of guilt and despair can be expressed.

Both GIM and IMT are distinguished by their orientation to patient resources. When dealing with fear-patients, GIM first uses music in the holding function. It assumes that fear can first be conquered when the individual is in possession of sufficient resources. Only then can the patient finds adequate strategies for coping with and managing fear in the imagination, while at the same time listening to music which might cause him to become afraid. Conflicts, disturbances and traumas stand in ever-changing relationship to each other on various physical, intellectual and spiritual levels of the body. On the whole, it can be said that GIM, like IMT, is a method which strives to allow these conflicts to be re-lived and processed emotionally. This strongly resembles the methods of Integrative Therapy.

The Understanding of Music

GIM allows music to be experienced very intimately. It becomes a co-therapist. It views the patient as a *musical being*, and assumes that music corresponds to spiritual forms, thus making healing possible. It is agreed that music and soul are related to each other in an analogue fashion, and that each movement of the soul and grounded in the body or marked and influenced by culture corresponds to a certain kind of music. This can be described as a "musical-bodily resonance" (Frohne-Hagemann 1999/2001, 252). A goal, both general and therapeutic, should be the ability to feel musically (again), if only because of music's ability to enrich and differentiate emotions.

When GIM is used within IMT, its methods can be modified strongly, leaving classical BMGIM behind. This is because the patient's world, biography, culture, experience of illness etc. is so strongly focussed, that music not found in traditional GIM programs (such as Jazz, hit-songs, Operetta) as well as other receptive methods can be used.

Areas of Emphasis

It is apparent that the possibilities of IMT in receptive therapy are greater in number than in BMGIM, and thus have a broader focus. As a *specific music therapeutic* method, on the other hand, GIM goes deeper. Long experience has resulted in the development of very carefully compiled programs of music. Most themes of life can be developed and treated within the time-frames and space made available by these programs. In this respect, GIM feeds IMT with nourishment and valuable ideas.

In GIM, work with culture is, as shown by the example of Julia, a personal possibility, not, however, in the way described in the Third and Fourth Paths of Healing. GIM is a more introverted, process, relating to exploration of the inner world of the patient. Music focuses on the experience itself. The assumption of a "universal function of music" (universal music) and the attempt to apply Bonny's programs in the same way to the GIM traveller universally can lead to misunderstandings. The *function* and *meaning* of a piece of music for an individual embodying a specific culture can easily be underrated. The music of Mozart and Beethoven is heard with pleasure throughout the world. However, music is heard differently according to context (see also the chapter by R. Tüpker). And the meaning of a certain context is dependant on many factors. GIM programs cannot be viewed as 'l'art pour l'art', or art for art's sake. Experience with bodily dimensions is one aspect. Another is digesting and evaluating what has been heard. This occurs in front of the background of embodied enculturement and socialisation. Programs of music must be compiled based on an analysis of the culture in which they are to be used. The compilation represents the art of overlapping and transfer.

The Therapist's Role

During the listening phase of GIM the role of the therapist is usually that of a "guide" or accompanist, facilitating the journey. Music acts as co-therapist. In receptive IMT, the therapist plays many roles simultaneously. These are not only dependant on whether active or receptive music therapy is indicated, but also on what form of receptive music therapy is applied on which "Path of Healing and Support".

Many uses of methods of Human Therapy were not able to be mentioned here. In the future much will have to be tried out and reflected upon with regard to the integration of different receptive methods within indication-specific and theoretically guided therapeutic processes.

Acknowledgement

The author would like to thank Elizabeth Franzen for the translation.

CH. 10: THE SOUND GUIDED TRANCE ACCORDING TO WOLFGANG STROBEL.

Receptive music therapy with sound archetypes – an in-depth psychological method

ANDREA SCHMUCKER

Introduction

"Sound-guided trance", developed and thus named by Wolfgang Strobel[1] 20 years ago, has several roots. It represents a synthesis of different therapeutic approaches, which are rooted in music therapy, hypnotherapy, psychoanalysis, and depth psychology. In essence, sound-guided trance is very close to shamanism, the world's oldest healing method. Both sound-guided trance and shamanism are rooted in therapeutic work with modified states of consciousness and use monotonous repetitive acoustic stimulation, which is produced "live" on traditional instruments. At different times and in different cultures shamans have used the magic power of archaic music in order to induce in their "clients" and themselves a different level of consciousness, to experience different forms of reality, to call on gods, ghosts or demons, to cure diseases or to retrieve lost portions of the soul. The most common means of "transport" for such a shamanic voyage into non-day-to-day realities is the drum, often called the "shaman's horse" (Drury 1989), and the rattle.

Sound-guided trance according to Strobel uses additional instruments and thus offers a very effective method within receptive music therapy. Playing the instrument in a special monotonous manner as well as ritualizing the hearing of the music produces an altered state of wake-consciousness, which allows access to unconscious and super-conscious levels of an individual's psyche. One can therefore constitute the "Musical Guided Affective Imagery", contrived by Hanscarl Leuner in the 60's and the so-called "Guided Imagery and Music" (GIM), developed in America by Helen Bonny in close co-operation with Stanislav Grof in the early 70's, as predecessors. Both are independent methods within receptive music therapy. They both, however, work with prefabricated (composed) music played via electronic media.

Inspired by the cooperation with his friend Tonius Timmermann and Tonius's experiments and results with the monochord's elemental sound structures, Wolfgang Strobel began, in the eighties, to analyze archaic energetic patterns and forces of further sounds. He researched the so-called sound archetypes of other

1 Wolfgang Strobel, Dr. med., medical specialist for psychotherapeutical medicine, medical specialist for psychiatry and neurology, psychotherapy, psychoanalysis, music therapist: manager of the institute for advanced training for music, body and trance therapy.

archaic instruments as well as their specific sound qualities and their effect on an individual in the context of their psychotherapeutic usability[2]. The novelty of the "sound-guided trance" method lies in the realization that the individual's experience is directly influenced by the type of sound used (Strobel 1992, 99). A specific sound with its specific psychological realm of meaning can therefore be used to focus on experiencing specific subject areas. The "sound-guided trance" therefore employs the awareness that "specific monochrome sound structures produced on archaic instruments resonate with specific topics in the subconscious and thus make them conscious. The sounds have a strong affinity to certain types of experiences such as prenatal, birth, early childhood, death and transcendence." (Strobel 1999, 221). The altered state of consciousness causes a regression of experience through which the suppressed (traumatic) experiences surface to the conscious mind, where they can be processed and worked with. Furthermore, it is possible to step into new realms of experience and facilitate individual growth.

In order for the reader to better understand the following, it should be emphasized that the "sound-guided trance" as described here was developed as an "uncovering" method for treatment of neurotic patients and people with borderline syndrome and it has also proven to be successful in self-encounter. The focus is on clients who are able to verbalize and work through issues on a level of consciousness. Sound-guided trance, or to be more precise, working with sound archetypes can, under certain circumstances, successfully be applied to psychiatric patients with psychotic disorders, people with disabilities or in coma vigil[3] as well as within child and youth therapy. The trance aspect moves to the background and some severe modifications to the method are necessary, which cannot be elaborated on within the framework of this work.

Trance: modified wake-consciousness

Formerly, the term "trance" described a state of reversed wake-consciousness. Still today, in popular language people refer to trance as being in a state of unconsciousness (= not being conscious). At the latest since Milton H. Ericksons hypnotherapy became popular in the seventies, the term trance has been used for all states of consciousness where the consciousness is not directed towards the outward world but instead inwardly. Since the normal wake-consciousness can be sustained and is merely modified, in scientific context it is commonly referred to as "modified wake-consciousness"

2 Strobel describes the results of this work for the first time in 1988 in his essay 'Klang – Trance – Heilung. Die archetypische Welt der Klänge in der Psychotherapie'.

3 Refer to the article by Jochheim, M.: Einfach Da-Sein dürfen. Musiktherapie mit bewusstseins- und wahrnehmungsgestörten Patienten. In: Baumann, M. u. Gessner, Ch. (2004): Zwischenwelten. Musiktherapie bei Patienten mit erworbener Hirnschädigung. Wiesbaden 2004.

Monotonous sounds and rhythms are excellent means of leading to such states of modified wake-consciousness and thus result in a centeredness of a higher apperception pointing inwards. Only when the trance has reached deeper levels of the consciousness can the archetypal impact of the sounds take effect. Individual reactions to a specific sound can vary significantly. Therefore, in order to reach a meaningful interpretation and adequate understanding of the multifaceted perceptions during a sound trance Strobel suggests allocating the sound experiences to certain levels of consciousness (Strobel 1992, 112). He identifies 7 levels of consciousness: levels 1 to 3 represent the normal state of wake-consciousness, levels 4 to 7 (which he takes from Grof in 1983) represent the altered state of wake-consciousness, whereby level 4 is understood as an intermediate stage.

Normal wake-consciousness:

1) Level of critical description of the external stimulus or impulse – the client tries to describe the external sound phenomenon (i. e. "I can hear a high pitched tone, it's very high and silvery.")
2) Level of day-to-day connotation – the sounds are connected to specific situations arising in day-to-day life (i. e. "That sounds like a lawnmower.")
3) Level of diffuse emotional perception – feelings are registered according to a like/dislike principle (i. e. "That is very pleasant" or "I do not like that.")

Modified wake-consciousness:

4) Level of abstract or aesthetic experiences – perception of anything from geometric patterns to psychedelic colors and forms.
5) Level of experiences that are to be interpreted psychodynamically – resuscitation of events of the individual's life story in concrete, real or metaphorical form
6) Level of pre- and perinatal experiences – experiences from the intrauterine period or from the time just before, during, or just after birth surface to the consciousness.
7) Level of transpersonal experiences – trespassing the boundaries of the I and of time and space (images of the collective unconsciousness, experiences of foreign cultures (without ever having been there), experiences of reincarnation, mystic, religious and transcendental experiences)

As stated before, the archetypal impact of the sounds only comes into effect in levels 5 to 7. When a patient does not advance into these deeper levels of the unconscious during the sound-guided trance, his or her reactions can not be attributed to these archetypal subject areas (Strobel 1992, 113).

The depth of trance alone however, does not guarantee an archetypal sound effect since there are also unspecific reactions to the different sound structures. If, for example, the patient has a current topic or problem at the top of his or her mind, then the topic doesn't really care by which stimulus it is brought to the surface and into the conscious mind. In this case, the specific effect of the sound archetype is invalidated. It is therefore not possible to ascertain with absolute certainty whether or not the experiences triggered by the stimulus stem from the realm of meaning of the specific sound. Furthermore, Strobel points out that according to the results of Dittrich's research (1985) there is a common core of experiences of modified stages of wake-consciousness which is independent from the type of stimulus that acts as trigger. The following phenomena are independent of any sound since they can already be associated with the state of trance: alteration in the way time, the body scheme and thought processes are perceived, loss of self control, hallucinatory apparitions. Known trance phenomena such as age regression, time distortion, visions, etc. can therefore appear with every sound. The complexity of the matter makes it obvious that sound-guided trance can only be applied appropriately and purposeful and its results can only be interpreted in a meaningful way when one has collected enough practical experience which enables one to make meaningful distinctions.

Sound archetypes and their specific impact

The term "sound archetype" actually refers to two situations: the energetic and physically measurable (objective) phenomenon of sound and the psychological (subjective) realm of meaning in the human experience which resonates with this phenomenon. With the help of the hermeneutic method of understanding interpretation, Strobel was able to identify conspicuous correlations in reactions to different specific sound structures. These correlations clearly correspond with archaic patterns in the human soul and have the ability to activate subject areas in the human subconscious. The term "archetype" in its meaning as a basic module within the human soul can be traced back to Johannes Kepler. In his time Kepler had already assumed correlations between musical archetypes and structures in the human soul (see Timmermann 1987, 65).

"Next to the unspecific trance-induced impact of the monotonous impulse on the experience there is also a specific impact caused by the sound *timbre*. For this reason I like to talk about *monochrome* sounds[4] which are produced on different instruments, represent energetic archetypes and can be attributed to characteristic psychological subject areas (Strobel 1992, 99).

It would be a mistake, however, to attribute the sound archetype solely to the instrument since it also heavily depends on the way the sound is played on the instrument (Strobel 1999, 104). When this differs, the impact is also different. Last but not least, the impact the sounds have also depends on the attitude, mood and centralized intention of the therapist. In this context, Strobel warns against a

4 'Monochrome sounds' are monotonously played sounds with a characteristic timbre.

"simplifying linear understanding of the sound impact", and points out (1992, 102) that "the process is a circular dialogue between the sound producing therapist and the reacting patient". This is one of the main reasons that he always works with sound and rhythm structures that are produced "live".

The following phenomenon is of primary importance in therapeutic work with sound archetypes, and thus is most emphasized during the therapy: the archetypal theme is most often distorted by a person's past traumatic life experiences. In this case, the archetype does not appear in the consciousness in its pure form but rather as a distorted version. As a reaction to the sound, the past experience resurfaces and blocks the archetypal theme – the archetype thus appears in the experience in its blocked form. This is where the therapeutic relevance lies in this method. If, for example, the sound of oneness with the world is being focused on and the patient has an issue with an early disharmonious relationship with his mother, these experiences will be the first to surface.

"Figuratively speaking, one could say that the person having the experience on his or her journey to the archetypal realm of experience is confronted with those obstacles (traumatic experiences) which block the way and make this realm inaccessible. It is only when these obstacles have been moved out of the way that the archetypal realm can be entered." (Strobel 1999, 105).

As long as a person cannot experience a certain type of sound archetype in its pure form he or she will not have access to the corresponding part of the soul. The specific sound is able to let these negative experiences which have blocked the path for the soul to this realm resurface to the conscious mind. With the help of thematically focused sound stimulation, the biographical situation can be relived and, if necessary, re-suffered. The therapist acts as guide and companion and, by maintaining a supportive and accepting attitude, can contribute substantially so that the patient can lovingly accept, and eventually overcome, the negative experience. Insofar as the sound always offers this healing experience on a symbolic and purely energetic level and consequently presents the soul with a new realm, it is a remedy.

The effective employment of "live" music sets a few requirements for the therapist. A trusting therapeutic relationship and knowledge of the sound archetypes are an essential prerequisite. The therapist needs to know how to play the different instruments and whilst doing so should be able to enter a state of centered attentiveness and maintain an empathetic inner attitude. This will enable him to get into resonance and communication with the patient.

Below, five sound archetypes will be described which W. Strobel has researched extensively in theory and practice. The effects of the ocean drum, the rattle, the shrutibox, the low-pitched singing bowl, the Javanese gong, the berimbao and the bullroarer (bush telephone) will have to remain unmentioned in this article.

The Monochord

The monochord is an instrument with 13 or more strings, all tuned to the same tone, strung across a resonating wooden box. By means of a continuous playing method a flowing key note is produced, over which the natural overtones are perceptible as "spheric sounds". The sounds relate to one another in a harmonic mathematic order and according to natural law, so that they can be perceived as an expression of a higher harmony. As long as the theme is not blocked, the sound of the monochord produces emotions of oneness with everything and even a feeling of limitless self. It is even possible to overcome the contradiction of feeling physically dissolved and supported at the same time. The focal point is the perception of oneness and in this context of oneness with the world, creation and the cosmos. Alluding to one's life story, oneness with the mother is representative in this context. If access to such an experience is disturbed, the sound of the monochord can cause those obstacles to enter the conscious mind. It is not uncommon for access to prenatal traumatic experiences (unity on a physical level) to become available.

The Frame Drum

The frame drum is used here as an example of the fact that the sound archetype is dependent on the way the specific sound pattern is produced on the instrument. The given connection between the drum-heartbeat meter with approximately 60 beats per minute and the heart rate of the human organism is easily comprehensible, as well as that a significant increase of this frequency can lead to restlessness and agitation whereas a decrease below 50 beats per minute can make a person become aware of the background of fear and panic attacks. If one goes into higher frequencies, much further from the human heart beat, this will have a completely different impact as is shown below.

a) The Heart Meter

If the "heart meter" is played on a frame drum in a warm and soft timbre and in a steady and continuous manner, a clearly circumscribed archetypal subject area arises: in essence, it revolves around the topic of being accepted and having meaning in the world. It is self-evident that this meter might represent the mother's heart beat, and thus cause early intrauterine experiences to resurface. Based on many experiences with regression, Strobel assumes that even in this prenatal state (from the 4th month onwards) the fetus is able to perceive, next to a physical and mental oneness with its mother, the existence of an I and a you on a preconscious level. It is thus able to perceive the dependence as well as the differentiation of its own life from its mother's heart beat.[5] With this perception of its own self an

5 Strobel 1996, unpublished manuscript

awareness of its own identity and a feeling of self-worth already start to develop in this early phase. Ideally, this prenatal phase is a time of experiencing complete and unconditional acceptance. Since this is rarely the case, however, a range of topics relating to a narcissistic difficulty can arise. The heart meter archetype of the drum is always applied in therapy when the central topic has to do with someone not having been accepted as an entity, or if acceptance had always been linked to some sort of preconditions (i. e. performance). As a result, this person cannot entirely accept himself (Strobel 1999, 113). In a larger sense, the heart beat meter represents a link to the earthly appearance of a person, to his individual being-in-the-world. It therefore refers to the passing of time, transience and continuity and brings structure, clarity and concretion. The constant recurrence of the consistent pulsation can be experienced as reliable, upholding and consoling, but also as relentless and merciless.

"The great therapeutic power in these continuous drum beats lies in the fact that it has the potential to permeate ones real self and the experience of unconditional love. Played with this intention, the drum has the capacity to wake up all negative past experiences, dissolve them and transform them into light."[6]

b) The Shaman beat

For millennia, the frame drum has been the most common means of transport into unordinary realities used by shamans of many cultures in order to go on internal journeys with the so-called "shaman beat" (Strobel 1999, 114). The frequency of this drum beat lies between 240 and 300 beats per minute (4–5 hertz) and corresponds with the theta waves of the brain, which appear when a human being is in a hypnotic state. Due to the analogy with the theta waves of the brain, Strobel calls this frequency "theta frequency" (ibid.). The distinguishing factor with the shaman beat is that it does not offer a descriptive subject area but has a rather unspecific character.

Paradoxically, one could say that the theme of this sound archetype is that it has none, and thus is open and neutral, and opens the gates to the unconscious. This form of powerful rhythmic stimulation produces an inner movement of the psyche. Because of its neutral character – and this is something the shamans intuitively knew and applied correctly – it qualifies very well as a means of trance induction with a specific intention: for shamanic work and intentions, i. e. for the search of the power animal, the resurrection of lost areas of the soul, the extraction of intruders, for healing rituals, etc. (ibid., 115) or for example in psychotherapeutic work as a support for verbally guided and managed imagination.

In a therapeutic phase during which no special theme or topic is present, the shaman beat can act as an open invitation for the next topic.

6 Strobel 1994, unpublished manuscript

The Gong Chau Lou (Tam-Tam)

Similar to the shaman drum, gongs have a long tradition as instruments in cult rituals as well as in shamanic use. Strobel refers the theme of this sound archetype solely to the Chinese gong chau lou, which he uses. He emphasizes that it cannot be transferred to other gongs since it is possible that these have a completely different characteristic. Through a very dense sequence of beats the chao lou unfolds an impressive sound volume and creates a steadily increasing overtone chaos. The experiences stimulated by this gong are very dynamic. The subject area of the gong archetype comprises processes of metamorphosis, passage or development between crisis and transformation up to those threshold situations where one condition is transformed into another followed by resolution and transformation. Right in the center, the big issues of birth and death present themselves – the experiences of dying and being born. Often it is about real – or in the metaphoric sense – situations of birth and death with dramatic escalation followed by resolution. It is not uncommon for the gong to activate the necessary energy in order for disease to be able to escalate into a healing crisis, or in order for fears which block the path to metamorphosis and reincarnation to be illustrated. In the most concrete sense, the gong subject matter is in demand when the focus is on perinatal topics (birth trauma), in the figurative sense, when the focus is on stagnation in a threshold situation. Here, the gong has a very broad range of use, considering that in therapy the focus is very often on threshold situations. The gong chau lou can function as a veritable "obstetrician" and can sensibly further the therapeutic process,

The Didgeridoo

This wind instrument used by the Australian Aborigines is considered to be one of the most archaic instruments of mankind and nowadays has even become popular in the western world. Its name is an echoism of the sound produced on it. By means of circular breathing (not uncomplicated but learnable), a homogenous and continuous keynote which can be modulated, is produced. Sound trance only uses this monotonous key note leaving aside all other modulations traditionally used by the aboriginal people. The archetypal themes of this sound are quite characteristic. On the surface, experiences with wild animals or ones that have to do with the element earth appear often. Sometimes the sound shifts the listener back to the early beginnings of mankind. According to Strobel's research, the emotional tinge of the sound of the didgeridoo is brutish, lustful, vital, powerful and archaic. In essence, the topic revolves around physicality, sensuality, and sexuality. This can be expressed as vitality, zest for life or as animalism, anger and aggression (Strobel 1999, 121). It is not uncommon for women to experience their female and for men to experience their male form of sexual power and sexual identity (or their problems with these). In addition, the sound can also stimulate perception and realization of the person's own ethereal body.

If the therapy deals with difficulties about being grounded, with physicality, sensuality, sexuality or aggression then, according to Strobel, the didgeridoo represents an adequate instrument to deal with this complex of topics and their background. In an ideal case, after working through, for example, hurtful experiences with sexual or bodily hostility on the one hand or sexual abuse or harassment on the other hand, it is possible to free the qualities of "physicality", "sensuality" and "sexuality" and assign them a positive connotation. As well as its sound archetypal effect, Strobel uses the vibrations of the sound of the didgeridoo as a medium for a therapeutic, healing intention (= energy)[7]. In this instance, the didgeridoo is played directly onto the body. The sound archetype only plays a secondary role in this work, but through its affinity with life energy and its tendency to activate the ethereal body, it has a very positive effect.

The high-pitched singing bowl

The high-pitched singing bowl is known for being able to centralize attention during meditation. This is self-evident when one hears its clear and piercing sound. Strobel discovered that the singing bowl, unlike any other instrument, has the capacity of giving access to transcendental areas. This, however, only becomes evident when it is not rung, as in sound trance, but instead rubbed with a stick on the outside rim, so that a continuous sound is created. Strobel is convinced that the singing bowl played thus has the strongest trance inducing potential of any of the instruments he uses and relates this not only to psychological but also to physical-physiological facts (Strobel 1992, 109). The sound of the singing bowl has the power to put rational thinking to sleep and to direct attention and perception to what is now present. In the therapeutic context it is able to focus in mindfulness on the center of the unconscious conflict. The archetypal subject area of the singing bowl has to do with the confrontation with a stringent, strong and predominant force or power from which one cannot withdraw oneself. Depending on biographical experiences, this power is experienced as positive or negative (Strobel 1999, 107). Whilst the positive scenario leads to an experience of happy surrendering (to life), all encompassing love, or even happy unison with the godly, the blocked form of the archetype experiences are always marked by painful or traumatic experiences (i. e. abuse, rape, war situations, strokes of fate, natural catastrophes, etc.) In certain therapeutic situations it is unreasonable to subject the patient to the stringent poignancy with which the topics are brought to the surface by the singing bowl.

The high-pitched singing bowl finds its best use in therapy when the concern is about the confrontation with a higher power, when the subject matter is about power and powerlessness, control and surrender. It is, for example, possible to work on very negative experiences of having been at someone's mercy, or to

7 Strobel 2000, unpublished manuscript

uncover an often hidden refusal of the exigent demands of life (power of destiny). All these negative experiences and the resulting attitudes stand in the way of being able to experience the happiness resulting from surrender to this higher power. The singing bowl is able to mediate this, once all obstacles have been removed.

No other instrument triggers so many transcendental experiences, or enables one to have the serendipitous experience of total surrender to a higher transcendental power (Strobel, 1999[8]).

Levels of experience in the sound-guided trance

Often, people think of trance as the experience of inner images and visions. Although this is relatively common, it does not necessarily have to be the case. Strobel emphasizes that "when there is too heavy a focus on optical hallucinations… not only these but also other therapeutically valuable levels of experience can be hindered or not paid attention to" (Strobel 1999, 133). For this reason, it is good to know all types of reactions which can appear during the sound-guided trance.

Thoughts and associations

Since thoughts and associations can already contain hints to unconscious topics and conflicts, it is advisable not to disregard these as trance-unrelated or as resistance, but rather to use them for the further process of experience

Emotions

In the case of emotional reactions, which can be very strong and cathartic, it is very helpful to honor these every once in a while with an attitude of acceptance and when necessary with encouragement ("everything is okay, just allow it to happen"), and to then bring to the fore the situation out of which these emotions initially resulted by posing focused questions.

Imagines – inner voice (optical, physical, acoustic, olfactory, gustatory or multi-sensory)

Internal images occur quite frequently, but if they do not appear it is advisable to ask the patient about his or her body sensations. A lot of people prefer to react on this level and might just need a hint in the right direction. Vehement reactions can occur here as well. Every once in a while, acoustic hallucinogenic phenomena occur which go beyond the perception of real sound. Less frequent are smell sensations, and even less common are taste sensations. Multi-sensory reactions do occur, meaning they pertain to several different sensory feelings at the same time (i. e. physical and imaginary).

8 unpublished manuscript

Spontaneous body movements and autonomous body processes

Sound-guided trance can also trigger spontaneous body movements and even lead to autonomous body processes (for example, the strong bodily reactions during the process of giving birth). Should this occur, it may become necessary to apply a suitable body-therapeutic approach (i. e. pressure, during the above mentioned birth process or real physical support).

From experience, intensive processes occur with patients with sufficiently stable ego-structure only when an appropriate protective frame exists. The resolution of old patterns doesn't necessarily have to happen in such a dramatic way. It can also happen very subtly and still be effective.

Setting and Development

One should not underestimate the vehemence of the surfacing experiences and should ensure a stable and secure setting. Sound-guided trance works better the more the therapist is able to take on an appropriate inner attitude and a guiding and protective function and thus, as a form of work-sharing, guarantees a connection to the external reality. This way, the client can give up that part of his attention directed towards the external and is therefore free to direct his awareness towards his inner worlds. This becomes even more effective when the therapist is able to partially immerse himself into the state of modified wake-consciousness because he achieves a better contact to the patient's level of experience as well as to his own empathetic and intuitive abilities (Strobel 1999, 100).

Strobel (ibid., 131) recommends, for a variety of reasons, that the sound-guided trance be verbally accompanied if possible. This means that *guidance* of the trance happens non-verbally and is entirely in the hands of the sound produced by the therapist. The therapist himself verbalizes solely *as a companion*. This guarantees the non-directive style of sound-guided trance. During sound-guided trance, therapist and client are therefore in verbal communication as the patient directly verbalizes his experience and the therapist, if necessary, intervenes on a verbal level (i. e. empathizes, queries, supports, encourages, etc.). The advantages of this direct verbalizing method lie mainly in the fact that the maintenance of the rapport implies more security. This allows the patient to get involved on a significantly deeper level. Verbal guidance also protects him from the danger of drifting off or falling asleep – later on he will be better able to recollect the experience. Taking part in the experience makes it easier for the therapist to be understanding and empathetic, and he can thus better support the therapeutic process. The speed at which the patient speaks, which is slower in trance, gives the therapist a good indication of the patient's depth of consciousness and can, by means of appropriate interventions, induct a deepening of the trance if necessary. This form of verbalizing can also be applied to group therapy when two people are working together, one of them as a companion.

At first, some people may have difficulties verbalizing, without losing the state of trance. Often, there is an underlying hindering assumption that it is not possible to verbalize the experienced without "getting out of it". An explanation and the encouragement to try it out can help. Only if this type of procedure proves too difficult does Strobel suggest letting the sound phase pass in silence and talking about it afterwards. The same applies for groups where hesitancy towards partner work is too strong.

The inner process of sound-guided trance follows a principle which corresponds with the scheme of trance pattern developed by Erickson and Rossi (1989). Strobel transferred this to the sound trance and added phase VI. He differentiates the phases as follows:

- *Phase I: focus of attention*
  In the beginning, the patient's attention is directed towards his own body and inner experiencing by means of some introductory sentences. When the sound begins, it captures the attention
- *Phase II: Invalidation of the common frame of reference*
  Through the unusual monotony of the sound, the normal frame of reference is invalidated
- *Phase II and IV: unconscious search for new experiences and unconscious process*
  The specific sound quality (the energetic sound archetype) triggers a search for new inner experiences in phase 3 and an autonomous process in phase 4. The sound archetype takes on the nondirective suggestions in a nonverbal manner and activates personal associations, images, etc.
- *Phase V: hypnotic reaction*
  As a result of the sound induced processes, the known trance-phenomena such as visions, age regression, modification of time, etc. appear automatically
- *Phase VI: Trance withdrawal*
  The withdrawal is either done by ending the sound stimulation and uttering verbal withdrawal suggestions or by a targeted change of the sound (as an example, if the homogenous sound of the monochord is changed into melodic phases of the sound scale, the patient is brought back to daily reality)

Strobel likes to integrate body-oriented methods. By integrating the body level, he supports the patient's ability of perception and trance, and advances or intensifies, as the case may be, the therapeutic process through different body postures, touching, with the help of different breathing techniques or movement patterns (including dance) through sensual expression, or even through active rhythmic music making or music sessions.

The effectiveness from an in-depth psychological viewpoint

"In psychotherapy, the trance induced, designed and guided by sound has two aims: on the one hand, the modified state of consciousness is used for regression of experience in order to make suppressed traumatic topics or covered up positive experiences conscious and thus resolvable. On the other hand, on an energetic or symbolic level the sound opens doors to new, as yet undiscovered realms of experience. This can bring stagnating development back into movement and support growth (Strobel 1999, 135).

a) Analysis of the disorder

As outlined above, monochrome sounds function as a means of uncovering in the sense of a life-activating dissociation of suppressed contents from the unconscious when unlimited access to redeemed form of the sound archetype is hindered. When the sound is used in this form it is a deeply (psycho-) analytical instrument. There is no danger that the conflicts and problematic areas will be "covered up" by music. On the contrary: the sound uncovers them and thus contributes by doing its analytical work. Under "analysis", Strobel understands (ibid.) in this context not intellectual research and fragmentation, but rather intensive experience and resolution (lysis) of suppressed contents which, not uncommonly, lead to a dissolution (analysis) of blocked energies via catharsis. Sound-guided trance enables the patient to perform an experience-oriented self research in which biographic material is not remembered or reconstructed but rather re-lived and "re-souled". Therefore, this method – different from classical psychoanalysis – functions largely without interpretation since the experience mostly appears convincing in its own right and is self-explanatory. However, in many cases an additional verbal working through of the experience following the sound trance assists in complete integration of the experience. The meaning of the experience can be better understood, and thus be anchored (and able to be remembered) in the normal wake-consciousness, and become useable in everyday life.

Strobel (1988) discovered that sometimes even in a single session, through the energetic quality of one and the same sound, different experiences from different periods of life, which can all be attributed to one single underlying theme (according to the sound archetype), can be fetched back into consciousness. His supposition was that life experiences from different times are apparently recorded, or at least can be recalled according to archetypal themes. He then found these results asserted in Grof's concept of COEX systems (= systems of condensed experience): these systems contain condensed experience (as well as memories and linked fantasies) from differing phases of life with one common denominator consisting of analogue patterns. They can lie respectively in a strong emotional meaning or intensive physical awareness of the same quality, or in another important element (Grof 1983). In this sense, the sound-guided trance allows different (traumatic) experiences of *one* COEX system to be reanimated and resolved. With the help of the sound, the appropriate time regression can appear by itself (spontaneously) which in verbal hypnotherapy has to be done by corresponding suggestions. Put simply, it is as though the sound poses a question which asks: "What are the experiences you have had in your life time regarding *this topic*?" When, during the treatment process, one stays with one sound archetype for a certain reason, it will keep posing this question until all the experiences modifying its underlying theme are brought to light. Therein lies the specific form of "working through" by means of the sound archetypes by which, in an ideal case, the specific theme will be redeemed. In order to clarify this using an example, the patient, upon hearing the sound of the drum beat in the heart meter, experiences a feeling of unconditional acceptance: "I am okay and loved because I exist."

b) Transference and relationship

Strobel (1992, 115f) also observed the phenomena described under the vantage point of transference and relationship. From this point of view, the sounds present themselves as objects of transference. The drum heart meter described above, for example, has many faces on the transference levels. At one time, it embodies the footsteps of the strict father who suppresses his son's wildness and aggression; another time it stands for the jealous mother and her begrudging attitude towards her daughter's creativity; or it becomes a crib which swings back and forth, not in a loving manner but rather factually mechanical, almost violently. It can be strict, demanding achievement, or even at a (slower) frequency of 50/min become a mercilessly rushing booster. It is only when the transference to the drum is resolved that the patient can build an (actual) relationship with the sound archetype beyond the projection and then, in the case of the drum, can experience a feeling of unconditional acceptance.

Differing from psychoanalysis, the therapist uses the sounds to expand the area of projection of his own person and adds the varying and characteristically structured projection areas (archetypal themes) of the sounds. In addition, the power of the sounds to activate experience offers the patient a targeted stimulation in order to bring unconscious conflicts to the surface of consciousness so that he can enter new realms of vibrancy and resonance.

In a very impressive example, Strobel (1999, 137 f) emphasizes the relationship between transference onto the sound of the drum and the relationship to the sound archetype: A woman in her late forties who rejected her physicality and femininity experienced the following at the sound of the drum: "I am standing outside. I am completely naked. I am a young girl. I am standing in a meadow surrounded by the wonders of nature. I am on my own." A hint of sadness appears on her face. "I am all alone surrounded by nature, there is no one else near or far. "I ask her what she wishes for. "It would be nice if there were more people, just like me. Now I see a procession approaching in the distance close to the hill. I think I need to hide so they don't see me the way I am. They are Catholics. They judge and despise me for being naked. It's immoral." I ask her if the sound of the drum is telling her that her natural nakedness is immoral. "That's strange, it says exactly two things. One beat keeps saying "yuck, that's immoral", the next beat comes from a different, from an archaic level and says "nakedness is something completely natural and self-evident". But then there is the other beat again that says "yuck", but I think that's my mother's voice."

Last but not least, therapy is always concerned with overcoming transference; this is nothing but a cleaning of perception from all emotional and mental preconceptions, from wrong convictions and associations. The aim is for the patient to be able to clear his perception from experiences and projections in order for to be able to enter into clear, authentic and real relationships (with the therapist, the sound archetype, with other people, with life). He thus reaches a higher level of consciousness.

When a patient has reached this stage, he can also profit from the fact that the sounds beyond the transference possibilities also expand the relationship spectrum to the therapist. This is helpful and essential for those patients who need a real therapeutic relationship level in order to become healthy again. For a better understanding, Strobel (1992, 116) exemplifies the expansion of the relationship possibility on the symbol level as follows: "A therapist playing the monochord actually does resemble a nourishing mother; with the drum he "plays" the role of the unconditionally accepting parents; at the gong he unites in himself the roles of midwife and obstetrician; with the didgeridoo he admits to sensuality and sexuality; and when he rubs the singing bowl he becomes a mediator of transcendental power."

c) New, healing experience

As just explained, the archetypal quality of sound allows access to 'good' and healing experiences after the traumatizing previous experiences have been resuscitated and resolved. These good and healing experiences were either hidden or non-existent. In the case of the latter, the sound offers the opportunity for a corrective or ripening new experience on a symbolic or energetic level respectively. Sometimes, the 'good' experiences were segregated (to protect them from the patient's destructive sides). The aim is to bring the 'positive' and 'negative' sides in contact with one another.

"The sound-guided trance can, however, convey totally new experiences. The enormously powerful effect of the sounds, in addition to the analytical effect, is enhanced by the extension of the repertoire of existing resources by means of catching up on missing qualities of experience. Often, it is those experiences beyond analysis which enable what Balint (1970) calls the new start. Erickson (Erickson & Rossi 1989, 527 ff) also knew that making use of existing resources is not enough when a patient lacks certain life experiences. In this case, it is the therapist's task to deliver substitutes in some form or other. This can be done quite elegantly in many different ways by using sounds." Strobel (1999, 136).

Functionality from a shamanic viewpoint

The relationship of the sound-guided trance and shamanism cannot be denied, as pointed out at the beginning of this text. On the one hand, this is where it has its roots, on the other hand sound-guided trance fulfills all criteria of a shamanic method according to the definition of Uccusic (1991) (cp. Strobel 1999, 138). This is mainly because the healing process essentially takes place on a level of "non-day-to-day reality".

Strobel draws the following parallel: the simple shamanic understanding of health and sickness (the shamanic psychopathology) is reduced to the concept that a person becomes ill either because he has too much of something inside (i. e. a foreign substance or body, a miasma, an "intruder" – or because he is lacking something (useful) – for example energy, emotions, lost or segregated parts of the soul. Whilst in the first case something has to be extracted and removed from the sick person, in the second whatever is missing needs to be replaced. For the following reasons sound guided trance is a shamanic healing method: on the one hand, the work has to do with bringing into consciousness and resolving negative 'energies'. These 'bad ghosts' are traumatic experiences, hindering convictions, energetic blockades. On the other hand, new positive qualities of experience are added via corrected new experiences: these can be healing experiences, for example being held, supported and loved, positive convictions, the integration of segregated emotions or parts of one's personality, access to the free flow of life energy, etc.

Similar to the way the shaman, as a powerful personality, works with magical objects, (their functionality is drawn from an energetic charging and their ritualistic use), the therapist using sound trance must have the intention to heal, before the nonverbal code of the sounds can become a "magical" cure, and the setting a ritual framework for action. The sounds thus represent symbols for communication which consist "not only of the scientifically measurable physical properties of sound, but also of the 'inner psychic power' of the person treating" (Strobel 1999, 140). The healing and inner psychic power of the 'magical' power of the sounds therefore lies in the interaction of the physical effect of the sound in conjunction with the conviction of the therapist. Strobel made the observation that knowledge about the meaning of the sounds and their continuous implementation has, in the course of years, strengthened the circumscribed valence of the sounds. He interprets the increase in their effect – similar to the increasing infusion of power into a shamanic object of power – as a result of a charging with a specific "bio-energy" due to its consequent function and use. If the therapist working in such a manner is prepared to use this powerful remedy responsibly (and not manipulatively in the negative sense of the word) and as an instrument of healing, then one can really call him a shaman of the new age.

"If one compares the therapeutic undertaking [of the sound trance] with a modern expedition, then the setting represents the vehicle, the monotony of the sound is the fuel and the sound timbre of the instruments is the direction or the country in which the journey is going. The undertaking is only realized through consciousness and the qualities of the driver (therapist) who is centered on the intention to reach the country" (ibid.)

The transpersonal dimension of sound archetypes

A truly remarkable quality of the monotonous sounds seems to be the tendency to transport us human beings into those transpersonal depth levels of consciousness in which we have contact with our spiritual dimension – whether we are open towards this or not. When working more intensively with this method – whether as therapist or as client – one cannot avoid confronting this topic sooner or later. Due to the complex experiences he had with sounds, Strobel himself was confronted with this elemental level of human existence, which resulted in a process of analysis lasting several years. This also included the question of whether the topic of transcendence is allowed to, can, should or even must have a place in therapy. He eventually made this area a focus of his personal interest as well as his therapeutic work. Eventually he came to the conclusion that without the inclusion of this dimension there can be no in-depth healing because in the end the source of illness is rooted in being separated from one's own godly nature and oneness.

The insights Strobel gained from his work with sounds he first saw confirmed in the concepts and results of 'transpersonal psychology', established by Ken Wilber[9] and Stanislav Grof[10] who grasped the areas of consciousness to a far greater extent than the traditional concepts of depth psychology. Nearly the same depth of experience that Grof described in the use of the psycholytic drug LSD, a much more massive substance (due to its chemical nature), can be had in sound trance (harmless in comparison). Grof defines the area of transpersonal experience as "...the experiential extension or expansion of consciousness surpassing the normal limits of the I, perceived as body as well as the limits of space and time" (Grof 1985, 64). Without the theoretical background of transpersonal psychology, many experiences had during work with modified states of wake-consciousness and thus with the method of sound-guided trance can not be permeated, sounded and understood.

9 Ken Wilber has combined several different approaches of western and eastern philosophy. Out of this synthesis, he developed a spectrum model of the human consciousness, which subdivides the consciousness into several layers of which we only recognize parts.

10 The theoretical framework of traditional psychoanalysis seemed too confined to Grof, due to his extensive therapeutic experiences with LSD, Thus, he developed a new model of the human psyche. This cartography or 'map of inner area' of the human psyche can be understood as an extended depth-psychological concept of the unconscious. In addition to the analytical-biographic level and the postnatal phases of psychic development, it includes pre- and perinatal. as well as transpersonal areas, as psychodynamic sources in its concept.

In the meantime Strobel has gone a step further and made the link of self-experience or therapy and spirituality a focus of his work. He combined psychoanalysis, depth-psychology, humanistic and transpersonal psychology as well as methods of different body therapies with the sound-guided trance, and integrated these into a solid spiritual concept of the world and humanity. He has offered further education in this method for over 10 years. This development could only take place as a result of his thirst for knowledge and open attitude during the research of sound archetypes.

Language is limiting, and barely able to express to what depths the soul can be reached when experiencing monochrome sounds. Nor can it express by what means this happens. In any case, by experiencing these particular sounds, one embarks on an intensive and also adventurous journey into one's own seemingly inscrutable inner self, into maybe known and unknown new areas of the soul. Its richness, otherwise experienced in dreams and poetry, appears and is made livable, perceptible and comprehensible; in its painful dimension as well as in its capability for ecstatic bliss. It is possible to experience a never before known quietness and inner peace, a being touched so deeply, that one really has the feeling that the true self is being sounded out, brought into the world and to a completeness which we might have always craved after, but which cannot be only of a worldly nature.

The difficulty of this article in expressing in words the spectrum and potential of the sound archetypes and their functionality within the receptive music therapy leads me to quote, in closing, Wolfgang Schroeder who remarked that one can "... capture the real dimension of this form of music therapy only by experiencing it..." (Schroeder 1999, preface).

Acknowledgement

The author would like to thank Nicola Ahrens for the translation.

CH. 11: EEG BRAINMAPPING OF TRANCE STATES INDUCED BY MONOCHORD AND RITUAL BODY POSTURES IN A RITUALISTIC SETTING

JÖRG FACHNER, SABINE RITTNER

Introduction

Work with trance-inducing sounds has become an intrinsic part of receptive music therapy in practice. Therapeutically intended altered states of consciousness enable an intensification of intrinsic perception, a weakening of psychic barriers of everyday-life consciousness, a more open association and imagination (Aldridge & Fachner 2006; Rittner & Hess 1996).

At the beginning of the eighties, some experienced music therapists in Germany perceived a growing interest in the effects of music from outside Europe and started experimenting with trance-inducing effects of monochromatic sounds of monochord, gong, dijeridoo, sound bowls etc., developing individual empirical concepts (Bossinger & Hess1993; Hess & Rittner 1996a; Oelmann 1993; Rittner & Hess 1996; Strobel 1988, 1994; Timmermann 1983, 1996). These first approaches were revised, further developed and also reviewed critically (Hartogh 2001; Hess 1999; Jungaberle 2003; Rittner & Jungaberle 2002; Zeuch 1999). Although the brain plays a decisive role in the experience of trance states, there is an astonishing lack of music therapy research into psycho-physiological aspects of sound-induced trance.

We would like to present an excerpt from an analysis of two trance inductions, i. e. one in recumbent position on a resounding body monochord (Rittner 1997) and one "ritual body posture" according to Felicitas Goodman (1989, 1992) accompanied by fast rattling sounds. The whole pilot study analysed four different methods of sound trance in a multi-perspective approach. The research design comprised visual and quantitative evaluations of a spontaneous EEG as well as psychometric measurements ("questionnaire on extraordinary states of consciousness" 5D-ABZ by Dittrich, Lamparter and Maurer (2002) and "Phenomenology of Consciousness Inventory" (PCI) by Pekala (1991a, 1991b). In addition we did a qualitative, content-analytical evaluation of written reports by participants on their experience.

This article presents the EEG evaluation of two induction methods. An extended electronic journal article (Fachner & Rittner, 2004) containing the coloured EEG brainmaps and audiovisual material can be accessed from the March 2004 issue available at http://www.musictherapytoday.com. In German it is available as an online article (Rittner & Fachner 2004) of the 'Musiktherapeutische Umschau' at http://www.musiktherapie.de/index.php?id=193.

EEG

The electroencephalogram (EEG), discovered by Berger in 1929, has lost none of its fascination (Berger 1991). Positron emissions tomography (PET), functional magnet resonance tomography (fMRT) and other procedures produce highly soluble images of the living brain; but the EEG with its temporal exactness is an ideal instrument to measure electrical processes in the brain, especially when listening to music. In addition, an EEG brainmapper provides a map of current intensities and wave speeds. Topographical presentations of main frequency ranges permit conclusions on functional interactions of brain regions and their levels of activity (Maurer 1989). Slow and large high-amplitude waves (Delta and Theta) e. g. are predominant in sleep, while in states of high concentration and alertness fast waves with small amplitudes (Beta) are dominant. Depending on vigilance and activity, there are various combinations of different waves. The Alpha-frequency band (8–12 Hz), the waves of which emerge when closing one's eyes, is discussed as a mediator and indicator between the high and low frequencies of the EEG, between the vigilant states of waking and sleeping (Basar *et al.* 1997; Schwendtner-Berlin *et al.* 1995).

Body Monochord

The body monochord is based on the design of the monochord invented about 15 years ago as a musical instrument for therapy purposes. It has the form of a double-walled wooden stretcher, with 26 strings of equal length and exactly the same tuning on the underside, so that a person lying on the instrument with eyes closed may perceive sound with the entire body, via skin, bones, vibration of body liquids, and auditory sense. Based on the keynote a, various "sound clouds" with overtones may be produced depending on the type of playing.

Ritual body posture with rattle induction

Primarily, the method of "ritual body posture and ecstatic trance"® is not so much a western music therapy procedure but rather an approach from anthropological research providing access to altered states of consciousness, where sound is used as an essential element of trance induction (see also Aldridge & Fachner, 2006; Rouget, 1985). An integration of this method into the clinical practice of music therapy and psychotherapy has turned out to be highly successful (see also Risch *et al.* 2001; Rittner & Jungaberle 2002).

A common factor of "ritual body postures" – as they are called by the anthropologist Felicitas Goodman– they are up to 32.000 years old – is that as a rule they are perceived as a considerable effort. In combination with the sounds of a rattle or frame drum of approximately 210 bpm (beats per minute) they produce a spontaneous burst of energy in the body. This allows inducing a controllable hallucinatory experience in the subject on all levels of perception (vision, auditory sense etc.).

The members of our investigation group assumed a specific sitting body posture to which they were not accustomed; Goodman studied this posture entitled "olmecic prince" (see Goodman 1989, 158–161; Gore 1996, 170–174). This posture was maintained for 15 minutes, accompanied by the rhythmic high-frequency sound of two calabash rattles, beaten with 210 bpm.

Fig. 1: Archaeological artefact of the so-called "olmecic prince" (location of find Tabasco/ Mexico, 1100–600 B. C., Source: Gore 1996: 170).

Fig. 2: Test person Tom in the body posture of the "olmecic prince"

Trance and EEG

The term "trance" (from lat. transire, change over to) has been defined in various, sometimes contradictory ways in literature (Fachner 2006; Meszaros *et al.* 2002; Pekala & Kumar 2000; Rittner 1999; Rouget 1985). We have used it here as a generic term for *"various physical-mental alterations that may occur in persons in altered states of consciousness independent of the cultural setting. Stimulus, techniques and ritual that induce and structure a trance depend on the socio-cultural context."*

(Hess & Rittner 1996b, 395). No EEG analyses on trance experience on the body monochord were found so far. Studies on DC-EEG and ritual body posture were published by Guttmann (1990, 1992, 1992).

Available studies on trance and pertinent alterations in the EEG did not focus on music and trance but reviewed individual differences in trance experiences between a variety of mainly verbal trance inductions (De Benedittis & Sironi 1985; Jaffe & Toon 1980; Meszaros *et al.* 2002; Oohashi *et al.* 2002; Park *et al.* 2002; Sabourin *et al.* 1990). It is interesting to note that more recent studies by Meszaros, Park and Oohashi come closer to the authentic situation, i. e. trance induction in situ, in their research design.

The question whether trance is a temporary state or a specific quality in persons addresses the state-trait discussion in psychology and has not been answered so far (see Meszaros *et al.* 2002, 500). Most studies assume differences in susceptibility to hypnosis, and subjects were psychometrically differentiated at the beginning. Sabourin e. g. compared 12 persons with high and 12 with low susceptibility to hypnosis respectively. At rest as well as under hypnosis, persons with high susceptibility to hypnosis had higher Theta amplitudes compared to persons with low susceptibility (Sabourin *et al.* 1990). For an overview and discussion on the above-mentioned studies see Fachner (2006).

Aims of the study

For the purpose of this study we assume that a specific state of consciousness may be induced and that the characteristics emerging in the EEG may be differentiated.

> *"In musical psychotherapy with sound trance, music (…) is effective in two directions: 1. Physiologically stirring (ergotropic) towards ecstasy by intensified rhythm in the field of perception (…) or 2. Physically calming and internalizing (trophotropic) towards enstasis with reduced field of perception and focussing via monochromatic sounds"* (Hess & Rittner 1996b, 401).

Ergotropic trance (*ecstasis*) in this context, in the sense of Fischer's mapping (Fischer 1971, 1976; Fischer 1998), means an alert, non-contemplative, wide-awake altered state of consciousness.

> Fischer says: *"The mapping follows along two continua: the perceptive-hallucinatory continuum of increasing central-nervous (ergotropic) excitement, and the perceptive-meditative continuum of increasing (trophotropic) damping."* (Fischer1998). *"Along the two continua, the sensory/motoric ratio increases. This means: the further you go along one continuum, the less will it be possible to verify the sensory element through random motoricity."* (ibid. 51)

Accordingly, a trophotropic trance is characterized by a rather relaxed, contemplative, apparently sleepy state, and also by a rather inhibited movement profile, and reduced reaction and willingness to perform (*enstasis*).

This study compares a presumably trophotropic induction (body monochord) with a presumably ergotropic induction (ritual body posture with rattling) in two test persons.

The EEG was expected to show differences of a trophotropic state via EEG synchronization, i. e. via deceleration of the main frequencies and increase of slower wave ranges: Delta from 0.3–4 Hz, Theta from 4–8 Hz and lower Alpha frequencies of 8–10 Hz (compare David *et al.* 1983; Schwendtner-Berlin *et al.* 1995).

Ergotropic states were expected to show in an EEG desynchronization and dominance of high-frequency waves (upper Alpha waves from 10–12 Hz, Beta-I from 12–16 Hz, and Beta II from 16–30 Hz).

Our research questions:

1. Are there intra-individual alterations in the topographical spontaneous EEG compared to undisturbed rest?
2. Which inter-individual differences or common factors may be detected between the two test persons?
3. Does our study reveal an increase in Theta waves in persons highly susceptible to hypnosis?

Research Methods

Topographical alterations of brain activities in two test persons were measured in a group setting with a topographical quantitative EEG brainmapping. Using a pre/post design, we compared artefact-free means of undisturbed rest (baseline state) with sound trance phases (altered state) induced by the body monochord or the ritual body posture with rattling.

Qualitative aspects of set and setting in this electrophysiological study

It is a well-known difficulty in physiological measurements that movements or activities in the course of a therapy may interfere with the precision of measurement data. EEG brainmapping requires a limitation to receptive sound perception with little movement. Ideally, the test persons were to be recumbent or sitting still in order to avoid movement artefacts in measurement results. The mobile NeuroScience BrainImager® used here was designed for EEG on intensive wards where reliable data collection is essential. Galvanic current separation and filter systems permit the recording of a solid EEG signal.

Measurements were taken in a therapy group setting (N=10). We attached specific importance to measurements being made in the ritual setting of a group well known to the test persons. Unlike an isolated laboratory situation, a group setting and familiarity with the experience will ensure that supportive socio-physiological factors influence the sound-induced trance experience for all participants (naturalistic design).

Most attempts to locate practical music therapy in a laboratory setting impair the authenticity of the situation. The documentation of significant moments in therapy on recording appliances in particular demands a sensitive approach. In the realization of such a qualitative electrophysiology study (see Fachner, 2004) the measuring instruments must be adjusted as close as possible to every-day practice in order to generate explorative data. Consequently, we collect our data in the immediate therapy situation and not under lab conditions. On the basis of such explorative data collection, later a test concept may be designed to review the tendencies revealed in exploration in a laboratory experiment under ideal technical conditions. Details and discussion may be obtained in Fachner (2001, 2004), Fachner and Rittner (2004) and Burgess & Gruzelier (1997).

Test persons

For this pilot study we selected volunteers with trance experience who were acquainted with the induction methods. The intention was to ensure a high degree of familiarity with the ritual setting and as little sensitivity as possible to the research situation. We focus mainly on the results for two test persons (TP), out of ten participants in total (male TP 1: Tom, female TP 2: Angelika).

Study design

After each of the four trance inductions, the test persons reported their experience in a written journal from which we quote. Two turns were performed, with an interval in between; each time a test person respectively was connected to the mobile brain imager in the group setting. Tom came first, Angelika in the second turn.

We examined a total of four different, tested, receptive music therapy procedures, the trance-inducing effects of which on the participants were measured and compared in the following order:

1. body monochord; designed by H. P. Klein (see Rittner 1997)
2. singing of monochromatic vocal sounds (see Rittner 1998)
3. Peruvian Whistling Vessels; old Peruvian whistles, traditional according to Statnekov (2003)
4. ritual body posture with rattle induction (according to Goodman 1989, 1992).

Results

Susceptibility to hypnosis

The PCI test that quantifies the occurrence of characteristic structures of altered states of consciousness via 12 main dimensions and 14 subscales is a method to determine retrospectively an individual's degree of hypnotic susceptibility (Pekala 1991a, 1991b). The hypnoidal score indicates in how far the experience of a situation resembles the experience of highly suggestible persons during hypnotic induction. The score for Tom on the integrated "Predicted Harvard Group Scale" (pHGS) shows him as "moderately hypnotizable" with 6,09, while Angelika may be termed "highly hypnotizable" with 7,78 points.

Body monochord

For the rest EEG (baseline) and the subsequent sound EEG (altered state), the test persons were placed with their backs on the body monochord, with a cap on their head containing 28 electrodes, from which cables transferred the data to the brainmapping computer next door.

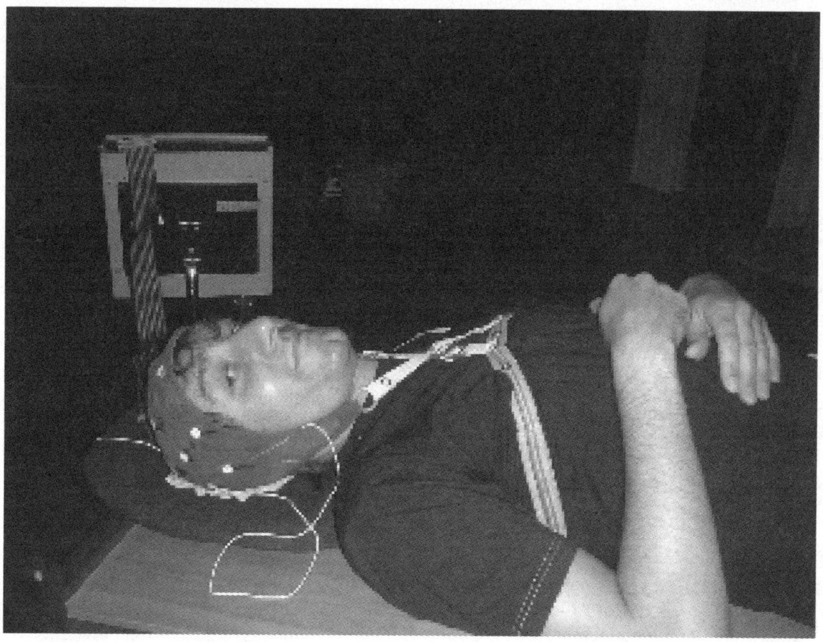

Fig. 3: Test person Tom lying on the body monochord

Neuropsychological functions

Both halves of the brain can be divided into a frontal and a posterior half by the central fissure in the middle. The functions of the two frontal “quarters” may be generally be described as motoric, intentional, planning, and as the hypothetic effective location of the “self”. The two posterior “quarters” have primarily sensory and receptive functions, are in charge of alertness-related processes and visual-spatial orientation. Details on functional correlations of brain regions may be followed up in the pertinent literature, i. e. by Kolb & Whishaw (1996).

EEG alterations TP 1 (Tom)

Compared to rest, the monochord derivation for Tom showed a decrease of the frontal Delta waves and parietal Theta and Alpha and Beta II waves. However, the fast Beta-II frequencies (16–30Hz) showed an increase in the frontal regions. Accordingly, the t-test comparison between rest and monochord revealed highly significant ($p<0.001$) differences on the Beta II frequency band from frontal to Gyrus Praecentralis.

The spectral band presenting the dominant peak frequencies and changes in frequency speeds showed an advancing desynchronization (increase of frequency speed) compared to rest.

While Theta and low Alpha frequencies were observed in frontal regions at rest, the monochord phase was characterized by the onset of a desynchronization, with a dominance of medium and high Alpha frequencies. This change in frontal frequency speeds was highly significant.

EEG changes TP 2 (Angelika)

In the case of Angelika, a decrease of Theta waves in temporal and frontal regions occurred compared to rest, while Alpha and Beta frequencies increased in parietal regions. In contrast to Tom a synchronization of the EEG to the frontal regions was recognizable in the spectral band during the monochord phase.

Changes were generally significant on the Alpha band, however not in frontal regions on the Theta band. Moreover, highly significant changes occurred in occipital regions on both Beta bands.

Ritual body posture with rattle induction

EEG changes TP 1 (Tom)

With the exception of the amplitude increase on the Beta II and the Alpha band, the amplitude mapping for Tom shows an increase of Theta and Beta I as well as a left-hemispheric and occipital desynchronization in the spectral band. The significance mapping for Tom also resembles that for Angelika.

EEG changes TP 2 (Angelika)

Compared to rest, the ritual body posture in Angelika combined with rattling reveals an increase of Theta waves from prefrontal and frontal and parietal-occipital along the vertex. Moreover, Alpha increases are to be found on the right, temporal-occipital and parietal. The Beta bands show distinct increases in parietal-occipital regions. The spectral band also represents a clearly visible increase in left-hemispheric frequency speeds.

In significance mapping, the contrast to rest is represented in highly significant alterations on the spectral, Beta I + II and the Alpha band.

Discussion

EEG correlate of the monochord experience

Both test persons showed an increase in Beta waves and a decrease in Theta waves during the monochord phase.

Diminutions in Theta waves, specifically in temporal regions (where primary auditory centres are located), while subjects were listening to music, were also found in a further study using this topographical EEG method. Fachner (2002) described this effect in a comparison of rest and music. Measurements with a direct-voltage EEG also revealed decreases in temporal regions (Altenmüller & Beisteiner, 1996; David *et al.*, 1969). Fachner found in his study with the NeuroScience BrainImager® that, in addition, the activity in the temporal regions is further dampened after consumption of a psychoactive substance (Cannabis). While the EEG signature of the substance was recognizable in synchronisation and Alpha wave increase, this study appears to show that reaction to trance induction – in the case of the monochord in particular – is rather specific to the individual test person.

Despite growing physical relaxation, the desynchronisation and increase of high Beta frequencies compared to rest suggests an active visual imagination in the case of Tom (*"A cloud rises in me and through the back of my head pulls me up to great heights ... I am flying, surrounded by clouds ... thousands of houses in green and lilac on a slope ... a beautiful sight..."*). The simultaneous decrease of Theta waves suggests increasing physical-mental alertness and an intentionally controlled imagination. The test person Tom influences his rather ecstatic experience.

In contrast, Angelika's EEG tends towards synchronization, induced by the Alpha increases. For her, the recumbent position on the monochord appears to promote a more relaxed and sensual body experience (*"... in me this turning movement ... as if I hovered in this rotation ... there were patches of haze or drifting veils and far away an unearthly music ... a feeling of calmness, of being sheltered..."*).

She seems to "drift" into an enstatic experience, a contemplation and deep physical relaxation. This was most obvious in the t-test in the highly significant change of the Alpha frequency in the comparison of rest and trance. Accordingly, the trance phase EEG revealed an increase in Alpha waves. Crawford underlined the correlation between Theta activity, high suggestibility and a reaction of frontal and limbic regions. Function-related hippocampus and amygdala activities (in deeper layers of the central brain) suggest a complex pattern of facilitation and inhibition of neural interaction in the limbic system of persons highly suggestible to hypnosis (in Sabourin *et al.* 1990). Since our two subjects turned out to differ in their suggestibility to hypnosis as a test result, i. e. revealed differences in facilitation and inhibition, this seems to influence the experience regarding tendencies towards ecstatic or enstatic experience. For Angelika, the hypoid score of the pHGS indicated "highly hypnotizable" (see above); she reacts more in the sense of a trophotropic trance with increasing low-frequency waves, while Tom reacts in the sense of an ergotrophic trance with increasing high-frequency waves.

The personal written reports reflect the effects of the monochord on both test persons in similar, subjective descriptions of hovering states, visions of cloud-like forms and changes in the body feeling. *"My impression is that I drift through space lying on the monochord" is Tom's description.* Angelika: *"They were very slow, but even movements … as if I hovered in this rotating movement … a tremendous space in grey and white, through which veils were drifting".*

EEG correlates of ritual body posture with rattling

Reports on experience

How to describe the experience of a "ritual body posture with rattle induction"? Exemplary excerpts from written reports by Tom and Angelika serve as illustrations. Angelika saw and perceived herself as a "volcano" in trance:

> I see the streams of lava in orange-red seeping over the black earth. It is still happening extremely slowly but evenly. Then I can feel a large opening in my lower abdomen through which lava comes out of me, too. I see it seeping out of me, can feel it in a very sensual way, and at the same time I am lava myself. After a long interval I hear the rattles again. They sound like thundering stones. My hands become rocks, which I throw away. Rocks keep growing, and I keep hurtling them away. I am still the volcano. All this does not feel very alarming but powerful. Then the movements of hurtling stones and of streaming lava cease. I feel light emerging in front of me. Everything is perfectly still, I am immobile, too. I can see tiny green plants sprouting from my hands, can feel them coming out between my fingers. – I feel full of power and content." (Further details in: Rittner 2004)

Tom identifies with the archaeological artefact of the "olmecic prince":

> "As soon as the rattling starts, I start to drift. I see figures and objects in front of me. An altar made of stone, in the middle of jungle. The images are more what I feel than what I see. Something bright and yellow on the altar .. the brightness becomes a crown, like the head dress of the "olmecic prince". The crown becomes larger and brighter. I see the very tall olmecic figure sitting in front of the altar. Creepers climb up all over it ... the whole place is ... grown over with plants. A tall, upright serpent ... looks at me, in the foreground. This is a very powerful, "knowing" place ... I see the earth as a rotating globe in green and blue. I watch it for some time and then I think: "and this is why the earth moves!" – The rattling stops, far too soon, a pity. I feel "dazed" for a long time. I feel I have taken in a lot of knowledge... the key to essential questions..."

Experience gained in altered states of consciousness becomes apparent e. g. in changes in thinking, emotionality, perception of meaning and a feeling of something unutterable (Ludwig 1966). A known effect is improved memory of what has been perceived during the ritual body posture. The increase in Theta waves and highly significant changes on fast frequency bands observed in Angelika, in visual regions specifically, may represent a more active access to image-like structures, analogous to a dream experience. The images and insights perceived or remembered in trance through spontaneous emotional intuition ("*I still am the volcano. All this does not feel very alarming but powerful...*") are possibly reflected here in the increase of Theta waves in the limbic system and of Beta waves in visual regions.

In 1990, Guttmann was the first to demonstrate in studies with the direct-voltage EEG that in the ritual body posture with rattle induction and simultaneously with the occurrence of Theta waves in the EEG, there was an unusual increase of cortical negativation (DC potential) of 2000–3000 microvolt (Guttmann 1990, 319). This indicates an overactive state of the cerebral cortex and in spontaneous EEG would be evident in a dominance of Beta waves. Guttmann coined the term "paradoxical arousal" or "relaxed high tension" for this phenomenon.

Park *et al.* (2002) found changes in the EEG in the case of a Salpuri dancer in comparing rest, listening to music and memory (of a previous dance). Salpuri is a traditional dance performed by medicine men in Korea. In the phase of remembering an ecstatic trance state in the dance, frontal increases of low alpha frequencies (8–10Hz) were found as well as frontal-occipital Theta increases, compared to rest. In the comparison of rest and listening to a piece of pop music, there was a highly significant increase in the frequency of high Alpha frequencies (10–12.5 Hz) over the entire cortex. This may have indicated a difference between a primarily physical trance experience and the enjoyment felt in listening to music. 9.5 Hz was the identified peak frequency in rest and memory of dance, with an increase of amplitude energy in the memory of dance. The peak frequency rose to 10 Hz in the process of listening to music, and high Beta frequencies increased. Park supposes that the Salpuri dancer *"reaches the altered state of ecstatic trance through suppression of frontal cortex functions and activation of subcortical functions"* (Park *et al.* 2002, 961), i. e. that trance is characterized by Theta frequencies, the dominance of which in the EEG suggests such activation.

Beta changes

The increase in high Beta frequencies, while a subject listened to music reported by Park is also known from other studies on music perception. Walker (1977) reported increased right-lateral activity while listening to classical music; Behne et al. (1988) reported occipital increases; Petsche (1993) found increases in posterior right-lateral coherence, and Bruggenwerth reported music-related, emotion-specific decreases or increases of posterior Beta activity (Bruggenwerth *et al.*, 1994). According to Petsche (1994), the Beta frequency bands indicate differentiations of music-related cognitive activity.

The conspicuous reaction of the EEG in both trance inductions with an increase of high Beta waves (16–30Hz) seems to be a further indication of the influence of trance triggered by sounds. Beta frequencies indicate changes in emotional states. Isotani *et al.* (2001) explored hypnosis-induced states of relaxation and anxiety and discussed the conspicuous reactions with high Beta frequencies and their EEG signature in emotional states.

Meszaros *et al.* (2002) interpreted the EEG for hemispheric differences and described a primarily right-hemispheric, parieto-temporal EEG reaction of the Alpha and Beta band in persons highly susceptible to hypnosis; he concluded that in the "*mainly emotion-focussed hypnotherapies*" (the same, p. 511), as expected, right-hemispheric changes will be dominant. In his study, persons with high, medium and low susceptibility to hypnosis all experienced an altered state of consciousness while listening to music in a relaxed position in an easy chair. Significant differences in the "Altered State Index" were only found for the areas imagination/hallucination (compare the same, p. 510).

Consequently, the Beta changes we found for the monochord as well as for the ritual body posture seem to illustrate the emotional reactions produced by the ritual and the sounds, which in the case of Tom resulted in an anterior right-hemispheric, and for Angelika in a posterior left-hemispheric change. It has to be mentioned that the high muscle tension, which is part of the ritual body postures, especially here in the neck region, has surely an influence on beta frequency range. This can be monitored with an EMG as well and should necessarily be investigated in future research. Therefore the interpretation of the Beta range in occipital regions has to be regarded as a tendency.

Conclusions

Returning to the research questions stated at the beginning, we found inter- and intra individual differences in comparing rest and trance induction. In this study with two test persons, highly significant differences were found in the topographical EEG comparing rest and trance. The profile becomes irregular in the case of the monochord. The female subject recumbent on the monochord showed a more trophotropic trance, indicated by an increase in Alpha waves, while the male subject showed a desynchronization and an increase of Beta waves, which suggests a more ergotropic trance. The data available do not explain whether these findings suggest gender-specific or mood-dependent differences, or differences in susceptibility to hypnosis.

Moreover, the topographical EEG showed a distinct difference between rest and sound-induced activations. The temporal regions of both test persons revealed a decrease on the Theta band.

Both subjects, however, showed similar reactions in trance induction through ritual body posture accompanied by rattling sounds. In both cases, there was a simultaneous increase in low and high frequency waves of the Theta and the Beta band. This state, described by Guttmann as *paradoxical arousal*, appears to be a specific reaction to this method of trance induction rediscovered by Goodman. We confirmed for a ritual group setting what Guttmann et al. discovered in laboratory tests as early as 1990: an ecstatic trance induced by sound and body posture is characterized by a "relaxed high tension".

A possible answer to our question concerning Theta increases in easily hypnotizable persons was only visible in body posture; but in the monochord test we also found a tendency toward synchronization and increased low frequencies in the easily hypnotizable subject. Increases in Theta and Alpha waves during the trance phase reported by other authors were most pronounced in the ritual body posture.

These results represent only a very small part of the entire data evaluated and are of an explorative nature. The last measurement phase covers, as expected, influences of the three previous trance inductions via singing, monochord, and listening to and playing of old Peruvian whistles. An ergotropic trance may well be characterized by an increase in high-frequency waves, and a trophotropic trance by an increase of low-frequency waves. The ritual body posture with rattles seems to cover both forms of reactions. To show more then a tendency of the beta range in the posterior regions an EMG has to be recorded during the postures as well.

Contrary to the concern of suffering loss of control in altered states of consciousness, our repeated findings of high Beta II elements illustrate that self-control is maintained in these methods of sound-induced trance and may even give way to a highly concentrated hyper alertness in the sense of an ergotropic trance. This is confirmed by the participating test persons as well as by our test results. A welcome effect of our study would be to reduce the fears deeply rooted in our society for cultural, historical and political reasons that trance is equivalent to loss of control and susceptibility to manipulation (Rittner 1999).

Acknowledgement:

We thank Prof. Eduard David, M. D., director of the Centre of Electropathology, University Witten/Herdecke, and former Chair of the Institute of Physiology, University Witten/Herdecke, who made the NeuroScience BrainImager® available to us for the purpose of this study.
We thank Christina Wagner for the translation.

CH. 12: REGULATORY MUSIC THERAPY (RMT)

Milestones of a Conceptual Development

CHRISTOPH SCHWABE

Observation is such a wonderful thing,
Of which we know only so little
we turn fully to the outside,
but just when we engage in it most
things appear to go on within us
That have only longed
To be unobserved

– *Rainer Maria Rilke*

The concept of *Regulatory Music Therapy* has evolved over time. This process, beginning in the sixties and continuing until today, appears to demonstrate both the validity and flexibility of the concept. In this paper, I will briefly discuss crucial aspects of this development.

Starting Points

In 2003, the Leipzig University Hospital celebrated its 50th anniversary. This is the place where *Regulatory Music Therapy* was born. The beginnings of *Regulatory Music Therapy* were embedded in a context where an established psychotherapy structure had departed from the zeitgeist of the early fifties, a time when psychotherapy had been closely connected to orthodox Pawlowian reflex theory (Schwabe 2003). The new approach advocated a new understanding of the patient as an active partner, not as an object to be treated. Only by himself and by means of his own activity is he able to resolve conflicts and overcome physical and psychological symptoms. This conceptual change resulted in the development of a psychotherapy concept, which Christa Kohler, head of Psychotherapy at Leipzig University Hospital (East Germany), and her colleagues called "Communicative Psychotherapy" (Kohler 1968).

An important assumption underlying this concept is that psychosomatic disorders are multi-factorial in nature, with potential causes ranging from psychological to social and biological aspects. Impairment regarding these aspects can lead to disorders in early childhood as well as in other developmental stages. This psychotherapy approach addresses biographical as well as situational aspects depending on the chronicity of the disorder. It uses a coordinated and complex array of methods including single and group therapy with verbal and nonverbal modes of action. The fundamental aspect of treatment is social interaction, or encounter, between therapists and patients using varying means of communication. Within this methodological diversity, music therapy plays an important role, equal to that of other psychotherapies. This complex form of psychotherapy relies on continuous and sophisticated communication between all individuals involved in the treatment, including nurses.

Starting Points for Music Therapy

In Leipzig, music therapy was expected to serve the following psychotherapeutic functions:

- Activation of emotional reflection skills
- Activation of social interaction skills
- Broadening of awareness
- Broadening of aesthetic values, regarding both perception and enjoyment

In order to meet these needs it was important to develop methods that worked in both dyads as well as in groups. This resulted in the development of a methodic system of music therapy, first published in 1969 (Schwabe 1969). *Regulatory Music Therapy*, at first only used in dyads, was part of this system. From the beginning, daily therapeutical reality showed whether methods worked and how they should best be applied. This also pertained to music therapy. It meant that methods depend on their contexts of application and implementation and have to be modified accordingly. This also meant that methods are capable of change. More specifically, they have to be flexible in order to be effective. As methods always show tendencies toward differentiation, and consequently toward rigidity, one has to take care that they do not enter orthodox rigor:

The flexibility that I had developed in dealing with the method system was due to the situational context, namely the foundation of a new psychotherapy approach in Leipzig. Also important in this regard was the fact that different leading figures shaped the development of a psychotherapy approach in Leipzig over the years. The concept of music therapy, however, was developed by only one person, namely the author himself. This particularly relates to the seventies in the 20th century (Schwabe 2003; Haase, Schwabe 2003;).

An important starting point for the development of Regulatory Music Therapy was the so-called contemplation hour during which patients could listen to music in their rooms, offered at Leipzig University Hospital as early as the fifties. Patients were supposed to enter an emotional state that would facilitate self-reflection and were encouraged to write down their thoughts afterwards (Wendt 1958). So-called serious music, chosen by the head doctor, was used.

The starting point, thus, was not to encourage patients to relax but to contemplate. This is important because until today *Regulatory Music Therapy* for various reasons is repeatedly misinterpreted as a music therapeutical relaxation technique. Relaxation effects can indeed be expected due to the state of mind required by actions taking place in *Regulatory Music Therapy*. They are, in a modified version, also intended (see Schwabe 1991b), but are not the essential and direct aim of RMT.

The Action Approach

From the beginning, *Regulatory Music Therapy* was based on a perception-psychological working approach (Schwabe, Haase 1998). This means that the psychotherapeutic approach, the action principle (cf. causality principle, Schwabe 1983), centers on a therapeutically induced encouragement of self-awareness. Self-awareness also includes an awareness of the surrounding context and calls for the activation or reactivation of an inner openness for the present physical, mental and psychological reality as well as for biographically relevant, possibly repressed experiences, by which this can enter consciousness. In the concept of *Regulatory Music Therapy*, the awareness of experiences is closely connected to an exact verbalization of those awareness objects that enter consciousness in the specific situation. When patients describe these objects, it helps them to give shape to those experiences. This supports a therapeutic process of confrontation with neurotic aspects, particularly with the defence of threatening material. This process leads to an increasingly differentiated awareness and thus to confrontation with those pathologically relevant experiences, which, depending on the specific indication, have to be worked through in a successful psychotherapy.

The description of awareness material is the opposite of awareness interpretation, that is, interpretation as common in psychoanalysis. It also excludes fantasizing and speculating as well as overgeneralizations drawn from single awareness aspects. It is a lengthy process, which also enables patients to overcome awareness constraints, shortcomings, and biases. The therapeutic principle of "awareness encouragement" leads to a broadening of awareness experiences and consequently to a changed experiential situation. This also includes a discovery of those aspects and domains that we call resources (Schwabe, Stein 2000). This short description might illustrate the far-reaching opportunities resulting from therapeutic action based on a perception-psychological action approach.

Implementations

For reasons of space, I can only refer to some fundamental didactical aspects in this paper. For more detailed information, the reader is referred to Schwabe (1979, 1988, 1987; Schwabe, Röhrborn 1996).

In what I call an "action offer", the therapist tells the patient what he can expect when he enters *Regulatory Music Therapy* and what he is expected to do. At the beginning the patient should put him or herself in a comfortable physical position, engage in a free flow of awareness, and experience thoughts, feelings, the body, and the music If possible, this should be done without corrective mental efforts, in a state of acceptance. A period of deep breathing and stretching follows the end of music. Afterwards, a conversation is initiated, and the patient is encouraged to describe his or her awareness experiences. The therapist selects the session music based on therapy criteria (Haase, Schwabe 2003; Schwabe 2003; Schwabe, Röhrborn 1996). A group therapy session is enriching in this process because all group members listen to manifold descriptions while sharing their awareness experiences. During this process, the group becomes important as sort of an experiential community. Within this community, individuals can learn that the same musical piece can result in very different awareness experiences, as verbalized by the group members, and that awareness descriptions can even be contradictory. Thus, individuals can experience both unity as well as difference among different individuals, leading to broadening and enrichment of life experiences in general. Although in those groups dynamic processes do occur that should be monitored closely by the therapist, the therapeutic process does not aim to actively initiate and reflect on group processes. The aim is rather to encourage each group member and to use the groups' potential for the encouragement of each individual. The developmental process within *Regulatory Music Therapy* is stimulated and maintained by the principle of "practice" or training. Psychotherapy trains different things, foremost is "relaxation". Training generally has a rather derogative connotation, which I hold to be unjustified. In the case of *Regulatory Music Therapy*, the aim is to practice a state of awareness, which also can turn into a state of living. In this regard, *Regulatory Music Therapy* has a function comparable to meditation.

The Music

Hans Peter Reinecke once said, "When different people speak about 'music' they usually mean different things" (Reinecke 1974). This statement from an important and insightful music sociologist who was very important for the development of German music therapy has not lost its validity. The national and international music therapy scene illustrates this point well.

In our music therapeutic concept, we do not prefer any particular kind of music. We regard "music" as a specifically human way of action and expression that music therapy is able to use in various forms (Schwabe 1978; Schwabe 2003; Schwabe, Haase 1998; Schwabe, Stein 2000). In *Regulatory Music Therapy*, we use recorded music that can be played using technical equipment.

Music is not only a specific language (Reinecke 1974; Schwabe 1986) but also a mental object, a specific "other", which individuals can experience through their senses and minds and which they are also able to describe. This object reality also represents other realities. Because of its character, music creates emotional reactions in individuals, which can vary enormously depending on the character of the music and the listening situation. Within this aspect, music becomes a specific "other" in the regulatory awareness process, broadening the horizon of awareness beyond one's own self.

When a patient experiences music, the therapeutic intention is to change the situation where he first expects the music's emotional effects, into a situation of active encounter. Thus, how an individual relates to music is no longer characterized by passive expectations directed at the music but by a conscious creation of an inner relationship. This process of change can stand for other changes in subject and object relations, which do indeed occur during the music therapy process. Following from this, one can imagine that the music selected by the therapist bears an enormous importance in this process. The selection of music may not occur randomly or be dependent on the personal taste of the therapist. This a challenging task, which requires intense training. Such training should teach profound knowledge not only of the musical repertoire, but also of the functional characteristics of musical structures. The latter refers not to the functionality of music in a sense of "pharmacological" effectiveness (Schwabe 1979) but to the creation of favourable starting conditions, so that an active process can be initiated.

Concert music, often also called "classical music", composed during the last 250 years is particularly suitable. This huge collection of music, found approximately between the composers Benda and Lutoslawski is not only a source of riches for the patient; it also presents the serious problem of how to deal with these riches. It might be a consolation for every music therapist engaging not only in improvisation but also in the study of this field of music that he can rely on a life-long never-ending source that can deeply enrich his or her own life. The oeuvres created during this era of musical production, unique in the world's history, represent all dimensions of human experience in diverse and varying ways, mostly without extra-musical conventional constraints. And technical reproduction makes them directly available to us (Schwabe, Stein 2000).

Developmental Steps

Two different approaches of action were present in the beginning. One aimed at a cathartic-affective release of emotions, short-term in nature and directed at repressed areas of inner conflict. Based on this approach "Reactivating Individual Music Therapy" was developed

(Schwabe in Kohler 1968; Schwabe 1969, 1971, 1986). The other approach aims at an "harmonization of the whole person" (Schwabe in Kohler 1968, 74). In contrast to the first approach, it is more meditative and constitutes the starting point for *Regulatory Music Therapy*. From the beginning it's inherent character was one of practicing, aimed at achieving a state of observing calm. Based on this, the aspect of awareness encouragement became increasingly important. It was oriented toward a free flow of awareness between the awareness domains of cognition and emotion, body and music (Schwabe 1969). At the beginning of the seventies *Regulatory Music Therapy* was applied widely in group contexts, both in in-patient as well as out-patient psychotherapy settings, and soon became an important alternative to "Intended Dynamic Group Therapy" (Höck 1981), which was predominant in Eastern Germany at that time. This process was advanced by seminars organized by the division of music therapy within the scientific community, the Society for Medical Psychotherapy in the GDR. The division of music therapy is the precursor of the Eastern German music therapy association, the "German Music Therapy Association East" (DMVO e. V.), which today is a society for music therapists in East and West Germany with about 300 members.

In 1979, the book "*Regulatory Music Therapy*" was published. It discussed the methodological principles of *Regulatory Music Therapy* developed thus far. It also contained an extensive study of the effectiveness of these methods (Hauschild 1979). At the same time, first ideas on modified applications of *Regulatory Music Therapy* were published (Mederacke 1979, 1993; Schwabe 1979; Stein 1979). The publication of this first book not only raised interest in the music therapeutical concept but also stimulated concrete activities toward a greater differentiation of methodological principles. Important in this developmental step were Röhrborn, head of the Erlabrunn Psychotherapy Clinic, and his team of psychotherapists. This process resulted in a second edition of the book "*Regulatory Music Therapy*" published in 1987. An important aspect of this differentiation was related to didactical applications. In a nutshell, clear training steps were presented by which patients would be guided through the treatment process. In this stage, applications and implementations of *Regulatory Music Therapy* became increasingly oriented toward the treatment of patients with psychosomatic disorders, also focussing on a depth-psychology oriented therapy of defence disorders. In addition, this approach relied on specific treatment conditions, namely continuous treatment within a group with a sufficiently large number of patients with adequate indication (Schwabe, Röhrborn 1996).

At the beginning of the nineties, psychotherapy structures and the health care system as a whole changed dramatically in Eastern Germany due to political changes. These vast changes were not only existentially threatening but also destroyed well-established in- and out-patient psychotherapy structures. Music therapy, among other existing and established treatment structures, was no longer, or less frequently used as a result of newly implemented health care system rulings. Thus, the essential field of application of *Regulatory Music Therapy* was suddenly missing. Things were also changing in in-patient institutions where *Regulatory Music Therapy* had been one of the standard methods of treatment especially with regard to patient clientele. This resulted primarily from an inflationary increase of free practices so that in-patient institutions could no longer administer previous treatment combinations and processes. This resulted in a considerable decrease in the domain of application of *Regulatory Music Therapy*. In contrast, especially in social care, a previously neglected area, interest in music therapy increased notably.

Thus, the present music therapeutical repertoire of methods had to be adapted to the new situation. Based on the well-founded single methods of music therapy, a more flexible action concept had to be developed that preserved the essential action approaches and principles but could be more effectively applied. An important point of reference in the restructuring and further development of our music therapeutical concept was the "causality principle" first formulated in 1983 (Schwabe 1983). Based on consistent conceptualisation, this methodological model allowed us to formulate indication-specific music therapy action approaches for very different treatments without running the risk of eclecticism. This conceptual process resulted in the development of the so-called "Social Music Therapy" (Schwabe, Haase 1998).

The Present

We know today that the psychotherapy approach of *Regulatory Music Therapy* is suited to application in two different ways. On the one hand, it can address the Ego and its defence mechanisms. This approach resembles the depth-psychological approach advocated for instance by Röhrborn (1993, 1994, 1995) in the eighties. It aims at self-reflection and tries to render "conscious present defence mechanisms and repressed experiences" (Schwabe, Röhrborn 1996, 54). On the other hand, individuals can learn to perceive and experience music as a coherent object in *Regulatory Music Therapy* (Reinhardt, 2002). To encounter a stable reality, music, in the context of an awareness experience cautiously supported by the therapist can result in a "turning away from one's own lability" and, thus, to a "reduction of anxiety" (Reinhardt 2002). This approach aims at rendering defence mechanisms more flexible through integration of disrupted experiences and the development of more mature defence mechanisms (Reinhardt 2002). It is indicated for personality disorders, such as borderline personality disorder, and is in its nature behaviourally oriented.

The second approach shortly depicted here has applications that reach far beyond the group of personality disorders. The experiences we have made over the last years (Haase, Schwabe 2003; Schwabe, 2000, 2002, 2003) have shown us that this treatment approach is effective not only with regard to a variety of disorders but also regarding non-clinical disorders or behavioural problem within the context of social work and education. This closely relates to the concept of resource oriented psycho- and music therapy described in more detail elsewhere (Schwabe, Stein 2000).

Method versus Concept

Initially, the development of our music therapeutical concept was embedded in the development of a complex psychotherapy structure, which was, like music therapy, just beginning. This resulted in the development of music therapy methods as integrative components of a complex psychotherapy concept. In the second phase the unity of this psychotherapy approach dissolved (Schwabe 2003). This brought us to postulate our own music therapeutical ideas within a methodology of music therapy (Schwabe 1978, 1980, 1986). The intention was to create methods of music therapy that were more flexible and which could, to a certain degree, – function independently to other psychotherapy concepts. In the third phase, in the nineties, highly differentiated methods of music therapy were disentangled from their dependence on specific treatment conditions. In order to apply methods flexibly in complex settings and to relieve them from the burden of strict application criteria we had to realize and describe their fundamental characteristics and nature (Schwabe, Haase 1998). This meant a departure from a rigid methodological concept.

Thus, *Regulatory Music Therapy* with its awareness-oriented action approach can function effectively in manifold combinations and diagnostic constellations. It has freed itself from an exclusively depth-psychology oriented context, which had become too narrow and too specific. It has grown and developed, and can be applied equally effectively in other therapy contexts, such as behavioural or humanistic therapy.

Acknowledgement:

I would like to thank Claudia M. Haase for translating this paper.

CH. 13: DYADIC REGULATIVE MUSIC THERAPY

Experiences from a Psychotherapy Ward of a Hospital

HELMUT RÖHRBORN

Regulative Music Therapy (RMT) was originally developed by Christoph Schwabe as individual psychotherapy focused on relaxation. In the 70s it was developed as a group music therapy method. Here, I would like to refer to the first edition of the Monograph by Christoph Schwabe (1979). In this phase, the author got acquainted with the method and was able to use it, initially with the focus on relaxation, on a psychotherapy ward of a hospital without the possibility of pre-selecting patients. In the beginning, it was only used as group psychotherapy. RMT in open groups as an additional relaxation method was used with patients not suited for psychodynamic group psychotherapy in the form of Intended Dynamic Group Psychotherapy developed by Höck (Höck 1981). After proceeding to work with closed groups, it became evident that with the help of the method, defense mechanisms and psychogenetic contexts were touched very quickly. This led to the development of a group psychotherapy concept with a symptom-centered approach. Symptom-centered means that through the encouragement of awareness of body, mind, and the external object music, access to psychogenetic contexts was possible, and via perception of the life of symptoms to the original intrapsychic conflict (Röhrborn 1987). Even though it could not be explicitly defined in this way in early years, this access to unconscious and therefore blocked-off mental contents characterizes the method as psychodynamic.

1. Essence of RMT, Indication and the Erlabrunn Concept of Symptom-Oriented Group Psychotherapy

1.1. About the essence of RMT

The essence of the method of RMT consists of the encouragement of perception of body, mind, and acoustics, here especially the perception of the music as "eines spezifischen Gegenübers ..., zu dem Kontakt hergestellt werden kann"[1] (Schwabe 2003b, 18). The instruction to be with the perception of the music and the body without defending against emerging thoughts, feelings, moods, memories, images, but integrating them into awareness, is similar to the instruction in the technique of free association. Every perception evokes emotional and mental, thus cognitive-emotional

1 Translation: "a specific vis-à-vis ... with whom one can make contact"

reactions. Perception is defined here as becoming aware of bodily sensations, mental processes and acoustic phenomena. Those cognitive-emotional reactions are again to be understood as perceptions. If they have a defensive character, if they are formed by fears, by unwanted thoughts and memories, they evoke defensive behavior which prevents the perceiving person from turning towards himself in an unbiased way. That blocks the way as it were to experiencing intrapsychic contexts. Defense mechanisms then appear in certain intrapsychic behaviors towards perceptions, which can be named in the following training conversation. An extended description would go beyond the scope of this contribution. I would like to refer to the second edition of the book "Regulative Musiktherapie" by Christoph Schwabe (Schwabe 1987) and to the revised and extended third edition by the editors Schwabe & Röhrborn (1996).

1.2. The concept of developmental levels of the ability of perception

A step by step approach to the encouragement of perception in Regulative Music Therapy was clearly developed especially in work with closed groups.

1. Invitation to perceive/extend perception during the music (Levels of perception: – body – feelings – memories, thoughts – music, outside noises) "Horizontal perceiving"
2. Invitation to differentiate perception – more and more clear perception/grasping/describing of single perceptions and sections of perception "Depth perception"
3. Invitation to perceive emotional reactions to the perceived "Grasping of emotional-cognitive reactions"
4. Invitation to differentiate between accepted and non-accepted perceptions and to grasping of intrapsychic reactions, disturbances like flight, fight, enduring, distraction "Confrontation with behaviors that support the symptoms"
5. Invitation to closely observe/describe non-accepted perceptions or disturbances with the result of realization of accepted behavior "Seduction into stress-reducing approach with experiences of disturbance"
6. Invitation to consciously turn towards and open to the disturbance with the result of allowing and accepting stress and perceiving psychogenetic contexts "The time of harvest"

Fig. 1: 6 levels of realization in Regulative Music Therapy

At level 1, the patient gets acquainted with the exercise, which is giving oneself over to perceptions and trying to let the inner eye wander without leading interference. By describing the perceptions in the following training conversation, the diversity of the possibilities of perception becomes clear to the trainee, who develops sensitivity for himself through further training.

At level 2, the variety of differentiated perceptions becomes also clear in smaller areas through describing smaller sections of perception or single perceptions. By remembering and describing the perceived, it also becomes possible to remember and to name those perceptions, which can be understood as cognitive-emotional reactions to the perceived. Here it becomes clear that every perception evokes reactions that range from very subtle feelings like indifference, astonishment, worry, to fear, and succeeding memories and thoughts about the perceptions.

Especially when working at level 3, individual defenses against perceptions can be grasped. That happens via exactly remembering and describing the feeling and thought reactions to the perceived. In addition to being able to give oneself over to and to observe perceptions, here there are groups of inner behavior. They are 1. fight against a perception, 2. flight from perceived to other more desirable and seemingly less burdening perceptions, and 3. enduring, an anguished need to perceive, a martyr's attitude. Here, even the most different paradoxes become clear and can be experienced. The trainee experiences that the resisted and the feared become stronger and are fixated into consciousness. Those that can be observed without resistance and endurance can become less important again and recede into the background (level 4).

At level 5, the trainee is, as it were, seduced into stopping those defensive actions, into getting interested in the disturbing, the feared, the onerous. This is done through the invitation to turn towards those perceptions which were reacted to with fight, flight, or enduring. That can lead to the fact that by perceiving the fear, it diminishes, that ideas lead to prior resisted memories and contexts, and that intrapsychic conflicts like, for example, the contradiction between a wish for closeness and fear of closeness can be re-experienced. This in return leads to awareness of conflicting material which can be dealt with in further therapeutic conversations (level 6 as "the time of harvest").

1.3. Indications and forms of realization of RMT

It follows that the basic indication must consider the patient's attitude towards illness, which relates only to bodily aspects. Because of the patient's restricted ability to perceive bodily and psychological dynamics, he shows a lack of insight into his own psychogenesis. This is often found in people with psychosomatic disorders with ineffective processing of the illness, if massive but resisted fear bocks the pathway to the person's own body and mind.

Defencies of the perceptive faculties in situate-emotional and physical areas
Defencies of perceptive faculties are found especially and pronounced as main pathogenic factors in • Axis II-Disorders • basic hysteroid structure (in the sense of difficulties in tolerating frustration, attitude of ambition, persistence) • basic depressive structure or depressive symptoms (in the sense of introversion, inhibition – aggressive inhibition, inhibited aggression –, being fixated on the depressive way of experiencing) • marked hypochondrical or phobic fixation, experiencing illness in relation to organs • situate-emotional dependency of symptoms which is rather in the appearance (and not perceivable by the patient) • psychosomatic illnesses and disorders

Fig. 2: Indication for RMT

For these patients, namely those experiencing illness in relation to organs without insight of psychogenesis, the Erlabrunn Concept of Symptom-Oriented Psychotherapy was developed, which proved to be very effective (Schwabe & Röhrborn 1996). In this concept, RMT in closed groups as the main therapy method is combined with verbal group therapy, Concentration-Relaxation as developed by Wilda-Kiesel (1993), movement therapy, active group music therapy, and unspecific receptive individual music therapy (so called "evening contemplation"), and other therapies in a high therapeutic density.

The realization of the described concept of stepwise encouragement of perception succeeds especially well in closed groups using other therapeutic factors of group psychotherapy, but it is not limited to this group concept. In the beginning, we worked with semi-open groups. Whenever RMT is used as one therapeutic component in other therapeutic concepts, both the semi-open group and work in dyads are useful. Independent from all variations of realization depending on the environmental conditions and the variables of patients, it is important that every individual proceeds according to the concept of levels of realization. That means sensitization for physical sensations and mental contents, changing attitudes and intrapsychic behavior towards symptoms, onerous memories, thoughts, and feelings in the sense of accepting perception, toleration, and inner distancing. This attitude can lead to relaxation, reduction of symptoms, self-awareness, and problem-solving. For the therapists, the concept of levels of realization offers an orientation for the setting of goals and for the necessary steps or tasks in the therapy sessions. It is not to be realized in a schematic way, but as guidance for action, comparison, and encouragement. Comments of patients in the training conversation are compared with the goals of the level. Comments of therapists serve to realize those goals. In this context, many modifications of the method are possible (Schwabe 2000; Schwabe 2003b). One of these modifications is dyadic RMT.

2. The Development of Dyadic RMT within the Erlabrunn Psychotherapy

As mentioned above, RMT was originally developed as an individual therapy method, then it was used primarily in group psychotherapy, and taught in trainings. For the author, the necessity to use RMT as individual therapy in a hospital came rather incidentally. In 1983, a 60-year-old patient who in the past had had several cardiac arrests with reanimations –thus clinically dead – was admitted into the hospital. On the surface, there was a fixation of awareness on his heart and the related constant fear of dying. It was almost impossible for him to leave his apartment. Because of his fears, he was unable to work in a group. Attempts to reduce the fear through necessary physical treatment and diagnostic, through a rational approach had failed in the past. Admitting him to our hospital was ultima ratio. As RMT was indicated for the time the patient was unable to work in a group, I decided to treat him individually. After 19 sessions, the patient could use the training concept successfully. The fears diminished markedly. Later he was again able to leave his apartment and even go cross-country skiing.

This experience encouraged us to use dyadic RMT more often, sometimes with in-patients, sometimes with out-patients, but always in those cases where for different reasons it was impossible to take the patient into our closed symptom-centered group psychotherapy concept with RMT as the main method. We first presented our experiences at a conference in Leipzig in 1992 (Röhrborn 1992). Christoph Schwabe expressed his worries that processes of transference and countertransference might get out of control in this more intense dyadic work. But we considered it to be similar to any other individual psychotherapy, which is done very intensively and in high frequency. Of course, those processes have to be taken into consideration. By orienting towards a shared task, which is the training with the music and clear exercises according to the levels of the training of perception, in my opinion malicious regression can be avoided.

3. The Differences between the Work with Regulative Music Therapy with Dyads and Groups

Both in groups and in dyads, the patient's realization of the stepwise perception training is necessary. Individual work is difficult, especially during the first sessions, because on one hand there are very suggestive and high expectancies of the therapy and the therapist, but they are not as readily visible as in groups. Thus they cannot be solved as quickly through processing. On the other hand, especially for patients with strong deficiencies in perception, so called alexithymic patients who show very abstract thinking and disabilities in emotional communication as well as in describing physical or mental sensations, the variety of descriptions of perceptions from the group is missing. This has to be balanced by the therapist's increased activity. Therefore, the therapist should offer possibilities of perceiving, and maybe, on occasions, give an example of a differentiated description of perception. Still, one has to observe the rule of abstinence, thus the therapist's own emotional problems do not belong into the therapy. The therapist has to convey to the patient through his actions, more so than in the group, what to also observe in memories. With this, he takes on part of the group activities.

It is advantageous that in dyads it is easier to measure out than in groups. For example, it is possible to encourage attention to disturbances quicker in the sense of paradox intention (so called behavioral strategies). By this I mean, for example, encouraging turning to and perceiving a disturbance as an interesting object of perception.

This emphasizes the relaxation character of RMT. It can be performed quite well if at level 3 one does not work with the same intensity, as though unconscious psychic contents should be explicitly brought into consciousness, thus as though aiming at bringing defenses into consciousness and changing them. At level 3, one always has to decide whether a relaxation method based on paradox intention and training of perception is taught, or if an intensive psychodynamic therapy should be conducted. This would then include processing conflicts that become conscious. Here, longer therapy sessions are necessary than when working on relaxation. The hallmark of the method, however, is the development of the perceptive faculty in both cases.

Thus, the foundation of the method is the strategy/concept of encouraging perception. There are other psychotherapy methods which use the "perception-oriented principle of action", the strategy of encouraging perception, for example Guided Affective Imagery developed by Leuner (1970) and Client-Centered Psychotherapy developed by Rogers (1977). Also, in RMT, according to circumstances and the situation of the patient, variations in the realization of the concept of encouragement of perception are known. Especially in the dyad in contrast to the closed group, a very individual procedure is possible. It is important, however, not to abandon the concept of encouragement of perception and the stepwise perception and non-defensive turning towards disturbances, towards the symptom and towards the emotional-cognitive reactions to the perceived – regardless of all variations of therapist, patient and environment. This is in accordance with the quote by Ernst Jürgen: "Auch in der Medizin ist die Taktik veränderlich, die Strategie unveränderlich"[2] (2000).

2 Translation: "Also in medicine are tactics changeable, but strategy unchangeable."

To control the therapy process, the "Erlabrunner Beurteilungsbogen zur Stundeneinschätzung bei symptomzentrierter Gruppenpsychotherapie"[3] (EBS) (Schwabe & Röhrborn 1996) was modified for use in dyads (ibid.). The application, however, was only successful in single cases. As far as I know, a wide application was not conducted. This might be related to the fact that individual therapy sessions have to be reported in detail, which serves a similar purpose. For scientific research, for the documentation of the process, the application is recommended. There is no difference in the selection of music for groups or dyads. For the role of the music, I refer to the literature (Schwabe & Röhrborn 1996; Schwabe 2003b).

4. On the Differential Indication of Group/Dyad

Here, no other criteria of differential indication have to be observed than for other group or individual psychotherapy. In addition to contraindications for group therapy like certain behaviors, very severe symptoms, severe physical disabilities, severe additional physical disorders, in the hospital there are also external factors. Sometimes social reasons are responsible for patients not being able to be expected to wait for the beginning of the next closed group. One has to consider well if the intensity of the group work and the additional experiences the patient can have in a closed group are less important than saving time through starting an individual psychotherapy immediately. The duration of inpatient individual psychotherapy usually is not short, but rather longer than the group concept.

Outpatient group therapy is seldom used, due to problems of organization and billing. In licensed outpatient clinics of hospitals, the small number of patients does not allow for closed groups. Therefore, in the outpatient clinic of the hospital, the decision for individual RMT is often made for formal reasons. If there is an indication for RMT but no possibilities for working in groups, individual treatment is necessary. However, in some places outpatient group psychotherapy is conducted. For example, in the private psychotherapy practice of Dr. Kunz in Lengefeld/Erz Mountains successful work is carried out with closed RMT-groups (Kunz 2003).

5. Experiences with Different Patient Groups

5.1. Somatoform Disorders

For patients with somatoform disorders, the indication of experiencing organ illness without insight into psychogenesis almost always applies. This is the biggest group of patients treated with RMT. Even though these patients are believed to

3 Translation: "Erlabrunn Rating Scale of Assessment of the Therapy Session for Symptom-Oriented Group Psychotherapy"

be very difficult in psychotherapy, they can be treated well with RMT. Once they become interested in body-awareness, and the connection between mental and physical processes is perceivable, they usually cooperate well. For the therapists, it is always a joy to see how people with fears of illness who seemingly lack fantasy and an emotional life, suddenly become open-minded, feeling, emotionally communicative, and enjoy the music. It can often be observed that ailments fail away when the fear of them, the fear of feelings can be perceived. Unfortunately, no empirical validation through prospective research exists yet.

5.2. Patients with difficulties relaxing

This is an area of outpatient treatment. It is common knowledge that rational and performance-oriented, hyper-accurate people do not work well with autogenic training. In this case, a relaxation method based on encouragement of perception like Regulative Music Training is recommended (Schwabe 1991b). Due to reasons of efficiency, it is often tried to teach the patient autogenic training without much effort. If this does not work, Regulative Music Therapy offers an alternative. Often, not only the ability to relax can be improved, but also changes in behavior can be achieved.

5.3. Patients with somatic disorders with insufficient processing of illness

Patients with chronic physical disorders often react with fear and defenses, sometimes also with denial to symptoms, illness, and changing patterns of daily life. The mental reaction to the illness often resembles in quality one of the definitions of neurosis from Bad Elster used in the GDR, the so called secondary psychological faulty development with a faulty attitude towards symptoms (especially development of expectation fears and avoiding behavior), towards the illness (secondary gain, chronification through medical doctors and the social system), and towards the way of living (neurotic arrangements) (Höck & König 1976). There are many similarities to patients with somatoform disorders. When working with this group of patients, it is very important to take care that the basic somatic disorder is considered properly, and that the patient does not get the impression that he is only treated as a mentally ill person and not also and primarily as physically ill. Among others, this means that much time is needed for education about the illness, maybe further diagnosis, and the encouragement to perceive physical symptoms. Levels 1 and 2 of the stepwise training of perception are especially important here. At level 3, when working with grasping and making conscious the fears of the symptoms, the work is very difficult, and a lot of patience and sympathy from the therapist is necessary. This is the same for patients with psychosomatic illnesses. Experience in the hospital shows, however, that these patients are only referred to psychotherapists in rare cases, usually when in a suicidal crisis.

5.4. Patients with chronic pain

What was said under 5.3. about patients with somatic illnesses is also applicable for patients with chronic pain. They are fixated on perceptions of pain and the fight against pain, the hopeless struggle to not feel pain. Fighting pain, very often all means of specific pain therapy with medication, injections, physiotherapy, etc. which are very much favored by the patients are included. However, this especially strengthens fixation on the experience of pain. Therefore, it is difficult to motivate patients with chronic pain to psychotherapy and to encourage them to change habitual defending behaviors towards pain, like fight, denial, and distraction. One also needs a lot of patience with this patient group. It is more pleasing if the approach towards pain changes from fear and fight towards a more relaxed perceiving, if the patient becomes interested in more things again, if social contacts improve, if, as it were, flowers smell and music resounds again. Improvement is evident if patients reduce their dosage of pain medication voluntarily.

5.5. Patients with personality disorders

During the past years, a growing number of patients with severe personality disorders, especially with emotionally instable personality disorders of the Borderline type enter hospital. Their symptoms are manifold: self-mutilating behavior, eating disorders such as anorexia nervosa and bulimia nervosa or mixed forms, substance abuse, inappropriate behavior, severe disturbances in interpersonal relationships as well as in relationships to the surroundings. Extreme fear of closeness, inability to have personal relationships with loss of the ability to distance oneself, clinging to the therapist followed by abrupt rejection and devaluation are frequent. Starting points in therapy therefore are building and forming the relationship between therapist and patient, as well as enhancing perceptive faculties. Patients with eating disorders and self-mutilating behavior have a markedly disturbed body-image and therefore bodily awareness. Up until now, there has been no royal road to therapeutic change. Working in groups with these patients is difficult due to relationship difficulties and the inability to stay in a community over a longer period of time. Group activities that last longer than 30 minutes often cannot be tolerated by the patients and lead to extreme reactions.

Therefore, work in dyads is focused initially; group activities are probably only possible later. In dyads, the therapist can proceed in a more differentiated way in relation to timing and the very fragile regulation of closeness and distance. One should especially avoid offering closeness to the patient without offering possibilities for escape. Of course, this also has consequences for he work with RMT in dyads. It should only start when there is a well established relationship between therapist and patient, even if RMT is indicated theoretically. In a rather factual atmosphere, the description of perceptions should be encouraged patiently according to the principle of remembering, describing and concrete naming by the patient. This can also protect against slipping into dissociative states. At the onset of dissociation, one should try to encourage factual description of bodily perceptions. One should especially avoid interpretations of perceptions and behavior. It is also very important to avoid intensive or intrusive inquiring if the patient describes very touching or shameful perceptions. The immense fear of certain mental contents but also of bodily perceptions, especially of losing boundaries seems to be central. Self-mutilating behavior results from different sensations or reasons. Some self-mutilating behavior has strong components of aggression against others, as unconscious punishment for behavior of the therapist or other people.. Some self-mutilating behavior is as a way of seeking attention (this is maybe the reason for epidemic self-mutilation in certain situations) and of forcing the patient who experiences loss of physical boundaries and unbearable scaring physical sensations to return to reality through pain and flowing warm blood. It is difficult to encourage the patient to turn slowly towards these physical sensations, to feel fears with the help of patiently practicing bodily awareness which can be supported by other methods like Concentration-Relaxation developed by Wilda-Kiesel (1993), without interfering in a panicked manner with self-mutilation. On the other hand, this seems to be a successful strategy. It is especially important not to work with RMT too early and in an overwhelming way with these patients. If working with RMT, it is important not to use emotionally challenging or disintegrating music selections. Lack of structure, the inability to structure one's day is one of the main problems of these clients. Therefore, work in the hospital with its holding structure and with clear, structure-building relationships that can also tolerate extreme behavior of the patients is so important. Before work with RMT is possible later in therapy, work with structured, predictable, emotionally clear, and shorter music is necessary.

The patient should work with a therapist with whom he has developed a strong enough relationship. In the training situation itself often strong fears of being at the mercy of someone or of being threatened arise. In addition to providing sufficient explanations before the start, the therapist should also make clear that he is not observing the patient but is training together with him. He should offer different possibilities of training like sitting, lying, or sitting in a reclining chair. He should discuss possibilities for protection like the patient stopping and turning towards the therapist whenever something becomes overwhelming. It is helpful to stress that one is not observing by turning one's back towards the patient or by offering him a place in the treatment room where he feels unobserved. I remember a patient who definitely wanted to lie down on the floor behind the desk because she was sure I could not see her there from my position next to the record-player. On the other hand, the presence of the therapist and being able to approach him any time also offers safety.

Especially work on level 1 and 2 of perception training offers the foundation for possible further processing of defenses and following change of behavior. Processing happens through the principle of remembering and describing, not through premature interpretation of defenses. More patience than usual is needed.

Despite the necessary adaptations of RMT for borderline patients, we do not see any reason to change from psychodynamic to cognitive-behavioral treatment as proposed by Schwabe (2003b) in a recent publication (see also the chapter by Schwabe in this book).

6. Differences between Inpatients and Outpatients

Inpatients treated with dyadic RMT are usually much more severely ill than outpatients. Rarely is the only treatment goal is relaxation. Frequent goals are a lessening of intense restriction of bodily awareness and finding a pathway to one's emotional life. Goals for the less severely ill outpatients are often being able to relax, and reducing unrest and sleeping disorders. For these patients, RMT in the sense of Regulative Music Training (Schwabe 1991) is very effective and helpful. However, treating patients with severe personality disorders with RMT in the outpatient clinic is problematic. It is at best useful at a very advanced state in therapy and in a very stable therapist-patient-relationship. In no case should the patient be referred to another therapist, for example to a music therapist unknown to the patient. This would be only possible on an inpatient ward where the music therapist is already known to the patient. In the outpatient clinic RMT is usually the main therapy method. On the inpatient ward, this is rarely the case. Here, RMT can be an important adjunct therapy for encouraging perception within the context of psychotherapy. If the patient is referred to a music therapist for this, there must be close contact between him and the verbal therapist. And, as mentioned before, the music therapist should already be known to the patient.

7. Closure

The description of dyadic Regulative Music Therapy must remain fragmentary for now. After a long period of development of RMT primarily as a group psychotherapy method, initially only few patients were treated individually. Even though the indication is theoretically well founded, adequate outcome-studies are still missing. A prospective study which would follow the course of therapy as well as short-term and long-term outcome would be desirable. Research instruments exist in part. Based on personal encounters, we can proceed on the assumption that many clinical psychologists and psychiatrists who learned to use RMT as group psychotherapy in the 80s have been using it since they began practicing privately. There are no reports of experiences with it. I hope, that inspired by the report of my experiences, other colleagues will also publish their experiences. There is an especially large interest in the treatment of severely ill patients with eating disorders, borderline personality disorder and self-mutilating behavior, but also with chronic pain, and with somatization disorders.

Acknowledgement

The author would like to thank Carola Maack for the translation.

CH. 14: EMOTION PSYCHOLOGY AND ITS SIGNIFICANCE IN REGULATIVE MUSIC THERAPY (RMT) AND THE BONNY METHOD OF GUIDED IMAGERY AND MUSIC (BMG)

THOMAS WOSCH

Up until now, music therapy and music psychology have hardly been recognized by emotion psychology as a sub-specialization of psychology. A notable exception is Volume 13 on Music and Emotion in the series, "Affective Science" published by the Oxford University Press (Juslin, Sloboda 2001). The series is edited by the leading emotion psychologists Davidson, Ekman and Scherer (USA, Switzerland). The volume on Music and Emotion even contains an article by Scherer himself, making it an interdisciplinary feature. Scherer put quasi-musical factors of speech at the centre of emotion psychological basic research in the study of emotion and language (Scherer 1990). The book also comments on the fact that overviews of music psychology do not contain chapters dealing with the fundamentals of emotions. In turn, the psychology of emotion does not make mention of music. This occurs despite the fact that emotion psychologists Gaver and Mandler had already indicated in 1987 that studies of music could be of enormous importance to the psychology of emotion in order to achieve a better overall comprehension of emotion (Gaver, Mandler 1987 in Juslin, Sloboda 2001, 3).

This article describes the emotion psychological basics of receptive music therapy. Exemplary reference is made to the two methods of receptive music therapy, Regulative Music Therapy (RMT) and the Bonny Method Guided Imagery and Music (BMGIM). The definition of emotion relevant to receptive music therapy methods must be clarified first. Then, two aspects of emotion, the classification of qualities of emotion and the process of emotions will be differentiated together with their references to these methods. The emotional process is particularly important to psychotherapeutic processes, including active music therapy (Langenberg 1996, Wosch 2002). Here and in studies dealing with music reception (Bonny 1983, Brüggenwerth et al. 1994, Gutjahr et al. 1994) however, only the process of a single emotion is examined. An emotional process encompassing all emotions (Machleidt 1994, 353; Wosch 2002, 253) and its importance for receptive music therapy has not yet been taken note of. This can only be made possible from the perspective of emotion psychology.

The Definition of Emotion and Receptive Music Therapy

In contemporary psychology of emotion (Scherer 1990, Izard 1994), emotion is chiefly defined in connection with motivation. The definition by Izard, applicable for psychology of emotion until this day, comprises two essential aspects. One aspect encompasses three inseparably entwined components of emotion.
These are:
"a) the experience or conscious perception of the emotion,
b) processes occurring in the brain and the nervous system, and
c) observable expression, particularly facial expression." (Izard 1994, 20)

Izard summarized these as phenomenological, neurophysiologic, and neuromuscular components of emotion (Izard 1994, 67). Expression of emotion in areas separate from the musculature of the face are disregarded.

Izard's second aspect states that emotions are "basic motivation systems of human behaviour" (Izard, Malatesta 1987, 494; Izard 1994, 19). This aspect is also reflected in Scherer's volume on emotion, as this volume deals with motivation and emotion (Scherer 1990), and emotion is regarded as a mechanism of adaptation (Scherer 1979, 212). This second aspect of motivation and mechanism of adaptation describes emotion as functionality. If, however, emotion is regarded as a fundamental system of motivation for human thought and behaviour, emotion has a mediating function in the psychic system from the outset. In contrast, a model has been developed in more recent German emotion psychology which grants emotion considerably more autonomy and reflection on the self. Compared to functionality in Izard and his universal definition of emotion, that is, assuming the same facial expression for individual emotions world-wide, the phenomenon of emotion is seen from a a person-centred perspective (Ulich 1992, 49). Contrary to Izard's definition, Ulich defines emotion excluding the factor of regulation of action and activity. He describes emotion above all as "being-touched" personally (Ulich 1992, 56). For Ulich, this element of emotion forms a component or rather a characteristic in the emotional complex. The four basic characteristics of emotion are the "moment of unity of body and mind", personal "involvement" or a direct sense of "being moved", the rather "passive" experience of feelings in the sense of "something happening to me", or the "close intertwining of interpersonal relationships", reaching through to the dimensions of "a particular culture and society" (Ulich 1992, 55–56). With this definition of emotion, Ulich orients himself to similar definitions and critical writings by Mandler (1979) and Lantermann (1983). Mandler has already been mentioned in the introduction as one of the few emotion psychologists who hoped to come to new and groundbreaking conclusions about emotion within emotion psychology, particularly as a result of musical research. The term "something happening to me", mentioned above, was created by Lanterman (Lantermann 1983, 405). Ulich carries this term further in a person-centred sense to a new quality of "being-touched". *Being-touched* versus *"something happening to me"* as separate characteristic of emotion gives the individual concerned a larger measure of participation, in what he is touched by and how he is touched.

This agrees with results of reception research in music. Gembris summarizes that apparently each individual has his own musical effect, so that the individual himself is the key to the actual experience of music (Gembris 1996). According to Gembris, this description particularly describes physiological characteristics, in that "the listener's individual reaction dispositions prove to be more decisive than the music itself." (Gembris 1996, 322). According to Ulich, each person has an individual, therefore person-centred, way of being touched by music. This, initially, also affects the neuro- or psycho-physiological (body and mind) level. An approach centred on the individual is emphasised in the latest results of American research on reception. According to these findings, social and socio-cultural factors play an ever-decreasing role in everyday music reception. Music is mostly heard when alone. The experience of music contributes significantly to autonomy if an individual is overtaxed by social duties. For young people, music has come to reflect the construction of the self, thus assuming the earlier role of group affiliation.(Sloboda, O'Neill 2001, 421; DeNora 1999, 51). The individual and therefore the psychological level take precedence over group and sociological levels. On a psychological level, *experience*, as a person-centered being-touched and emotional befall takes centre stage opposite functionality for other, universal schemes of effectiveness. This applies in the same way to both emotion and music reception. For Ulich's definition of emotion, experience for the sake of experience, or art for art's sake, is central to defining emotion. Parallel to this, a change can be noted in current reception research in music psychology from the use of the term emotion to those of "musical experience" and "experience of emotions" (Vink 2001, 145–146). In both cases, experience, as opposed to functionality of emotion, is emphasized both for emotion and for musical experience. Ulich's fourth characteristic of emotion, the relationship component, is directly related to central therapeutic points of receptive music therapy methods. Ulich elaborates on this component in the person-centred sense. "In feeling, it is not the objective properties of the object that are experienced, but the type of relationship" (Tunner 1982, 215 in Ulich 1992, 52). With this definition, he is unique. Izard does not discuss this component, but treats the phenomenological aspect in a universal way, as applying to all individuals, for example in the examination of facial expressions accompanying individual emotions, identical the world over (Izard 1994, 109–114). Ulich, on the other hand, offers two person-centred qualities: "being touched" and "something happening", applied to current music reception, and, for some time, to music therapy. With these three characteristics, being touched, "something happening" and the relationship component Ulich's definition of emotion appears to acquire a special relevance for music therapy in general as well as for receptive methods in particular.[1]

1 Especially in the last Tunner-Ulich quotation, "feeling" could easily be replaced by "musical experience in music therapy" and "of the object" by "of music".

The receptive methods, RMT and GIM, mentioned above, refer to emotion in both different and similar ways. GIM considers emotion from the client's point of view as an important element within the images arising within him. On the other hand, emotion is an independent and separate factor within the therapeutic process of GIM (Goldberg 1999, 117–118). In GIM, interaction between music and emotion is assumed for both meanings. Goldberg wrote: "Music ... may be an archetypal representation of emotion, born of creative genius, and therefore able to touch deep unconscious layers of emotion in the listener" (Goldberg 1999, 118). Here the parallelism of emotion and music described above appears to be interaction. Two processes become clear: the universal anchoring of emotion according to Izard with archetypal content described here, and the criterion of being-touched according to Ulich. In other emotion psychological works, Goldberg refers to Tomkins (1962) and Plutchik (1984) in whose tradition Izard stands (Izard 1994; Ortony, Turner 1990). Goldberg refers also to Mandler, who is repeatedly mentioned in connection with Ulich (Goldberg 1999, 118).

This person-centred determination of emotion appears to form the emotion-psychological basis for the principles of GIM. First, this applies to changes which Bonny had made to Leuner's Katathyme Imaginative Psychotherapy (KIP) based on the characteristics of musical experience (Kiel 1993). It was not possible to use the standard images of KIP as a gateway into GIM. Set figurative images and person-centring or rather the subjectivity of musical experience were incompatible. Thus, client's person-centered events and images from initial GIM interviews or previous therapy sessions replaced standard images as an entrance to the actual imagination as guided by music. Secondly, Bonde puts the significance of the client's personality at the centre of attention for imagery guided by music. Bonde describes the function of music as a "projection screen" for the client's unconscious content (Bonde 2002, 118). This makes person-centring the key to the experience of music in GIM. Bonde, however, concedes that for those GIM therapists who consider music as an "archetypal field of energy" the focal point of therapeutic changes lies in the mythical structure of music, the relationship object according to Ulich (Bonde 2002, 119). In this distinction, an older theoretical image of emotion in the latter, and a newer image in Bonde's position are visible. This may also explain the ambivalence in the emotion-psychological works of Goldberg, which can be assigned to the older or newer emotion theory together with Bonde's two clearly separate positions. On the one hand, this is person-centring according to Ulich with the central position of the client, for whom music becomes the projection screen of his own experience. On the other hand, mythic-universal musical structures effect therapeutic change on the individual human being in the client's stead. These changes have a general character and are similar in their effects to universal forms of expression and functionality as described by Izard.

As a common denominator for both positions of GIM, Bonde, however, mentions transpersonal experience. If musical experience is ultimately considered as experience, being touched and "something happening", clearly contrary to the regulation of action and activity, this can be assumed to be the basis of GIM for the experience of emotion interacting with music. In the end, this makes Ulich's definition of emotion more applicable to GIM than Izard's. An exception regarding a universal definition of emotion according to Izard are those areas of GIM giving precedence to archetypal structures within the musical experience.

Literature on RMT does not explicitly contain theoretical emotion psychological studies. Individual principles and details of RMT, however, clearly anchor this receptive music therapy method within the definition of emotion according to Ulich. To this belongs the term of "allowing to happen", central to RMT (Schwabe 1987, 159 and the chapters by Schwabe and Röhrborn in this book). With the realization of allowing to happen in the client's process of perception an unambiguous reference is made to "something happening to me" within emotional experience. In addition, the description of moments of unity of body and mind is named in two levels of perception: bodily perception on one level, and thoughts, moods and feelings on another. These are to be combined in the therapeutic process of RMT. Body, thoughts, moods and feelings are perceived in a more differentiated manner in their combination in the therapeutic process of RMT (see the chapters by Schwabe and Röhrborn in this book). Relationships, differing from person to person, can be identified, and thus leading directly to therapeutic change. It is in these relationships that moments of unity of body and mind, i. e. a basic characteristic of emotion, are consciously perceived. Furthermore, special importance is placed on the separate contemplation of emotion within the perception description during the third phase of RMT. In this phase, it is possible to discover and capture reactions to feeling (Schwabe, Röhrborn 1996, 63). Individual emotions as reactions to feelings are allocated a position that is to be achieved first within the process of therapy and perception in RMT. According to this understanding of RMT, emotion is neither a system of motivation (Izard 1994, 19) nor a starting point for the regulation of action according to Izard. Rather, emotion stands at the end of an experience process not previously consciously perceived. This process of experience consists of intertwined perceptions, at the end of which emotion leads to the core of experience. Therefore, dealing with emotion in RMT strongly bears the character of an experience located at the end of a (micro-) process. This position also affects the therapeutic process of RMT as a whole. This is described as a "process of encountering the self, especially the emotional side of one's own person"(Schwabe, Röhrborn 1996, 44). In contrast to GIM, we are not looking at the interaction of music and emotion here; the radius is even more restricted to the interaction of the individual and his emotions. This can be regarded as an even stronger focus on the person-centred side of emotion, as differentiation occurs again within this area. Furthermore, as a result of RMT, an "increasingly more conscious and controlled dealing with one's own emotionality" (Schwabe, Röhrborn 1996, 44) can be achieved. Finally, emotion is not viewed as a system of motivation, but as an autonomous phenomenon perceived consciously during the process of RMT. Later, instead of being considered a means of regulation even this was seen to be too regulative.

This can only occur if emotionality is not only confronted, as in GIM, but also, taken one step further, if this phenomenon is confronted with the aim of changing within the musical experience while at the same time distancing oneself from it. This gives the client an extremely strong position within the therapeutic process.
The finality of the phenomenon of experience per se, emotion, becomes the key to therapeutic change as emotion perception in RMT and in dealing with this autonomous phenomenon. In the end, it is a discovery of and dealing with being touched. This being touched takes place above all in the encounter of the self mentioned above, with the focus on meeting one's own emotions. According to Ulich, this is "our relation to 'something'" (Ulich 1992, 56). This something is, in RMT and many psychotherapeutic methods including GIM, the relation to one's own self. Being touched by the self appears to be the quadrate of being touched in an emotion psychological perspective, which then closes the circle. The self forms the object of being touched. At the same time, the person is touched by the object. These moments can constitute emotion-psychological pivotal moments. Regarding the process of RMT, however, other relations and relationships are also described. This refers especially to the beginning of the relationship to music, which occurs solely on an auditive level. In this relationship beginning, an "inner performance of movement" (Schwabe 1987, 99) occurs, representing a second form of being touched. In this case, it is touch by the medium of music in time. Here one can see similarities to partial structures of music in GIM as mentioned above.
Archetypal basics of music, however, are not described in the literature on RMT, which again suggests a rather person-centred image of music. On balance, Ulich's definition of emotion also appears as the theoretical basis of RMT within emotion psychology. This refers to the moment of unity of body and mind, "something happening to me" and being touched. Emotional-psychological characterizations as seen by Izard's cannot be discerned here. The therapeutic process of RMT goes beyond experience itself by directly formulating the desired level of dealing with being touched and defining this as the therapeutic goal. Initially it seems as though experience itself stands too much at the centre of attention, as its further significance for the client plays a smaller role than the quasi-structural regulation of person-centred experience.
As stated earlier Mandler and Gaver, emotion psychology can generally gain huge amount of knowledge from the study of music. We can then conclude that for the receptive methods GIM and RMT a theory regarding the basics of emotion which has only played a minor role up until now is actually more relevant than the differential emotion psychology's definition of emotion favoured by emotion psychology at the present. The features of musical experience and those of the psychotherapeutic approaches of GIM and RMT build rather on a person- and experience-centred basis of emotion (Ulich) with a final character than on a universal and motivation-oriented basis of emotion with functional character (Izard).

The Classification of Emotion Qualities and Active Music Therapy

After the definition of emotion for receptive methods of music therapy like RMT and GIM has been clarified, the next aspect to be discussed is the distinction between various emotions. Principles of receptive methods emphasise different aspects of emotions like anxiety, happiness, and yearning, which represent various phenomenological or experienced qualities of being touched. Before these differences can be explained, however, a common frame of reference for emotions to be differentiated must be clarified. This occurs based on emotion psychology. For this, the relevant definition of emotion as person-centred being touched, moment of unity of body and mind, "something happening to me" and quality of relation is used.

The distinction between different emotions in emotion psychology is widely distributed. In 2002, a study counted as many as 22 different systems for naming emotions (Wosch 2002, 27–34). 19 of these come from differential emotion psychology, and include between two and eleven basic emotions. In addition, the systems of five basic feelings (Lungwitz 1970; Machleidt et al. 1989), the world-wide naming of 56 emotions (Schmidt-Atzert, Ströhm 1983) and the classification of 24 emotions (Mayring 1992) are mentioned. Differences between the systems are already made clear by the use of the terms 'basic emotions', 'basic feelings' and 'emotions'. Further terms like fundamental emotions, primary emotions and self-reflexive affects broaden this spectrum (Wosch 2002, 39). However, the attempt to name different emotions in the sense of person-centred experience qualities to be differentiated (Mayring 1992; Wosch 2002) shows similarities between the 22 different systems. One of these similarities is that 19 of the 22 systems contain the emotions of anxiety/fear and anger/fury. Another similarity is that Mayring's classification, based entirely on Ulich's definition of emotion (Ulich, Mayring 1992), includes all differentiated emotions from the other systems, with the exception of Schmidt-Atzert and Ströhm's system[2]. Remarkably, Mayring divides the 24 classified emotions into four groups, nearly corresponding to Lungwitz and Machleidt's five basic feelings (Lungwitz 1970; Machleidt et al. 1989). Only the emotions of anxiety/fear and anger/fury, differentiated in almost all emotion systems and clearly differentiated in their phenomenology within the basic feelings (see below) are included in the same group in Mayring. These and further steps are elaborated on elsewhere (Wosch 2002, 17–45) and lead to the formation of a frame of reference of various emotion qualities, as seen in Table 1. Short-term intense emotions (affects), of longer-lasting emotions of medium intensity (feelings) and long-lasting emotions with constant intensity (moods) are not further differentiated here. The different qualities of being touched, of "something happening to me", of the moment of unity between body and mind and of the quality of relationship

2 Only 24 of 56 emotions collected by Schmidt-Atzert and Ströhm comply with the characteristics of an emotion based on Ulich's definition. .

are described as emotional qualities.[3] In Table 1, the emotional qualities of envy, jealousy and disgust are omitted. These three do not appear in the systems of emotions in music therapy mentioned below and cannot be clearly assigned to the characterizations of the five classes of emotion qualities.

Table 1: Five-part classification of qualities of emotion (see Wosch 2002, 38, 253)

Emotions of intention and affection	Emotions of anxiety and aversion with avoidance	Emotions of anger and aversion with approach	Emotions of sadness (mourning) and discomfort	Emotions of joy and well-being
Interest, love, sympathy, pride, yearning	Anxiety, fear, shyness	Anger, fury, rage, contempt, hate	Mourning, melancholy, dejection, shame, loneliness, sense of guilt, emptiness	Joy, pleasure, happiness, contentment, relief

These five classes of emotional qualities are referred to repeatedly in literature on music therapy. This applies to active music therapy (Priestley 1994; Bunt, Pavlicevic 2001; Wosch 2002) in particular and, at times, to GIM (Bonde 2001). Before this is discussed, the five classes will be characterized according to the sources of emotion psychology already mentioned. Machleidt describes the emotional quality of intention as “a feeling of hunger in the broader sense“(Machleidt et al. 1989, 44). In its quality of experience, this “feeling of emptiness“(Lungwitz 1970, 531) characterizes “curiosity, wish, craving, desire, yearning, etc” (Machleidt 1994, 352). Referring to the quality of relationship, Machleidt writes: “An individual experiencing intentional feelings is held by the object, fascinated…” (Machleidt et al. 1989, 44). The self has been virtually captured. In contrast, the emotional quality of anxiety is described as a “feeling of restriction” (Machleidt et al. 1989, 56; cf. Latin: angustus = restricted). The emotional characteristic of “something happening to me” may take on existential proportions in the sense of being threatened. Anxiety may be compulsively directed at particular objects (Machleidt et al. 1989, 56), but this includes “embarrassment, reserve… flight” towards the object of anxiety in the quality of relationship for the affected person, or an aversion to the object (Mayring 1992, 138). According to Machleidt, the emotional quality of anger is closely related to the Latin aggredior, or approach (Mayring 1992, 151). This results in a Janus-faced experience of energy (Machleidt *et al.* 1989, 85). in One direction indicates the painful experience of separation and farewell in (Lungwitz 1970, 532), the other shows the approach to the object or the object of anger. Lungwitz sees here an inseparable moment of unity of body and

3 In Ulich, the definition of emotion focuses mainly on the dimension of emotional feelings (Ulich 1992, 55).

mind, particularly as mental and physical components can least be separated in this quality of emotion (Lungwitz 1970, 532). In this emotional quality, the self is partially strengthened. The emotional quality of mourning is experienced as a "feeling of loss" (Machleidt 1994, 354). In its quality of relationship it represents "feelings of farewell, of redemption, of abandonment, of loneliness or also ... of dejection..." (Machleidt 1994, 354). In every-day experience, this emotional quality can be perceived clearly or less consciously as being touched. In its quality of relationship, mourning is sometimes more strongly directed to the self than to the object of mourning. The emotional quality of joy is marked as a "feeling of satisfaction, of completion, of fulfilment, of happiness... of delight, etc." by Machleidt (1994, 354), and as feeling of well-being by Mayring (1992, 138). When referring to delight, for example, experienced here as well-being and fulfilment, it must be differentiated from "appetite" (Machleidt et al. 1989, 44), which must be assigned to the emotional quality of intention. The self rests completely in itself in the emotional quality of joy.

In active music therapy, these five classes of emotional qualities play an important role in particular in the characterizations described above. Priestley describes seven different emotions as the basis of therapeutic action in analytical music therapy (Priestley 1994, 31–36). These are the three different kinds of anxiety, anger, guilt, and sorrow, or mourning, as well as the triad of love, joy and tranquillity (Priestley 1994, 31–32). All seven values of the differentiated emotions which, according to Priestley, contain the totality of the emotional spectrum (Priestley 1994, 29) are viewed according to their positive as well as negative aspects. Thus, for example, anger is described in a positive sense in connection with a constructive struggle against one's own values and therefore as a source of necessary changes. In a negative sense it manifests itself in violence (Priestley 1994, 31). The positive aspect is emphasised especially in the characterization above. On the whole it can be said that the emotional qualities of anxiety, mourning and joy are differentiated by Priestley, and that intention, or love is positioned closely to joy. The spectrum of the five emotional qualities is, however, neither exceeded nor restricted by this. The extensive field of emotions in analytic music therapy according to Priestley corresponds completely to the differentiations in Table 1.

This correlation becomes even clearer in one of the most recent studies of active music therapy and improvisation by Bunt and Pavlicevic (Bunt, Pavlicevic 2001). They examined the interaction of music and emotion of five (!) emotions (according to GIM): happy, sad, affectionate, angry and anxious (Bunt, Pavlicevic 2001, 189–190). In three cases, all five emotions appear literally as an expression of different emotional qualities in Table 1. Happy appears below the subsumed emotions of the emotional quality of joy. Affectionate is clearly understood as the feeling of affection in the sense of Table 1 and the subsequent characterization of the five emotion qualities.[4] In another study, music therapeutical improvisations were analysed based on the five emotion qualities in Table 1 (Wosch 2002). This made a visualisation of miniscule emotional processes possible (Wosch 2002, 111–112). These processes included alterations between two different emotional qualities of the player within a single improvisation (Wosch 2002, 252). As a result, an improvisation was not viewed here as the *state* of a single emotional quality, but as the *process* of several emotion qualities, in contrast to the study by Bunt and Pavlicevic. Changes in the client's relationship qualities were immediately related to this process. A turning towards the self could be observed during the transition from intention to anger within one improvisation. During the course of the entire therapy, the experience of anger represented a threshold. Once past this threshold, the client was able to approach the self, both mourning and joyful (Wosch 2002, 237–241). Thus, meanings in the "traditional", stringent change of the five emotion qualities could be further differentiated within the "course of experience" (Machleidt 1994, 353). In particular, the musical experience offers an emotional component within the auditory sense. This has not yet been sufficiently considered by emotion psychology up until now. The differentiation of emotions is bound in particular to visually perceptible facial expression (Izard 1994; Krause 1990; Ekmann, Friesen 1969). This is frequently referred to as a *state*. In so doing, the relationship between different emotional qualities as part of an "entirety of emotions" is lost. However, the time-medium music suggests the study of change in emotional qualities because of the constant alteration, which occurs within one "state of emotion". This is the only way in which a theory such as the course of experience (Machleidt 1994) can be studied empirically (Wosch 2002). Ulich's definition of emotion can thus be complemented by the component of constant change of emotional qualities inherent to emotion, while taking musical expression into consideration.[5]

4 The basis of this differentiation of emotion qualities goes back to Sloboda and Juslin (Sloboda, Juslin 2001, 77). In short improvisations, these qualities were played separately and judged by raters.

5 In the totality of the change of all different emotion qualities, a constant growth of the self is achieved in the therapeutic process (Wosch 2002, 243).

Emotional Qualities and Different Approaches within Receptive Music Therapy

Table 2: Mood-Wheel Bonde (Wigram, Nygaard, Pedersen, Bonde 2002, 59)[6]

1	2	3	4	5	6	7	8	9
dignified	dark	tender	quiet	graceful	bright	active	agitated	vigorous
serious	melan-cholic	dreamy	tranquil	sprightly	happy	energetic	exhilarated	aggressive
spiritual	sad	sentimental	lyrical	whimsical	cheerful	straight-forward	dramatic	majestic
sober	tragic	yearning	serene	delicate	gay	extrovert	passio-nate	martial
awe inspiring	blue	mellow	soothing	humorous	optimistic	encouraging	triumphant	exalting

For active music therapy it was able to be demonstrated that emotional qualities are differentiated. This is substantiated by emotion psychology. Among the receptive methods, GIM and RMT, this is true for GIM only in part. For the selection of music in GIM, Bonde describes the mood-wheel (Wigram, Nygaard, Pedersen, Bonde 2002, 59), originally developed by Hevner (Hevner 1936), with an extension. In a study, Hevner presented 66 different moods, which, unlike Lungwitz and Machleidt, she did not regard as entities (Hevner 1936, 250) but as an expression of particular characteristics of music, summarized in groups or categories. These categories include similar characterizations in the sense of similar shade of feeling (Hevner 1936, 250) and partly include emotions in the sense indicated above. Bonde shortened Hevner's 66 differentiations in eight categories to 40, made some changes and added a ninth category for the characterization of popular music (Number 7). These nine categories are listed in Table 2.

Not all of the designations in this mood-wheel correspond to characteristics of emotions in the sense mentioned above. Differentiations such as dramatic, passionate or sombre, here called moods, do not meet the core of emotion as concrete experience and relationship quality. Rather than the process itself, evaluations or impressions are described from a neutral outside perspective. Hevner used her list of adjectives mainly in the study of musical expression, which is not apparent in

6 In Frohne-Hagemann 2003, "frightening" is mentioned additionally in Category 2. This is not explicitly mentioned by Bonde or Hevner. For this reason "frightening" is not dealt with here. This has a special significance further in the text. Other sources also emphasize the omission of frightened, among others, in Hevner (Gabrielsson, Lindström 2001, 244).

one-to-one emotional correspondence. Therefore, a great number of the adjectives are not found in Table 1. Nevertheless, several categories by Bonde and Hevner are very similar to the classifications in Table 1. Individual emotions are named directly within the categories. This concerns category 2, "sad", and category 6, "happy" by Hevner (Hevner 1936, 265). Category 2 is very similar to the emotional quality of mourning mentioned in Table 1. Category 3 is characterized predominantly by the emotional quality of intention with "yearning", but also with affectionate (see Bunt, Pavlicevic in the last subchapter). Categories 4 and 6 as well as 5 in part resemble closely the emotional quality of joy and the feeling of well-being. Categories 7, 8 and 9 are characterized greatly by the emotional quality of anger. Category 1 appears to represent more of a transcendental level of experience, which is not included in Table 1.[7] In regarding all nine categories, it is remarkable that the emotional quality of anxiety is not represented at all by Hevner or Bonde. It therefore affects the classification of moods for the selection of music in GIM. The absence of anxiety, however, does not only seem to find its expression in this, but seems to emerge from the basic principle of action of GIM in general. Bonde describes that GIM, a form of receptive music therapy, chooses to work in a trophotropic way (Bonde 2002, 116). Bonde makes reference here to an article by Bonny on music and consciousness from 1975 (Bonny 1975 / 1999). Here, Bonny depicts an ergotropic and a trophotropic path to the self within a scheme of states of consciousness (Bonny 1999, 173–174; with reference to Fischer 1971).

The ergotropic path leads to the self by means of perception via sensibility, creativity, anxiety, the only emotional quality mentioned, and stages of schizophrenia as well as ecstasy. The trophotropic path leads to the self via relaxation, meditation and tranquillity (even yoga) (ibid.). The path of relaxation and thus the trophotropic path are mentioned as the key to action in GIM. In this way, the ergotropic path to the self and the anxiety explicitly connected with it are evaded from the outset. In the place quoted, however, Bonny mentions EEG measurements, which particularly show a pattern of anxiety for imagination, central to GIM. Bonny describes an increase of the EEG-theta activity before falling asleep during most types of imagery (Bonny 1999, 174–175). According to Machleidt's EEG measurements, however, it is the emotional quality of anxiety which is characterized by an increase in theta-activity (Machleidt 1994, 356). When these results are viewed together, one can form the hypothesis that for the affected person, images within the emotional quality of fear are not directly experienced as angst-filled defence mechanisms resulting from the feeling of being touched. . Furthermore, this would mean that the trophotropic path of GIM including "anxiety-free" music would be made possible

7 Here, the immediate religious dimension and level of GIM with its principles becomes clear. The mythical structures of GIM mentioned above are given another aspect .

by the principle of imagery.[8] This train of thought could provide an explanation for the interpretation of a short case study of GIM.

Goldberg describes a young man, who during his first GIM session accompanied by the second movement of Beethoven's Fifth Piano Concerto suddenly sees his deceased father and abruptly interrupts the music-guided imagery (Goldberg 1999, 125). In this situation, the young man experiences sudden overpowering fright, anxiety and shock experienced as "something happening to me". This makes it impossible to continue the music-guided imagery session. In the second session, the past is experienced in the same image, in which the young man directly experiences sadness and tears during the music-guided imagery (Goldberg 1999, 126). The emotional quality of sadness, characterized by a decline in all areas of performance in EEG patterns (Machleidt 1994, 356), often appears in GIM case descriptions (Bruscia 1996, Wigram et al. 1999, etc.). During GIM, this can be experienced in the same way as other emotion qualities.

In contrast to GIM, RMT anxiety is named specifically as an emotional quality. This does not refer to the selection of music in RMT but the direct perception of emotions or reactions to emotions by the client. Frankl, founder of Logotherapy, must be mentioned here as part of the theoretical foundation of RMT (Frankl 1999). His paradox intention is used by RMT in the fifth phase (Röhrborn, this book). The central starting point of the development of the paradox intention was the anxiety of expectation. The "neurotic-anxious expectations"(Kriz 1994, 217–218) were also confirmed as the original cause of anxiety and obsessional neurosis in later studies of logotherapy. The client recognizes the emergence of anxiety, intensified by himself in RMT. By this, restricted experience, which according to emotion psychology means a restricted spectrum of emotional qualities is widened and becomes more extensively accessible within the framework of the self. Before this can be possible to a full extent, the perception of "personality- and symptom-specific anxieties" in the third phase of RMT (Röhrborn in this book) plays a repeated role in the experience and therapy process of RMT. Therefore, the emotional quality of anxiety has great significance for the action of RMT. This is found neither in the basic principle of GIM nor in the emotional classification of musical selections in GIM.

The RMT process is thus characterized as ergotropic according to Bonny, and contains the above-mentioned emotional quality of anxiety. In RMT, however, relaxation phenomena can also be encountered. The letting-happen of RMT, as mentioned above causes a loosening of anxiety fixations or rather a clear "reduction of anxiety" (Reinhardt 2002 in Schwabe 2003, 27) in RMT. Anxiety is not trophotropically "evaded" by means of images, but confronted in the state of awareness of perception.

---

8 At this place it would be interesting to examine whether Category 1 in Table 2 contains anxiety moments of unity of body and mind and intensifies them, how anxiety is experienced as "something happening to me" without, however, being experienced as an existential threat in the sense of anxiety as a phenomenon.

The especially successful indications for RMT therefore include excessive ambitions, introversion as well as phobic and hypochondriac fixation on physical symptoms (Hofmann 1996, 110–113). Especially at the beginning of the therapeutic process, clients repeatedly experience anxiety (Rudloff, Schwabe 1997). The complete openness for all forms of perception in the initial phase of RMT is repeatedly experienced as insecurity with regard to everyday perception behaviour. "Disturbed" perceptual behaviour is weakened in RMT in favour of an emotionally wider and more accessible perception of self. Thus, the ergotropic path of RMT passes sensitization, creativity and anxiety, corresponding completely to Bonny and Fischer. Subsequently, however, it does not lead to the self via schizophrenic stages and ecstasy (here, the contraindications for RMT are to be observed) but perceives, accepting and always starting from perception, the actual state as reality divided into many smaller pieces, (Lacan 1980, 216)[9] and the self with a broad spectrum of emotion qualities. At this point, a state characterized as ergotropic is experienced trophotropically, and involves an increased experience of pleasure and of relaxation.

In the emotional process, which, according to Machleidt (1994) and Wosch (2002), runs from intention via anxiety, anger and mourning to joy as stages of different relationship qualities with regard to an object, RMT can start from the point of blockage caused by the emotional quality of anxiety. Emotion psychologically, RMT thus carries out a therapeutic process which starts with the restricting "something happening to me" and leads to the experience of emotions as moments of unity of body and mind with its procedural component. GIM appears to avoid the point of anxiety in the emotional process through its trophotropic action.[10] Even at the end, the complete experience of emotion represents a moment of unity of body and mind. With its meditative principle and, above all, its spiritual category of experience (Table 2, No. 1), however, its starting point lies in an extra-emotional area which serves as a beginning for individual qualities of emotion of the self via images.

Summary

Current emotion psychology offers two basic images of emotion. One image shows emotion as a complex encompassing universal phenomenological, neuropsychological, and neuromuscular components. In addition, it is a fundamental system of motivation of the human being. It constitutes the current focus of emotion psychology. . A second definition describes emotion as a complex of moments of unity of body and mind, "something happening to me", being touched, and a relationship component as well as, a person-centred phenomenon. Especially for receptive music therapy,

9 At the same place Lacan also calls the real an "object of anxiety par excellence".

10 Emotional qualities characterized above all as trophotropic in the emotional process are emotions of mourning and joy, which possess a final process character.

the latter provides an extensive and relevant basis. At the same time, it contains a strong analogy between emotion and music.

Emotion psychological differentiation of qualities of emotion may be carried out in active as well as for receptive music therapy using the five emotion groups of intention/affection, anxiety/dislike, anger/dislike and approach, mourning/ uneasiness, and joy/well-being. In order to complete the definition of emotion, research in active music therapy as well as the attention given to musical expression as a component of the strong focus on facial expression up until now seem to make it necessary to add a procedural component to the qualities of emotion. In the characterization of musical selections and according to the basic principles of GIM, which are predominantly trophotropic, all emotional qualities are of importance except anxiety. In contrast, this emotional quality plays a special role in the therapeutic process of RMT. The ergotropic path of RMT based on perception as a fundamental therapeutic process appears to be necessarily connected to anxiety. This opens the possibility of being touched from a much broader spectrum of emotions as result of a process. In contrast, based on emotion psychological criteria the spiritual mood is characterized in the mood-wheel of GIM as extra-emotional. This opens a path to an emotional experience of body and mind. An empirical examination of this theoretic differentiation is yet to be conducted. Such examinations would further clarify questions of indication and questions of music selection between RMT and GIM. Emotion psychology offers a comprehensive setting, which in turn promises encouraging theoretic feedback from music therapy to emotion psychology.

Acknowledgement

The author would like to thank Elizabeth Franzen for the translation.

CH: 15: METHODOLOGY OF MUSIC THERAPY AND DEPTH RELAXATION (DRMT)

HANS-HELMUT DECKER-VOIGT

A credo

Relaxation and depth relaxation lead into trance. Every intense reading or identification with a novel's protagonist leads into trance. Every deeper immersion into an image from a painter or a picture of a landscape or a face can lead into trance. Every daydream implies being in a state of trance. In particular, every intense musical experience leads to trance. One of the most effective trance-inducing methods is the connection of musical experience with relaxation (as a means of self-treatment), or depth relaxation (as a therapeutic goal). This is as true for the individual as for the group or society. It is effective enough even to be used in a negative way for mass manipulation, but is also optimal as a healing tool.

Definition of trance and therapeutic trance

Trance is a natural experience that often takes over our entire psychological system. Trance is 'an experience of subjective reality that is often more "real" than real reality' (Manfred Prior in an address to hypnotherapists in the *Milton H. Erikson Institut*, Hamburg 1994). We experience this subjective reality as blending with the so-called "normal" reality, and vice versa. Each individual sways between these two "realities" according to their own rhythm, and the changes between "waking consciousness" and "altered waking consciousness" are distinguishable by measurable physiological changes. Between modern brain research and psychotherapeutic trance work, a new field of research has developed, based on one of the most ancient shamanistic techniques. Ancient magic, modern psychology and brain research meet in receptive music therapy. Essential to all these methods is, as in all modern relaxation and depth relaxation techniques, the absence of anxiety in the presence of the therapist. Only when the patient is free of anxiety inner human resources really be mobilised. Qualitative statements such as this are supported by quantitative psychological and medical research in the field of stress management. Stress provokes an increase in cortisone, which hinders the brain's ability to connect emotional qualities with verbally encoded knowledge. Trance and therapeutic trance, however, effect a synchronistic fluidity in emotional experience and memory and their transfer to the verbal therapeutic speech concerning life issues being dealt with in the therapy. The therapist's presence also has an effect on the overall setting, and it must be taken into account that even "positive" effects of this can actually contradict the aims of the therapy; it may invoke a "euphoric intensity" which may have an especially disturbing influence on problem-centered or dysfunction-oriented work. But common to music trance work and music psychotherapy are the necessity for an atmosphere as free from anxiety as possible, a warm climate of empathy allowing free-floating consciousness, and sensory and mental openness to the therapeutic setting. Peter Hess and Sabine Rittner have provided an overview of these implicit factors (Hess & Rittner 2003).

Definitions of "relaxation/depth relaxation/pain-management therapy"

A definition of terms is here necessary because, as *Depth Relaxation Music Therapy* (DRMT) exclusively employs complex musical structures, or music played (performed) by the therapist ("semi-improvised" music), and is to be used only for relaxation because of the emotional associations it holds for the patient. This is incongruent with the usual definitions of "deep" or "depth" relaxation. The literature differentiates three levels in which music is used in the context therapy or self-healing:
1. Relaxation
2. Depth Relaxation
3. Pain-management therapy

1. Relaxation with music

For people who are unable to relax without the aid of an external medium (music, visual images, sounds from nature, etc.) can perceive a constant stimulus as "sensory overload". Such patients usually choose music according to their own specific preferences in consultation with the therapist, and revised as necessary. The more precisely and variedly the patient and therapist can choose music which effectively enables relaxation, the more independently can the patient use "his" music in his everyday life to positively influence the psycho-physical unity of body, mind and soul. This level of experience is defined as occurring on the "relaxation" level. Today's booming market in "relaxation media" is to be attributed to this, although, from a medical perspective, the therapeutic use of music for relaxation developed primarily in the context of the patient-therapist (/doctor) relationship. "Relaxation with music" is today popularly but erroneously associated with "self-treatment", rather than considered as a part of therapeutic treatment. The conception of music as an element in therapy is increasing in medical schools (for example the work of Ralph Spintge and Roland Droh), as is its everyday use in German clinics (Droh & Spintge 1983). DRMT, as herein described, has been recommended by a goverment run employers's body (the BfA *Bundesversicherungsanstalt für Angestellte*) for use in the treatment of heart patients in a currently running research project in a rehabilitation clinic in Berlin, the *Curschmann-Klinik*.

2. *Depth Relaxation with music*

Harm Willms (1977) and later Christoph Schwabe (1991) have further differentiated "Depth Relaxation" from "relaxation". When the state of "relaxation" can no longer be attained due to high stress (preparing for examinations, or before a medical operation for example), the necessity of "Depth Relaxation" arises.
Specifically, *Depth Relaxation* is induced by a doctor or therapist

- using speech
- the music is not determined by the patient's emotional preferences, rather aimed at creating a stress-relieving feeling-world in the patient.

The methods and procedures of *Depth Relaxation* can be defined as implying a therapeutic setting with the therapist integrated in an on-going, developing therapeutic relationship, in the sense of an "I – Thou" relationship as described by Martin Buber (Buber 1983). The central role that this relationship plays is markedly different from other therapeutic uses of music, and from private use of relaxation music, where the recording invites the recipient into a state of auto-communication.

3. *Music and pain-management (audio-analgesia)*

The main fields in this area are:

- music in the waiting room
- music for pre-operative relaxation (use in dentistry is a well researched example)
- music during operations
- music in the post-operative stage
- music for pain prevention

The patient would be provided with specifically suitable music through headphones. Details can be found in specialist literature.

The methods of depth relaxation in music therapy described in this essay work, like other relaxation techniques I know, exclusively with trophotropic (calming) music. There may be exceptions where ergotropic (lively, energising) music could be used, for example where a patient due to musical socialisation already associates a specific piece of such music with relaxation. (For example, a lively German folksong worked as a lullaby for a 68 year old patient, because his father had always played it on the record player when he returned from shift work at the child's bedtime). The entire process is, however, induced and orientated through the work of the therapist, who is also prepared for problem-centred or problem-management discussions after treatment.

The "Building Blocks" of DRMT

After two years of ambulant and six years of stationary practice, I developed a seven step methodology, each element of which can be used, where necessary, in any order, and can be integrated with other relaxation techniques in problem oriented and problem solving work. Each "building block" can, and indeed must be employable in an open order, as each stage of treatment must be oriented to the physical and psycho-emotional condition and characteristics of the patient. Each step is flexible:

- from simple relaxation work (independently or as an introduction to active improvised music with patients),
- through depth relaxation before a stressful medical intervention or examination, (for example, balloon angioplasty in a heart clinic, or chemotherapy; where necessary, follow up work with any results or consequences that are causing distress),
- to conflict-centred, solution-oriented, issue-based work, dealing with any remaining issues on the psycho-social and psycho-dynamic level that the medical problem may have triggered,
- and to preparation for life after leaving hospital, and dealing with the possibilities of relapse.

The steps can be followed in any order and can be combined with any of the other components of the complete therapy, for example, with counselling, active music therapy, psycho-social counselling, pastoral care, occupational therapy.

The Seven Steps and their context

I. Sensitisation to the feeling of "comfort" in the body
II. Sensitisation to the breath
III. Sensitisation to feelings, mental images, thoughts
IV. Sensitisation to the auditory perception of music
V. Re-orientation to the "here and now"
VI. Reflection of these experiences and their transference into everyday life through connecting questions
VII. "Rolling back"

Each of these steps has been influenced by the work of Milton Erikson's psychotherapy, in terms of responsibility of the patient for his own growth, the continuously supportive tenor of the verbal accompaniment, which I define as a "the therapist's moderation of the patient's contribution" (see Erikson 1981). Erikson has also influenced my personal methodology of accompanying the patient into trance. **Steps I and II** (sensitisation to body comfort and breathing) have emerged from experience with other relaxation techniques, for example autogenic training and work with guided imagery. **Steps III (and V)**, (sensitisation to feelings and images), are based on the methodologies of psychoanalytical and humanistic psychology, using associative material from the patient. Other influences have been art therapy, especially *Ausdruckstherapie* ("expressive art therapy"), developed by Paolo J. Knill (Knill 1993), and *Medien und Ausdruckstherapie*, ("media and expressive art therapy"), which I developed with Knill starting in 1975(Decker-Voigt 2002). **Step IV** (sensitisation to auditory perception) uses methods for sensitisation to the auditory environment similar to those used in music pedagogy at the primary level, as developed by Küntzel-Hansen in the 1970's (Küntzel-Hansen 1971). Eriksonian hypnotherapy also integrates such sensitivity (Erikson & Rossi 1989a), as do various body work modalities (Bio-energetics, for example). This step works towards a greater receptivity to music that characterises the entire DRMT approach. Together with the other steps, this step has many possibilities for modification, from its use of recorded or improvised music on the one hand, to the way it relates to problem centred work on the other. **Step V** (re-orientation to the here and now) is also based on experience with various relaxation methods – from autogenic training to Gestalt therapeutic approaches. The strong emphasis on the patient's self motivation and involvement in the forming of the overall therapy is influenced again by Erikson's hypnotherapy. The term "re-orientation" is used to make a clear distinction between "induction" (the guidance into trance in the first four steps) and re-entrance into "everyday reality", emphasised in the work of Mary Priestley (Priestley 1982). Here, the patient is guided out of the trance state, explicitly using the same sequence of steps each time. ("Induction" refers to steps leading into trance; "re-orientation". **Step VI** (reflection of experiences in everyday life) has the broadest range of possible techniques. It could be limited to simply identifying and naming the patient's associative material (with the same general aims of normal relaxation therapy). Here, the therapist can guide the patient in the meaning the patient draws for him/herself out the therapeutic experiences, and can offer other meanings in a humanistic psychoanalytic way, (perhaps laying emphasis and gaining a perspective on past experiences). The therapist may also, during the musical-receptive experience, directly pose questions relating to the present or planned life concept of the patient. The problem/conflict centred approach of DRMT is not oriented on any procedural principles; rather it focuses exclusively on the psychodynamic and physical condition and character of the patient. Included here are components of Theme Centred Interaction psychotherapeutic counselling. In this step, it is decided to what extent DRMT will remain in the realm of relaxation work, or develop into solution-oriented psychotherapeutic work. **Step VII** ("rolling back"), builds bridges between the protected world of therapy (time for the patient, his/her fantasies and resources) and the "outside" world (the workplace, the apartment, etc.).

Preparation to the Seven Steps

Discovering ("uncovering") ones inner state

The learning implied in the first step, the development of awareness of one's inner condition, inner well-being, sensitivity to feelings of "comfort" in the body, (and the implied awareness of sensations of well-being and otherwise), forms a basis for work in the steps that follow. For this reason, it is worth taking some time to examine these steps more fully.

The offer of relaxation (regardless of technique or modality) in the area of either prevention or education and training, give the patient an active choice. The patient does not encounter me as "patient", rather, is guided by an expectation of experiencing something comfortable. The same is true for the person who buys a relaxation CD from the book or music store (or pharmacy/ drug store).

In all these cases, the term "relaxation" has positive associations and implies the patient's ability for self-healing. No one in an adult education course or in rehabilitation is surprised by an offer of relaxation or comfort. This is, however, not so with heart patients. A heart attack or heart disease, admission to a heart clinic, the swift progression of treatment, examination and interventions has only recently been finished. The entire treatment, from injection to bypass operation, balloon angioplasty, and open-heart surgery, is experienced as a traumatising intervention on the body from the outside, and is associated with fear of death, fear of losing one's health and the loss of a life-concept. Patients with such an experience in the recent past would experience the suggestion to "just relax... now!" as foreign and absurd, and would wonder if the therapist has any idea of what they have suffered. This disturbance might strengthen the patient's resistance and may close him/her off to trance work permanently.

DRMT includes the current psycho-emotional and physical state of the patient in the invitation to trance oriented relaxation work, in accordance with the therapist's perception or the patient's descriptions. For this "meeting the patient where he is" on the body-mind-soul unity level, a verbal exchange is necessary before beginning with **step 1** (sensitisation to body comfort). Often the current medical diagnosis is in the foreground, and the physical condition can be used as a starting point. The importance of the heart patient's awareness of his physical condition (whether self-perceived or perceived with guidance from the therapist) cannot be overestimated. It is the foundation of all the psycho-emotional work that follows. For the patient, it also distinguishes the holistic approach of music psychotherapy from the "clinical" world of the heart clinic, and its "functional" approach. This initial step of the patient becoming sensitive to his inner condition is a kind of "induction into the induction", and brings the motivation to continue with the further steps. It is comparable to the pre-induction talk in Eriksonian hypnosis, developed by Manfred Prior (Prior 1963: 289)

Verbal picture of discovering/uncovering ones inner condition

Introductory talk:

"How would you describe your inner feelings, your state of mind?"“
"How do you experience yourself at the moment? (... after this terrible night/... before the approaching medical examination/... after yesterday's letter from your employer/... before you wife comes to visit ...) -according to whatever is the most important issue the patient is facing.

I prefer to use expressions from fairy tales ("Once upon a time", "there will be", "it is now") or parables and stories, as Erikson used. I also often use word-plays to avoid standard answers to the standard question "How are you?" Manfred Prior's "helping questions" (Prior 2002) and my work with association-rich word plays can often form a good basis for the later work with 'tone-play' in free improvisation. For patients who are reluctant or uncertain in the area of verbalisation, I invite them to try a short musical improvisation on the theme of "my inner condition". This happens before the receptive stage with music, and provides the patient with the opportunity to experience different aspects of their own musical expressiveness with improvised and receptively experienced music.

The experience that one's own improvised music, as well as specially chosen recorded music, also has symbolic associations with one's inner state deepens the experience of music and turns chosen recorded music into a kind of instrument for personal expression. The methods of music therapy are often variously graded ("Do we listen to music here? Or do we play music?"). Often, a patient will play a musical structure in the 'one minute sound-picture' that he/she will request as recorded music a short while later. Elements such as tempo and dynamic, sound, rhythm and structure can re-appear in the therapist's verbal induction into musical receptivity. Patients' difficulties, sensitive areas or other hindrances can also be integrated into "enjoyable experience you now wish to allow yourself." Patients with a musical background can often feel restricted in playfully making their own music, and can be simply invited to choose from a selection of recorded music to express their current inner situation and feelings.

Musical illustration of inner condition

Improvised musical „one minute sound-picture“

„Would you, perhaps like to try to express with musical instruments, how you are feeling at the moment? A one minute musical piece.“

Imaginative musical picture of inner state

„Which piece of music occurs to you, in portraying an answer to the question, ‚How am I feeling today'?" (If the therapist is to improvise a piece for the patient, there should be a discussion of the patient's wishes for the character of the music.)

Whether an adagio or an agogic outburst – regardless of what the patient does, it expresses something of his inner situation and can provide material for later discussion or be integrated into the induction. ("Maybe you can imagine bringing the sounds you have just played, with you into the time frame of the present, where you have the opportunity to experience something pleasant?"). The aim of the exercise is to integrate the musical expression of the answer to "How am I feeling?" into the induction. Often, the invitation to take problematic or uncomfortable feelings or sensations into more pleasurable relaxation experience can help the patient integrate what he has experienced in the therapy into his everyday life (seventh step).

For patients not as comfortable with verbal expression, drawing with crayons and markers on DIN A-3 paper can be employed. For me, these also belong to the equipment of music therapy.

Vignette:
(Followed by a discussion of the picture, or transference into a musical picture.)

Drawing/painting one's inner state

"Perhaps you might like to find an answer to the question "How am I feeling?" with markers or crayons – a 'one minute picture'.

A heart patient spoke slowly about her terrible night (before balloon angioplasty later that day), her speech dragging, and trailing off into unended sentences. Her drawing of "how am I feeling" shows her in bed in her room, with shelves in the background, rising to the ceiling, filled with medicine bottles, and in the middle a window looking out to the Baltic Sea. When she starts to talk about the picture, her speech suddenly becomes lively. Previously, the patient managed a shop selling organic produce. She had contact to many organic farms, and her world view was that of "green" politics, alternative lifestyle, etc. Her feelings that morning were not so much characterised by fear of the approaching

> operation, but by the feeling that she would be betraying her ideology and self concept by having the operation and being dependent on machines, and later having to take part in medical and training programmes for the rest of her life, "as well as the relaxation therapy I have to keep doing regularly".

Further work dealt with this basic underlying feeling of having betrayed her philosophy of life. In turn, she also felt betrayed by that philosophy and lifestyle. Where she had expected reward, she had a feeling of being punished. This feeling had medieval overtones and hindered her acceptance of her illness and, consequently, the possibilities for healing. By using drawing materials rather than musical instruments, she was able to express herself on a primarily personal/self-oriented manner, rather than through the more social medium of music. To invite patients to express themselves musically necessarily means inviting them to experience socialising effects: every musical expression or reception – improvised or heard – connects participants in a group socially, or connects a patient with a therapist. No one can play a sound in a room without it being heard by others present, or without sharing the experience of listening with them. (The use of headphones is, of course, an exception.) Music, therefore, is forced socialisation, and this can be a barrier to its use in some situations. Drawing, on the other hand, can allow a patient more privacy in feeling and bringing something more slowly and un-selfconsciously to expression, rather than immediately producing musical sound that necessarily involves others and impels the patient into social contact. When a patient indicates a need for "time to himself". I leave or do not enter on the musical level.

Before the treatment, I always discuss with the patients that we are not only bringing problems and discomfort into awareness and acceptance, but also searching for positive moments of comfort, and that the work with relaxation belongs to this. Enticement and coaxing are important elements in trance and relaxation work with acutely ill heart patients. ("Maybe it would be good for you. I am here to accompany you. ")

The final question before beginning the induction into step one is:

> "What do you think you might need in order to allow yourself to especially enjoy the next experience?"

This question allows the patient to become active. He checks his inner perceptions of bodily comfort, and considers, even in the middle of his illness, how he can prepare himself for greater comfort. The therapist can also depersonalise the question:

> "Is anything still needed before we start?"

This is recommended when the patient reacts with resistance to the induction when the question is directed explicitly to him. In my experience, by leaving the question open, the patient tends to focus more on the situation, rather than on problems and difficulties irrelevant to the session.

A case study showing step four illustrates the interdependence between theory and practice. The other six steps will be illustrated in Decker-Voigt 2006 (in preparation).

Step Four

Sensitisation of auditory perception

"When the flow of the breath is more familiar to you, then we will wander with our inner eye, using it to gather what we are hearing at this moment. Maybe there are familiar or new sounds inside the room we are sitting in; perhaps even sounds from within the body, where inner organs are working for us; we allow all these sounds, within, from without, and now we take in the sounds of the music we are hearing and let them work on our inner being, as we allow the tones to come, and to let them go – maybe the sounds bring inner pictures with them, or thoughts, or feelings, we allow all these to come and to go, or peacefully to come to rest, leaving their impressions, feeling the music, now, and allow yourself to adjust your body to a more comfortable position at any time you wish."

The music receptivity phase starts here as the therapist switches on the sound system, or begins to play improvised music, from 3 minutes to at most 8 minutes. If the playing time is longer, experience shows that the patient may have difficulties with re-orientation. In accordance with the case history and the introductory discussions (inner awareness), I make verbally clear the problem or tasks that the patient earlier identified, and bring them to the foreground, as the background to the problems (the personality structures and character dynamics) can be better dealt with after the "softening up" that occurs during the inner "wandering" through the body and the arising formulation (and occasionally solution) of problem material through the medium of music.

Here is a summary of the outward conditions necessary for a secure music reception work:

- The session room needs to be acoustically suited, like a music therapy room, to improvised music. There should be no disturbance from outside noise.
- Lighting should be soft: avoid disturbance from wandering shadows cast by direct sunlight; electric lighting should be indirect.

- Bedside work with a patient in hospital is, of course, an exception to these rules.
- Always test equipment before stating, and do any pre-programming.
- Position your seat where you can easily reach the sound system without cause unnecessary noise disturbance.
- Patients with less experience in meditation and relaxation can sit on ergonomic (not too soft) chairs to begin with, and later go into trance in a lying position. (Again, excepting bedside work in a hospital.)
- Always start with the music soft, and slowly increase the volume manually (or by remote control).
- To help patients concentrate, always allow a little silence before playing the music, so that the music "comes out of silence".

The time-frame of 3 to 8 minutes is oriented to:

- Inter-subjective experience in various similar clinical projects, which have shown what duration is most supportive for patients ("Please, no longer" or "Please, no shorter")
- Observational experience of the minimum time in which muscular relaxation is induced, and the maximum time possible without causing difficulties in the re-orientation phase.

Function and Selection of Music

In selecting music suitable for the patient, and in accordance with the intentions of the therapist, a preliminary talk with the patient is necessary. (Or a talk with the patient's relatives if the patient is not capable of verbalising.) The enjoyment of a piece of music on an emotional level is in effect the induction of trance.

As suggested earlier, a school student's daydream, an immersion into a picture is the beginning stage of a trance, of a change in "waking consciousness". Indicators for this "altered waking consciousness" or trance-like state are to be observed in every concert hall, art gallery, library, classroom, when a person is "lost" in the experience or in thought: respiration becomes shallower, muscle tone changes- the swallowing reflex lessens and the motor system reacts to the experience. In a clinical setting, music selected for an individual patient would be used as a support for trance inducement, understood and used as an amplifier of the trance experience. The result can be similar to what Martin Buber (1983, 1997) calls "the Third" (*der Dritte*): the successful encounter; and what Paolo J. Knill and I see in terms of an artistic medium that the creator first creates, and which itself then creates the creator (Knill 1993).

Recorded music which the patient brings (often symbolising important times or events in the patient's biography) can also often induce trance as successfully as therapist-chosen or improvised music.

In a group therapy setting, the patient chooses his "soul-favourite" by exploring selection according to the parameters he decides upon (rhythm, dynamic, tone, melody and structure, – to name the elements of music discovered in developmental psychology). After a short rehearsal, the other patients perform his "soul-favourite".

The result is often a great improvement in the cohesion of the group, with which the recipient patient can identify; his fellow patients who are "performing" for him also identify more strongly with the group. This effect – the change in the group dynamic – has a further therapeutic effect for the recipient patient, in which the other patients literally "play" a part.

In the central receptive phase of the trance (after sensitisation of auditory perception) music, DRMT (as with most music therapy modalities) takes on the function of transference of associative material, which can be worked on in the post-trance discussion in terms of their deep-psychology/phenomenological aspects.

Background: through deep relaxation, music can often release traumatic material, which can only rise to consciousness in a safe context. Before the DRMT begins, therefore, problem-centred and problem-resolving therapeutic methods and possibilities must be in place in this mixture of music therapy and psycho therapeutic counselling.

This mixture of receptive music therapy (for the patients) and active music therapy for co-patients/therapists is oriented to music especially selected by the patients (the "soul favourites"). In my experience a strong sense of self involvement is created through the active selection of pieces, and therefore deepens the trance state.

94% of 105 documented music therapy sessions in the *Curschmann-Klinik showed* trophotropic oriented music structures with a duration of 3 to 8 minutes (either recorded or improvised music).

I have recorded (together with the former chief physician Friedrich-Karl Maetzel of the *Curschmann-Klinik*, now professor for *Propaedeutik der Medizin* at the *Hamburger Institut für Musiktherapie*) a practical example of the seven steps in a self-treatment CD with a handbook, for heart patients as part of a project for the *Curschmann Rehabilitation Klinik (Timmendorfer Strand)* (Decker-Voigt/ Maetzel 1998). This self-help package was intended for patients leaving the clinic. After their return home, the CD functioned as a reminder of the therapist, his voice and the therapeutic climate of the therapeutic setting during his stay in the clinic. If a particular patient found the receptive music therapy treatment especially valuable, then the music from the treatment would be edited and burned onto a CD, and given to him upon leaving. This is not only a music recording, but also a concrete symbol of the patient's "own" music, bridging his healing experiences in the clinic with his home life. Music, by its nature, reaches pre-verbal aspects of the psyche and therefore has an effect on the earliest (pre-verbal) traumas experienced by the individual. In patient feedback two and six months after leaving the clinic, this CD proved to be important as a trigger and support structure for the seven steps of DRMT being internalised and transformed into a self-help method, comparable to therapist guided, later, self directed processes, like autogenic training, for example.

Acknowledgement

The author would like to thank Mahina Strömer for the translation.

CH. 16: RECEPTIVE MUSIC THERAPY WITHIN ANTHROPOSOPHIC MUSIC THERAPY

MONICA BISSEGGER

Historic Aspects

Anthroposophic music therapy (Stückert 1997; Bissegger 2001), and especially receptive music therapy or "listening therapy", as it is also called, is decisively influenced by Rudolf Steiner's comments about music (see: "The Inner Nature of Music", GA 283). Various elaborations of his indications about music were to build an important foundation for Anthroposophic music therapy. **Anny von Lange** (1887–1957) e. g. began to study music phenomenology, having been stimulated by Goethe's sketch of his 'Tonlehre' (Theory of Musical Tone) and by Rudolf Steiner's manifold elaborations on music. A pianist and composer, Anny von Lange herself did not work as a therapist. However, through intensive work on the individual tone, intervals, rhythms, different keys, the seven-foldness and the twelve-foldness in music, the connection of tones with the planets, the planetary scales, etc., she created an essential foundation for the therapeutic use of music. Her work is summarized in the two volumes of "Man, Music and Cosmos". The musician *Wilhelm Doerfler* (1899–1980) also left behind the results of his intensive phenomenological studies in three volumes called "Das Lebensgefüge der Musik" (1994). The music scientist *Hermann Pfrogner* (1911–1988) was very interested in the healing effect of music (i. e. "Living tones", 1981) and cooperated at the beginning of the 60's with *Karl Koenig* (1902–1966) and *Hans-Heinrich Engel* (1921–1973), two physicians who practiced medicine in curative education, as well as with the music therapists *Maria Schüppel* (*1923), *Veronika Bay* (*1922), *Johanna Spalinger* (*1926) and *Christof-Andreas Lindenberg* (*1932).

Engel has been described as a person, who had not only a vast knowledge, but also a wealth of therapeutic intuition at his disposal (1999). He applied this intuition in the medical realm as well as in the therapeutic use of music. Engel occupied himself intensely with the fundamental elements of music and composed individual music pieces for therapeutic use with children with special needs, as well as archetypal tonal sequences related to the anthroposophic study of the human being. These individual therapeutic music pieces were played to the child by the music therapist over weeks, or sometimes even months with breaks in between and only then developed further by Engel. Astonishing results were recorded, especially with the very needy children.

Maria Schüppel, who influenced the development of Anthroposophic music therapy decisively, had a special gift of being able to connect inwardly with and listen into a person, based on a foundation in the study of man given by Rudolf Steiner. She had the talent of putting the impression she perceived into music and of developing a "listening therapy" out of this (Stückert 1997).

Receptive music therapy was of great importance especially at the beginning of Anthroposophic music therapy. Even though now decreasing, it was and still is the practice to write and use individual composed music pieces therapeutically, based on music phenomenological studies and the phenomenological observation of the individual illness of a patient. Nowadays it is more common to use music as a 'listening therapy' that arises in the moment as free improvisation, but is based on the same phenomenological foundations.

Listening

In order to be able to understand the effect of receptive music therapy, we have to enter into the listening realm as such.

Considering our different sense organs, we notice that the senses of sight and smell are oriented towards the front. We stretch our noses forwards to be able to smell better. Tasting happens a little more inwardly. Listening is placed the furthest back. It is not oriented towards the front but to the sides. We even lean back a little, to be able to hear a noise better, if we don't yet know where it comes from. The eye is as an organ located in a cave in the head that opens towards the outside, the ear is in a cave that opens towards the inside, surrounded by solid bones. Furthermore, we find that the eye has a limitation in space. We can see till the boundaries of space. The ear can go beyond those boundaries. The eye searchingly touches the surface; the ear penetrates into the depth of matter and discovers how it is sounding. So we can say listening is, as opposed to seeing, much more oriented towards the inside (McKeen 1996/Soesmann 1995).

If we focus on listening, ideally while lying down, we have the strange experience that we are not listening with our ears, but with our whole body. The sound envelopes us and sounds through us entirely. The ear as an organ overcomes the airy being of a tone and therefore its physicality and we can experience the tone that has become an etheric tone within us as a resonance of the outer tone. This resonance is a musical experience that is connected to the realm of feeling. From the realm of feeling, this experience penetrates into the ether body, the body of life, which enlivens our physical body. Thus we can also experience the musical tone with the etheric body. We can therefore understand the experience of listening with the whole human being. We can also understand how listening to music can evoke a sense of well being, independent from the memories the music might bring up in connection with our own biography (Steiner GA 283).

Whenever we occupy ourselves with listening, it is essential that we pay attention to the after-image of the sound. As we concentrate on the "after-sound", we can meet this experience only in amazement. It is as if we have been allowed to enter into a greater world, which goes far beyond previous personal experience. It is easier to understand, through such an experience, when Rudolf Steiner speaks about the physical music being only an image of a spiritual reality and man being able to experience the sounding of the spiritual world into the physical through music (Steiner GA 283/102).

In a therapy session, we can enhance this inwardness of the listening experience by playing behind the patient. The actively playing music therapist is no longer in the field of vision of the patient. The patient can concentrate fully on listening. The listening experience will be therefore deepened. Another therapeutic option could be to walk around the patient, while playing for example a hand bell or a gong. The patient feels surrounded by the sound. Many patients like to close their eyes, while listening; by inactivating the sense of vision, one intensifies listening.

It's not always possible for a patient to enter the realm of listening. Maria Schüppel says: "Often we have to create the path towards listening" (Stückert 1997). The ability to concentrate on music and to experience the sound's after-image needs practice and can therefore become a therapeutic goal.

The Music

In his book "The Inner Nature of Music" (GA 283), Rudolf Steiner draws a comparison: as the shadow of a human being is not the real human being, so is the music we make in this world only a shadow of a higher music, an image of a spiritual reality. He further describes how man unconsciously experiences the harmony of the spheres, while sleeping: "The soul lives during the night in these sounds of the spheres ... In the creative musician the perceptions of the night consciousness struggle through during the day consciousness and become memories ... All that men know as the art of music are the expressions, imprints, of what is experienced unconsciously in the sphere harmonies . . . It is the in-streaming of tones from a spiritual world which man experiences in the musical art." (GA 102, June 11, 1908, English translation by 'The Anthroposophic Press').

Maria Schüppel describes music from the therapeutic point of view this way: "Music is a spiritual substance, which man can absorb in his soul and can feel its structuring effect" (Stückert 1997).

Occupying oneself in a phenomenological way with the qualities of music, one realizes how tremendously manifold music is (Steiner GA 293; v. Lange 1968; Doerfler 1994; Pfrogner 1981; Ruland 1981; Bindel 1985; Beckh 1987; Husemann 1989; Hoerner 1993; Felber/Reinhold/Stückert 2003). One can discover different qualities of the intervals, the keys, the scales, the tonal systems, the music epochs, the musical forms, the rhythms, the harmonies, even of the individual tones, etc. What is the difference between the sound of an ascending sixth and a descending one? How is the key of D major different from E major? How is a melody with no semitone steps? How do I experience the rhythm short-long differently than long-short? What effect does a change of measure have in a song? What is special about a 6/8 measure or a 7/8? What differentiates the tone C from B? Intense occupation with those musical qualities, advancing from a subjective to a more and more objective perception, to an "objective discernment" (Ruland 2003) will enhance ones experience of music greatly (Bissegger 2001).

What kind of music is played in a therapeutic situation? The music, which is played live only, ranges from pieces from music literature to freely improvised music that arises out of the moment, to especially composed therapeutic music pieces.

The Choice of Music

Music literature is chosen according to the situation of the patient. The following questions can be decisive in making the right choice: Is the music meant to free the soul from heaviness within or to intensify the sensitivity of the soul? Should the music be rhythmically light, upbeat and swinging, or rather measured and focusing? Should the music be melodically easy to follow, with short phrases? Or can it be a more complex melody with different moods? Should the music have more of a waking quality, or be relaxing? Which music style fits best the momentary situation of the patient? Could it be an old Gregorian hymn, which can remind us of a prayer? Or is it a piece from the Baroque or the Classical period that expresses much more soul moods? Or should it be maybe a well known folk song that brings up old memories? In the way we perform a piece, e. g. loudly, quietly, faster, slower, lighter or denser, we can create variations, transitions, and sequences. Composed pieces can also be played with a free prelude, interlude or postlude, or one related to the piece. When working with free improvised music, the therapist can pick up moods, vocal expressions and movements of the patient. This can be based on a more questioning or a more answering attitude and can encompass all the musical qualities the therapist has at his/her disposal. One can look for a suitable rhythm, a melody that picks up on the mood of the patient, maybe a certain interval or tone, etc. The improvised music can develop into a direct dialog between the therapist and the patient, which develops further from one moment to the next. Especially in situations where there is no verbal communication possible this can become an important tool.

Composed therapy music can be a piece of music, which has an archetypal character and can be used for different patients, or a piece of music, which is especially composed for one specific patient. An example of the first kind of therapy music follows: a piece by Maria Schüppel for alto-lyre (originally played in a round with soprano- and alto-lyre) called "Mercury Bath" This music has a light, sparkling and enlivening character. The 7/8 measure and the ever-changing major and minor triads bring a mobility that enhances the enlivening effect of it.

In specifically composed music therapy, the therapist tries to connect the overall impression of the patient with a therapeutic goal and composes this into the music. Here follows an example by Maria Schüppel from music therapy for a

3 ¼ year old boy with cerebral palsy. In addition to being spastic, he is also blind, moderately hard of hearing and has a weak overall condition. He cannot sit up, hold his head up, crawl or talk. The music that is printed here is only one part of the whole therapy:

The music is played on soprano-lyre; in the last part a voice is added. The descending sequence of fifths has an incarnating character. The overlapping fifths are played in various rhythms and create finally a flowing melody, supported by the voice singing vowels.

The Music Instruments

In Anthroposophic music therapy many different music instruments are used and put in connection with the human being (Bissegger 2001; Felber/Reinhold/Stückert 2003; Reinhold 1996). In receptive music therapy, the alto-lyre is used in particular. The **lyre** is an instrument with similarities to a harp. Its tonal range is a little more than three octaves (E to F' or A"). Because of its light tone, which leaves the listener very free, the lyre is the instrument most commonly used in receptive music therapy, especially in work with seriously ill, comatose or dying patients. Since especially those patients are in a situation of extreme openness and vulnerability, it is of great importance to use an instrument, which can be played very softly and transparently. The unchallenging nature of the outer sound gives the patient the possibility of being open to what comes towards him and to allow himself to be 'touched' by it. In his tremendous vulnerability, the patient has to guard himself against noises from the outside, which means that he withdraws inwardly, a disposition one can often observe on intensive wards. Through the sound of the lyre, the soul can become 'wide' again, can open up and turn towards the world. The patient can find himself again as an individual.

In the neonatology we use the **Kinderharfe** (children's-harp) instead of the lyre. The Kinderharfe is a small stringed instrument, which can be played very gently. Its tonal range is much smaller than a lyre, reaching from D' to E'' (B''). Corresponding to a little child, the darker tones, available on the lyre, are not played on this instrument. Furthermore, the Kinderharfe is not tuned chromatically, like a lyre, but is pentatonic, which eliminates semitone steps and the centeredness on a key note. A light, suspended mood arises, that corresponds to the situation of a small child (Bissegger 2000).

Next to the lyre/Kinderharfe, the **singing voice** has a very central place in receptive music therapy. With the voice, the singer as a person is much more directly present than he is when playing an instrument. His soul-spiritual being sounds through the voice. Therefore with singing one can build a bridge to another human being much more directly. Even unconscious or semi-conscious patients can be addressed by singing (Bissegger 1999a). Because of its personal imprint one has to use one's voice very consciously. The voice has to be freed from a too personal emotional timbre and put into the 'service' of the other person, which means it is not about expressing one's own wellbeing, but about a questioning search for the wellbeing of the other person. It is not always an easy undertaking to make this step, since one's own wishes, even though they are in relation to the patient, quickly come into the foreground (the wish that the patient would wake up, open his eyes, come into contact, etc.). The voice has to be so well trained, that one can sing also very quietly, nearly inaudibly. The less a patient is incarnated, which means the less he is still connected to his physical body with his soul-spiritual being (unconscious or dying patients), the quieter, 'less substantial' the sounds have to become.

In a therapeutic context, I often combine the lyre and the voice. I start with the lyre to help the patient to tune in, but also to tune in myself. A patient who can't react verbally or with facial expressions, who has a disturbed consciousness, is often surrounded by a lonesome mood that can also affect me. A first 'tuning in' with the lyre can help me to overcome this mood and to engage gradually with the patient. Playing the lyre also helps to get a feeling for the patient. How is his listening capacity? Does he have a soulful access to the music? Does his soul start to 'vibrate'? What mood is he in? When a certain contact has been established and I can feel his readiness towards the music and my presence, I add my voice. I use the voice only once I feel that he is ready for it. Until then I stay with the more objective playing of the lyre. There are also situations when I step to a bedside and recognize that I have to stay very close to the patient; that I maybe have to come into direct contact and put my hand on his arm or his hand. In a situation like this I start directly with the voice and stay with it.

English hand bells are another kind of instrument used in receptive music therapy (Reinhold 1997). Hand bells are amazingly soft and warm sounding instruments that create a large sounding space. Through the striking movement when being played they have a more requesting character than stringed instruments. A similar sound experience comes from forged **gongs** that are also used in receptive music therapy. When one chooses to work with a wind instrument and therefore puts the emphasis more on the melodic element than on the sound, one uses mostly a **gemshorn**, most often the tenor-gemshorn (made of a cow's horn). The bass-gemshorn or the subbass-gemshorn can be used as well. When working with special needs children, with the goal of stimulating their listening activity through different sounds, one can use many different instruments, such as the **kantele, choroi-flute, finger cymbals, chrotta, bowed psaltery,** etc.

The Application of Receptive Music Therapy

In Anthroposophic music therapy, receptive music therapy is considered a therapeutic situation in which the patient is not engaged outwardly and does not play an instrument himself, as opposed to active music therapy. The patient is totally focused on the listening experience, which is strictly speaking also a very active process. The listening experience can be followed by a conversation about this experience, if possible. Images and feelings that arise while listening to the music can be reflected on and brought into the personal life context.

In music therapeutic practice, the application of receptive or active music therapy is tuned to the situation the patient is in at a time. Receptive music therapy is used with patients who can not handle an instrument actively. These are unconscious, semi-conscious, very weak or dying patients, small children and children or adults with special needs.

In work with very ill, weak patients, receptive music therapy is in the foreground. It can be combined, however, with a short phase of active music therapy, in which the patient plays just a few sounds, for example on a bordun-lyre, a small stringed instrument, tuned to one chord. To play actively can have an enlivening and encouraging effect on the patient.

With patients who can participate in active playing, receptive music therapy is used only partially. If used, listening to music can serve as a way to tune in before the patient enters himself in an active phase of playing. The listening can also follow an active phase, to round off a therapeutic session. The goal can be to deepen a desired inwardness through taking back outer activity. With children who normally love to be active themselves, especially with hyperactive children, it can be an important step in the therapeutic process to weave in short receptive phases in order to create a moment of rest from all outer activity.

In receptive therapy, we always deal with music that is directly played by the therapist. Experience shows that seriously ill patients don't like to listen to electronically produced sounds, but experience live music as being pleasant. Therefore we use no recorded music. The directly, live produced tone can unfold its own character fully. A 'true' sense perception is the result and with that comes an enlivening of the senses. Through this kind of sense perception, we enhance a deepened, soulful experience that also has effects into the physical body. The therapist, who is fully present in each moment, can adjust his playing at any given moment to the needs of the patient. He can enter fully into the situation. This will be more and more important, considering the highly technical development of medicine otherwise.

Realms of Applications

Receptive music therapy, next to active music therapy, is applied in Anthroposophic medicine in the following areas:

- Intensive Care
- Internal Medicine
- Gynecology
- Oncology
- Palliative Care
- Psychiatry
- Psychosomatics

- Geriatrics
- Pediatrics
- Pediatric Intensive Care
- Neonatology
- Curative Education
- Social Therapy

Indications

The following indications can be named, among others:

- Unconsciousness
- Disturbance of consciousness
- Feeblemindedness
- Lack of concentration
- Difficulty in breathing
- Disturbances of heart function and circulation
- Physical and emotional pain
- Physical and emotional weakness
- Loss of motivation
- Agitation
- Bi-polar Illness
- Schizophrenia

Goals

Goals can be grouped in the following three areas:
Physical level

- Pain relief
- Relaxation of breathing
- Deepening of breath
- Harmonizing of heart function and circulation
- Muscle relaxation
- Enlivening
- Forming
- Building up and strengthening of life forces
- Balancing and harmonizing of different organ functions

Soul level

- Calming
- Relaxation
- Inwardness

- Strengthening of experiential and sensitive faculties
- Feeling of safety
- Feeling of support
- Being touched
- Experiencing care

Spiritual level

- Strengthening of concentration
- Strengthening of hopefulness
- Strengthening of courage
- Integration in bigger life context
- Experiencing of higher content
- Connection to the spiritual world
- Resume connection to a higher world
- Finding of wholeness
- Experiencing of ones own being
- Experiencing of 'truth'
- Encounter with the archetypes

An important goal of receptive music therapy is to connect to one's Ego. Through the active listening process the patient finds a way to an inner quietness. He experiences lightness inwardly. At this moment, he encounters himself. He encounters his ego, the inner core of his personality.

Perception of a Patient and the Therapeutic Attitude

People who are seriously ill, for whom receptive music therapy is especially indicated, are in a situation where they are emotionally open, but also vulnerable. Lying in bed brings a person into a situation where he is more receptive. Experiences can go very deep. The possibility of distancing oneself inwardly, however, has become much less. This great sensitivity has to be dealt with consciously by the therapist. It is recommended for any music therapist to listen to live played music, once while lying down, once while sitting up. One will notice immediately that one's sensitivity of perception is greater while lying down. While sitting up, we listen more analytically, 'with the head', when lying down, we can distance ourselves less. Details lose their importance. We listen as a 'whole being'.

Receptive music therapy is decisively influenced by the therapist's ability to perceive the patient. From this exact perception arises how and what we are playing and therefore the possibility of 'reaching' the patient. The perception has to encompass the whole human being in all his realms of being: The therapist tries to tune into the patient through asking himself different questions. Is the patient's physicality for example rather delicate and small, or rather large and dense (physical level)? Does the patient appear weak and exhausted, or lively? Does his skin indicate good circulation, or does it have a yellowish or grayish appearance? Is his breathing quiet and regular, or fast, irregular and shallow (realm of life forces)? How is his emotional appearance; light and bright, or heavy and dark; withdrawn or open (soul level)? What kind of personality does one encounter (spiritual level)? The overall impression and the way in which the physical, etheric, soul and spiritual level of a person come together, create an overall picture. This overall picture can transform, in a musically trained therapist, into a musical picture and can flow into an in the moment originating piece of music or into an individually composed music.

It is not easy to find answers to questions concerning the soul and spiritual level when working with semi-conscious or unconscious patients. Their ability to express themselves in words, gestures or mime might be very limited, or nonexistent. Observations are limited then to the first two levels, and one gets only a 'notion' of the other two levels. Still, it is of the outmost importance to make this endeavor since one will not otherwise get a full picture of the individual's overall personality. But how can I get a perception of the soul and spiritual level of a seriously ill patient? The so-called 'subsidiary exercises' by Rudolf Steiner, which are mentioned as part of the Anthroposophic path of inner schooling, can be a help (Rudolf Steiner GA 245). Of the given six exercises (Thought control/ concentration of thought –initiative in action – equanimity – positivity – freedom from prejudice – inner balance), the following qualities are especially important for strengthening a therapeutic attitude: equanimity, positivity, freedom from prejudice and inner balance. When practicing equanimity, the goal is to use one's forces of sympathy and antipathy in such a way, that they are not only an expression of ones own being, but also a tool to be able to perceive and take in the well being of the patient. When practicing positivity, the goal is to see the patient not only with all his incapability, but to recognize his possibilities and resources, which are the seeds for the future. To be natural and unprejudiced is a prerequisite for being able to discover something new or different. An open attitude of wonder, which distances itself from the immediate urge to put everything into known phrases, will lead to the realization of new experiences. Through equanimity of one's own soul forces, one achieves an inner balance and, therefore, a comprehensive perception becomes possible.

In addition to working one's own therapeutic attitude, we have a special possibility of training our capacity of perceiving through the music. It is my experience that music with its spiritual dimension can be a help in feeling oneself into the soul-spiritual being of a semi-conscious patient. Music with its immaterial qualities seems to come very close to the state such a person is in. Sometimes it is possible to enter into a 'higher', spiritual encounter.

Case study: Intensive Ward

For this case study I would like to use the patient's own words first. Mrs. Smith (name changed) has put her experiences in writing herself.

Waking Up on the Intensive Ward

"It was arranged with the physicians that I would have to stay for two to three days on the intensive ward after the success of the abdominal operation. So that's where I woke up, weak, hooked-up, but without pain, thanks to modern intensive care. Next to me were ticking and beeping noises, I was supervised by a medical apparatus. Still heavily sedated, I dosed through the second half of the day and the following night.

In the morning, great joy, the loving nurse from the day before was again on duty. But the morning got long, in my body I felt a strange mingling of heaviness and insensibility, my stomach being a yawning numb nothingness. The outside seems to be infinitely distant. To be on an intensive ward is to be disempowered.

At this moment, a woman comes to my bedside, gently and with a strong, clear gaze, introduces herself and asks: "May I play to you on the lyre?" I am incredulous with amazement, for moments, outside traveling through vast soul realms. I experience happiness, devotion and thankfulness. Never in my life will I forget this encounter. I lie back, close my eyes and listen. I listen to the tones, in a way that I have never before experienced tones, it is as if my soul is listening.

Quietly, the music therapist disappears, and I stay surrounded by the sounds for a long time. The room is peaceful; an angel seems to have stopped by. Full of astonishment, I notice later that I have felt no pain, heaviness or other bodily sensations. There were only those sounds that had gently lifted me up.

The night I spent sleepless, I am surrounded by constant beeping and running, I feel sick and have to throw up. The next morning brings no improvement. The strong painkillers deprive me of day-consciousness. As soon as I wearily close my eyes, forces threaten to pull me out of my body, I sink into my bed, and a black heaviness lies over my consciousness. I struggle, catch myself with optical perceptions, and start to name things in my room loudly at times. The doctor, who is alarmed, checks my neighbor, the apparatus, and states: "Everything is all right."

The music therapist comes to my bedside again. The familiar sounds fill the room, I start to relax, I rather keep my eyes still open, but finally I close them exhaustedly. Anxiously, I wait for what is going to happen. Miraculously, nothing threatening happens, no, the heaviness is transformed into gentle hovering and harmony. I am carried by the tones. I can give myself completely to the sounds, let myself fall. Peace enters. Love, love to this strange woman germinates.

By and by, the sounds disappear, the body calls for attention again, the old struggle starts anew. At lunchtime, the physicians reduce the pain medication drastically, due to my pleading. Slowly my head awakens, freed from its anesthetized clinched state; I can feel my stomach again – painfully. But I prefer to live with an aching stomach then with a dead head.

Side remark: I am not a musician, on the contrary I am, musically speaking, a blank page.

Patients in intensive care are in a, for themselves, difficult state (Bissegger 1999a). They are in a totally strange, unknown, noisy environment, a cool atmosphere, surrounded by different apparatuses, depended on help from strangers. "The outside seems to be infinitely distant. To be on an intensive ward is to be disempowered." A good encounter with a care-person can build up vital trust. To listen to sounds, to music, played in the moment, just for this one patient in a life threatening situation, played in utter devotion of one person to the other, can become an extraordinarily deep experience. "I listen to the tones, in a way that I have never before experienced tones, it is as if my soul is listening." The uncertainty, all that is threatening can disappear for a time. A feeling of being carried, being held of peace, of devotion arises. Pain can be forgotten and the feeling of well being can come. This feeling of well being can be of great importance for the further development of the healing process, because feelings of hope, of trust and of courage to face life can arise from it.

Mrs. Smith, who has fine, dark brown hair and a transparent, pale skin, was lying in bed quietly and concentrated. Because of her weakness, there was no conversation possible. After being introduced, she closed her eyes again immediately. I sat down with my lyre and tried to feel myself into her situation. Which sounds should I play for her? Which sound does she need in this moment? Which tone should I start with? It isn't always easy to answer this question in a room on the intensive ward. Many noises mix, often a certain tone is dominant, from which I have to distance myself inwardly, in order not to get influenced by it. I finally choose the tone E and quietly begin to play large intervals upwards and downwards (fifths, sixths, octaves and ninths) starting on E spreading across all three octaves of the instrument. The swinging measure of 6/8 played as a short-long rhythm with an up-beat, tunes in well with the rhythm of inhaling and exhaling. The large intervals have an expanding effect and can on the one hand dissolve the cramped emotions a little, so the body with its physical pain and heaviness will be less noticeable; on the other hand, I try to tune myself with those intervals into the soul mood of the patient. Mrs. Smith has, as I experience it, not quite come back to herself due to the long operation. Through narcosis, one gets pulled out of ones body artificially. This has to be overcome after waking up, in order to be able to find oneself again on a soul-spiritual level in a healthy way. Gradually, I condense the large intervals and add smaller intervals in my improvisation, tuning myself into the soul mood of the patient. Through contracting the sounds, I try to help Mrs. Smith to experience herself again in her personality, to find to herself, in order to access those forces that will guard her against what is happening. Playing on the lyre I change to D as a key-note and pick up a melody in D major, which I accompany with my voice, humming. Doing this, I have left the wide open mood and have arrived into a clear melody with a harmonic structure, which addresses, supported through the singing voice, the listener directly on an emotional level. After I finish playing, Mrs. Smith is breathing more quietly and her facial expression is relaxed.

When I meet her the second time, Mrs. Smith already seems to be more present, but still very transparent and vulnerable. Again a verbal exchange is not yet possible. I begin to play the lyre in a similar way to the first time. The large sounds and wide breaths, this time beginning on D, become smaller without loosing the breathing mood. After a while, I arrive in the Dorian mode, a mode that brings a certain darkness with its minor third, but also stays bright through the major sixth. Since I feel how intensely Mrs. Smith is listening, it is easy for me to play. It 'plays by itself'. I feel very grateful. I let the improvisation flow into an old hymn. I add the voice and hum the melody without the words. Through this old hymn with its wonderfully moving melodic phrases, the listening space widens and the soul realm becomes noticeable. "I am carried by the tones. I can give myself completely to the sounds, let myself fall. Peace enters."

Acknowledgement

The author would like to thank Christina Porkert for the translation.

CH. 17: THE THERAPEUTIC USE OF THE VOICE AND SOUND AT THE BEGINNING OF LIFE

MONIKA NÖCKER-RIBAUPIERRE

The music market has become saturated with more and more recordings to therapeutically accompany a child through his intra-uterine life, birth, and further his development. The spectrum encompasses rich, even "medicinal" musical offerings, especially during pregnancy. These recordings are supposed to enhance the mother-infant bonding process and help the fetus to be relaxed and healthy. These commercial selections are deceptive, ignoring a cause and effect principle that is not so easy to replicate. On one hand, many nurses and parents on neonatal intensive care units (NICU) play calming music for these infants – from suitable classical music to dolphin singing or the sounds of ocean waves. They have heard that these are good for premature babies and have the feeling they are doing something to the make the child's life more bearable in this highly technological environment. This is easy to understand, but needs to be clearly differentiated from therapeutically working with music.

The following is a professional, therapeutic example of the use of sound as used by music therapists in a NICU – research and clinical practice. Different receptive, music therapeutic possibilities will be presented and critically evaluated, based on bio-medical, physiological conditions, and the physiological affects of music.

I would like to broaden the concept of music therapy beyond our German understanding of it. In other countries, especially the USA, music therapy is seen as the pure functional use of music subsumed under scientific assumptions. I divide this into medical music therapy and music psychotherapy. Both receptive starting points begin with the physiological effect of music on the human organism, but differentiate in their views on the situation of the premature infant and its treatment.

Intrauterine Development

Intrauterine development is a continuum, beginning with the union of egg and sperm. A tiny organism develops through further cell division. Eight weeks later, it is 12 mm long and shows its first movement. The development of the central nervous system and sensory organs then follow a genetic plan in programmed stages. At this time, it is to be assumed that each sensory organ is reacting and ready to receive information, which it will need.

The entire pre-natal and onset of post-natal development is essentially formed through physical experiences. It is a time of constant integration and differentiation of an endless variety of multi-sensory, environmental information from the *Body-I* (Fröhlich 1994) or *Body-self* (Zieger 1999). The concept of the *Body-I* represents a condition of the body and soul, inner and outer, subject and object, inseparable and not opposed to one another. The *Body-I* consists of autonomic experiences, the unity of sensory impressions on an elementary level under the inclusion of the intero- and proprioreception, as well as the archaic unconscious and deep sleep (Gustoff & Hannich 2000). The one is simultaneously the other, anchored in the world as a unit, protecting the developing child. Any therapy with the young infant needs to take this situation into consideration.

The development of affect is an indicator of the development of sensory organs and their integrative function, as well as the observations of fetal movement and the reaction to external stimulus. Change in mood as a pre-form of affect is only noticeable through autonomic changes in heartbeat, breathing or movement. Affect expresses itself through autonomic reactions and is stored as such in the *Body-I*. When there is no integration of these early affects through relationship experiences, psychological disturbances can occur which often become clear years later during psychoanalysis with children (Maiello 2004) or adults (Janus 1990).

Diverse research has shown music therapy to be significant, especially for patients not able to speak or adequately communicate (Nöcker-Ribaupierre 1995; Aldridge 1996; Gustorff & Hannich 2000). The physiological basis is found in the phylogenesis and ontogenesis of the hearing system and has been verified through brain research (Grothe 1995). Processing music is centrally found in both hemispheres of the brain and in the brain stem (formatio reticularis). Information coming through the ear is processed in the brain stem before it is transferred to the cortex. This means that hearing in humans is not bound to a functioning cortex because the primary integration center exists sub-cortically. This center allows the human to be influenced, autonomically, emotionally, and motivationally. This path also functions when the cortex is not yet developed or is damaged. On the other hand, the auditory system is fully functional in the 18th week of gestation (Rubel 1984). In the 24th week one can observe the fetus reacting to extra-uterine sounds (Birnholt & Bencerraf 1983), sometimes even in the 19th week (Hepper & Shahidullah 1994). It is unknown at what age the fetus stores acoustical stimulation, although one can observe it reacting during an ultrasound. This more academic question is not of particular importance for therapy as the biomedical relationship theories (Zieger 1999) and psychoanalytical theories (Maiello 2004) stress that subject and object, perception and the processing of stimulus are not yet separate.

In addition, when standing in front of a 500 g infant that is hard to identify as a living human among the life support cables, one needs time to feel and recognize what the infant wants to say. In this isolation, the baby seems to be expressing a silent suffering and infinite loneliness. In using therapeutic sounds, it will be necessary to preserve and remain true to what one can see and observe.

The Acoustical Environment

The acoustical environment of the unborn child is structured through the continual low frequencies of the ventricle and intestinal sounds of the mother's womb along with her heartbeat and breathing. This continuum is unpredictable and can be disturbed by the mother's voice when she speaks or sings, through other voices further away, by music the mother is listening to or playing herself, or through natural noises in the environment. The unborn child perceives this entire spectrum in different intensities through sound transmission via bones or vibration. The healthy newborn shows a strong preference for what it has heard before birth, which it recognizes and can differentiate from new acoustical stimulation. This includes the mother's heartbeat and blood flow, her voice, the voices and noises of normal everyday life and also stories and music (De Casper & Fifer 1980; Fernald 1982; DeCasper & Spence 1986; Righetti 1996).

Patients on an intensive care unit are in the middle of an enormous amount of technology, light and noise (a constant noise level between 50–50 dB and the unpredictable alarms can go up to 110 dB, without any means of a trusted and understandable possibility for communication. We can only begin to observe and possibly understand their state of consciousness, feelings and development with an EEG, variations in heart beat, levels of oxygen saturation, visible reflexes, agitation or unrest and autonomic reactions. Signs of stress, anxiety or agitation can be observed and measured through physiological parameters. We now know that this routine treatment with continuous bright lights and excessive noise causes stress. Patients must often be sedated in order to handle it and reduce the stress induced physiological effects. Premature infants react exactly as adults – with observable and measurable aversion to life in this un-physiological environment. They show reduced oxygen saturation and pulses, apnea and bradycardia, wide fluctuations in blood pressure, increased excitement and agitation, crying, and sleep disturbances. As a result, premature infants use an enormous amount of energy in dealing with this stress, which they would normally be investi[illegible] in their growth and development. This is a major reason why intensive care [illegible] searching for methods to reduce stress or simply avoid it.

For just these reasons, music has b[illegible] intensive care units for the last 15 years (Spintge & Droh 1987; G[illegible] nnich 2000; Schwartz 2004). Spintge's medical research is based on b[illegible] nd includes the effects of brain physiology and emotions. He recom[illegible] edicinal effects of individually selected music for reducing the level [illegible] hormones, balancing breathing, rhythmic reduction of muscle tension, lo[illegible]g of pulse, blood pressure, oxygen need, and metabolism. Thus, music reduces the sensation of pain and lowers anxiety (Spintge & Droh 1987).

When music is used in the first days of life to mask the noise level and stress for premature infants and ill newborns, physiological parameters indicate the music does reach these children. One can actually follow how they are emotionally touched by it.

Assuming that emotions are a part of the central regulating program of human behavior and thus necessary for development, the use of music on an intensive unit can be justified.

The Therapeutic Use of Sound at the Beginning of Life

Since the end of the eighties, especially in the United States, there have been numerous multi-modal and purely acoustical studies of music with premature infants. These publications describe the physiological reactions of infants to specific types of music. Results of these early research phases show that from the beginning, music has observable and positive quieting effects (Schwartz 2004). Since 1991, studies in music therapy have described significant results in relationship to momentary physiological parameters, as well as child development. These studies deal exclusively with receptive listening from cassette recorders. This functional area is called "medical music therapy" as it is focused on the physiological parameters of the infants during hospitalization (Loewy 2004; Schwartz 2004).

Medical Music Therapy

The selection of music used in these American studies, then and now, are the Brahms' *Lullaby*, commercial lullabies, specially composed music with womb sounds (i. e. circulation and heart beat), lullabies with guitar or strings or a capella vocalises, female voices, singing and speaking, male voices, and the spoken and sung voice of the infant's mother.

As stated before, all of these studies demonstrate partially effective and significant results in the reduction of observed stress behavior and general quieting (Busnel 1986; Caine 1991). These include a significant rise in oxygen saturation (Collins & Kuck 1991; Cassidy & Standley 1995; Standley & Moore 1995); an increase in weight (Chapman 197[illegible] [illegible]ine 1991); a more rapid weight gain in girls compared to boys (Coleman [illegible] a shortening of length of hospitalization (Caine 1991) or significantly [illegible]e (3–5 days) (Coleman et al. 1998).

Medical music therapy [illegible]ven to have long term effects. In two American hospitals in whic[illegible]tinely used on the NICU, a quicker growth in head circumference w[illegible] in direct correlation to the use of music (Schwartz 2004; Standley 1998). [illegible]evant, as the early loss of intrauterine environment has an effect on brai[illegible]wth and maturation (Hüppi 1996). Early work on prenatal intrauterine sound stimulation also had an effect on the growth of head circumference and increased the ability to develop (Logan 1991). As head circumference during the first two years is an accurate indicator for brain size (Sheth 1995), a reduced growth in the skull (which can not be made up later) has a definite negative effect on cognitive ability. Reduced head circumference is a strong indicator for reduced intellectual abilities as of eight years (Hack 1991).

A further problem for long term prognosis of very premature infants is the later development of hyperactivity and ADD. The results of the music therapy studies are also important here as they show that in general music reduces stress reactions (Spintge & Droh 1987). Stress induced hormones in plasma (ACTH, cortisol, β-endorphins) can cause damage to the neural network. This can explain the high rate of ADSD.

Live Music for the Infant

Joanne Loewy describes another possibility for using music therapy in the NICU – live music for the newborn. She has developed a practical program for stable premature infants (older than 32 weeks). Called "environmental music therapy," it is exact, structured, and differentiated. It includes a special use of music therapy in which the therapist's goal is to reduce environmental noise and stress. It is not enough to simply play a particular piece of music in a certain tempo. The pitch of the peeping machines, the voices of the nursing staff, and the rhythm of the chaotic, acoustical surroundings need to be evaluated before any music therapy interventions can begin, and be further evaluated during the intervention. The therapist's live music is solely based on what is happening in the actual situation. This is decisive in what the therapist does. She may sing a lullaby to put the infant to sleep; use a Gato drum to alleviate respiratory difficulties by imitating the child's rhythm of breathing; quiet him with an ocean drum and humming/singing; or support bonding (when the baby is lying with its mother) with music and soft humming/singing (Loewy 2004). Another person has a central role here: the therapist who is playing for the child.

Both of the following methods assume that mother and child are inseparable in this stage of development and include the mother in the therapy.

Relationship Oriented Music Therapy: Making Music for Mother and Child

Monica Bissegger plays for both mother and child. She wants to create an atmosphere of security and safety in the form of a "sound blanket" with only live sounds. The mother holds the child on her breast. When the infant is too premature, she stands next to the incubator. The therapist attempts to transcribe the state of the child and the atmosphere in the environment into an improvisation, humming or singing with the accompaniment of a pentatonic lyre. A "blanket of sound" is developed, offering mother and child security, safety, and closeness. When the mother is ready, she can sing along. They can *tone* together or the therapist lets the mother sing. In this way, the mother has an active role in the bonding process and with the help of the therapist can re-establish her relationship with her infant. The child can also breathe, mimic, and move in the dialog (Bissegger 2000).

Auditive Stimulation with the Mother's Voice

Finally, I would like to speak about my own musical psychotherapeutic use of Auditive Stimulation with the mother's voice. The purely functional use of sound and its positive and supportive effects on development justify this encompassing method of treatment. My original use of receptive methods developed in order to offer the infant a different acoustical impression than the un-physiological one in the NICU – something he would recognize from before that would offer him some security – his mother's voice. This voice would reduce stress and offer positive stimulation. His mother would be free to tell stories, read him something or sing. Her voice would be recorded and over a six-week period, played five times daily in his incubator, when there were no other disturbances.

I conducted two research studies. In the first one, we observed the immediate effect of the mother's voice on the infant and follow-up development of the children up to 20 months. In a further project, we tracked the development until the children started school at the age of six.

The results showed that the children visibly and measurably reacted to their mother's voices as of the 26th week of gestation (when no illness or medication prevented outer stimulation). In addition, it was clear the mother's voice had a quieting effect on her infant which resulted in a significant rise in the measured transcutaneous partial pressure of oxygen. At five months, the babies showed an important increase in their verbal and motor development. At 20 months, these children had a motor and verbal development jump compared to the children in the control group. The six-year olds demonstrated slightly better results in IQ tests and speech development, but significant improvement in understanding speech (Nöcker-Ribaupierre 1995, 2004).

During this study, auditory stimulation developed into a more encompassing therapy form, including the psycho-dynamics of what had happened and its influence on the bonding of mother and child. It became very apparent that the mother and child could not be treated as separate entities in this very early phase of development. A large body of literature has proven this (Bowlby 1969; Winnicott 1965; Klaus u. Kennell 1976; Ainsworth 1976; Eagle 1984; Stern 1985; Fedor-Freyberg 1987; Janus 1990). A premature birth is a traumatic event for both. Both must be treated in order to find a way for optimal development. I would like to explain this further:

The Mother: A premature birth usually entails a caesarian. The mother often sees her infant one or two days later when she able to visit the NICU. Although she may have seen photos, and the baby's condition has been explained to her, she is usually deeply shocked, frightened, and feels helpless when she sees her child for the first time. In addition to helping her deal with her grief over the disrupted pregnancy and early birth, she also needs support to actively do something. She has been separated from her child. It is no longer a part of her body, more like an object lying across from her. When she has an opportunity to do something, to give of herself, she can begin to bond with her infant. This is possible through her voice, the voice her baby knows from her womb – a trusted sound, a new way back to her child. She can speak to her child and experience how he reacts. This whole process will take a form and further develop – a deciding factor for a newly won form of communication and bonding with her baby. It is for this reason and from observations and research with full term, healthy infants, who above everything else prefer their mothers' voices (Standley & Moore 1995) that we used this form of auditory stimulation therapeutically.

The Child: In order to understand the psycho-dynamics of the life of a premature infant, we must look at the new analytical theories and models in infant research. Stern's studies on bonding (1985) demonstrate a genetic determination of awareness, showing an infant can participate in different social and cognitive experiences from the beginning. Stern sees this as a principle of development, which includes others right from the start. The physiological regulation of its life is dependent on the infant's ability to socially interact. Vitality affects play a deciding role. The mother's vitality affect reaches the child through her voice. The child reacts to this voice. This explains how it is possible for the premature infant in his incubator to allow an emotional space for her voice, a space for their relationship – where it can further develop. Infants feel this and clearly react to it.

Sandra was born at 28 weeks gestation with life threatening medical problems. She had to be immediately placed on a ventilator and in the NICU. Her mother came to visit her the next day. She sat silently in front of the incubator, full of fear with little hope that her child would survive. However, she gladly accepted the offer of recording her voice. But her voice was flat and toneless. She spoke haltingly, slowly and softly. She began to visit Sandra daily and spoke with her more and more. With time, she stabilized psychologically and was pleased about her daughter's development. She cautiously began to help with her care. When Sandra was 34 weeks old, she began to cry when she heard her mother's voice on a cassette, but not when her mother was directly speaking to her. Due to her more positive emotional state, her mother's voice had become stronger and positive. We replaced the old recording with a new one. From this moment, Sandra turned her head towards the loud speaker, whenever she heard the new recording of her mother.

A second aspect lies in the ability of the child to react to acoustical impressions. We observed the infant always reacting with his full attention to his mother's voice in comparison to eventually growing used to the technical noises. He reacted when he wasn't ill or sedated or sound asleep. He always turned his head towards the source of her voice. As in the first study, definite times were set for the auditory stimulation and he waited for the voice. Eagle (1984) explains this as a newborn's desire to establish contact with objects in his world, which are not necessarily the same as meeting his needs. For this reason, I directed my music therapy methods towards the child as well as his mother – and, thus their relationship.

The musical medium is the mother's voice, non-verbal, emotional. Its musical parameters include content, its psychological effect with its special, unmistakable sound for each child, its melody and rhythm, this side of any explanation. All of this makes it a carrier of prenatal emotional interaction.

As in other areas of receptive music therapy, one should use standard, original or improvised music according to the needs and desires of the client or at least symbolically. We assume that in these earliest, pre-mental, pre-verbal period, sound and rhythm do not have any symbolic meaning for the child. The premature infant is not yet capable of symbolizing. Symbolizing requires inner representation, which need memories and a certain level of consciousness. The symbolic value of music during therapy with adults, which plays such a decisive role, is not applicable here. The infant is still in a pre-conscious and pre-symbolic world. Rhythm and sound accompany the beginning of early childhood experience and can establish a relationship through the mother's voice. After the dramatic interruption of the pregnancy due to the premature birth, her voice allows the child the possibility of maintaining a continuum of this primary acoustical representation. In this situation, the mother's voice is on one hand a continuation from this intrauterine period, and on the other, a symbol for their relationship. When the intention of the therapeutic intervention is to support the mother-child relationship, the therapeutic medium can neither be composed music nor the use of other sounds.

Discussion

The above-described receptive methods are the results of careful quantitative research. There may be reservations or objections to this type of work. Some feel there should be a musical prescription for premature infants written without the involvement of the child. Of course, the current state of development of the child must always be taken into consideration. For example, an infant of 25 weeks gestation (beginning of 6th month) who weighs about 600 grams is not in any way able to breathe or take nourishment on its own. It will need a ventilator and to be hooked up to numerous monitoring machines. In the middle of all of this, it is almost impossible to feel or experience the baby as an individual. It will be observed, controlled and nursed around the clock. The intensive unit consists of a large room, easy to observe, with many incubators and all the necessary machines all next to each other. There is no possibility for any privacy or a sense of a protected environment.

Nursing staff and music therapists who work with these children are there to help each of them. They carefully observe how the baby reacts to each sound and are ready to modify it according to the child's needs. Their clear goal is to support these infants' development with necessary and more humanizing stimulation in the middle of this high- tech environment. The observation of the child's development is primarily possible through physiological parameters, but also through the direct, observation of the mimic and movement of each child. Each therapist working on a NICU observes the reaction of each individual child carefully, reacting to the child as his own person.

The chosen music also follows criteria, corresponding to the development of the child. In depending on the cultural similarities of lullabies, the music follows rhythmic, melodic and harmonic parameters, instruments are used accordingly, the mother's voice or other trained female voices chosen, and the volume individually modified. We know the actual behavior for every stage of development exactly. At 34-36 weeks, the infants are so far developed that they are able to respond to stimulus with predictable reactions. At about this age, children clearly show that they are no longer completely satisfied with recorded voices. They want it in connection with tactile stimulation – stroking, holding or being carried. They also show signs of their first development with a constant object: when they have experienced both the mother's voice and face over a longer period of time, they are can fall asleep with a story read or lullaby sung by the mother on a cassette. Stern recommends that voices and faces should come together – this means they should appear together (Stern 1977). This development of a cross-modal awareness clearly occurs four weeks before the approximate birth date.

When the babies are stable enough to exist without mechanical intervention, they are often placed in smaller, more intimate rooms in which it is easier to have active music in a dialogue with them (Shoemark 2004).

Finally, I would like to add my personal comments. In her psychoanalytical research (1992), Piontelli observed children from the beginning of their intrauterine life until their third year. She did this through ultra sounds and direct observation and was able to conclude that pre- and post birth behavior was mostly concurrent. For example, after acoustical stimulation, a fetus pulls back into a "corner" of the uterus, thumb in mouth. A child will later react shyly and also pull back. This indicates that the intrauterine fetus is not going to *become* the future child, but rather it already *is* an individual (Maiello 2004). This holds for every premature child and demands our respect and empathy in our contact with each one of them.

Conclusion

Receptive music therapy is the only possible way of working with premature infants on a NICU. As different as the above methods are, they have something in common: music therapy supports and helps premature infants, physiologically and emotionally. This can be observed and measured with regard to their momentary condition and future development. Music relaxes, reduces stress, supports development and can be used as a preventive measure to reduce the future damaging effects of premature birth up to the beginning of school (Achenbach *et al.* 1993). In addition, the mother's voice supports the mother-child re-bonding process, building a basis for their future life together. In other words, it is well proven in neonatology that working with receptive music therapy with music, singing and sounds offers positive results for helping the infant and mother in the moment and for the future.

Acknowledgement

The author would like to thank Susan Bawell Weber for the translation.

CH. 18: STORIES WRITTEN UNDER MUSICAL INDUCTION: A TOOL OF PSYCHO-DIAGNOSIS, PSYCHOTHERAPY AND RESEARCH

LONY SCHILTZ

1. Introduction

My training as a psychoanalytic Music Therapist (DU Paris-V) followed 20 years of psychotherapeutic practice using a combination of psychoanalysis and humanistic approaches. Therefore, once I began to work with Music therapy, I was able to observe that the therapeutic process evolved much more quickly and with greater fluidity with the serious disorders of adolescence with whom I worked. I began to ask myself why this was the case. This initiated my scientific study of the therapeutic process itself, and is the foundation for several research projects I undertook.

Psychoanalytic music therapy works on the principle of free association on both musical and verbal levels. Just as the free flow of thought is not refrained, the free flow of musical and poetic associations should not be limited. The desired stability doesn't come through rules and prescriptions to the making of music, but through the creation of the therapeutic relationship that allows expressing frightening, destructive contents of the patient's psychic world within a playful and anxiety-free context. The therapist's attention is focused as much on the manifestations of the unconscious as on the coping strategies of the person being treated. The goal is the re-establishment of the capacity for symbolic thought, and the imaginative and cognitive working out of repressed emotions. This capacity is disturbed in many cases of serious psychopathological, social or psychopedagogic problems. In French psychoanalytic literature, one calls this a weakening of mentalization (Marcelli & Braconnier 1999) or a disturbance in the subjectivation process (Cahn 1998; Richard 2001).

2. Writing under the induction of music as a part of psychotherapeutic work with youths

In the last years, I have treated young patients with a mixed method of music therapy, combining active music-making with writing stories under musical induction. In this treatment method it is the creative act of writing itself, not the act of listening to music, which becomes the focus of attention. The music is only perceived in the background, and it works rather preconsciously and unconsciously than in the clear focus of consciousness. I first developed this method in order to help youths who were experiencing a profound blockade of authentic emotions and desires (Mc Arthur 1988; Schiltz 1995). During a long-term follow-up study that became the basis of my doctoral thesis in clinical psychology, I investigated afterwards the effects of this music therapeutic method on adolescents suffering from conduct disorders (Schiltz 1999).

It seems to me that the connection between undirected musical improvisation and writing stories under musical induction favours an elaboration of self-representation and a distancing from dysfunctional thoughts and emotions. With unstable, ego-weak youths, classical receptive music therapy (for example Escande 1993), which means listening to music and becoming aware of one's own feelings and thoughts in a state of relaxation does not induce the same in-depth work as the formal effort of constructing a story, thus integrating primary and secondary thought processes. That is why the story must be written while the patient is listening to music, and not afterwards when it risks becoming an account of the fantasies that were experienced primordially. In the first case, the various musical impressions are worked on progressively at the level of fantasy, while in the latter case it is a simple reconstruction.

Within an individual music therapy session, making music (alone or in a musical dialogue with the therapist) alternates with writing stories under musical induction. This yields a fruitful reciprocal action; the atmosphere described in a story can be used as the starting point for an improvisation, and the story becomes more authentic because of the easing of tension induced by music making and the facilitation of access to unconscious images and representations.

The verbal process, which follows directly after the artistic production, stays on the poetic level of analogous speech and uses symbols and metaphors produced by the patient. During the therapeutic process personal meanings are discovered. One's own story is seen in a new light. By means of a quasi-experimental design I could prove (2002a) that with this method a restructuring of the personality in borderline patients is possible within a one to two year period of therapy. Projective testing methods showed that more mature defence mechanisms gradually replace the earlier splitting, the primitive idealisation, and the projective identification. Let me remind the reader that the psychodynamic interpretation of borderline functioning is that the structural level of personality is characterised by the overriding of archaic defence mechanisms (Dulz and Schneider 1996). The symbols and images surfacing from the stories, and during the free association phase, may have archetypical features; at the important turning points of their evolution the patients produce exactly those images which are of existential importance for them, and which anticipate their future evolution (Schiltz 2002b).

In my evaluation study of music therapy[1] I have shown that musical and poetic creativity evolve parallel to each other, and that the complexity and structure of musical play is correlated to originality, artistic processing, and the quality of the

1 It was a controlled follow-up study with 50 persons belonging to the clinical and to the control group. The treatment was done in individual sessions; it lasted from 6 months to 2 years.

language in the stories (Schiltz 1999). This statistically proven connection leads to the assumption that a basic capacity for symbolic thought exists, which can express itself in musical as well as in poetic creations and thus explains this parallel evolution. This capacity comes from the child's early preverbal thinking that makes learning language possible (Richard 1990).

To find the proper music, I used an empirical approach. When I chose rock or pop music, which the teenagers loved and heard from morning till evening, they wrote only very conventional stories. The best results were achieved with the three following musical styles: baroque and early classical music; ethnic music; and romantic music. Because of my clinical experience, I have to exclude the idea that a specific piece of music has specific effects due to its structural characteristics alone, independent of the mood of the listener, as some researchers have assumed in the past. The listener projects his/her own feelings and imagination into the music. But at the same time, there are also collective themes, which appear frequently in relation to the different musical styles, but not in relation to individual pieces of music.

With the help of phenomenological-structural analysis[2]2 (Mucchielli 1983), I succeeded in showing collective group structures in some subgroups of borderline disorders (Schiltz 2003a, 2003b) for the music styles mentioned above. During the course of therapy, there was an evolution of the thematic contents of the stories of the clinical group towards those of the control group. At the same time, the stories progressively acquired greater differentiation and individualisation. A summary of the results of the statistical computation is shown in the following table (for all differences, p. = at least < .05).

Table 1: Development during music-therapy treatment

Variables	Pretest	Evolution	Posttest
Formal Structuring	N > B	B → N	n. s.
Temporal Structuring	N > B	B → N	n. s.
Long lasting Temporal Perspectives	N > B	B → N	n. s.
Differentiation of Vocabulary	N > B	/	N > B
Triviality of Content	B > N	B → N	n. s.
Passivity of Hero	B > N	B → N	n. s.
Controlled Aggressiveness	N > B	B → N	N > B
Primary Aggressiveness	n. s.	/	n. s.
Depressive Mood	N > B	B → N	B > N

B = Borderline Group; N = Neurotic Groupe; n. s. = non significant; (adapted from Schiltz 2003a)

2 This method of qualitative analysis belongs to the humanities in general and allows drawing latent significant structures from human behaviour, as well at the level of fantasy, of language but also of action. It also enables us to work out collective themes in the artistic production of individuals.

Most interesting is the seeming paradox in the evolution of the categories concerning aggression and depression. It is the relationship between the secondary and the primary expression of aggression that changes during the course of the therapy, the controlled expression of aggressiveness becoming more frequent while the expression of archaic aggression remains at the same level. The increase of depression in the borderline group is a sign of emotional growth, because depressive themes only appear in the stories once impulsiveness decreases on the level of actual behaviour.

There is a many-layered interaction between the personaltiy of the individual, the stage of the therapeutic process, the musical style, and the elementary characteristics of the musical parameters; nevertheless it is possible to discern common characteristics on one single level. The development of a general model of this reciprocal action, including the psychopathological components, would be an interesting subject for future research.

3. The suitability of musically induced stories as a projective testing method

I have been using projective personality tests like the Rorschach and the TAT3 in the personality diagnosis for a long time, and I prefer the holistic psychoanalytic interpretation method (Brelet 1986; Chabert 1995) to the summing up of separate components. When I compared the stories written under musical induction with the TAT, I noticed that the former reflect partly similar, partly complementary aspects of the personality. Thus, the stories cannot only be included in the psycho-diagnostic inventory at the beginning of therapy, but can also document the psychological development of the patient during therapy and in the posttest session. For this reason I use them especially to reveal to the patient hidden developmental possibilities and his/her own progress. I also use the testing methods of Rorschach and TAT in this way,not to make psychopathological symptoms the centre of attention, but to put the patient in contact with the healthy part of his/her personality and to strengthen his/her self-confidence. By comparing stories from different stages of the therapy, I make self-healing tendencies aware to the patient. It is interesting that there is a drifting of the temporal perspectives in the stories: past difficulties can only be worked on literally if the danger of a breakdown is overcome, and if, on the other hand, the heroes of the stories implement latent possibilities within the patients themselves for which they have not yet achieved the necessary maturity in real life.

3 Thematic Apperception Test, Murray

3.1. Clinical illustration: Stories which are written at important turning points of therapy

Literary re-working of a survived danger:

> "She cried, cried… cried the whole night through till the evening, till the last light in the neighbourhood was out. In her solitude she was totally desperate and no one could imagine her situation. In other people's eyes she seemed to be happy, even though her husband had died ten years ago. But she had suffered much; she had had a big loss and had become depressive. She wanted to die, but didn't have the courage. No one had ever tried to scratch off the layer of colour, which hid the true picture; no one had the idea that behind this idyllic facade the black colour of death and the red colour of life lay hidden.
> So one day she went into the forest, on a winter day full of snow, covered in her black coat, which she had worn on her husband's burial day. She held a dagger in her right hand. In the middle of the forest she stopped and let her life gush out of her body." (Vivaldi: The Four Seasons)

This story originates with a girl of fourteen years who suffered from a narcissistic flaw. It was written immediately after the patient had gone through an extremely serious interpersonal crisis. Especially noteworthy is the theatrical setting of the story, in which the unbearable loss of the love object is emphasized by means of archaic mechanisms such as idealisation and the magic of colour. On paper, the suicide could be presented dramatically, whereas in real life this could be avoided.

Symbolic elaboration of new developmental possibilities:

> "Deep in the forest it was dark. Here, there was a lake. On the surface of the water, the moon and the fir trees were reflected; these were the very trees that could be seen growing on the edge of the lake. At times, one can recognize everything exactly, and the theatre play is like a film. But sometimes, when there are gusts of wind, one sees the fir trees swing back and forth. At that moment everything seems frightening, and from far away one hears the howling of a wolf.
>
> If one goes on further, one comes to a waterfall that flows downward, slowly and peacefully. Above on the rocks where the water is quiet, a wolf is revealed; the moon is in the background. Although it has a frightening appearance, it is friendly. It remains seated and looks at me. Suddenly I have the feeling that it is laughing at me. It comes closer and licks my hand. I stroke it and feel completely happy, as if this is what I had always wanted. Wolves are my favourite animals. Suddenly I wake up and realize that is was only a dream. Since then I return to my friend in the forest every night." (Beethoven: Violin Concerto)

The psychic development of this young girl appears through the choice of symbolic themes in several parts of the story. Firstly, the repression of feelings and impulses (the moon shining, the lifeless landscape), then the anxiety produced by her own desires (the gusts of wind, the howling of the wolf) and finally the acceptance of the dark side of her personality. The well-known archetypal motifs of fairy tales (Bettelheim 1984) often appear in stories written under musical induction, and yet these motifs are not simply reproduced. In this example, the female process of individualization during adolescence is put in relief. The passionate longing conveyed by the tone of the violin corresponded in this case with the inner feelings of the young girl.

The effect of the music has to be understood within the context of a lengthy therapeutic process in which verbal psychotherapy also plays a large role. Let me stress once more that it certainly is not the specific structure of either baroque or classical music that affects the patient. Rather, the significant therapeutic value of music is shown in the interaction between it and the pre-existent life story and personality structure of the patient, as well as in the dynamics of the therapeutic relationship.

3.2. Visual and musical stimuli of the imagination

What is the difference between TAT and the stories written under musical induction? What does a visual stimulus do to our imagination, in comparison with a musical one? In the former case, the stimulus is a precise picture that theoretically could be interpreted in many ways, but that nevertheless seems to favour a specific kind of interpretation, for example through the appearance of the figures, their ages, their behaviour, their facial expression (Mucchielli 1983). Music, on the other hand, has no meaning in the linguistic sense; the meaning is constructed by the person who listens. Since the dynamics of music give it the possibility of reflecting any features of life, it becomes an ideal background onto which one's most interior conflicts can be projected.

In comparison with TAT, the variety of stories is much greater, even if, as described above, different styles can call up common cultural associations. For example, ethnic music is often associated with a feast, regardless of which land it comes from. Whether the feast is associated with a cruel scene of sacrifice, a drinking orgy, or a cult dance of some kind depends on the listener. As a reaction to romantic music, young people often write stories with themes of love or adventure. Baroque music often has a balancing and structuring effect in the case of patients suffering from acute anxieties; but there are exceptions to this rule. The selection of musical pieces depends on the clinical intuition of the therapist. At all times during the treatment, I use various musical styles, but only after a structured therapeutic relationship has been established which can serve to compensate any possible destabilizing effect of special music pieces.

The archetypal figures occur earlier and more frequently in the stories written under musical induction than in TAT. They concern the relationship of the Ego to the Ego Ideal and to idealized or demonised parental figures. They are above all more oriented towards the future and show the patients their wishes and hidden developmental possibilities at a time when the stories of TAT more strongly reflect current intra-psychical conflicts (Schiltz 2005).

4. Stories has an instrument of research

I would like to present some of the areas in which the use of stories written under musical induction have proven to be a promising tool for research.

4.1. The specificity of borderline disorder looking at the example of the double

Research into the archetypal figure of the double appearing in the stories of young borderline patients shows that in different clinical subcategories during the use of music therapy a complimentary approach to the initial problematic occurs, and that this development reveals itself in new character traits of the double (Schiltz 2003a).

4.2. Overcoming life crises

In working with elder people, the search for a renewed reason for living and the integration of an altered self image was facilitated by writing stories under musical induction. A comparison between strategies for overcoming the crisis of adolescence and the crisis of the third age showed interesting parallels and differences in the coping strategies which appeared in the stories.

Table 2: The coping strategies at different stages of life

Variables	Level of Significance	Direction of Change
Artistic Elaboration	n. s.	
Humoristic Elaboration	P< .01	AG > JG
Cognitive Elaboration	P< .05	AG > JG
Dramatic Elaboration	P< .05	AG < JG

AG : Group of elderly people; JG : Group of adolescents (adapted from Schiltz 2003d)

The tendency to choose artistic solutions, that is, the inclusion of aesthetic aspects, is identical in both groups.

Older patients tend to use humour more often,, as they use cognitive strategies that involve access to a general perspective that is greater than one's own destiny. The dramatic solution –the presentation of inner conflicts as if they were a scenario – is preferred by younger experimental subjects.

4.3. Working with gifted underachievers

The deep restriction of symbolic thinking combined with self-doubt, feelings of emptiness, and a complete lack of intrinsic motivation appeared in the stories of gifted students suffering from school failure. At the same time, the patients' positive advancements with the help of the above-mentioned methods have been documented. School results used as outside validity criteria improved in a highly significant manner (Schiltz 1995, 2004a).

4.4. The treatment of cognitive disturbences of adult psychiatric patients

Finally, I would like to mention a broad research program of which I am the director from 2004 to 2008 at the Public Research Center for Medicine and Health, funded by the National Research Foundation in Luxembourg. Among others, the efficiency of music therapy with patients suffering from schizophrenia, or from other cognitive disturbances linked to depression and anxiety will be investigated. Most of all, we are interested in the effect of music on the ability to concentrate, on logical structuring and fluency of thought, as well as on the volutional capacities of the patient. The treatment is a combination of active and receptive music therapy as described above. The evaluation is based on semi-structured interviews, observational frames and psychometrical and projective tests.

Conclusion

The reinvigorating effect of music on physical and psychic levels has been documented for a long time. A temporary heightening of the feeling and mood situation of the patient does not suffice, however, to induce permanent changes. If this were so, numerous uprooted youths whose only leisure time activity is often listening to music for hours, would be able to help themselves. But if the personal effort and formal work of music making and writing stories within the reassuring atmosphere of the therapeutic relationship comes into play, many new cognitive and affective solutions and coping strategies can develop. These can enrich the conscious life, and can even lead to structural change. This statement is particularly important for preventive work with youths in whom the first signs of psychopathological disturbance in the ability to function is observable.

It is banal to say that music therapy develops creativity. The creativity involved in the artistic expression of the patient is, however, not the main aim. Rather, this form of creativity is the goal of artistic education. In the therapeutic field, it is fluency of thinking and the creative approach used to deal with anxiety-provoking material from one's own intrapsychic world, which is important.

Acknowledgment

I express my greatfulness to Dr. Dana Rufolo who helped translating this text.

REFERENCES

Abrams, B. (2002a): Transpersonal Dimensions of the Bonny Method. In: Bruscia, K. E. & Grocke, D. E. (eds.): Guided Imagery and Music: The Bonny Method and Beyond. Gilsum, NH, 339–358

Abrams, B. (2002b): Methods of Analyzing Music Programs used in the Bonny Method Guided Imagery and Music. In: K. E. Bruscia and D. E. Grocke (eds): The Bonny Method and Beyond. Gilsum NH, 317–335

Achenbach,T. M.; Howell, M. S.; Aoki, M. F.; Rauh, V. A.(1993): Nine-Year Outcome of the Vermont Intervention Program for Low Birth Weight Infants. In: *Pediatrics* 91(1), 45–55.

Adorno, Th. (1962): Einleitung in die Musikpsychologie. Frankfurt

Aigen, K. (2002): Playin' in the band. A qualitative study of popular music styles as clinical improvisation. New York, Nordoff-Robbins Center for Music Therapy. Steinhardt School of Education. New York University

Ainsworth, M. (1976): Attachment as Related to Mother-Infant Interaction. In: Rosenblatt, J., Hinde, R.; Beer, C.; Busnel, M. (ed): Advances in the Study of Behavior. Vol. 8. New York, 1–51

Åkerlind, A. (2003): Five weeks in the Spectrum Program – narratives of five patients. (In Swedish): Final paper presented for certification as a licensed psychotherapist. SAPU psychotherapy training institute. Stockholm

Aldridge, D. (1996): Music therapy research and practice in medicine: from out of the silence : David Aldridge. London

Aldridge, D. and G. Aldridge (1999): Life as Jazz: Hope, Meaning, and Music Therapy in the Treatment of Life-Threatening Illness. In: Dileo, C.: Music Therapy & Medicine: Theoretical and Clinical Applications, MD, American Music Therapy Association. Silver Spring, 79–94

Aldridge, D., Fachner, J. (eds.) (2006): Music and altered states – Consciousness, transcendence, therapy and addictions. London

Altenmüller, E., Beisteiner, R. (1996): Musiker hören Musik: Großhirnaktivierungsmuster bei der Verarbeitung rhythmischer und melodischer Strukturen. In Musikpsychologie – Jahrbuch der Deutschen Gesellschaft für Musikpsychologie, Wilhelmshaven, 89–109

Ansdell, G. (2001): Musicology: Misunderstood Guest at the Music Therapy Feast? Music Therapy in Europe. In: di Franco, G. Ruud, E., Wigram, T., Aldridge, D. (eds.): The 5th European Music Therapy Congress (Napoli, April 2001). Rome, ISMEZ, 17–34

Balint, M. (1970): Therapeutische Aspekte der Regression. Stuttgart

Balint, M. (1973): Therapeutische Aspekte der Regression. Die Theorie der Grundstörung [Orig. London 1968]. Reinbek bei Hamburg

Banister, P., Burman, E. et al (1998). Qualitative Methods in Psychology. A Research Guide. Buckingham Philadelphia, Open University Press.

Basar, E., Schurmann, M., Basar Eroglu, C., Karakas, S. (1997): Alpha oscillations in brain functioning: An integrative theory In: *Int J Psychophysiol*, 26(1–3), 5–29.

Beckh, H. (1987): Die Sprache der Tonart in der Musik von Bach bis Bruckner. Frankfurt

Behne, K.-E., Lehmkuhl, P. & Hassebrauck, M. (1988): EEG-Korrelate des Musikerlebens, part II. In: Behne, K. E., Kleinen, G. & de la Motte-Haber, H. (eds.):Musikpsychologie. Wilhelmshaven, 95–106

Behne, K.-E. (1984): Befindlichkeit und Zufriedenheit als Determinanten situativer Musikpräferenzen. In: *Musikpsychologie,* 1, 7–21

Behne, K.-E.(1999): Zu einer Theorie der Wirkungslosigkeit von Hintergrund-Musik. In: *Musikpsychologie,* 14, 7–23

Berger, H. (1991): Das Elektroenzephalogramm des Menschen – (Kommentierter Reprint des Erstdruckes von 1938, Halle ed.). Frankfurt am Main

Besseler, H. (1926): "Grundfragen des musikalischen Hörens". Jahrbuch der Musikbibliothek Peters (32), 35–52

Bettelheim, B. (7/1984): Kinder brauchen Märchen. München

Bindel, E. (1985): Die Zahlengrundlagen der Musik im Wandel der Zeiten. Stuttgart

Birnholtz, J. C.; Benaceraff, B. R. (1983): The Development of Human Fetal Hearing. *Science*, (222), 516

Bishop, S. (1994): The use of Guided Imagery and Music with Adult Female Survivors of abuse in an inpatient psychiatric setting. KS: Bonny Foundation.

Bissegger, M. (1995): Anthroposophische Musiktherapie am Beispiel der Inneren Medizin in der Filderklinik. In: *Musiktherapeutische Umschau*, Göttingen, Vol. 16, 4, 289–298

Bissegger, M. (1999a): "... dem andern begegnen..." Musiktherapie auf der Intensivstation. In: *Einblicke. Beiträge zur Musiktherapie*, 9, 69–78

Bissegger, M. (1999b): Musiktherapie bei frühgeborenen Kindern und ihren Müttern. Ein Pilotprojekt mit Unterstützung der A.-T.-Kindstiftung. Hamburg. unpublished

Bissegger, M. (2000): Musiktherapie bei frühgeborenen Kindern und ihren Müttern. In: Aldrige, D. (ed.): Kairos V, Beiträge zur Musiktherapie in der Medizin. Bern, 26–39

Bissegger, M. (2001): Anthroposophische Musiktherapie. In: Decker-Voigt, H.-H. (ed.): Schulen der Musiktherapie. München, 357–386

Blake, R. L. & Bishop, S. R. (1994): The Bonny Method of Guided Imagery and Music in the treatment of Post Traumatic Stress Disorder (PTSD): with adults in a psychiatric setting. In: *Music Therapy Perspectives*, 12(2), 125–129.

Bonde (forthcoming): Imagery, metaphor, and perceived outcome in six cancer survivors' BMGIM therapy. A qualitative research monograph. Gilsum NH

Bonde, L. O. (1997): Music Analysis and Image Potentials in Classical Music. In. *Nordic Journal of Music Therapy* 6(2), 121–128

Bonde, L. O. (2000): Metaphor and Narrative in Guided Imagery and Music. In: *Journal of the Association for Music and Imagery* 7, 59–76

Bonde, L. O. (2002): GIM Selections. Database. Available as a pdf file at http://www.musik.aau.dk/research/musikterapi/gim-resource-center/index.htm

Bonde, L. O. (2002a): Models and Methods of Music Therapy: Guided Imagery and Music – The Bonny Model. In: Wigram, T., Pedersen, I. N. & Bonde, L. O.: A Comprehensive Guide to Music Therapy. London, 115–121

Bonde, L. O. (2002b): New Resources in GIM. In: *Nordic Journal of Music Therapy* 11(2), 193–196

Bonde, L. O. (2002c): Theoretical Foundations of Music Therapy: Music as Analogy and Metaphor. In: Wigram, T., Pedersen, I. N. & Bonde, L. O.: A Comprehensive Guide to Music Therapy. London, 97–111

Bonde, L. O. (2003): Rapport over projektet "Receptiv musikterapi med udskrevne cancerpatienter. En effektundersøgelse med fokus på stemning (mood) og livskvalitet (pilot-undersøgelse)". Aalborg, Institut for musik og musikterapi AAU

Bonde, L. O. (2004): Bibliography on Guided Imagery and Music (GIM) and Related Topics. Database. Institute of Music and Music Therapy, Aalborg University. Available as a pdf filde at http://www.musik.aau.dk/research/musikterapi/gim-resource-center/index.htm

Bonde, L. O. (2005): The Bonny Method of Guided Imagery and Music (BMGIM) with Cancer Survivors. A psychosocial study with focus on the influence of BMGIM on mood and quality of life. Unpublished PhD dissertation. Aalborg. University. available as a pdf file at http://www.musik.aau.dk/research/musikterapi/gim-resource-center/index.htm

Bonde, L. O. ($^{2nd. ed/}$2005a): Researching the music. In: Wheeler, B. L. (ed.): Music Therapy Research. Quantitative and Qualitative Perspectives. Gilsum NH, 489–525

Bonde, L. O. (2005b): 'Finding a new Place'... Metaphor and Narrative in One Cancer Survivor's BMGIM Therapy. In: *Nordic Journal of Music Therapy* 14(2): *137–154*

Bonde, L. O. (in press): "To draw from bits and pieces a more supportable narrative". An introduction to Paul Ricoeur's theory of metaphor and narrative and a discussion of its relevance for a hermeneutic understanding of music-assisted imagery in The Bonny Method of Guided Imagery and Music (BMGIM). In: *Canadian Journal of Music Therapy*.

Bonde, L. O. and Pedersen, I. N. (1996/2001): "Grounding Image Potentials in the Musical Experience. Reflections on a Tape Analysis of "Creativity I"." Col Legno 2001: http://www.musik.aau.dk/collegno/collegno.dk.html

Bonny, H. and Mardis, L. K. (1994): Music resources for GIM Facilitators: A Discography of Core Programs. Olney. MD,

Bonny, H. & Pahnke, W. N. (1972): The Use of Music in Psychedelic (LSD): Psychotherapy. In: *Journal of Music Therapy*, 9, 64–87.

Bonny, H. (1975): Music and Consciousness. In: *Journal of Music Therapy*, 12, 121–135

Bonny, H. (1976): Music and Psychotherapy. Dissertation, Baltimore, Maryland

Bonny, H. (1978a): GIM monograph #1: Facilitating GIM sessions. Salina, KS: Bonny Foundation.

Bonny, H. (1978b): GIM monograph #2: The role of taped music programs in the GIM process. Salina, KS: Bonny Foundation.

Bonny, H. (1980): GIM Monograph #3: Past, present and future implications. Salina, KS: Bonny Foundation.

Bonny, H. (1983): Music Listening for Intensive Coronary Care Units. In: *Music Therapy*, 3 (1), 4–16.

Bonny, H. (1999): Music and Consciousness. In: *Nordic Journal of Music Therapy*, 8 (2), 171–179

Bonny, H. (2002): Twenty-one years later – a GIM update. In: Summer, L. (ed.): Music & Consciousness – the Evolution of Guided Imagery and Music. Helen Lindquist Bonny. Gilsum NH, 141–154

Bonny, H. (2002): Music & Consciousness: The Evolution of Guided Imagery and Music. Gilsum NH

Bossinger, W., & Hess, P. (1993): Musik und außergewöhnliche Bewusstseinszustände. In: *Musiktherapeutische Umschau*, 14 (3), 239–254

Bowlby, J (1969): Attachment and Loss. New York

Brelet, F. (1986): Le TAT. Phantasmes et situations projectives. Paris

Brüggenwerth, G. & Gutjahr, L. & Kulka, T. & Machleidt, W. (1994): EEG-Veränderungen emotionaler Reaktionen auf Musik. In: *EEG-EMG*, 25, (2), 117–125.

Bruhn, H., Oerter, R., Rösing, H. (ed.): (1993): Musikpsychologie. Ein Handbuch. Reinbek bei Hamburg

Bruhn, H.; Frank-Bleckwedel, E.-M. (1994): Rezeptive Musiktherapie. In: Bruhn, H., Oerter, R., Rösing, H. (eds.): Musikpsychologie. Ein Handbuch. Reinbek b. Hamburg, 412–417

Bruscia, K. E. (1987): IAP. Improvisational Assessment Profiles. In: Bruscia, K.: Improvisational Models of Music Therapy. Springfield, Illinois, 401–496

Bruscia, K. E. (1994): IAP. Improvisational Assessment Profiles. Kartlegging gjennom musikkterapeutisk improvisation. Sandane

Bruscia, K. E. (1995): Manifestations of Transference in Guided Imagery and Music. In: *Journal of the Association for Music and Imagery,* 4, 17–35

Bruscia, K. E. (1996): Embracing live with Aids: Psychotherapy through Guided imagery and music (GIM): In: Bruscia, K. (Ed.): Case studies in music therapy. Gilsum, 581–602

Bruscia, K. E. (2002): Boundaries of GIM and Bonny Method, In: Bruscia, K., Grocke, D. (eds.): Guided Imagery and Music – the Bonny Method and Beyond. Gilsum, NH.

Bruscia, K. E. (2002): A Psychodynamic Orientation to the Bonny Method. In: Bruscia, K. E., Grocke, D. E. (ed.): Guided Imagery and Music . The Bonny Method and Beyond. Gilsum, 225–244

Bruscia, K. E. (2002): Developments in Music programming for the Bonny Method. Guided Imagery and Music. In: Bruscia, K. E. and Grocke, D. E.(eds.): The Bonny Method and Beyond. Gilsum NH, 307–315

Bruscia, K. E. (2nd ed /2005): First-Person Research. In: Wheeler B. L. (ed.): Music Therapy Research. Quantitative and Qualitative Perspectives. Gilsum NH, 379–391

Bruscia, K. E. and Grocke, D. E. (eds) (2002): Guided Imagery and Music: The Bonny Method and Beyond. Gilsum NH

Buber, M., (1983): Ich und du. Heidelberg

Bunt, L., Pavlicevic, M. (2001): Music and emotion: Perspectives from music therapy. In: Juslin, P. N. & Sloboda, J. A. (eds.): Music and emotion. Theory and research. Oxford, 181–203

Burgess, A. P., Gruzelier, J. (1997): How reproducible is the topographical distribution of EEG amplitude? In: *Int J Psychophysiol*, 26(1–3), 113–119

Busnel, M. C., Mosser, Ch., Relier, J. P. (1986): Preliminary results on the effect of acoustic stimulations on premature infants. In: *Pediatric Research* 20, 1056

Bydlowski, M. (dir.): La recherche clinique en psychopathologie. Paris

Cahn, R. (1998): L'adolescent dans la psychanalyse. L'aventure de la subjectivation. Paris

Caine, J. (1991): The Effects of Music on the Selected Stress Behaviors, Weight, Caloric and Formula Intake, and Length of Hospital Stay of Premature and Low Birth Weight Neonates in a Newborn Intensive Care Unit. In: *Journal of Music Therapy*, 28 (4): 180–192

Canacakis, J. (2000): Ich sehe deine Tränen. Trauern, Klagen, Leben können. Stuttgart

Carlsson, M. (2001-02): Kundalini and the Bonny Method of Guided Imagery and Music. In: *Journal of the Association for Music and Imagery*, 8, 35–55

Cassidy, J. W.; Standley, J. M. (1995): The Effect of Music Listening on Physiological Responses of Premature Infants in the NICU. In: *J of Music Therapy*, 32 (4), 208–227

Chabert, C. (1995): Contribution des méthodes projectives. In: Bourguignon, O./ Bydlowski, M. (eds.): La recherche clinique en psychopathologie. Paris, 93–110

Chapman, J. S. (1979): Influence of Varied Stimuli on Development of Motor Patterns in the Premature Infant. In: Anderson, G.; Raff, B. (Hg.): Newborn Behavioral Organization: In: *Nurs Res and Impl.* New York, 61–80

Clark, M. F. (2002): The Evolution of the Bonny Method of Guided Imagery and Music. In: Bruscia, K., Grocke, D. (eds.): Guided Imagery and Music – the Bonny Method and Beyond. Gilsum, NH.

Clarkson, G. (2002): Combining Gestalt Dreamwork and the Bonny Method. In: Bruscia, K. E., Grocke, D. E. (eds.): Guided Imagery and Music. The Bonny Method and Beyond, Gilsum, 245–256

Coleman, J. M.; Pratt, R. R.; Stoddard, R. A.; Gerstmann, D. R.; Abel, H. H. (1998): The Effects of Male and Female Singing and Speaking Voices on Selected Physiological and Behavioral Measures of Premature Infants in the Intensive Care Unit. In: *International Journal of Arts Medicine*, 5 (8), 4–11

Collins, S. K.; Kuck, K. (1991): Music Therapy in the Neonatal Intensive Care Unit. In: *Neonatal Network* 9 (6), 23–26

David, E., Berlin, J., & Klement, W. (1983): Physiologie des Musikerlebens und seine Beziehung zur trophotropen Umschaltung im Organismus. In: Spintge, R. & Droh, R. (eds.): Musik in der Medizin – Neurophysiologische Grundlagen, Klinische Applikationen, Geisteswissenschaftliche Einordnung. Berlin, 33–48

David, E., Finkenzeller, P., Kallert, S., & Keidel, W. D. (1969): Akustischen Reizen zugeordnete Gleichspannungsänderungen am intakten Schädel des Menschen. In: *Pflügers Archiv* (309), 362–367

De Benedittis, G., Sironi, V. A. (1985): Deep cerebral electrical activity during hypnotic state in man: Neurophysiologic considerations on hypnosis. In: *Rivista di Neurologia*, 55 (1), 1–16

de la Motte-Haber, H./Kopiez, R. (1995): (eds.): Der Hörer als Interpret. 7 Schriften zur Musikpsychologie und Musikästhetik, Frankfurt a. M.

DeCasper, A. F.; Fifer, W. P. (1980): Of Human Bonding: Newborns Prefer their Mother`s Voices. In: *Science*, 208: 1174–1176

DeCasper, A. J.; Spence, M. J. (1986): Prenatal Maternal Speech Influences Newborns' Perception of Speech Sound. In: *Infant Behavior and Development*, 9, 133–150

Decker-Voigt, H.-H. (2006): "Musiktherapeutische Tiefenentspannung (MTE)" Lilienthal

Decker-Voigt, H.-H. (2004): Entspannungstechniken und rezeptive Musiktherapie. "Kursbuch Musiktherapie". München

Decker-Voigt, H.-H./ Maetzel, F. K. (1998): "Selbsthilfe zur Herz-Kreislaufstärkung", CD/ Handbuch in der Reihe "Musik und Gesundsein", Hamburg und New York

Decker-Voigt, H.-H., (2002): The Thorny Path Leading to the Healing Arts in Medicine. In Levine, S. K. (ed.): Crossing Boundaries, Explorations in Therapy & the Arts, Toronto

DeNora, T. (1999): Music as a technology of the self. In: *Poetics*, 27, 31–56

Der Neue Brockhaus, Band 3 (1985 a): Wiesbaden

Der Neue Brockhaus, Band 5 (1985 b): Wiesbaden

Deuter, M. (1992): Spätere Versionen frühkindlicher Erfahrungen in der Improvisation. In: *Materialien zur Musiktherapie*. Vol 5. Zwesten, Steinfurt: Institut für Musiktherapie und Morphologie, 35–41

Dittrich, A. (1985): Ätiologie-unabhängige Strukturen veränderter Wachbewusstseinszustände. Stuttgart

Dittrich, A., Lamparter, D., Maurer, M. ([2]/2002): 5D-ABZ – Fragebogen zur Erfassung außergewöhnlicher Bewusstseinszustände. Zürich

Dogiel, J. (1880): Über den Einfluss der Musik auf den Blutkreislauf. Archiv für Anatomie und Physiologie. Abteilung Psychologie, 416–428

Dörfler W. (2/1994): Das Lebensgefüge der Musik, Vol. I, II, III. Dornach

Draguns, J. G. (1996): Ethnocultural Considerations in the Treatment of PTSD: Therapy and Service Delivery. In: Marsella, A. J., Friedman, M. J., Gerrity, E. T. & Scurfield, R. M. (eds.): Ethnocultural Aspects of Posttraumatic Stress Disorder: Issues Research and Cultural Applications. Washington

Drewes, R./ Schemion, G. (1991): Lernen bei Musik: Hilfe oder Störung? – Eine experimentalpsychologische Analyse einer pädagogisch-psychologischen Kontroverse. In: *Musikpsychologie,* 8, 46–66.

Droh, R., Spintge, R. (ed.) (1983): Angst, Schmerz, Musik in der Anästhesie. Basel

Drury, N. (1989): Der Schamane und der Magier. Reisen zwischen den Welten. Basel

Dulz, B., Schneider, A. (²/1996): Borderline Störungen. Theorie und Therapie. Stuttgart

Eagle, M. N. (1984): Recent Development in Psychoanalysis. A Critical Evaluation. New York

Edgar, I. R. (1994): Imagery Fields: the Cultural Construction od Dream Interpretation in Three Contemporary British Dreamwork Groups. In: Internet: www.dur.ac.uk/i.r.edgar/cultdream.thesis.html

Ekman, P. & Friesen, W. V. (1969): Nonverbal leakage and clues to deception. *Psychiatry,* 32 (1), 88–106

Eliade, M. (1999): Schamanismus und archaische Ekstasetechniken. Frankfurt/Main

Engel, H.-H. (1999): Musikalische Anthropologie. Anregungen zum Studium der Anthroposophischen Musiktherapie. Revised by Maurer, M., Schneider, H., Spalinger, J.. Dornach,

Erickson, M. H., Rossi, E. L. (1981/1989): Hypnotherapie. Aufbau, Beispiele, Forschungen. München

Escande, M., (1993) :De l'écoute musicale à la psychothérapie. In: *Bulletin du Groupe Toulousain de Psychanalyse*, 5, 4–15

Fachner, J. (2001): Veränderte Musikwahrnehmung durch Tetra-Hydro-Cannabinol im Hirnstrombild (E-Book on Music Therapy Info CD-ROM ed. Vol. III). Witten. University Witten/Herdecke

Fachner, J. (2002): Topographic EEG changes accompanying cannabis-induced alteration of music perception – Cannabis as a hearing aid? In: *Journal of Cannabis Therapeutics,* 2 (2), 3–36

Fachner, J. (2004): Cannabis, brain physiology, changes in states of consciousness and music perception. In: Aldridge, D. (ed.): Case Study Designs in Music Therapy. London, 211–233

Fachner, J. (2006): Music and altered states of consciousness – an overview. In: Aldridge, D. & Fachner, J. (eds.): Music and Altered States – Consciousness, Transcendence, Therapy and Addictions. London, 15–37

Fachner, J., Rittner, S. (2004): Sound and trance in a tiualistic setting visualised with EEG Brainmapping. Music Therapy Today Online. Retrieved 18. January, 2006, from http://www.musictherapyworld.net/modules/mmmagazine/showarticle.php?articletoshow=93

Fedor-Freyberg, F. G. (1987): Pränatale und perinatale Psychologie und Medizin. Alvjö/Schweden

Felber, R., Reinhold, S., Stückert, A. (2/2003): Anthroposophische Kunsttherapie, Vol. III: Musiktherapie und Gesangstherapie. Stuttgart

Ferguson, D. N. (1960): Music as Metaphor. The Elements of Expression. Minneapolis

Fernald, A. (1982): Acoustic Determinants of Infant Preferences for "Motherese". Unpubl. doct diss. Oregon

Ferrara, L. (1984): Phenomenology as a tool for musical analysis. In: The Musical Quarterly 70 (3), 355–373

Fischer, R. (1971): A Cartography of the Ecstatic and Meditative States. In: *Science*, 174, 897–904

Fischer, R. (1971): A cartography of the ecstatic and meditative states. *Science,* 174 (4014), 897–904

Fischer, R. (1976): Transformations of consciousness. A cartography, II. The perception-meditation continuum. In: *Confin Psychiatr*, 19 (1), 1–23

Fischer, R. (1998): Über die Vielfalt von Wissen und Sein im Bewusstsein. Eine Kartographie außergewöhnlicher Bewusstseinszustände. In: Verres, R., Leuner, H. C., Dittrich, A. (eds.): Welten des Bewusstseins. Berlin, 43–70

Foa, E. B., Keane, T. M. and Friedman, M. J. (2000): Effective treatments for PTSD. Practice Guidelines from the International society for Traumatic Stress Studies. New York

Forinash, M. and Gonzalez, D. (1989): A phenomenological perspective of music therapy. *Music Therapy* 8(1), 35–46

Frankl, V. E. (1999): Theorie und Therapie der Neurosen. Einführung in Logotherapie und Existenzanalyse. München

Fricke, Jobst (1989): Der Klang der Musikinstrumente nach den Gesetzen des Gehörs: Wechselwirkung Mensch – Instrument. In: *Das Instrumentalspiel.* Wien/München, 275–284.

Fricke, Jobst (2003): Systemische Musikwissenschaft. In: Niemöller, K. W. (2003): Systemische Musikwissenschaft. Festschrift Jobst Fricke. Frankfurt a. M., 13–24

Fritsch, J.; Sherokee, I. (1995): Unendlich ist der Schmerz. Eltern trauern um ihr Kind. München

Fröhlich, A. (1994): Pädagogische Überlegungen zum Thema Bewusstsein und Bewusstlosigkeit. In: Bienstein, C., Fröhlich, A. (eds.): Bewusstlos. Düsseldorf

Frohne, I. (1981): Das Rhythmische Prinzip.– Grundlagen, Formen und Realisationsbeispiele in Therapie und Pädagogik. Lilienthal

Frohne-Hagemann, I. (1990/1999): Integrative Musiktherapie als psychotherapeutische, klinische du persönlichkeitsbildende Methode. In: Frohne-Hagemann, I. (ed.): Musik und Gestalt. Klinische Musiktherapie als integrative Psychotherapie. Paderborn, 99–120 (reprinted edition 1999. Göttingen, 101–123)

Frohne-Hagemann, I. (1990/2001): Integrative Musiktherapie und ihr psychotherapeutisches Selbstverständnis. In: Frohne-Hagemann, I. (2001): Fenster zur Musiktherapie – Musiktherapie-theorie 1976–2001. Wiesbaden, 97–114

Frohne-Hagemann, I. (1991/2001): Zur Funktion der Musik in der Integrativen Musiktherapie. In: Frohne-Hagemann, I. (2001): Fenster zur Musiktherapie. Wiesbaden, 115–123

Frohne-Hagemann, I. (1996): Musiktherapie vor dem Hintergrund integrativer Theorie und Therapie. In: Decker-Voigt, H.-H. (ed.): Schulen der Musiktherapie. München, Basel, 157–182

Frohne-Hagemann, I. (1996/2000/2001): Das musikalische Lebenspanorama (MLP): – narrative Praxis und inszenierende Improvisation in der Integrativen Musiktherapie. In: *Einblicke, Beiträge zur Musiktherapie*, ed. by Berufsverband der MusiktherapeutInnen (BVM), 10, 59–73

Frohne-Hagemann, I. (2001a): Ästhetik und Leiblichkeit als Meta-Konzepte integrativer Musiktherapie. In: Frohne-Hagemann: Fenster zur Musiktherapie – Musik-therapie-theorie 1976–2001, Wiesbaden

Frohne-Hagemann, I. (2001b): Die Bedeutung von Musik, Traum und Imagination für die ästhetische Aneignung von Wirklichkeit. In: www. frohne-hagemann.de

Frohne-Hagemann, I. (2002): Vom Sinn und Unsinn des Nachnährens. In: Moreau, D. v./ Wölfl, A. (eds): Zur Idee des therapeutischen Nachnährens – was kann Musiktherapie leisten?. Wiesbaden, 11–28

Frohne-Hagemann, I. (2003): Das Musikalische Gefühlsspektrum (in Anlehnung an K. Hevner). Berlin [unpublished seminar paper]

Frohne-Hagemann, I. (ed.) (2004): Rezeptive Musiktherapie – Theorie und Praxis. Wiesbaden

Frohne-Hagemann, I., Pleß-Adamczyk, H. (2005): Indikation Musiktherapie bei psychischen Problemen im Kindes- und Jugendalter. Musiktherapeutische Diagnostik und Manual nach ICD 10. Göttingen

Gabrielsson, A. & Lindström, E. (2001): The influence of musical structure on emotional expression. In: Juslin, P. N. & Sloboda, J. A. (eds.): Music and emotion. Theory and research. Oxford, 223–248

Gaver, W. W., Mandler, G. (1987): Play it again, Sam. In: *Cognition and Emotion*, 1, 259–282

Geiger, E. M. (2004): GIM – The Bonny Method of Guided Imagery and Music. Imaginative Psychotherapie mit Musik nach Helen Bonny. Eine Übersicht. Frohne-Hagemann, I. (ed.): Rezeptive Musiktherapie – Theorie und Praxis. Wiesbaden, 89–110

Gembris, H. (1981): Teilprobleme der Forschung und Praxis in der rezeptiven Musiktherapie. In: *Musiktherapeutische Umschau*, 2 (2), 93–105

Gembris, H. (1987): Forschungsprobleme der Musiktherapie am Beispiel des Themas "Musik und Entspannung". In: *Musiktherapeutische Umschau, 8, (4), 300–309*

Gembris, H. (1990): Situationsbezogene Präferenzen und erwünschte Wirkungen von Musik. In: *Musikpsychologie,* 7, 73–95.

Gembris, H. (1993): Zur Situation der rezeptiven Musiktherapie. In: *Musiktherapeutische Umschau*, 8 (4), 193–206

Gembris, H. (1996): Rezeptionsforschung. In: Decker-Voigt, H.-H., Knill, P., Weymann, E. (eds.): Lexikon Musiktherapie. Göttingen, 321–326

Gembris, H. (1999): 100 Jahre musikalische Rezeptionsforschung. Ein Rückblick in die Zukunft. In: *Musikpsychologie,* 14, 24–41.

Goldberg, F. (1992): Images of Emotion: The Role of Emotion in Guided Imagery and Music. In: *Journal for Music and Imagery* 1, 5–18

Goldberg, F. (1994): The Bonny Method of Guided Imagery and Music (GIM): as individual and group treatment in a short-term acute psychiatric hospital. In: *Journal of the Association for Music and Imagery* 3, 5–18.

Goldberg, F. (1995): Lecture: "Reflections and Connections". Workshop at the Creative Arts Institute. Asilomar, CA.

Goldberg, F. (1995): The Bonny method of guided imagery and music. In: T. Wigram, B., Saperston, B., West, R. (eds.): The Art and Science of Music Therapy: A Handbook. Chur, 112–128

Goldberg, F. (2002): A Holographic Field Theory of the Bonny Method of Guided Imagery and Music (BMGIM). In: Bruscia, K. E., Grocke, D. E. (eds.): Guided Imagery and Music. The Bonny Method and Beyond. Gilsum, 359–378

Goodman, F. (1989): Wo die Geister auf den Winden reiten. Trancereisen und ekstatische Erlebnisse. Freiburg

Goodman, F. (1992): Trance – Der uralte Weg zu religiösem Erleben. Rituelle Körperhaltungen und ekstatische Erlebnisse. Gütersloh

Gore, B. (1996): Ekstatische Körperhaltungen. Essen

Gouk, P. (2000): Musical Healing in Cultural Context. Aldershot, England

Grocke, D. E. (1999): A Phenomenological Study of Pivotal Moments in Guided Imagery and Music (GIM) Therapy. Faculty of Music, The University of Melbourne

Grocke, D. E. (2002a): The Bonny Music Programs. In: Bruscia, K., Grocke, D.: Guided Imagery and Music – the Bonny Method and Beyond. Gilsum, 99–136

Grocke, D. E. (2002b): The Evolution of Bonny's Music Programs. In: Bruscia, K., Grocke, D.: Guided Imagery and Music – the Bonny Method and Beyond. Gilsum, 85–98.

Grof, S. (2/983): Topografie des Unbewussten. LSD im Dienste tiefenpsychologischer Forschung. Stuttgart

Grof, S. (1985): Geburt, Tod und Transzendenz. Neue Dimensionen in der Psychologie. München

Gustorff, D., Hannich, H. J. (2000): Jenseits des Wortes. Bern

Gutjahr, L. & Brüggenwerth, G., Güvenec, O., Wilcken, C., Machleidt, W., Hinrichs, H. (1994): Die Wirkung altorientalischer Musik im EEG. *EEG-EMG*, 25, 126–129

Guttmann, G. (1990): Zur Psychophysiologie der Bewusstseinssteuerung. Meditation – Trance – Hypnose: Wurzeln und biologische Korrelate. In: Bandion, J. (ed.), Einheit der Vielfalt. Wien

Guttmann, G. (1992): Zur Psychophysiologie des Bewusstseins. In Guttmann, G. & Langer, G. (eds.): Das Bewusstsein. Multidimensionale Entwürfe. Wien

Guttmann, G., & Langer, G. (1992): Das Bewusstsein – Multidimensionale Entwürfe. Wien

Haase, U., Schwabe, C. (eds.) (2003): Konzept und Offenheit. Musiktherapie in Theorie und Praxis. Materialien zum wissenschaftlichen Symposium der Akademie für angewandte Musiktherapie Crossen, November 2002. Crossen

Hack, M., Breslau, N., Weissman, B., Aram, D., Klein, M., Borawski, E. (1991): Effect of Very Low Birth-Weight and Subnormal Head Size on Cognitive Abilities at School Age. In: *The New England Journal of Medicine*, 325 (4), 231–237

Hanks, K. J. (1992): Music, Affect and Imagery: A Cross-Cultural Exploration. In: *Journal of the Association for Music and Imagery*, 1, 19–31

Hartogh, T. (2001): Die Rezeption monotonaler Klänge. Eine empirische Untersuchung zur Klangwirkung des Monochords. In: *Zeitschrift für Musik-, Tanz- und Kunsttherapie*, 12 (3), 111–119

Hegi, F. (1998): Übergänge zwischen Sprache und Musik. Die Wirkungskomponenten der Musiktherapie. Paderborn

Helmholtz, H. von (1863): Die Lehre von den Tonempfindungen als physiologische Grundlage für die Theorie der Musik. Braunschweig

Hepper, P. G.; Shahidullah, B. S. (1994): Development of Fetal Hearing. In: *Archives of Disease in Childhood*, 71, 81–87

Hess, P. (1999): Musiktherapie mit archaischen Klangkörpern. In: *Musiktherapeutische Umschau*, 20 (2), 77–92

Hess, P., Rittner, S. (1996a): Trance. In: Decker-Voigt, H. H., Knill, P. & Weymann, E. (eds.): Lexikon Musiktherapie. Göttingen, 395–398

Hess, P., Rittner, S. (1996b): Verändertes Wachbewusstsein. In Decker-Voigt, H. H., Knill, P. & Weymann, E. (eds.): Lexikon Musiktherapie. Göttingen, 398–403

Hess, P., Rittner, S. (1996): "Verändertes Wachbewusstsein" . In: Decker-Voigt, H.-H../ Knill, P. J./ Weymann, E. (eds) (1996): Lexikon Musiktherapie, Göttingen, 398–404

Hevner, K. (1936): Experimental studies of the elements of expression in music. In: *The American journal of psychology*, 48, 246–268

Höck, K. (1981): Konzeption der intendierten dynamischen Gruppenpsychotherapie. In: Höck, K., Ott, J., Vorwerg, U. (eds.): Theoretische Probleme der Gruppenpsychotherapie, Psychotherapie und Grenzgebiete, (Vol. 1). Leipzig

Höck, K. (1981): Konzeption der intendiert dynamischen Gruppenpsychotherapie. In: Höck, K., Ott, J., Vorwerg, U. (ed.): Theoretische Probleme der Gruppenpsychotherapie, Psychotherapie und Grenzgebiete, Vol. 1. Leipzig

Höck, K., König, W. (1976): Neurosenlehre und Psychotherapie. Jena

Hoerner, W. (3/1993): Zeit und Rhythmus. Stuttgart

Hofmann, R. (3revised ed./1996): Indikation zur Regulativen Musiktherapie. In: Schwabe & Röhrborn: Regulative Musiktherapie. Entwicklung, Stand und Perspektiven in der psychotherapeutischen Medizin. Stuttgart, Jena, 105–113

Hüppi, P. S., Schuknecht, B., Boesch, C.; Bossi, E., Felblinger, J., Fusch, C., Herschkowitz, N. (1996): Structural and Neurobehavioral Delay in Postnatal Brain Development of Preterm Infants. In: *Pediatr Res*, 39, 895–901

Husemann, A. (2.rev.ed./1989): Der musikalische Bau des Menschen. Stuttgart

Hutterer-Krisch, R. (2001): Behandlungsfehler in der Psychotherapie. In: Hutterer-Krisch, R. (ed.): Fragen der Ethik in der Psychotherapie: Konfliktfelder, Machtmissbrauch, Berufspflichten. Wien, New York

Isenberg-Grzeda, C. (1998): Transference Structures in Guided Imagery and Music. In: Bruscia, K. E.(ed.): The Dynamics of Music Psychotherapy. Gilsum NH, 461–480

Izard, C., Malatesta, C. Z. (1987): Perspectives on emotional development I. In: Osofsky, J. D. (ed.): Handbook of infant development. New York, 494–554

Izard, C. (1994): Die Emotionen des Menschen. Weinheim

Jaffe, J. R., Toon, J. H. (1980): EEG and polygraphic changes during hypnotic suggestibility. In: *Journal of Electrophysiological Technology*, 6 (2), 75–92

Janata P. et al. (2002): The Cortical Topography of Tonal Structures Underlying Western Music. In: *Science*, Vol. 298, 2176–2170

Janus, L. (1990): Die Psychoanalyse der vorgeburtlichen Lebenszeit und der Geburt. Pfaffenweiler

Jerneizig, R., Langenmayr, A., Schubert, U. (1991): Leitfaden zur Trauertherapie und Trauerberatung. Stuttgart

Jung, C. G. (1959): Basic writings of Jung. Garden City, New York

Jung, C. G. (1964): Approaching the Unconscious. In: C. G. Jung (ed.): Man and His Symbols. New York

Jung, C. G. (1969): The Structure and Dynamics of the Psyche. Collected Works, 8. London

Jung, C. G. (1988): Bewusstes und Unbewusstes. *Beiträge zur Psychologie*, Frankfurt/Main

Jung, M. (2001): Probleme der Organtransplantation aus der Sicht der Integrativen Therapie. In: *Integrative Therapie* 3, 218–246

Jungaberle, H. (1999): Music and metaphor – Understand the Transmission from Music to Language in Therapy. Paper given at the 9th World Congress of Music Therapy Music Therapy: A Global Mosaic: Many Voices, One Song". Washington D. C. November 17–22, 1999.

Jungaberle, H. (2001): New steps in musical meaning – the metaphoric process as an organizing principle. In: *Nordic Journal of Music Therapy* 10 (1), 4–16

Jungaberle, H., Altieri, P., Gerloff, E., Kurze, K., Verres, R. (2003): Töne strömen ein. Beiträge zur Musikpsychologie des Monochords. In: *Musiktherapeutische Umschau*, 24 (4), 319–332

Jünger, E. (2000): Sämtliche Werke in 18 Bänden. Vol. 3: Strahlungen II. Stuttgart

Juslin, P. N. and J. A. Sloboda (2001): Psychological perspectives on music and emotion. In: Juslin, P. N., Sloboda, J. A. (eds.): Music and emotion. Theory and research. Oxford, 71–103

Juslin, P. N. & Sloboda J. A. (eds.) (2001): Music and emotion. Theory and research. Oxford

Justice, R. W. (1994): Music Therapy Interventions for People with Eating Disorders in an Inpatients Setting. In: *Music Therapy Perspectives*, 12 (2), 104–110.

Karow, D./Rötter, G. (2000): Eine Studie zur analgetischen Wirkung von Musik. In: *Musikpsychologie*, 16, 84–101

Kasayka, R. (1991): To Meet and Match the Moment of Hope: Transpersonal Elements of the Guided Imagery and Music Experience. Unpublished PhD dissertation. New York University

Kasayka, R. (2002): A Spiritual Orientation to the Bonny Method: To Walk the Mystical Path on Practical Feet. In: Bruscia, K. E., Grocke, D. E. (eds.): Guided Imagery and Music. The Bonny Method and Beyond. Gilsum, 257–272

Kast, V. (1982): Trauern- Phasen und Chancen des psychischen Prozesses. Stuttgart

Kast, V. (1997): Wenn Geburt und Tod zusammenfallen: Trauer aus der Sicht der Therapeutin. In: Lutz, G., Künzer-Riebel, B. (eds.): Nur ein Hauch von Leben. Lahr

Keil, C. and Feld, S. (1994): Music grooves: essays and dialogues. Chicago, IL

Keiser, L. H. (1986): Conscious Listening. An annotated guide to the ICM taped music programs. Savage, D, Institute for Music and Imagery.

Kiel, H. (1993): Guided Imagery and Music. In: *Musiktherapeutische Umschau*, 14 (4), 327–340

Kivy, P. (1990): Music Alone. Philosophical Reflections on the Purely Musical Experience. Ithaca and London, Cornell

Klaus, M. H., Kennell, J. H. (1976): Maternal-Infant-Bonding. St. Louis

Knill, P. J., (rev.ed./1993): Ausdruckstherapie. Künstlerischer Ausdruck in Therapie und Erziehung. Lilienthal

Kohler, C. (1968): Kommunikative Psychotherapie. Jena

Kohler, C. (ed.) (1971): Musiktherapie. Theorie und Methodik. Jena

Kolb, B., Whishaw, I. Q. (1996): Neuropsychologie. Heidelberg

König, K. (4/1995): Sinnesentwicklung und Leiberfahrung. ed. by. Arnim, G.. Stuttgart

Körlin D. and Wrangsjö, B. (2002): Treatment Effects of Guided Imagery and Music (GIM) in Therapy. In: *Nordic Journal of Music Therapy*; 11(1), 3–15.

Körlin, D. (1999): Spontaneous Peak Experiences in Guided Imagery and Music Groups – A Catalyst for Working Through Psychodynamic Issues. Proceedings of "Exploring the Spiritual Dimension", Conference, Department of Psychology. Stockholm University.

Körlin, D. (2002): A Neuropsychological Theory of Traumatic Imagery in the Bonny Method of Guided Imagery and Music (BMGIM): In: Bruscia, K., Grocke, D. (eds.): Guided Imagery and Music – the Bonny Method and Beyond. Gilsum, NH., 379–416

Körlin, D., Nybäck H., Goldberg, F. (2000): Creative Arts Groups in Psychiatric Care: Development and Evaluation of a Therapeutic Alternative. In: *Nordic Journal of Psychiatry*; 54, 333–340

Koschnik, W. J. (1992): Standardwörterbuch für die Sozialwissenschaften, 2 volumes. München

Kötter, E. (1996): Zu Bezügen zwischen den Benennungen von Affekten in der Barockmusik und Begriffen der heutigen Emotionspsychologie. In: *Musikpsychologie,* 12, 75–88

Kramer, J., Alstad, D. (1993): The Guru Papers: Masks of Authoritarian Power. Berkeley

Krause, R. (1990): Psychodynamik der Emotionsstörungen. In: Scherer, K. R. (ed.) (1990): Psychologie der Emotion. Vol. C IV, 3. Göttingen, 630–705

Kreitler, H., Kreitler, S. (1972): Psychology of the Arts. Durham, N. C., USA

Kriz, J. (1994): Grundkonzepte der Psychotherapie. Weinheim

Kühn, M. (2001): "The times they are a changing ..." (Bob Dylan): Sehnsucht nach der Musik im Medienzeitalter. In: *Musiktherapeutische Umschau*, 22, (2), 83–92

Kümmel, W. F. (1976a): Gesundheit und Krankheit unter dem Aspekt der "musica", part 1. In: *Musiktherapie. Zeitschrift für die musiktherapeutische Forschung und Praxis. Musik & Medizin*, 10, 31–36

Kümmel, W. F. (1976b): Gesundheit und Krankheit unter dem Aspekt der "musica", part 2. In: *Musiktherapie. Zeitschrift für die musiktherapeutische Forschung und Praxis. Musik & Medizin*, 11, 29–35

Küntzel-Hansen, M. (1971): Wir hören und lernen Musik. Hannover

Kunz, W. (2003): personal notice

Lacan, J. (1980): Das Ich in der Theorie Freuds und in der Technik der Psychoanalyse. Olten

Lakoff, G. and M. Johnson (1980): Metaphors we live by. Chicago and London

Lange, v. A. (1968): Mensch, Musik und Kosmos. Anregungen zu einer goetheanistischen Tonlehre, Vol. I, II. Freiburg

Langenberg, M. (1996): Affektivität. In: Decker-Voigt, H.-H., Knill, P., Weymann, E. (eds.): Lexikon Musiktherapie. Göttingen, 3–4

Langer, S. (1954): Philosophy in a new key: A study in the symbolism of reason, rite, and art. New York, N. Y.

Langer, S. (1984): Philosophie auf neuem Wege. Frankfurt am Main

Lantermann, E. D. (1983): Handlung und Emotion. In: Euler, H. A., Mandl, H. (eds.): Emotionspsychologie. München, 273–282

Laughlin, C. D., McManus, J., Shearer, J. (1993): Transpersonal Anthropology. In: Walsh, R., Vaughan, F. (eds.): Paths Beyond Ego. The Transpersonal Vision. New York.

Lecourt, E. (1988): La musicothérapie. Paris

Lecourt, E. (1997): Voix et émotion, recherche collective. In: *La Revue de Musicothérapie*. XVII, 2/3, 63–65

Lehmann, A. C. (1994): "Habituelle und situative Rezeptionsweisen beim Musikhören – eine einstellungstheoretische Untersuchung". In: *Schriften zur Musikpsychologie und Musikästhetik*, 6. Frankfurt a. M., 129ff

Lewis, K. (1999): The Bonny Method of Guided Imagery and Music: Matrix for Transpersonal Experience. In: *Journal of The Association for Music and Imagery* 6 (1998–99), 63–85

Lewis, K. (2002): The development of Training in the Bonny Method of Guided Imagery and Music (BMGIM) from 1975 to 2000. Guided Imagery and Music. In: Bruscia, K. E. and Grocke, D. E. (eds.): The Bonny Method and Beyond, Gilsum NH, 497–517

Loewy, J. (2004): A Clinical Model of Music Therapy in the NICU. In: Nöcker-Ribaupierre, M. (ed.): Music Therapy for Premature and Newborn Infants. Philadelphia,159–176.

Logan, B. (1991): Infant Outcomes of a Prenatal Stimulation Pilot Study. In: *Prenatal and Perinatal Psychology Journal*, 6 (1), 7–31

Lothrop, H. (1998): Gute Hoffnung, jähes Ende. München

Lu, F. G., Lim, R., Mezzich, J. E. (1995): Issues in the Assessment and Diagnosis of Culturally Diverse Individuals. In: Oldham, J. & Riba, M. (ed.): Review of Psychiatry, Vol. 14. Washington, D. C., USA

Ludwig, A. M. (1966): Altered States of Consciousness. In: *Arch Gen Psychiatry*, 15(3), 225 –234

Lungwitz, H. (1970): Lehrbuch der Psychobiologie. Erste Abteilung. Berlin

Lutz, G., Künzer-Riebel, B. (ed.) (1997): Nur ein Hauch von Leben. Lahr

Machleidt, W., Gutjahr, L., Mügge, A. (1989): Grundgefühle. Berlin

Machleidt, W. (1994): Ist die Schizophrenie eine affektive Erkrankung? In: *Psychologische Beiträge*, 36, 348–378

Machleidt, W. (1999): Affekttypologie schizophrener Psychosen. In: Machleidt, W., Haltenhof, H., Garlipp, P. (eds.): Schizophrenie – eine affektive Erkrankung? Stuttgart, 99–112

Maiello, S. (2004): On the Meaning of Prenatal Auditory Perception and memory for the Development of the Mind: A Psychoanalytic Perspective. In: Nöcker-Ribaupierre, M. (ed.): Music Therapy for Premature and Newborn Infants. Philadelphia, 51–66

Mandler, G. (1979): Denken und Fühlen. Paderborn

Marcelli, D., Braconnier,A. ([5]/1999): Adolescence et psychopathologie. Paris

Marr, J. (2000): The Effects of Music on Imagery Sequence in the Bonny Method of Guided Imagery and Music. Faculty of Music. Melbourne, 171ff

Maslow, A. H. (1968): Toward a Psychology of Being. New York

Maurer, K. (ed.). (1989): Topographic mapping of EEG and evoked potentials. Berlin

Mayring, P. (1992): Eine Klassifikation der Gefühle. In: Ulich, D., Mayring, P.: Psychologie der Emotionen. Stuttgart, 136–164

McArthur, D. S., (1988): Birth of a Self in Adulthood. Nortvale

McKeen, T. (1996): Wesen und Gestalt des Menschen. Aufsätze und Vorträge zur anthroposophischen Menschenkunde und Medizin. Stuttgart

Meadows, A. (2002): Distinctions between the Bonny Method of Guided Imagery and Music (BMGIM) and Other Imagery Techniques. In: Bruscia, K. E., Grocke, D. E. (eds.): Guided Imagery and Music: The Bonny Method and Beyond. Gilsum, NH, 63–84

Mederacke, I. (1979): Regulativ-aktive Musiktherapie bei Kindern mit Herz-Kreislauf-Schäden. In: Schwabe, C., Röhrborn, H.: Regulative Musiktherapie. Jena, 206–221

Mederacke, I. (1993): Regulatives Wahrnehmungstraining mit Musik – Praxis mit körperbehinderten Kindern. In Decker-Voigt, H.-H., Eschen, J. Th., Mahns W. (eds.): Kindermusiktherapie. Hamburger Jahrbuch (Vol. 3). Lilienthal, 97–110

Merriam, A. P. (1964): The Anthropology of Music. Evanston, IL, USA

Meszaros, I., Szabo, C., Csako, R. I. (2002): Hypnotic susceptibility and alterations in subjective experiences. In: *Acta Biol Hung*, 53 (4), 499–514

Metzner, S. (1999): Tabu und Turbulenz. Göttingen

Metzner, S. (1996): Guided Imagery and Music. In: Decker-Voigt, H.-H., Knill, P. J., Weymann, E. (eds.): Lexikon Musiktherapie. Göttingen, 122–124

Metzner, S. (2004): Einige Gedanken zur rezeptiven Musiktherapie aus psychoanalytischer Sicht. In: Frohne-Hagemann, I. (ed.): Rezeptive Musiktherapie – Theorie und Praxis. Wiesbaden, 27–38

Möller, H.- J. (1976a): Was macht die Musik mit den Lebensgeistern? Musik und Therapie in der Geschichte: Die Theorie des Athanasius Kircher. In: *Musiktherapie. Zeitschrift für die musiktherapeutische Forschung und Praxis. Musik & Medizin*, (3), 35–36

Möller, H.-J. (1976b): Die harmonischen Proportionen der Gegensätze. Musik und Therapie in der Geschichte: Die Harmonie als Ordnungsprinzip des menschlichen Körpers im Corpus Hippocratium. In: *Musiktherapie. Zeitschrift für die musiktherapeutische Forschung und Praxis. Musik & Medizin*, (4), 40–41

Mucchielli,A. (1983): L'analyse phénoménologique et structurale en sciences humaines. Paris

Müller, R. (1990): Musikalische Rezeptionsstrategien und Differenziertheit des musikalischen Urteils in verschiedenen sozialen Situationen. In: *Musikpsychologie,* 7, 129–146.

Müller, R. (2000): Die feinen Unterschiede zwischen verbalen und klingenden Musikpräferenzen Jugendlicher. In: *Musikpsychologie,* 15, 87–98

Muthesius, D. (1990): Denkt man doch im Silberhaar gern' vergang'ner Zeiten. In: *Musiktherapeutische Umschau*, Vol. 11, 2, S. 132–140

Niedecken, D. (1988): Einsätze. Material und Beziehungsfigur im musikalischen Produzieren. Hamburg

Nijs, M. (1999): Trauern hat seine Zeit. Abschiedsrituale beim frühen Tod eines Kindes. Göttingen

Nöcker-Ribaupierre, M. (1995): Auditive Stimulation nach Frühgeburt. Stuttgart

Nöcker-Ribaupierre, M. (1999): Premature Birth and Music Therapy. In: Wigram,T.; De Backer, J.(eds.): Clinical Application of Music Therapy in Developmental Disability, Pediatrics and Neurology. London, 47–68

Oberhoff, B. (ed.): (2002a): Psychoanalyse und Musik. Eine Bestandsaufnahme. Gießen

Oberhoff, B. (ed.): (2002b): Das Unbewusste in der Musik. Gießen

Oberhoff, B. (ed.): (2003): Die Musik als Geliebte. Gießen

Odgen, T. H. (1997): Über den potentiellen Raum. In: *Forum der Psychoanalyse* 13, 1–18

Oelmann, J. (1993): Klang, Wahrnehmung, Wirkung. Zur therapeutischen Arbeit mit Gongs und Tam-Tams in rezeptiver Therapie. In: *Musiktherapeutische Umschau*, 14 (4), 289–305

Oerter, R., Rösing, H. (eds): Musikpsychologie. Ein Handbuch, Reinbek b. Hamburg, 412–417

Oerter, U. (1993): Rezeptive Musiktherapie als Lehrangebot. Eine Zusammenschau auf Grund der Einschätzungen von StudentInnen und DozentInnen. In: *Musiktherapeutische Umschau*, 14 (4), 340–349

Oohashi, T., Kawai, N., Honda, M., Nakamura, S., Morimoto, M., Nishina, E., et al. (2002): Electroencephalographic measurement of possession trance in the field. In: *Clinical Neurophysiology*, 113 (3), 435–445

Ortony, A., Turner, T. J. (1990): What's basic about basic emotions? In: *Psychological Review*, 97, 315–331

Palm, G. (2001): Jetzt bist du schon gegangen, Kind. München

Park, J. R., Yagyu, T., Saito, N., Kinoshita, T., Hirai, T. (2002): Dynamics of brain electric field during recall of Salpuri dance performance. In: *Percept Mot Skills*, 95 (3 Pt 1), 955–962

Pavlicevic, M. (1997): Music Therapy in Context. Music, Meaning and Relationship. London

Pedersen, I. N., Bonde, L. O., et al. (2002): Theoretical Foundations of Music Therapy. In: Wigram, T., Pedersen, I. N. and Bonde, L. O. (eds.): Analytical, Pschodynamic and Transpersonal Theories. A Comprehensive Guide to Music Therapy. London, 71–97

Pekala, R. J. (1991a): Phenomenology of Consciousness Inventory (PCI) Form I (1999), U. O., Trans.) West Chester PA. MID-Atlantic Educational Institute

Pekala, R. J. (1991b): Quantifying Consciousness: an empirical approach. New York,

Pekala, R. J., Kumar, V. K. (2000): Operationalizing 'trance' I: Rationale and research using a psychophenomenological approach. In: *American Journal of Clinical Hypnosis*, 43 (2), 107–135

Perilli, G. (2002): A theory of metaphor in the Bonny Method of Guided Imagery and Music (BMGIM). In: Bruscia, K. E., Grocke, D. E. (eds.): Guided Imagery and Music: The Bonny Method and beyond, Gilsum, NH, 417–448

Petsche, H. (1987): Gehirnvorgänge beim Musikhören und deren Objektivierung durch das EEG. In: *Musikpsychologie,* 4, 7–28

Petsche, H. (1993): Zerebrale Verarbeitung. In: Bruhn, H., Oerter, R., Rösing, H. (eds.): Musikpsychologie. Reinbeck bei Hamburg, 630–638

Petsche, H. (1994): The EEG while listening to music. In: *EEG-EMG-Z Elektroenz Elektrom*, 25 (2), 130–137

Petzold, H. G. (1988): Integrative Bewegungs- und Leibtherapie. Ein ganzheitlicher Weg leibbezogener Psychotherapie. Integrative Therapie, Schriften zu Theorie, Methodik und Praxis, Vol. I/1, Paderborn

Petzold, H. G. (2001): Das biopsychosoziale Modell kritischer Humantherapie und Kulturarbeit – Theorie, Praxis, Wirksamkeit. Jubiläumsausgabe *Integrative Therapie*, Paderborn

Petzold, H. G. (2002): Zentrale Modelle und Kernkonzepte der "Integrativen Therapie". In: www.fpi-publikationen.de/polyloge/petzold-kernkonzepte-polyloge-02-2002.htm

Petzold, H. G. (1993a): Das "neue Integrationsparadigma" in Psychotherapie und klinischer Psychologie und die ‚Schulen des Integrierens' in einer ‚pluralen therapeutischen Kultur' (1992): In: Integrative Therapie. Modelle, Theorien und Methoden für eine schulenübergreifende Psychotherapie, Integrative Therapie, Schriften zu Theorie, Methodik und Praxis, Vol. II/ 2, Paderborn, 927–1039

Petzold, H. G. (1993b): Integrative Therapie. Modelle, Theorien und Methoden für eine schulenübergreifende Psychotherapie, Integrative Therapie, Schriften zu Theorie, Methodik und Praxis, Vol. II/1, 2, 3, Paderborn

Petzold, H. G. (1993c): Frühe Schädigungen – späte Folgen? Psychotherapie und Babyforschung, Vol. 1, Paderborn

Petzold, H. G. (1993d): Die Kraft liebevoller Blicke. Psychotherapie und Babyforschung, Vol. 2, Paderborn

Petzold, H. G., Wolf, H. U. et al. (2000): "Integrative Traumatherapie" – Modelle und Konzepte für die Behandlung von Patienten mit "posttraumatischer Belastungsstörung". In: v. d. Kolk, B., Mc. Farlane, A., Weisaeth, L. (eds.): Traumatic Stress. Grundlagen und Behandlungsansätze. Paderborn, 445–579

Pfrogner, H. (2/1981): Lebendige Tonwelt. München

Piontelli, A. (1992): From Fetus to Child – An Observational and Psychoanalytic Study. London

Plutchik, R. (1984): Emotions and Imagery. In: *Journal of Mental Imagery*, 8, 105–112

Pohlen, M. (1999): Was ist Psychotherapie als Wissenschaft? In: *Forum der Psychoanalyse 15, 71–80*

Porat, R., Meltzer, B. (1998): Images of War and Peace. In: *Journal of Sandplay Therapy*, VII/2, 24–70

Priestley, M. (1982): Musiktherapeutische Erfahrungen. Stuttgart

Priestley, M. (1994): Analytical Music Therapy. Phoenixville

Prior, M. (2002): Mini-Max-Interventionen", 15 minimale Interventionen mit maximaler Wirkung. Heidelberg

Reddemann, L. (2002): Imagination als heilsame Kraft. Zur Behandlung von Traumafolgen mit ressourcenorientierten Verfahren. Stuttgart

Reinecke, H. P. (1974): Musikpsychologie und musikalische Kommunikation. Berlin

Reinhardt, A. (2002): Regulative Musiktherapie bei Borderline – Persönlichkeitsorganisationen nach Clarkin. Unpublished. paper, Akademie für angewandte Musiktherapie Crossen. Crossen

Reinhold, S. (1993): Musiktherapie in der Intensivmedizin. In: Glöckler, M., Schürholz, J, Walker, M. (eds.) ([3]/2004): Anthroposophische Medizin. Stuttgart, 88–94

Reinhold, S. (1996): Anthroposophische Musiktherapie. Eine Hinführung. Aus der Schriftenreihe: *Soziale Hygiene* 157, Bad Liebenzell, 22–37

Reinhold, S. (1997): Englische Handglocken. In: *Musiktherapeutische Umschau*, 18 (1). Göttingen, 25–34

Reinhold, S. (2/2002): Musiktherapie für Sterbende. In: Treichler, M. (ed.): Den Sinn des Todes fassen. Mut zur Begleitung Sterbender. Stuttgart, 95–105

Rejzlik, W. (2001): Musikpräferenzen Jugendlicher unter besonderer Berücksichtigung der massenmedialen Verbreitung von Musik. Dissertation. Wien.

Richard, J. F. (1990): Les activités mentales: comprendre, raisonner, trouver des solutions. Paris

Richard, J. F. (2001): Le processus de subjectivation à l'adolescence. Paris

Ricoeur, P. (1984): Time and narrative, Vol. 2. Chicago

Righetti, P. L. (1996): The Emotional Experience of the Fetus: a Preliminary Report. In: *Pre- and Perinatal Psychology Journal*, 11(1), 55–65

Risch, M., Scherg, H., Verres, R. (2001): Music therapy for chronic headaches. Evaluation of music therapeutic groups for patients suffering from chronic headaches. In: *Schmerz*, 15 (2), 116–125

Rittner, S. Fachner, J. (2004): Klang und Trance im EEG -Brainmapping verschiedener Tranceinduktionsmethoden im rituellen Setting. Musiktherapeutische Umschau Online. Retrieved 18. Januar, 2006, from: http://www.musiktherapie.de/index.php?id=193

Rittner, S., Hess, P. (1996): Klangtrance. Trance. Veränderte Bewusstseinszustände. In Decker-Voigt, H. H., Weymann, E., Knill, P. (eds.): Lexikon Musiktherapie. Göttingen,169–173

Rittner, S., Jungaberle, H. (2002): Sounding systems – Different Approaches to the valuation of Music Psychotherapy Groups. In Aldridge, D., Fachner, J. (eds.), Music Therapy in Europe – Proceedings of the the 5th European Music Therapy Congress in Castel Dell'Ovo, Naples, Italy 20.–24. April 2001 (E-Book on Music Therapy Info CD-ROM ed., Vol. IV, 1514–1543). Witten, University Witten/Herdecke

Rittner, S. (1997): Die Arbeit mit dem Ganzkörper – Monochord in der Musikpsychotherapie. In: Berger, L. (ed.): Musik, Magie & Medizin. Paderborn, 110–117

Rittner, S. (1998): Singen und Trance – Die Stimme als Medium zur Induktion veränderter Bewusstseinszustände. In: Gundermann, H. (ed.): Die Ausdruckswelt der Stimme. Heidelberg, 317 –325

Rittner, S. (1999): Bewusstseinsforschung. In: Verres, R., Schweizer, J., Jonasch, K., Süßdorf, B. (eds.): Heidelberger Lesebuch Medizinische Psychologie. Heidelberg

Rittner, S. (2004): Seelen-Wege: Der Körper als Gefährt für Reisen in andere Wirklichkeiten. In: Tucek, G. (ed.), Musik und Medizin – Beiträge zur Musik- und Therapieforschung 1995–2004 (CD-ROM Edition). Wien

Robson, C. (2002): Real World Research. A resource for Social Scientists and Practitioner-Researchers, Oxford

Röhrborn, H. (1987): Der symptomzentrierte Psychotherapieansatz der RMT. In: Schwabe, C. (1987) (ed.): Regulative Musiktherapie. Stuttgart, Leipzig

Röhrborn, H. (1992): Regulative Musiktherapie in der Dyade. Unpublished paper

Röhrborn, H. (1993): Zum Psychotherapiekonzept der Regulativen Musiktherapie (RMT) nach Schwabe. In: *Musiktherapeutische Umschau,* 14 (2), 134–141

Röhrborn, H. (1994): Regulative Musiktherapie im Kontext eines tiefenpsychologisch orientierten Gruppenpsychotherapiekonzepts. Presented at the 13th Meeting of the Work Group Clinical Psychology in Rehabilitation Centers. Bad Wildungen - Reinhardshausen

Röhrborn, H. (1995): Regulative Musiktherapie im Kontext eines tiefenpsychologisch orientierten Gruppenpsychotherapiekonzepts. In: Bürckstümmer, E., Burmeister, G., Wintzler, G., Würther, K. (eds.): Psychotherapie in Rehabilitationseinrichtungen. Regensburg

Rouget, G. (1985): Music and Trance. A Theory of the Relations between Music and Possession. Chicago

Rubel, E. W. (1984): Ontogeny of Auditory System Function. In: *Annual Review Physiology* 46: 213

Rudstam, G. (2002): Att synliggöra det osynliga. Final paper presented for certification at the "Expressive Arts" institute. Stockholm

Rueger, C. (1991): Die musikalische Hausapotheke für jedwede Lebens- und Stimmungslage von A-Z. Genf, München

Ruland, H. (1981): Ein Weg zur Erweiterung des Tonwesens. Basel

Ruland, H. (2003): Musik als erlebte Menschenkunde. Borchen

Ruud, E. (1980): Music Therapy and its Relationship to Current Treatment Theories. St. Louis

Ruud, E., Mahns, W. (1991): Meta-Musiktherapie. Wege zur einer Theorie der Musiktherapie. Oslo

Sabourin, M. E., Cutcomb, S. D., Crawford, H. J., Pribram, K. (1990): EEG correlates of hypnotic susceptibility and hypnotic trance: Spectral analysis and coherence. In: *International Journal of Psychophysiology*, 10 (2), 125–142

Salber, W. (1989): Der Alltag ist nicht grau. Bonn

Salber, W. (1991): Gestalt auf Reisen. Bonn

Sander, F. (1927): Experimentelle Ergebnisse der Gestaltpsychologie. In: Sander, Friedrich/ Volkelt, H. (eds.) (1967): Ganzheitspsychologie. München

Schafers, M. (1988): Klang und Krach. Eine Kulturgeschichte des Hörens. Frankfurt a. M. [Orig. Toronto 1977]

Scherer, K. R., Wallbott, H.G. (1990): Ausdruck von Emotionen. In: Scherer,K.R. (ed.): Psychologie der Emotion, Vol. C IV, 3. Göttingen, 345–422

Scherer, K. R. (1979): Entwicklung der Emotionen. In Hetzer, H., Todt, E., Seiffge-Krenke, I. (eds.): Angewandte Entwicklungspsychologie des Kindes- und Jugendalters. Heidelberg, 211–253

Scherer, K. R. (ed.) (1990): Psychologie der Emotion. Vol. C IV, 3. Göttingen

Schiltz, L. (2005): Dysfonctionnements cognitifs liés aux pathologies limites à l'adolescence. Étude comparée de quelques tests projectifs. Neuropsychiatrie de l'Enfance et de l'Adolescence. 53, 3; 107–113

Schiltz, L. (1995): De l'utilisation de la musicothérapie avec des adolescents souffrant d'un blocage du fonctionnement pulsionnel. D. U. art en thérapie et en psychopédagogie. Université René Descartes. Paris-V. Paris

Schiltz, L. (1999): Musique et élaboration imaginaire de l'agressivité à l'adolescence. Evaluation d'une expérience thérapeutique. Thèse de doctorat en psychologie clinique. Université René Descartes. Paris-V. Paris

Schiltz, L. (2002a): Musiktherapeutische Behandlung jugendlicher Borderline Patienten. In: Petersen, P. (ed.): Forschungsmethoden Künstlerischer Therapien. Methodische Grundlagen, Projekte, Vorschläge. Stuttgart, 385–402

Schiltz, L. (2002b): Archétypes signalant la reprise du processus de subjectivation. In: *La Revue de musicothérapie.* XXII, 1; 8–11

Schiltz, L. (2003a): Some Epistemological considerations about Musictherapeutic Research. In : Schiltz, L. (ed.) Epistemology and Practice of Research in the Arts Therapies. Luxembourg, 45–55

Schiltz, L. (2003b): L'organisation limite de la personnalité à l'adolescence. Considérations diagnostiques et thérapeutiques. Tome 1. Rapport de recherche R et D. Luxembourg. 221–226

Schiltz, L. (2003c): La fonction du double à l'âge de la quête d'identité. In: *La Revue Française de Psychiatrie et de Psychologie Médicale.* VII, 80 , 51–55

Schiltz, L. (2003d): Musicothérapie et quête de sens à l'âge adulte avancé. In : Sudres, J. L. Roux G. et al. (dir) : La Personne âgée en art thérapie. De l'expression au lien social. Paris,

Schiltz, L. (2004a): Le blocage cognitif, émotionnel et motivationnel des élèves surdoués en situation d'échec scolaire grave. Résultats d'études cliniques et expérimentales sur la "résignation apprise". In: *La Revue française de Psychiatrie et de Psychologie médicale,* VII, 79, 39–44

Schiltz, L. (2004b): Musicothérapie et processus de symbolisation chez les adolescents à fonctionnement limite. In: *La Revue française de Psychiatrie et de Psychologie médicale.* VII, 73, 17–20

Schmidt-Atzert, L., Ströhm, W. (1983): Ein Beitrag zur Taxonomie der Emotionswörter. In: *Psychologische Beiträge*, 25, 126–141

Schroeder, W. (1999): Zum Geleit für Strobel, W. : Reader Musiktherapie, Klanggeleitete Trance, musiktherapeutische Fallsupervision und andere Beiträge. Wiesbaden

Schumacher, K., Muthesius, D., Frohne-Hagemann, I. (2005): Die Geschichte der psychotherapeutisch orientierten Musiktherapie in Berlin – ein historischer und systematischer Überblick. In: Müller, T. (ed.): Psychotherapie und Körperarbeit in Berlin. Geschichte und Praktiken der Etablierung. Husum, 261–290

Schumacher, K. (1991): Musiktherapie mit autistischen Kindern als menschliche Begegnung. In: *Der Kinderarzt*, 22 (9), 1439–1443

Schumacher, K. (1999): Musiktherapie und Säuglingsforschung. Zusammenspiel und Einschätzung der Beziehungsqualität am Beispiel eines autistischen Kindes, Europäische Hochschulschriften, Reihe 6, Vol. 630. Frankfurt/M., Berlin, Bern, New York, Paris, Wien

Schumacher, K.; Calvet-Kruppa, C. (2001): Die Relevanz entwicklungspsychologischer Erkenntnisse für die Musiktherapie. In: Decker-Voigt, H. H. (ed.): Schulen der Musiktherapie. München,102–124

Schumacher, R. (1982): Die Musik in der Psychiatrie des 19. Jahrhunderts. Marburger Schriften zur Medizingeschichte, Vol. 4, Frankfurt

Schwabe, C. & Haase, U. (1998): Die Sozialmusiktherapie (SMT). Crossener Schriften zur Musiktherapie (Vol. VII). Akademie für angewandte Musiktherapie Crossen

Schwabe, C. & Röhrborn, H. ($^{\text{3.rev.ed.}}$/1996): Regulative Musiktherapie. Entwicklung, Stand und Perspektiven in der psychotherapeutischen Medizin. Stuttgart, Jena

Schwabe, C. & Stein, I. (eds.) (2000): Ressourcenorientierte Musiktherapie. Materialien zur Tagung "Musiktherapie – Lebensgenuss – Freude – ?". Crossener Schriften zur Musiktherapie (Vol. XII): Akademie für angewandte Musiktherapie Crossen

Schwabe, C. (1969/$^{\text{2nd rev.ed.}}$1972/$^{\text{3rd rev.ed.}}$1973): Musiktherapie bei Neurosen und funktionellen Störungen. Jena, Stuttgart

Schwabe, C. (1978, $^{\text{2nd rev.ed.}}$/1980, $^{\text{3rd. rev.ed.}}$/1986): Methodik der Musiktherapie und deren theoretische Grundlagen. Leipzig

Schwabe, C. (ed.) (1979,): Regulative Musiktherapie. Jena, Stuttgart ($^{\text{2nd rev.ed. ed.}}$/1987. Stuttgart, Leipzig)

Schwabe, C. (1983, $^{\text{2nd rev.ed.}}$/1991a,): Aktive Gruppenmusiktherapie für erwachsene Patienten. Leipzig/ Stuttgart ($^{\text{3rd. rev.ed.}}$1997. In: Crossener Schriften zur Musiktherapie, Vol. IV. Akademie für angewandte Musiktherapie Crossen)

Schwabe, C. ($^{\text{3rd}}$ /1991b): Entspannungstraining mit Musik, Regulatives Musiktraining/ Anleitung zur gezielten Selbstentspannung. Leipzig/ Stuttgart

Schwabe, C. (1996): Regulative Musiktherapie. In: Decker-Voigt, H.-H. et al.(eds.): Lexikon Musiktherapie. Göttingen, Bern, Toronto, Seattle, 317–320

Schwabe, C. (2000): Anwendungsmodifikationen von Regulativer Musiktherapie und Regulativem Musiktraining. Crossener Schriften zur Musiktherapie (Vol. XI): Akademie für angewandte Musiktherapie Crossen

Schwabe, C. (2003a): Konzeption als Prozess oder als Dogma. In: Haase, U. & Schwabe, C. (eds.): Konzept und Offenheit. Musiktherapie in Theorie und Praxis. Materialien zum wissenschaftlichen Symposium der Akademie für angewandte Musiktherapie Crossen. Crossener Schriften zur Musiktherapie (Vol. XIII)

Schwabe, C. (2003b): Regulative Musiktherapie (RMT): Die Entwicklung einer Methode zu einer Konzeption. Crossener Schriften zur Musiktherapie (Vol. XIV): Akademie für angewandte Musiktherapie Crossen

Schwabe, C. et al. (1971): Physiologische und psychologische Untersuchungen zur rezeptiven Einzelmusiktherapie. In Kohler, C. (ed.): Musiktherapie – Theorie und Methodik, Jena/Stuttgart, 51–71

Schwartz, F. J. (2004): Medical Music Therapy fort he Premature Baby – Research Review. In: Nöcker-Ribaupierre, M. (ed.): Music Therapy for Premature and Newborn Infants, Philadelphia, 85–96.

Schwarzer, G. (2000): Musikalische Wahrnehmungsentwicklung: Wie Kinder Musik hören. In: *Musikpsychologie,* 15, 60–76

Schwendtner-Berlin, H., Berlin, J., David, L., Fachner, J., Böving, S. F., David, E., et al. (1995): Gesetzmäßigkeiten in der Psychologie veränderter Bewusstseinszustände. In: *Curare*, 18(2), 361–368

Sheth, R. D.; Mullett, M. D.; Bodensteiner, J. B.; Hobbs, G. R. (1995): Longitudinal Head Growth in Developmentally Normal Preterm Infants. In: *Archives of Pediatric Adolescent Medicine* 149, 1358–1361

Shoemark, H. (2004): Family Centered Music Therapy for Infants with Complex Medical and Surgical Needs. In: Nöcker-Ribaupierre, M. (ed.):Music Therapy for Premature and Newborn Infants. Philadelphia,141–158.

Short, A. E. (1992): Music and Imagery with Physically Disabled Elderly Residents: A GIM adaptation. In: *Music Therapy*, 11(1), 65–98.

Siegel, D. J. (1999): The Developing Mind – Toward a Neurobiology of Interpersonal Experience. New York

Skaggs, R. (1992): Music as Co-therapist: Creative resource for change. In: *Journal of the Association for Music and Imagery* 1, 77–84

Sloboda, J. A., Juslin, P. N. (2001): Psychological perspectives on music and emotion. In: Juslin, P. N., Sloboda J. A. (2001): Music and emotion. Theory and research. Oxford, 71–104

Sloboda, J. A., O'Neill S. A. (2001): Emotion in everyday listening to music. In: Juslin, P. N. & Sloboda. J. A.: Music and emotion. Theory and research. Oxford, 415–429

Smeijsters, H. (1999): Grundlagen der Musiktherapie. Theorie und Praxis der Behandlung psychischer Störungen und Behinderungen. Göttingen

Soesmann, A. (1995): Die zwölf Sinne – Tore der Seele. Stuttgart

Spering, M. (2001): Current Issues in Cross-Cultural Psychology Research Topics, Applications, and Perspectives. Institute of Psychology, University of Heidelberg, Germany. In: Internet: http://www.psychologie.uni-heidelberg.de/ae/mitarb/ms/cross-cultural%20psy.pdf

Spintge, R., Droh, R. (1987): Effects of Anxiolytic Music on Plasma Levels of Stress-Hormons in different Medical Specialities. In: Pratt, R. R. (ed.): The Fourth International Symposium on Music, Rehabilitation and Human Well-Being. Lanhan, USA, 88–101

Standley, J. M. (1998): Effect of Music Intervention on Head Circumference of Premature Infants: a Post-Hoc Analysis of Music Research in Neonatal Intensive Care. Paper presented at the National Convention of American Music Therapy Association. Cleveland, OH

Standley, J. M.; Moore, R. (1995): Therapeutic Effects of Music and Mother's Voice on Premature Infants. In: *Pediatric Nursing* 1, 90–95

Statnekov, D. K. (2nd/2003): Animated Earth. Berkeley

Stein, I. (1979): Regulatives Musiktraining – Entwicklung und Anwendung bei Studenten. In Schwabe, C. (ed.): Regulative Musiktherapie. Jena, Stuttgart, New York, 226–245

Steiner, R. (4/2001, GA 102): Das Hereinwirken geistiger Wesenheiten in den Menschen. Dornach

Steiner, R. (5/1989, GA 283): Das Wesen des Musikalischen und das Tonerlebnis im Menschen. Dornach

Steiner, R. (Sonderausgabe, GA 245): Anweisungen für eine esoterische Schulung. Dornach

Stern, D. N. (1977, 2nd/2002): First Relationship. Infant and Mother. New York [in German (1994): Mutter und Kind: die erste Beziehung. Stuttgart]

Stern, D. N. (1985): The Interpersonal World of the Infant. New York

Stern, D. N. (1990): The diary of a baby. New York, [in German (1994): Tagebuch eines Babys: Was ein Kind sieht, spürt und fühlt). Stuttgart]

Stern, D. N. (1992): Die Lebenserfahrung des Säuglings. Stuttgart

Stern, D. N. (2000): Das präsymbolische Denken beim Kleinkind. Einige Implikationen für die Psychotherapie. In: Salvisberg, H. Stiegler, M. Maxeiner V. (eds.): Erfahrung träumend zur Sprache bringen. Bern, 101–114

Stern, D. N. (2004): The present moment in psychotherapy and everyday life. London

Stige, B. (2002): Culture Centered Music Therapy. Gilsum NH

Straus, E. (1956): Vom Sinn der Sinne. Ein Beitrag zur Grundlegung der Psychologie. Springer, Berlin/Heidelberg. Reprint of the 2. edition 1978

Strobel, W. (1988): Klang – Trance – Heilung. Die archetypische Welt der Klänge in der Psychotherapie. In: *Musiktherapeutische Umschau*, 9, 119–139

Strobel, W. (1992): Die klanggeleitete Trance. Eine analytisch orientierte Form nonverbaler Hypnotherapie. In: *Hypnose und Kognition*, 9, 98–117

Strobel, W. (1999): Die klanggeleitete Trance in der Psychotherapie. In: Strobel, W.: Reader Musiktherapie. Klanggeleitete Trance, musiktherapeutische Fallsupervision und andere Beiträge, Wiesbaden, 99–142

Strobel, W. (1999): Schöpferische Psychotherapie. In: Strobel, W.: Reader Musiktherapie. Klanggeleitete Trance, musiktherapeutische Fallsupervision und andere Beiträge. Wiesbaden, 193–225

Stückert, A. (1997): Verschiedene Aspekte der Musiktherapie auf anthroposophischer Grundlage. München

Stumpf, C. (1883/1890): Tonpsychologie. 2 volumes. Leipzig

Stumpf, C. (1911/1979): Die Anfänge der Musik. Hildesheim

Summer, L. (1981): Guided Imagery and Music with the Elderly. In: *Music Therapy*, 1, 39–42.

Summer, L. (1988): Guided Imagery and Music in Salina, KS: Bonny Foundation. The Institutional Setting. St. Louis

Summer, L. (1989): Defining Guided Imagery and Music Lecture: Bonny Foundation Level I GIM Training. Wichita, KS.

Summer, L. (1995): Melding Musical and Psychological Processes: The Therapeutic Musical Space. In: *Journal of the Association for Music and Imagery*, 4, 37–48

Summer, L. (ed.) (2002): Music & Consciousness – the Evolution of Guided Imagery and Music. Gilsum, N.H.

Summer, L. (2002): Group Music and Imagery Therapy. In: Bruscia, K., Grocke, D. (eds.): Guided Imagery and Music – the Bonny Method and Beyond. Gilsum, NH, 297–306

Suzuki, D. T. (1988): Studies in Zen. London, Sydney, Wellington

Tatarkiewicz, W. (1979): Geschichte der Ästhetik, Vol. 3. Basel

Taylor, K. (1995): The Ethics of Caring: Honoring the Web of Life in Our Professional Healing Relationships. Santa Cruz, CA, USA

Teirich, H. R. (1958): Musik in der Medizin. Stuttgart

Tesch, R. (1990): Qualitative Research: Analysis Types and Software Tools. London

Thesen der Kasseler Konferenz (1998). In: *Musiktherapeutische Umschau 19 (3) 232–235*

Timmermann, T. (1983): Klangstrukturen und ihre psychische Wirkung. München

Timmermann, T. (1987): Musik als Weg. Zürich

Timmermann, T. (1996): Ethnologische Aspekte in der Musiktherapie. In Decker-Voigt, H. H., Knill, P. & Weymann, E. (eds.): Lexikon Musiktherapie, Göttingen, 87–90

Tomkins, S. S. (1962): Affect, imagery, consciousness: 1. The positive affects. New York

Toomey, L. (1996–97): Literature Review: The Bonny Method of Guided Imagery and Music. In: *Journal of the Association for Music and Imagery,* 5, 75–103

Treurniet, N. (1981): Psychoanalyse und Selbstpsychologie. In: *Psyche,* 39, 905–941

Troué, N./Bruhn, H. (2000): Musikpräferenzen in der Vorpubertät – Wandel von der Elternorientierung zur Peergruppenorientierung. In: *Musikpsychologie,* 15, 77–86

Tunner, W. (1982): Subjektive Distanz, Richtung und Zeit. In: *Gestalt Theorie*, 4, 207–216

Tüpker, R. (1999): Musik – eine Zaubermacht? Kritische Untersuchung zur Bedeutung der Musik im Märchen. In: *Musiktherapeutische Umschau*, 20, 231–248

Tüpker, R. (2002): Wo ist die Musik, wenn wir sie nicht hören? In: Oberhoff, B. (ed.): Das Unbewusste in der Musik. Gießen, 75–102

Tüpker, R. (2003): Selbstpsychologie und Musiktherapie. In: Oberhoff, B. (ed.): Die Musik als Geliebte. Gießen, 99–138

Uccusic, P. (1991): Der Schamane in uns: Schamanismus als neue Selbsterfahrung, Hilfe und Heilung. Genf/München

Ulich, D. (1992): Begriffsbestimmungen und Theoriediskussion. In: Ulich, D. & Mayring, P. (1992): Psychologie der Emotionen. Stuttgart, 28–57

Van Tienhoven, A. H., van Waning, A., Veen, G. (2001): Culture, Trauma, Transference and Counter-Transference: A Working Model for the Complex Interaction between Refugee

Client and Therapist. Presentation at the VI International Conference for Health and Human Rights, Cavtat, Kroatien. In: Internet: www.ishhr.org/conference/articles

Ventre, M. (2002): The Individual Form of the Bonny Method of Guided Imagery and Music (BMGIM): In: Bruscia, K. E., Grocke, D. E. (eds.): Guided Imagery and Music . The Bonny Method and Beyond. Gilsum, 29–36

Verdeau-Paillès, J. (3/1993): Le bilan psychomusical et la personnalité. Coulay

Vink, A. (2001): Music and Emotion. Living apart together: a relationship between music psychology and music therapy. In: *Nordic journal of music therapy*, 10 (2), 144–158

Walker, J. L. (1977): Subjective reactions to music and brainwave rhythms. In: *Physiological Psychology*, 5 (4), 483–489

Walsh, R., Vaughan, F. (1993): Paths Beyond Ego: The Transpersonal Vision. New York

Ward, K. (2002): A Jungian Orientation to the Bonny Method. In: Bruscia, K. E., Grocke, D. E. (eds.): Guided Imagery and Music. The Bonny Method and Beyond. Gilsum, NH, 207–224

Wehmeyer, G. (1974): Erik Satie. Regensburg

Wellek, A. (1930/31): Zur Typologie des Gehörs und des Musikerlebens überhaupt. In: *Zeitschrift für Musikwissenschaft* 13. Leipzig, 21ff

Wellendorf, F. (1999): Jenseits der Empathie. *Forum der Psychoanalyse 15, 9–24*

Wendt, H. (1958): Musik und Schlaftherapie. In: Teirich, H. R. (ed.): Musik und Medizin. Stuttgart, 105–112

Wigram, T., Nygaard-Pedersen, I., Bonde, L. O. (2002): A Comprehensive Guide to Music Therapy. London, Philadelphia

Wigram, T., Saperston, B.,West, R. (eds.) (1999): The Art & Science of Music Therapy. Amsterdam

Wilber, K. (1977): The Spectrum of Consciousness. Wheaton, Illinois

Wilber, K. (1979): No Boundary: Eastern and Western Approaches to Personal Growth. Boston, London

Wilber, K. (1980): The Atman Project. A Transpersonal View of Human Development. Wheaton, Illinois

Wilber, K. (1995): Sex, Ecology, Spirituality. Boston

Wilber, K. (1997): The Eye of Spirit: An Integral Vision for a World Gone Slightly Mad. Boston

Wilda-Kiesel, A. (1993): Die Konzentrative Entspannung. Studienbücher für Medizinische Berufe, Lern-Ausbildungssysteme GmbH. Reinbek bei Hamburg

Willms, H. (1977) (ed.): Musik und Entspannung. Stuttgart

Winnicott, D. J. (1965): The Maturational Process and Facilitating Environment. London

Winnicott, D. W. (1985): Vom Spiel zur Kreativität. Stuttgart

Witzel, M. (1999): Anmerkungen zur Integrativen therapeutischen Arbeit mit Musik von J. S. Bach: In: *Integrative Therapie* 2–3. Paderborn, 251–288

Wolcott, H. F. (1995). Transforming qualitative data: Description, analysis and Interpretation. Sage

Wosch, T., Frommer, J. (2002): Emotionsveränderungen in musiktherapeutischen Improvisationen. In: *Musik-, Tanz- und Kunsttherapie*, 13 (3), 107–114

Wosch, T. (2002): Emotionale Mikroprozesse musikalischer Interaktionen. Eine Einzelfallanalyse zur Untersuchung musiktherapeutischer Improvisationen. Münster

Wosch, T. (2003a): Der Weg zur Freude. Musikrezeption, Improvisation und Emotion im Kontext aktueller Musikvermittlung. In: Petrat, N., Kafurke, R., Schöne, K. (eds.): Mit Spaß dabei bleiben. Musikästhetische Erfahrungen aus der Perspektive der Forschung. Essen, 95–108

Wosch, T. (2003b): NeoM – a research-network on emotion in music therapy. In: Aldrigde, D., Fachner, J. (eds.): Info-CD Rom V – Music therapy world

Yalom, I. D. (1995): The theory and Practice of Group Psychotherapy. New York

Yehuda, N. (2002): Multicultural Encounters in Music Therapy – A Qualitative Research. In: Voices: A World Forum for Music Therapy, http://www.voices.no/mainissues/Voices2(3):Yehuda.html.

Zeuch, A. (1999): Schöpfer eigener Wirklichkeiten. Die Klangmeditation mit dem Monochord. In: *Musik-, Tanz- und Kunsttherapie*, 10 (4), 175–185

Zieger, A.(1999): Wieviel Gehirn braucht der Mensch? Dialogaufbau mit Menschen im Koma und apallischen Syndrom. In: Neander, K.-D. (Hg.): Musik und Pflege. Urban & Fischer, München/Jena, 9–38.

THE AUTHORS

Monica Bissegger, teacher and Music Therapist (BVAKT). Trained in Anthroposophic Music Therapy at the Musiktherapeutische Arbeitsstätte e. V. in Berlin, Germany; Director: Maria Schüppel. Since 1990 Music Therapist in Filderklinik, Filderstadt, Germany. Guest Teacher in various music therapy training programs. Fields of experience include: Internal Medicine, Pediatrics, Gynaecology, Psychosomatics (children and adults), Intensive Care (children and adults) and Neonatology.
Address: Filderklinik, Im Haberschlai 7, D-70794 Filderstadt, Germany
E-Mail: m.bissegger@filderklinik.de

Lars Ole Bonde, PhD, is Associate Professor in Music Therapy at the Department of Communication and Psychology (Division of Music Therapy) at Aalborg University, Denmark. He holds a Masters Degree in Musicology and Scandinavian Literature and later trained as a music therapist (FAMI, MTL). As a researcher, he has specialized in the therapeutic understanding and analysis of music in music therapy (using improvisation as well as pre-composed music) and in the phenomenology and hermeneutics of the musical experience. He is currently involved in cancer care projects, including the establishment of an international network for research in music therapy in oncology. He has published extensively and internationally in the fields of music therapy, music education and music theatre.
E-Mail: lobo@hum.aau.dk

Hans-Helmut Decker-Voigt, Prof. Dr., M.A. (Expressive Therapy Lesley College/ Cambridge USA) was born in 1945. He is currently director of the Institute for Music Therapy at the "Hochschule für Musik und Theater in Hamburg", and honorary President of the "Weiterbildungsakademie für künstlerische Psychotherapien der Herbert von Karajan-Stiftung in Berlin". He is also Director of the Music Therapy Division of the Clinic "Gut Wienebüttel", an academic teaching institution and part of the Institute at the Hamburg Hochschule. He is the author and publisher of 60 books on music therapy. In addition, he is the editor of the half-yearly publication, "Musik und Gesundsein" (Music and Being Healthy).
Address: Hochschule für Musik und Theater, Harvestehuder Weg 12, D-20148 Hamburg, Germany. www.decker-voigt-archiv.de.
Information about training seminars in DRMT can be obtained through the "Akademie der Herbert von Karajan-Stiftung Berlin c/o Institut für Musiktherapie der Hochschule für Musik und Theater Hamburg", Harvestehuder Weg, 12, D-20148 Hamburg
www.rrz.uni-hamburg.de/musikmed

Jörg Fachner, Dr. rer medic. Dipl. Ped., is Senior Research Fellow and holds the Chair for Qualitative Research in Medicine at the University of Witten Herdecke in Germany. He is managing editor of the music therapy research and service site: www.MusicTherapyWorld.net and editor of the E-Journal: www.MusicTherapyToday.com. Formerly, he worked as a

research assistant in physiology, in sensory and movement research. He studied from the University in Dortmund. He holds a degree in social- and education science in Wuppertal and graduated as an educationalist in rehabilitation from the University in Dortmund). In 2001 he finished his doctoral thesis on music perception in an EEG investigation at the Chair for Qualitative Research in Medicine and has recently published a book on music and altered states. His research interests, publications and scientific memberships focus on qualitative research aspects of music, therapy and medicine and music physiology, as well as psychology, youth und pop culture, altered states of consciousness, transcultural psychiatry and anthropology of the body.
Address: c/o Faculty for Medicine, University Witten/Herdecke, Alfred-Herrhausen Str. 50, D-58448 Witten, Germany
E-Mail: joergf@uni-wh.de http://www.musictherapyworld.net

Isabelle Frohne-Hagemann, Dr. phil., born in1947, Integrative Music therapist, licensed psychotherapist and supervisor in private practice in Berlin, GIM-Fellow (Bonny Method of Guided Imagery and Music Fellow), Assistant Professor of Receptive Music Therapy and GIM at the "Institute of Music Therapy of the University of Music and Theatre in Hamburg"; former head of the study program "Integrative Music Therapy", training therapist and supervisor at the European Academy of Psychosocial Health and Promotion of Creativity (Fritz Perls Institute), Hückeswagen; Co-founder of the "Institut für Musik, Imagination und Therapie, Berlin (IMIT)", Member of the lectorial board of the "Music Therapy Annual" ed. by the "Berufsverband der Musiktherapeuten in Deutschland" (BVM), mumerous publications in the field of Music Therapy
Address: Forststraße 50, D-12163 Berlin, Germany
www.frohne-hagemann.de;
E-Mail: i.frohne-hagemann@t-online.de

Edith Maria Geiger, born in 1964, Dipl. Music Therapist, licensed psychotherapist for children and adolescents, GIM-Fellow and Primary Trainer for GIM (AMI: Association for Music and Imagery). Co-founder of the "Institut für Musik, Imagination und Therapie, Berlin (IMIT)"; GIM-training, private practice for music therapy and psychotherapy in Berlin, Germany
Address: Albrechtstr. 115, D-12167 Berlin.
E-Mail: edith_geiger@freenet.de

Dag Körlin, MD, PhD, born in 1945, Bonny Method of Guided Imagery and Music Fellow. Recently defended his PhD thesis "Creative Arts Therapies in Psychiatric Care" on BMGIM and the Spectrum Group Program described in this chapter (in this book, or in the corresponding chapter), certified psychotherapist.
Address: Parkvägen 32, S-18352 Täby, Sweden,
E-Mail: dag. korlin@telia.com

Carola Maack, M.A., FAMI (Fellow of the Association for Music and Imagery) Music Therapist, Psychotherapist and Supervisor in private practice, clinical emphasis on trauma therapy. Primary Trainer of the Bonny Method of Guided Imagery and Music (BMGIM). Lectureship at the University of Applied Sciences Frankfurt, Germany.
Address: Institut für imaginative Psychotherapie und Musik, Lohbergenweg 39, D-21244 Buchholz, Germany
E-Mail: c.maack@t-online.de.

Susanne Metzner, Prof. Dr. sc. mus., born in 1958, Music Therapist, Social-pedagogue, Musician, registered Psychotherapist for Children and Adolescents, Supervisor; clinical experiences in working with children, adolescents and handicapped people, with oncological and psychiatric patients; 1991-2002 taught at the Institute of Music Therapy at Hamburg University of Music and Theater, since 2001 Professor at the University of Applied Sciences Magdeburg-Stendal; Guest Teacher at Sejong University (Seoul), Temple University (Philadelphia), Aalborg PhD Programme (Denmark), Universität der Künste (Berlin); 1994-2003 President of the Professional Association of Music Therapists in Germany, since 2003 member of the scientific board of the Professional Association of Music Therapists in Germany; since 2003 co-founder and member of the scientific board of the "Magdeburger Akademie für praxisorientierte Psychotherapie" (training programs for psychotherapists).
Address: Hochschule Magdeburg-Stendal, FB SGW, Postfach 3655, 39011 Magdeburg, Germany. http://www.sgw.hs-magdeburg.de/musik/
Private address: Bismarckallee 45, D-22926 Ahrensburg

Monika Nöcker-Ribaupierre, Dr. phil., Music Therapist, specializes in auditory stimulation after premature birth, (NICU, University Children's Hospital and Harlaching Hospital, Munich/Germany), and music therapy with developmentally disabled children. She is chairperson of the postgraduate Music Therapy Training in Munich/Germany, lecturer at Ludwig-Maximilian-University in Munich, member of the International Society for Music and Medicine ISMM and of the Scientific Board of "Musiktherapeutische Umschau" and General Secretary of the EMTC (European Music Therapy Confederation). In 2004 she edited the book "Music Therapy for Premature and Newborn Infants" (Barcelona Publ.)
Address: Wehrlestr. 22, D 81679 Munich, Germany
E-Mail: mnoeckrib@aol.com

Sabine Rittner is a licensed Psychotherapist and Music Therapist at the University Hospital of Heidelberg, Department of Medical Psychology. She teaches medical students, nurses and doctors and works with outdoor psychotherapy clients, mostly psychosomatic, chronically ill and cancer patients. Specialist in the field of altered states of consciousness, she integrates Voice Therapy, Bodywork, Gestalt, Hypnotherapy (Milton Erickson) and Trauma Therapy in her work. Her research focus is the effects of the voice, of sound and trance in Psychotherapy and traditional healing rituals. Recent research projects: Brainmapping of trance states in a ritualistic therapy setting. And: Field research on the use of the voice in healing rituals of the Shipibo tribe in the peruvian amazon jungle. She is an internationally well known speaker, teacher and author.

Address: Institut für Medizinische Psychologie, Universitätsklinik Heidelberg
Bergheimer Straße 20, D-69115 Heidelberg, Germany
E-Mail: Sabine_Rittner@med.uni-heidelberg.de
www.SabineRittner.de

Helmut Röhrborn, Dr. med., Department Head, consultant in psychosomatic medicine and psychotherapy/psychoanalysis, internist. Member of the scientific advisory board of the journal "Musiktherapeutische Umschau". Main focus in music therapy: receptive and regulative music therapy by Schwabe.

Professional Address: Klinik für Psychotherapie und Psychosomatik
Kliniken Erlabrunn GmbH, Am Märzenberg 1 A, D-08359 Breitenbrunn, Germany
E-Mail: h.roehrborn-@erlabrunn.de
Private address: Steinbachweg 1, D-08359 Breitenbrunn OT Erlabrunn, Germany
E-Mail: Helmut.Roehrborn@t-online.de

Lony Schiltz, Dr. phil habil., doctor of clinical psychology, Music Therapist, Head of research projects at the Centre de Recherche Publique-Santé, Luxembourg, Head of studies of the post graduate curriculum in arts therapies (Master of Science) at the University of Luxembourg.

Professional address: Dr. Lony Schiltz
CRP-Santé, 18, rue Dicks, L-1417 Luxembourg
E-Mail: lony.schiltz@education.lu
Private Address: Dr. Lony Schiltz, 10, rue Gabriel de Marie L-2131 Luxembourg

Andrea Schmucker, Master's degree in Germanic studies, sociology and Romanic studies Teacher of Tai-Chi, Training in Body Therapy (Neo-Reich). Since 1996 working partnership with Wolfgang Strobel. Since 2000 active member of training team in Strobel's Institute for Music, Body and Trance Therapy.

Address: Oberer Geisselring 10, D- 97236 Lindelbach, Germany .Tel.: [0049] 9303-99816
E-Mail: andreaschmucker@web.de
Also : Institute for Music, Body and Trance Therapy:
Dr. Wolfgang Strobel, Zeppelinstrasse 78, D-97074 Würzburg, Germany
Tel.: [0049] 931-72477, Fax [0049] 931-8808567
E-Mail: anando@wolfgang-strobel.de, www.wolfgang-strobel.de

Christoph Schwabe, Dr. phil. habil., University Lecturer, Teaching Music Therapist, Foundation, Development and Extension of an individual Concept of Music Therapy, without a one-sided association with any particular existing School of Psychotherapy. 1960-1980: Clinic for Nervous Diseases, University Leipzig. 1980-1992: Hochschule für Musik "Carl Maria von Weber" Dresden. 1992 he founded the Akademie für angewandte Musiktherapie Crossen in Bad Klosterlausnitz. Co-Founder of the "Deutschen Musiktherapeutischen Vereinigung Ost e.V.". Numerous publications in the field of Music Therapy. Editor of the book series, „Crossener Schriften zur Musiktherapie" (Writings on Music Therapy, Crossen)

Address: D-04626 Vollmershain Nr. 32, Germany
Tel./Fax: 034496-22431
E-Mail: schwabe.christoph@gmx.de

Birgit Süselbeck-Schulz, Graduate in Integrative Music Therapy. Long experience as an intensive care nurse. Work as Music Therapist with coma patients. Natural practitioner (German: "Heilpraktiker") of classical homeopathy
Address: Graf-Recke-Weg 38, D-40489 Düsseldorf, Germany
E-Mail: birgit.sueselbeck@gmx.de

Rosemarie Tüpker, Priv. Doz. Dr. phil. Dipl. Music Therapist (BVM), Psychotherapist (HP), postdoctoral lecture qualification. Works as Music Therapist in psychosomatics, Since 1990 director of the diploma course in music therapy at the University of Münster, Germany. Co-Founder of the Institute for Music Therapy and Morphology (IMM) and the Society of Psychological Morphology (GPM). Main Research Focus: Morphological and psychoanalytical principals of music and music therapy, methodology of research, improvisation, music and therapy with the elderly.
Address: Institut für Musikwissenschaft und Musikpädagogik, Philippistr. 2, D-48149 Münster, Germany.
E-Mail: tupker@uni-muenster.de; www.uni-muenster.de/Musiktherapie

Thomas Wosch, Dr. phil. (PhD), born in 1966, MT-DMVO, Lecturer in music therapy at the Magdeburg-Stendal University of Applied Sciences, Germany, Discussion Editor of www.voices.no, guest teacher at National University Zaporizhzhya/Ukraine (head of developing MA music therapy), German Academy of Developmental Rehabilitation Munich, Germany, and of the international PhD-program in music therapy at Aalborg University, Denmark; Research: microanalysis in music therapy, emotional processes, alexythymia effect research, E-learning, music therapy with the Crossen approach; focus of clinical practice: psychiatry; www.sgw.hs-magdeburg.de/musik/pages/team/wosch/wosch.html, co-founder of the music therapy program in Magdeburg / Germany;
Address: Dr. Thomas Wosch, Hochschule Magdeburg-Stendal (Magdeburg-Stendal University of applied sciences), FB SGW, Breitscheidstr. 2, D-39114 Magdeburg, Germany.
E-Mail: thomas.wosch@hs-magdeburg.de

SUBJECT INDEX

INDEX OF NAMES (IN THE TEXT)